CHILDREN OF TH

Giving Birth To A God
& The Science of Child Rearing

By Fudia Muhammad

To Sis. Alexis - I Beautiful Queen - I pray that God continues to protect you and surround you with Peace. May you produce greatness from your mind + your womb. May you find value in this book!.

Peace + Love,

Published by Bashirah House Publishing - First Edition, 2019
Layout/Indexing: Traci C. Muhammad (Phoenix, AZ)
Interior/Layout: Rodney 'Asaad' Muhammad (Phoenix, AZ)

ACKNOWLEDGMENTS

I thank Allah (God) for making His love unmistakable by coming in the Person of Master W. Fard Muhammad; and for raising The Most Honorable Elijah Muhammad to be a divine Leader, Teacher and Guide so all of humanity may benefit. It is true that The Most Honorable Elijah Muhammad produced many brilliant and exceptional students, but there is one who stands alone as his Lead student, The Honorable Minister Louis Farrakhan. The sole reason the *thought* of this book ever took shape is due to the concepts and lessons contained in his *How to Give Birth to a God* lecture series. I am so grateful to Allah (God) for inspiring The Minister's love and directing his will to study such a profound subject matter. As a result, he has changed the lives of countless individuals and families for the better; and given me a *healthy* obsession with all things related to this subject.

I thank Allah (God) for my husband, Robert, whom I love dearly – he is my best friend and confidant; and has been on this journey with me for decades. We are grateful to Allah (God) for blessing us with four beautiful children. They are all truly remarkable young gods, who are my daily motivation for striving toward righteousness every single day. They serve as immediate reminders as to why this subject matter is so important.

It has been a long, humbling, exhilarating and challenging task to attempt to write this book. I have gained the upmost respect for all writers who pen books of substance to better the condition of our world by increasing the knowledge of others.

The original manuscript of this work was completed nearly twenty years ago, but I never seriously pursued publishing. Though much has been changed and added to this latest version, the foundation is the same. Therefore, a special thanks go to Sister Captain Emeritus A'ishah Muhammad (Chicago) and her staff for their review of the original manuscript and encouraging words. I also must thank Brother Jeffrey Muhammad (Austin, TX) for his critique and editing of the original manuscript, and Sister Richa Muhammad (Austin, TX) for contributing profound information. A tremendous appreciation to Brother Willie Muhammad (Austin, TX) for compiling invaluable Final Call newspaper articles and to my wonderful sister, Yankain Turay, for spending so much 'computer time' with me. I am also grateful to my former sister-in-law, Jenniffer Muhammad, for sharing critical counsel regarding the potential release of this book all those years ago.

To my dear Brother, Jesse Muhammad (Houston, TX) – though I have thanked him more times than I know at this point, it is still not adequate to just say, 'thank you.' Brother Jesse is the reason why this book is no longer an intention or a goal but is now a reality. When I needed it most, he offered his award-winning platform to me – no strings attached. The overwhelming love and feedback I received from posting my weekly column, *Children of the Most High*, on his blogsite, www.BrotherJesseBlog.com, gave me the confidence and encouragement needed to push forward with this book. I am so grateful to Allah (God) for Brother Jesse and his beautiful wife, Sister Shareefah – they have a special inclination and desire to continually encourage, promote and to help others.

I also send a huge THANK YOU to all of the Believers of Muhammad Mosque No. 64 – Austin, Texas; they are second to none. I thank you for your love and support, but especially for creating and maintaining an environment that helps the righteous to keep striving in the cause of truth.

And last, but certainly not least, I thank my beloved mother and father for giving me the gift of life and opportunity. I thank my extraordinary mother for nurturing me until I could do for myself; but for also continuing to be there every single time I have needed her.

Everyone who had anything to do with making this book a reality has my deepest gratitude and appreciation.

I love you all,

As-Salaam Alaikum (Peace Be unto You).

Contents

INTRODUCTION

The year, 2017, marked the 30th anniversary of what may arguably be the most profound, impactful and life-changing lecture series delivered by anyone in modern history. On Sunday, July 26, 1987, the Honorable Minister Louis Farrakhan, gave a lecture that would become the first installment of a five-part lecture series titled, ***How to Give Birth to a God***. During this series of lectures, the Honorable Minister Louis Farrakhan mentioned that he had been studying the subject matter for then fifteen years, prior to delivering the lectures. His extensive study on this topic was clearly evident with every word he spoke. The Minister's divine proficiency of scripture, history, biology, psychology, and metaphysics – coupled with his wise understanding of the woman and her direct connection to God, resulted in a lecture series of unparalleled guidance and direct application for both men and women.

During Part Two of this five-part lecture series, the Honorable Minister Louis Farrakhan made a powerful declaration to the Sisters, *"You can change the world with your womb!"* This single statement capsulizes the message that the Minister so beautifully delivered all of those years ago – and based on the condition of this world, it is a message that must be reignited in the consciousness of our people. It is difficult to disagree that the world is in a terrible condition. One could also, then, agree that the condition of the world is a direct result of the condition of the mindset of the people who inhabit it. This mindset was not created in a vacuum, for there are no persons – living or dead – that did not come from the womb of a woman. Simply put, the nations of the world, comprised of thinking people, cannot rise any higher than their women. Why?

The Honorable Minister Louis Farrakhan explains that the woman is blessed with two wombs. Not only does she possess the physical womb (often called uterus) that houses the baby during pregnancy, but she also possesses a mental womb – the mind – that directly feeds the growing baby spiritually and mentally. Both wombs are majestic and created by Allah (God) to be extraordinarily powerful, giving the woman the ability to produce a god or to produce a devil. Both wombs must be at their optimum in order to give birth to a god – a child that will grow to one day change the condition of our world for the better, and not continue to perpetuate the wickedness that pervades the earth.

The Bible reads, *"I have said, Ye are gods; and all of you are children of the most High"* (Psalm 82:6 KJV). If this is true, and it is; then what happened? Why have we as a people not actualized our god-potential? The Honorable Minister Louis Farrakhan said, *"It is not that you don't have the potential, the capacity, but you don't have the knowledge. And because you don't know how to do what you are born into the world to do, you miss your task."* During his lecture series, the Minister shared the prerequisite knowledge with all of us.

Preparation is the key. In order to get the physical womb at its most desirable state to produce the desired goal – a god – we should begin at least one year prior to conception. For most, it is common knowledge today that our physical bodies must be cleaned-up. We must immediately stop smoking and eliminate all drugs and alcohol. We must quickly wean ourselves off of all over-the-counter drugs and unnecessary medications that can be replaced with proper food and nutrition. We should invest in a copy of ***How to Eat to Live: Books I & II*** by the Most Honorable Elijah Muhammad and practice the diet he describes, which was given to him by God in Person, as a prescription for our ills and to give us abundant life. Exercise is also paramount because being healthy and physically fit will help to minimize

2

complications during pregnancy and give the body the strength required to endure the physical burden of bearing life.

What is not common knowledge to most is that the mind must also be prepared before conception so that when we are blessed to conceive, we will be deliberately focused and engaged in assisting God to create human life. This serious preparation for getting the mind – the second womb – into a state to produce a god cannot be neglected, because this womb affects the spiritual and mental development of the growing baby, inside the physical womb. This process should also begin at least one year before conception, but the more time we invest in our spiritual and mental development – the greater the benefit for our children.

The Minister also emphasizes that our heart-felt desire to produce a child for God must be forefront. It is important to understand that we cannot intentionally produce what we do not desire to produce, so the first essential attribute that the mental womb must obtain is the desire to produce a child for God. Not a child that possesses the characteristics of a Tamerlane, a Hitler, or a Jeffrey Dahmer – all born of a woman – but a child that possesses the characteristics of Moses, Jesus, and Muhammad – also, born from women.

Living a clean physical life reflects living a clean spiritual life and vice versa. But amazingly, the mind is so powerful that whether or not adequate time was taken to prepare the physical body, a focused-determined mind can overcome the physical. If the desire is present, it can feed our will. Our desire to produce a god will inspire us to bow down to The God that can bring it about. So, the Honorable Minister Louis Farrakhan said that as soon as we know there is life in the womb, we should be as Mary's mother and make a **vow** that we will devote our child to the service of God; and ask Him to accept the child from us. There is simply no substitute for prayer. More than anything, it is our sincere supplication to God during pregnancy that

3

impresses itself on the brain of the forming child. The Honorable Minister Louis Farrakhan said, *"Now look at what she [Mary's mother] did. She formed it with a vow, so her desire to please God started writing on the brain of the child that was being fashioned from her blood. You, woman, can make the child a mental giant or you can make it an imbecile; but it is what you think and what you desire that writes on the brain. And the child comes forward from the darkness of the womb with a predisposition toward a certain reality."*

We can change the world by producing gods from our womb. A god is one who has force and power to change reality by creating a new and better reality. A god has mastery over self and environmental influences. A god can manipulate the forces of nature. A god is supreme in his or her field of endeavor. This means that a god is also extraordinarily knowledgeable and wise.

In Part Four of ***How to Give Birth to a God***, the Honorable Minister Louis Farrakhan recounts a Japanese woman who produced four geniuses as a result of reading to each baby while the babies were still in the womb. The first direct instruction ever given to Prophet Muhammad (PBUH) was – "Read." Reading not only stimulates and energizes the thought processes of the mother, but also that of her child. The Minister advises us not to read foolish fairytales and nursery rhymes that promote falsehood, not godhood. We should read the most beautiful scriptural narratives to our growing baby combined with books that have a focus on nation-building disciplines.

This introduction is just a mere snapshot of the Divinely guided lessons shared by the Honorable Minister Louis Farrakhan, but hopefully, this information makes it easy to see how thirty-plus years later, the Minister's timeless message continues to reverberate in the hearts and minds of a new generation. Over the decades, the Honorable Minister Louis Farrakhan has never wavered in making it clear to our people, particularly Black women – that we are chosen by Allah (God) to produce a brand-new reality on this earth. This can be achieved when we actively co-operate and co-create with the same God who meticulously designed the exquisite womb of the woman as a replica of His own self-creation, from the triple darkness of space, which is the womb of the universe.

We are blessed to serve a Benevolent God who did not leave us alone to figure it all out. He gave us proper guidance and a specially-prepared guide. Yes, we were given instructions and guidance on how to live and how to manage every area of life, including – how to rear our children. Through the mathematically precise study of nature, science, the Scriptures, the Teachings of The Most Honorable Elijah Muhammad and the words and living example of The Honorable Minister Louis Farrakhan, we have exactly what we need!

PREFACE: WHAT IS A GOD?

In 1987, The Honorable Minister Louis Farrakhan electrified audiences with a lecture-series titled, *"How to Give Birth to a God."* The certainty and passion with which the Minister delivered this five-part lecture series left no doubt that it was completely inspired by God. Over the decades, this series has motivated and encouraged many to make serious changes by applying the specified recommendations, so they may one day produce their own little gods. Yet, there are others who are unfortunately blocking a multitude of potential blessings, unable to get beyond one word in his lecture title – God! No surprise as to who has the biggest reservations – the so-called religiously devout: *'What does he mean, give birth to a god? That's impossible, sacrilegious, and blasphemous.'* So, let's deal with that first.

Giving birth to a god does NOT mean giving birth to the Supreme Being – Allah (God). It does not mean giving birth to the Creator of the Heavens and the Earth; that's been done. It does not mean giving birth to the One who is Possessor of power over all things; can tune-in to over seven billion minds without confusing a thought and controls every atom in the Universe. We are not referring to The One God we pray to for protection and guidance, or to demonstrate our gratitude. Nor are we referring to giving birth to The One with Supremacy in knowledge, wisdom, understanding, and power. He has no equal – no partners – no associates.

The Bible reads, *"I have said, ye are gods; and all of you are children of the most High"* (Psalm 82:6, KJV). The Honorable Minister Louis Farrakhan explains, *"Now Brothers and Sisters, the greatest goal of all is to meet with or to form a perfect union with, Almighty God Allah. When there is a perfect union with God and when we become one with our Creator, then the Attributes of God come right across our own personality and character, so that we become one with the Source of life, so that when you see the person, you are actually looking at God...If you can become one with the Creator, join with Him in a perfect union, which is a great struggle, then His Attributes, His own unique Personality, will impress Itself upon you and His own being will come across your being, so that you die, He lives, in you – through you. When they see you, they see Him, for you are in Him and He is in you"* (Self-Improvement: The Basis for Community Development).

The Most Honorable Elijah Muhammad said, *"Whenever you look at a Blackman, you are looking at God."* Black men and women are direct descendants of Allah (God), the Creator of the Universe. Our physical and spiritual essence can be traced directly back to The Most High. We are the Original people of the planet Earth. To give birth to a god is the activity of returning to the nature in which we were created in order to actualize our god-potential. At present we are unrecognizable as His children because we have been made other than ourselves. This is why there is a need for prophets and messengers – they are commissioned to guide the people of God back to the straight path after deviation from His principles and commandments.

So, what is a god? A god exudes the highest degree of submission on all planes of existence – spiritually, mentally and physically; pursuing his or her purpose in life. Physically, a god is strikingly beautiful! He or she looks different from all others. Their level of discipline in areas of diet, exercise, and belief manifests itself in their physical appearance. Many bear witness that they have a perpetual shine or glow – the mark of submission. A god is healthy and physically strong – he or she has the potential to live as long as the old patriarchs we read about in the Scriptures. The original people are capable of living for several centuries and still maintain all faculties of reason and function. We know that it is difficult to comprehend such longevity when we continue to marvel at those who manage to reach the century mark, but a person one hundred years old is a mere baby.

Mentally, a god is what this world would call a genius and may want to study how his brain works. He is extraordinarily knowledgeable and wise. He is not only academically advanced, but The Honorable Minister Louis Farrakhan said that a god has the mental strength of a prophet and a seer. Some gods are born with the gift of prophecy while others develop it through an intensive study of history and current events. This means that a god, who is at one with his Creator and the Universe, will know tomorrow's headlines, today.

A god uses 95 to 99 percent of his mental capacity. Minister Jabril Muhammad wrote, *"The human mind has grades. There is nothing irrational in believing that there are realms, or mental levels, beyond the experience most of us live on"* (This Is the One). Those gods who have reached the most advanced of these realms or mental levels are those who can communicate with other gods telepathically. They have also literally mastered mind over matter; moving objects with just their thoughts (telekinesis or psychokinesis). They can manipulate the weather and other forces of nature and can even travel anywhere in the world without leaving their seat.

A god experiences a spiritual apex when he forms a perfect union with the Supreme Being. Morality, integrity, and an impeccable character come with ease to a god. His greatest desire is to live a life pleasing to Allah (God), while fully realizing his own divinity. To be human and divine is NOT an oxymoron – in truth, it is only when we can accept our own divinity that we will be able to manifest our true selves. Some gods are so spiritually advanced, ascending to such a degree that they can self-heal and heal others without the aid of doctors or medicine.

A god understands and begins to pursue his purpose in life at an early age. He or she is superior in their field of endeavor. A god is powerful and courageous; willing to *"stand up against the odds and deliver the people from the oppressor"* (HMLF). A god has force and power to change reality by creating a new and better reality. He or she can both call into existence and control their own circumstances because they have mastery over self and environmental influences. We can produce these gods in one generation or sometimes more; but the process must begin now if we desire, at some point, to experience our human potential.

It is wonderful to learn about the advanced sciences and mathematics which allowed us to build the pyramids, but we cannot stop there – the Black man and woman put all the planets into orbit; the moon and all the stars. If this all sounds like fantasy or fiction, it is only because we have fallen so far from our Father that we cannot fathom an elevated plane of existence. Not to mention we have been lied to about the reality of God. The Most Honorable Elijah Muhammad teaches that God is not a spook, spirit or a mystery. He is a flesh and blood, breathing, living human being; which means we can be like Him. The only difference between Him and us is that He is **Supreme** in Knowledge, Wisdom, Understanding, and Power. Take it or let it alone!

SECTION 1: Preparation Before Conception

"O people, keep your duty to your Lord, Who created you from a single being and created its mate of the same (kind), and spread from these two many men and women. And keep your duty to Allah, by Whom you demand one of another (your rights), and (to) the ties of relationship. Surely Allah is ever a Watcher over you."

Holy Qur'an 4:1

IN THE BEGINNING:

The Most Honorable Elijah Muhammad said, *"A Nation Can Rise No Higher Than Its Woman."* Whatever condition our men or Nation is in, is a direct reflection of our women. Both men and especially women must begin with understanding the value and sacredness of the female when preparing to produce a child for Allah (God).

The woman, particularly, the Original Black woman is majestic – possessing powers so incredible, we should be in awe every time we are blessed to be in her presence. The very essence of her being is directly from the Originator of the heavens and the earth. Biblically, we are taught that the female is the product of man's rib and therefore inferior to the man. But it is this misinterpretation and so many others which lead to the mistreatment of women and accelerates the fall of humanity from our honored position of being the Glory of God.

Sisters: We must reconnect ourselves to the Source of our very existence and fall in love with Allah (God) all over again. It is not enough to just believe that we are the key to the Kingdom of God; we must **know** with absolute certainty; otherwise, our way of life will not reflect this reality, which has proven to be detrimental. The reformation of the Nation must start with the woman, so it is incumbent upon the woman to change, now! What do we look like demanding that our men be respectful, treat us like queens and shower us with adoration; but our speech, our dress, and our actions indicate that we are unworthy? There is no need to ask the man to change – we must change first, then he will be compelled to respond accordingly.

The Honorable Minister Louis Farrakhan stated that if the Black woman does not rise, humanity, not just her race; but all of humanity is lost.

This may seem to be a heavy burden placed on one specific group, but the Holy Qur'an assures, *"Allah places not on any soul a duty beyond its scope."* The Most Honorable Elijah Muhammad understood this and therefore focused 75% of his work with the woman. Just the same, Prophet Muhammad (Peace Be Upon Him) expressed that mothers should be honored three times before the father is honored once.

Minister Farrakhan said, *"It is only when we have produced a reformed female, filled with the love and spirit of Allah (God) that we will be able to produce a superior Nation. Likewise, the female is so important because she is the first nurse and the first teacher of the child."* Teaching a man equates to teaching an individual; but when you teach a woman, you teach a Nation.

The Most Honorable Elijah Muhammad is an extremely wise man who unfortunately has been tragically misunderstood. We can no longer afford to be so foolish as to discard his wisdom – we must study it, so that we may extract the immeasurable value contained in it.

There are three things the enemy said he would never teach his former slaves: (1) the science of warfare, (2) the science of business, and (3) the science of mating. Notice that we did not say: how to shoot a gun, how to start a business, or how to reproduce. To be able to science something is to have the ability to master it. If giving birth to a god is scientific (and it is), then we also need to know how to mate scientifically. It begins with working on self.

One of the most important elements in preparation before conception is to first have the desire to give birth to a god present. The Honorable Minister Louis Farrakhan teaches that desire feeds the will. Praying **before** pregnancy that the children we will one day be blessed to conceive will help to change the awful condition of our world, will naturally motion us to make the proper changes needed to manifest the desire.

I remember before I was married when I first heard these Teachings, I prayed to Allah (God) to one day bless me with children who were reflections of Him. I also prayed that if I would not be blessed to give birth to gods, but rather destined to bear children that were enemies of righteousness; then I did not care to have children at all! Today, as I reflect on that prayer, it may not have been proper, but it was definitely sincere. It is not my place to recommend such a supplication to anyone, but I wanted to give an example of the level of seriousness and intensity of our desire when beginning the process of giving birth to a god. We must desire this as much as the water we drink and the air we breathe.

THE VOW:

"When a woman of Amran said: My Lord, I vow to Thee what is in my womb, to be devoted (to Thy service), so accept (it) from me; surely Thou, only Thou, art the Hearing, the Knowing. So when she brought it forth, she said: My Lord, I have brought it forth a female – and Allah knew best what she brought forth – and the male is not like the female, and I have named it Mary, and I commend her and her offspring into Thy protection from the accursed devil" (Holy Qur'an 3:34-35).

The woman of Amran, in the above verse, is the Mother of Mary, grandmother of Jesus. Most of us probably do not generally reflect on any of Jesus' family members before Mary and Joseph. Although we do not give it much thought, we naturally understand that if Jesus had a mother, then he certainly had a grandmother and many more great forebears in his divine lineage. It is remarkable and certainly worth studying the mindset and the way of life of those who created the environment that would ultimately give birth to one of the greatest men in the annals of history. In the Holy Qur'an, Allah (God), allows us access into the mind of Jesus' grandmother. Using just the two aforementioned verses, we gain so much knowledge, wisdom, and understanding about the two most essential prerequisites to giving birth to a god – desire and prayer.

Jesus' grandmother, like so many of the women during her time, desired to be *the* woman that possessed *the* womb that Allah (God) would bless to produce *the* Deliverer. Can you imagine having that honor bestowed on you as a mother? It was indeed a coveted position and one of great honor, respect and adoration among the righteous.

As mothers, we get excited and want to celebrate and share every wonderful accomplishment or skill that our children manifest – no matter how insignificant it may seem in the eyes of others; we are Proud! Why? Because deep down we hope that it is an indication that our child is on the right path towards one day making a positive contribution to the world. Jesus' grandmother did not just want a child that would contribute to the world, she wanted to give birth to that One who would make the most transformative contribution, ever.

Desire: According to Merriam-Webster dictionary, **desire** means, *"to long or hope for: to express a wish for: to request: to invite."* Some synonyms of **desire** are *"to crave, to hanker, to yearn, to covet."* This woman of Amran was so desirous of giving birth to the Deliverer, that she was not taking any chances. As soon as she knew that she was blessed with life in her womb, she went right away to Allah (God) in supplication and prayer – vowing to Him that the child she was carrying would be devoted to the service of God. A **vow** is a binding, sacred and solemn promise. Vows are not to be given lightly for they are in-fact lawful contracts. The Honorable Minister Louis Farrakhan said, *"When you make a vow – that is not only your desire; that is your will combined with your determination. I vow. I'm determined that what I make – what is in my womb – is to be devoted to YOU."*

Evidently, Jesus' grandmother must have been a righteous and prayerful woman prior to her pregnancy. She had to have experienced having her prayers answered by Allah (God) many times before because when she gave birth and saw that her child was a female, she was surprised and confused. This confusion arose because she prayed during pregnancy and she not only had faith but a profound expectation that her prayer would indeed be answered. This must have been based on the fact that she had been blessed to have had her prayers answered in the past. Her prayers were indeed answered, as she would soon come to understand. But at that moment, she expressed concern (but never disappointment) to Allah (God) that the baby she had so well-prepared in the womb to be devoted to His service and had begged Him to accept from her was not the expected gender.

Allah (God) comforted her and eased her anxiety. Allah (God) is the Best Knower, so He knew in advance exactly what she would produce. *"The male is not like the female."* Allah (God) required a special female first; a pure vessel that would then produce the male Deliverer. Understanding this, Jesus' grandmother – a woman of Amran – then prayed for both her daughter AND her future grandson. She entrusted both Mary and Jesus into Allah's (God's) protection from the accursed devil. Powerful!

As Black women, we must understand that in all of this there are signs and lessons for us. We will never produce great children if we do not first and foremost have a profound desire to do so; long before we are pregnant. This desire then feeds our will to clean up our lives spiritually, mentally and physically.

Secondly, the moment that we are aware that life is in our womb, we must *pray, pray, pray*. Pray to Allah (God) and make our solemn vow. We should devote ourselves to prayer continuously throughout our pregnancy. Our prayer, however; should not stop at the child growing in our womb but should extend to future generations beyond the one that we are presently producing – never having any doubt or thought in our mind that we will not receive the answer to our prayers.

THE DESIRE OF WOMEN:

Theologians and Biblical scholars have discovered that one of the names of Jesus was, *The Desire of Women*. Minister Farrakhan explained that this did not necessarily mean that all of the women were attracted to Jesus, but rather they desired to be the one whose womb would bring forth the

Messiah. If we desire to produce a child like Jesus, then we must think, act and live our lives in a manner similar to his mother, Mary.

Mary is called the Mother of God. That is a powerful title. How extraordinary does a woman have to be in order to be worthy of such honor? There is an entire chapter in the Holy Qur'an titled, Maryam – it is the 19th chapter. Maryam or Mary is the standard by which every woman should try to equal herself up to. Why? The Holy Qur'an reads, *"O Mary, surely Allah has chosen thee above the women of the world. O Mary, be obedient to thy Lord and humble thyself and bow down with those who bow"* (3: 41-42). Mary was a Black woman who actually existed. But bigger than that, she is a sign and a representation of the Original Black woman today – take it or leave it! At present, Allah (God) has chosen the Black woman above the women of the world!

We must take a closer look at Maryam and the actions she took to prepare herself to give birth to Jesus, one of the greatest men to walk the earth.

WHO CAN FIND A VIRTUOUS WIFE?

The Book of Proverbs (NKJV) reads, *"Who can find a virtuous wife? For her worth is far above rubies. The heart of her husband safely trusts her; so, he will have no lack of gain. She does him good and not evil all the days of her life"* (31: 10-12). The next 19 verses go on to describe in great detail the divine characteristics and noble qualities of a virtuous wife. There are many Biblical versions and translations of this same verse asking: *"Who can find a virtuous woman"* (KJV); *"A wife of noble character who can find"* (NIV); *"A worthy woman who can find"* (ASV)? However, the New King James Version gets right to the heart of the inquiry – a man is looking for a wife. He's not just looking for any woman; not a girlfriend, a boo, a lover, or a one-night stand – for she's easy to find. But this particular translation implies that the wife the man seeks is very difficult to find because he also requires that she be virtuous.

When a man is seeking a wife, the one woman whom he will commit to for the rest of his life; the one he will adore, maintain and protect, and whom he desires to bear his children, his standards are justifiably raised. Now, virtuous means many things indeed. It means, *righteous, moral, decent, noble, respectable, etc*. But virtuous also means *pure, innocent, untouched, chaste, celibate* – a virgin. Hmm. This scripture makes a lot more sense today than it did centuries ago because, in the 21st century, a virtuous or virgin wife is far more difficult for a man to find.

Now before my modern feminist Sisters get all bent out of shape, let's reason. If we are being completely honest with ourselves and listen to the nature in which God created us and not the noise of the world; every mature woman with a less than virtuous past has regrets and wishes she had done things differently. The fact is new brides still dress in white symbolizing virginity and purity; every groom desires a wife that no other man has ever been with, and every parent desires for their children to remain virgins until marriage (just ask them). Why is that?

In his lecture, ***How to Give Birth to a God: Part 5***, The Honorable Minister Louis Farrakhan said, *"Once in your life, Sister, you have your virtue. And after it is gone, you can't get it back again – that virginity, that's what I'm speaking of. And really, you can only love once; really perfectly. Only God can bring it back the second time and make it as sweet as the first love, or sweeter. But without God, when you get a woman that has already been used and abused, she never gives the man the second time what she gave the man the first time..."*

According to the Law of God, premarital sex is forbidden. Is Allah's (God's) way antiquated; or are we just guilty of using deceptive intelligence to justify our disobedience and rebellion against a divine command? We could be charged with perpetrating a fraud when we elevate and extol the blessed "virgin" Mary while very few strive to emulate her example. The Most Honorable Elijah Muhammad did not tip-toe around his mission concerning the sacredness of our women and girls. The Honorable Minister Louis Farrakhan said, *"Most of the little girls in the University of Islam were virgins – and that's just a fact. You could find more virgins in the University of Islam than you find among the nuns. And it was the virtue of the women and girls that the Honorable Elijah Muhammad felt was more valuable than increased knowledge at the expense of your chastity. Because virtue and chastity build character in a woman, but education doesn't necessarily build your character."*

Therefore, the Honorable Minister Louis Farrakhan along with other Believers were asked by the Most Honorable Elijah Muhammad to sacrifice sending their daughters away to college until he could finish building the university-level of MUI, which would allow them to be educated *"in an environment that would protect the righteousness that he had inculcated in them since they were little girls."* The Minister obeyed the Most Honorable Elijah Muhammad's instructions, but there was a Brother who sent his daughter away to college anyway. The Minister said, *"The Honorable Elijah Muhammad told me to tell that man that if anything happened to his daughter while she was in the 'devil's institution,' he would hold him thoroughly responsible. And if she violated the law of God while she was there; not only would she be punished, but the double punishment would come to him."*

The Most Honorable Elijah Muhammad was not anti-education; in fact, he wanted the Sisters highly educated and taught us that an ignorant

22

woman is a sin. But he had a much broader far-seeing mission. Therefore, he understood that the type of education that was being offered at most colleges and universities was not worth corrupting our girls; they are priceless – *far above rubies*. Proper education will not only build-up the mind; but it will also build virtue, character, and righteousness. Being highly degreed, yet immoral makes us fit for the devil's world, but of little value to God. Allah (God) wants the woman to assist Him in the creation of human life; a new man and a new woman who will establish His kingdom on earth.

For a woman, sex is not simply a physical act. The woman is a receiver. When she gives herself to a man, she receives him in return. She receives him emotionally, mentally, spiritually and physically. And if what she receives is not of God; she does not benefit, but instead suffers a tremendous loss. And what she loses is no longer available. Unless Allah (God) intervenes, the next man will have a difficult time navigating through all of her baggage, which is stuffed with the burdens of all her past experiences. So, Mother Tynnetta Muhammad said that it takes about three years for a woman who has been intimate with a man to be completely free of him on every level before she can begin a new relationship burden-free.

This is not a world that encourages young girls to value their virginity and to remain chaste until marriage. *So, who can find a virtuous wife?* She is indeed difficult to find, but not impossible. In the midst of a rebellious nation, there is a man who, like his father before him, is fighting to produce a Nation of women and girls who understand their sacredness and delight in pleasing God. The Honorable Minister Louis Farrakhan teaches women and girls that not only should we strive mightily to maintain our virtue; but we should also be ready and willing to fight, kill and die to protect that virtue if any man tries to take what we are not willing to give. That's the value of a virtuous woman in the eyes of God and in the eyes of righteous men.

Let's take every opportunity we have to encourage our young girls to be proud of their virginity; giving them the assist they all need to walk the uphill road, so they will continue to be pure reflections of God.

SHE SCREENED HERSELF:

"And mention Mary in the Book. When she drew aside from her family to an eastern place; So she screened herself from them. Then We sent to her Our spirit and it appeared to her as a well-made man" (Holy Qur'an 19:16-17).

There are so many intricate facets in the life of Mary, the Mother of Jesus that extensive time really must be taken to study her, by those of us who desire to see a profound change in the lives of our people and all of humanity. The Holy Qur'an confirms that Mary's exalted status is given to her by God Himself. She was chosen by Allah (God) and purified by Him. The angels told Mary that Allah (God) chose her above the women of the **world**! (Holy Qur'an 3:41)

If we are reading the scriptures of both the Bible and Holy Qur'an as mere history books, then we are missing their true value and relevance in our present-day lives. According to the Most Honorable Elijah Muhammad, most of what we read in both Books is not history, but prophecy – being fulfilled in the present time. This is why the Holy Qur'an describes Mary and her son, Jesus, as "a sign." The Honorable Minister Louis Farrakhan said this particular sign *"is pointing to something bigger than itself."* So, Mary and Jesus represent something bigger coming in the future. A sign is also an *"event whose presence or occurrence indicates the probable presence or occurrence of something else."* Signs, particularly divine signs, must be analyzed because they are used *"to convey information or instructions."*

If Mary was chosen above the women of the world, this means she was anointed with a rank that was higher than the mother of Abraham, the mother of Moses, and even the mother of Muhammad. There are 66 books in the Bible, only two are named after specific women – the Book of Ruth and the Book of Esther. In the Holy Qur'an, there is only one chapter (book) out of 114 named after a specific woman. Since the Qur'an was revealed to Prophet Muhammad (PBUH), one may think that this honor should go to the mother of Muhammad; but the 19th chapter of the Holy Qur'an is named Maryam, after the Mother of Jesus.

Mary is revered in both Christianity and Islam. She was an exemplary model of virtue and righteousness – prepared by her mother in the womb to live her entire life in a manner that glorified God. The enemy wants us to continue to believe that both Jesus and his mother were Caucasian – though the Bible (Revelation 1:14-15) and historical evidence clearly contradicts this notion. Not only was the historical Mary an Egyptian Black woman, but her impeccable standard serves as a sign for the present-day Black woman if we would only follow her example. The Honorable Minister Louis Farrakhan said, *"Mary had to be one heck of a woman because she was always found praising Allah (God): '...**My soul doth magnify the Lord, And my spirit hath rejoiced in God my Saviour' (Luke 1:46-47)**. From this, we can see that the very essence of this woman is that she was **God-fearing**...So, if you want to produce a righteous giant, study Maryam – chapter 19 of the Qur'an is given to her. Study her life. Pattern your life after her life and I guarantee you, we will change the world."*

Mary understood that she belonged to God. The Black woman belongs to God. Allah (God) revealed to Mary in advance that she would give birth to a pure boy. She knew that in order to properly prepare she had to screen herself from her family by drawing aside to an eastern place. Historically that means that she retreated to Bethlehem of Judea (Palestine). She had to protect the life of her son from those who sought to kill him; but before his birth, she had to also protect herself from an element within her family and community that may have had a negative influence on her pregnancy and subsequently, her son. Jesus was destined to be pure, which means the environment surrounding Mary's pregnancy and his birth had to be ideal.

We too have been visited by God in Person and from His mouth, He said that He is going to make a new people by first making a new woman. This is why 75% of the mission of the Most Honorable Elijah Muhammad is with the woman. The scriptures do not say that Mary was pure, but that she was *purified* – implying that one can undergo a process of purification or transformation. It is never too late!

Mary's decision to "screen" herself is a bigger sign of the need of the Black woman to do the same. A screen on a window or door allows the fresh air and warm sunlight to enter the room but keeps the insects and pests out. To screen oneself is to *"conceal, protect or shelter"* oneself from any person, place, thing, or **thought** that would adversely affect the development of the new life. Sometimes this includes family and friends. It also includes staying away from movies, funerals, the nightclub, and other negative elements while pregnant. Like Mary, we can be in the world, but not of it. But what is our eastern place? It is true that the sun rises in the east; all of the prophets of God came from the east, and the holiest cities are in the east – but our eastern place is not physical, it's spiritual – it's with God. Mary, a prayerful woman was fiercely protective of her spirit and transferred this to her new baby. Solitude can have its benefits.

Another key prerequisite to being qualified to be chosen above the women of the world was that Mary had to remain chaste until she met one worthy of her. Mary grew up under the strict law of Moses. It is interesting that in order to help her maintain her virtue and grow up living a life pleasing to God, she was put into the charge of a righteous man, Zacharias; not a woman. The Holy Qur'an reads, *"So her Lord accepted her with a goodly acceptance and made her grow up a goodly growing, and gave her into the charge of Zacharias"* (3: 36).

This is significant to our condition today because it is going to take righteous men who understand and value the sacredness of the female, to stand up and take their rightful place as the spiritual and physical maintainers of women. Men who are protectors and not violators of women and girls. Our men must be like the angels who contended with one another over who would have charge over Mary – that's how precious she was in the sight of godly men. Brothers must grow to see the potential for every Black woman to produce a god and determine to make their communities sanctuaries for women and girls to *"grow up a goodly growing."* The Black woman, our present-day Mary, deserves nothing less than a well-made man imbued with the spirit of God. Only then, will we produce new people and establish the Kingdom of God on Earth!

In his lecture, *How to Give Birth to a God (Part 5)*, the Honorable Minister Louis Farrakhan quoted words from a Caucasian scholar during a colloquium at Harvard – the scholar said, *"I am convinced through our study and research that neither the white man, nor the white woman will save the world. I am convinced that the Asian man, nor the Asian woman will save the world. And I am equally convinced that the Black man will not save the world. But all of my research and scholarship says that if there's going to be a savior coming, it'll come from the Black woman."*

Anytime Allah (God) needs a man like Moses, Abraham, Muhammad or Jesus; He does not produce the man without first producing a woman with extraordinary qualities who He will co-operate and co-create with to bring forth this type of man. We are that woman. However, our greatest enemy, ignorance, has kept us blind to our true identity. We all have the ability to produce children in the likeness and image of God but make no mistake about it – this requires all-out sacrifice.

GO NOT NEAR FORNICATION:

Fornication is an act that can be defined in both secular and non-secular terms. The difference in each respective position is exposed by the subtleties within the definitions. The broader secular world defines fornication as simply, *"sexual intercourse between people not married to each other."* However, the non-secular or religious definition of fornication is, *"unlawful or illicit sexual intercourse."* Fornication, according to the latter definition is against the law – God's law. In the United States, the laws are governed by men and women, not by God; so those who commit fornication are not criminally prosecuted or fined. However, this does not mean there are no consequences. According to the law of God, fornication is *"forbidden, prohibited, unsanctioned, illegitimate, felonious, unauthorized, illegal and criminal."* In other words, fornication is NOT allowed. The Bible goes so far as to equate fornication with adultery, homosexuality, incest, and bestiality – wow!

Whether or not we agree with comparing fornication with the aforementioned, we should ask ourselves why God views fornication with such disdain and contempt. A clear indication of the gravity of a specific law is the punishment rendered when it is violated. The Honorable Minister Louis Farrakhan wrote, *"The Honorable Elijah Muhammad taught us why fornication is an ugly thing in the Sight of Allah, and punishable in the dominate Islamic world by death. Isn't that something? It's punishable by death – that's how heavy a crime it is!"* If we lived and were governed by a theocracy (society ruled by the laws of God) – Christian, Muslim or Jewish – the punishment for fornication could very well be death.

Though some countries, in the dominate Islamic world, put both the adulterer and fornicator to death, the Holy Qur'an does not actually prescribe death. Yet, the number of lashes from flogging that the violator is sentenced to is so great that death could easily be the result of such a judgment. Death is irrevocable and irreversible; therefore, Quranic law requires that at least four witnesses of the crime of fornication or adultery be provided. Keep in mind that in most cases when a person violates a known law, it is done undercover and out of the sight of others; so, it is very difficult for there to be any additional witnesses much less four of them. So, in the eyes of Allah (God), though the violation is severe, there is still evidence of His Mercy.

Those of us who are striving to be counted amongst the righteous Believers and followers of God's path are not interested in man's law if they contradict God's law. For a Believer, a crime that requires the violator to pay with his or her blood is one we should fear. If understood, the very language in the Holy Qur'an provides protection, for those who desire to adhere, from ever falling victim to fornication. It reads, *"And go not nigh [near] to fornication: surely it is an obscenity. And evil is the way"* (17:32). Maulana Muhammad Ali's footnote to this verse reads, *"The Qur'an not only forbids fornication but enjoins men not to go **near** it, thus avoiding all those opportunities which are likely to tempt one to fall into the evil. Hence it is that Islam discourages the too free intermingling of the sexes."*

Teenagers and adults do not "accidentally" have sex with people whom they are not married. In fact, married people do not accidentally have sex. Consensual intercourse is the result of desire and environment; both must exist at the same time. Allah (God) gave men and women a natural desire for one another that begins to manifest during adolescence. Though passion is natural, it must be restrained until marriage. This is done by deciding to be mindful of the environment we allow ourselves and our children to be exposed to and engaged with. This keeps us obedient to the Holy Qur'an, which warns us not to even approach the environment or get near the activities which can lead to fornication.

Good manners protect good morals. Typically, children do not leap from innocent angels to promiscuous teens overnight. There is a gradual build-up. First, seemingly harmless behavior is allowed – private conversations, intimate questioning, holding hands, daring suggestions… It's the same with adults, but adults quickly graduate from having coffee together to having an intimate evening out. If we allow ourselves to indulge and go near these activities, nature will propel us towards breaking the law forbidding fornication. Youth is not an excuse. We cannot feign ignorance of the law because we were *'too young to understand.'* If it is done away from public view, in the darkness of secrecy and we attempt to hide our actions from those in authority; then we knew it was wrong and are held responsible for our actions.

In the Nation of Islam, we do not physically harm those who fall victim to this law. To execute such a harsh punishment at this time would be unjust due to the chronic spiritual and mental handicap which continues to plague us after 400 plus years of captivity. However, there is a consequence – one to five years away from the circle of Believers. Yet, the greater consequence for any person who commits fornication is that they are weakened physically, mentally and spiritually. What we abuse or misuse, we lose. This means that the egg and sperm are not only physically weakened, but their divine potency is also weakened. Most know that women are required to protect their virtue and remain chaste, but the Holy Qur'an gives the same instructions to the man. A man produces the seed of life daily – when he is careless and promiscuous, his seed is steadily weakened with every violation. This means that future children are directly affected by the transgressions of their parents to this divine law. Fornication used to be as taboo as incest; one day soon, it will be again.

We believe that everyone can benefit from the good manners and restrictions that the followers of the Most Honorable Elijah Muhammad strive to maintain in order to protect good morals and keep from going NEAR fornication. Here are just a few: Lower your gaze when speaking directly to the opposite sex; do not stare at sisters or watch the movements of their body; do not watch sexually explicit movies or listen to sexually explicit songs; do not feel, rub or pat sisters; do not lust; do not display adornments, but dress modestly; do not strike (stomp) your feet loudly, calling attention to yourself; do not remain in the company of those who are drinking heavily or using drugs; avoid functions not conducive to righteous conduct; do not engage in inappropriate private conversations – in person or online; do not leave daughters alone with any male; and adults should not be alone in private with the opposite sex, who is not a blood relative.

It was Jesus who raised the bar and desired for his followers to correct immoral behavior by first elevating their thinking. Since every action is first preceded by thought, Jesus said, *"But I tell you that anyone who looks at a woman lustfully has already committed adultery with her in his heart"* (Matthew 5:28, NIV). This bears witness to the Book of Proverbs, *"For as he thinketh in his heart, so is he…"* Again, we can avoid fornication by not going anywhere near it; and we avoid going near it by controlling our thinking. Yes, Allah (God) is ever-Forgiving and the Most Merciful, but He reminds us, *"Repentance with Allah is only for those who do evil in ignorance, then turn (to Allah) soon, so these it is to whom Allah turns (mercifully). And Allah is ever Knowing, Wise. And repentance is not for those who go on doing evil deeds, until when death comes to one of them, he says: Now I repent; nor (for) those who die while they are disbelievers. For such We have prepared a painful chastisement"* (4: 17-18).

VIRTUE & ATTIRE

The Honorable Minister Louis Farrakhan stresses that we must strengthen our families through marriage and this will equal a strong Nation. We must live our lives in accordance with the laws of Allah (God). He forbids us to indulge in our lower desires. As previously stated, fornication (sex before marriage) has no place in the Kingdom of God. We must keep chaste and restrain our sexual passion for the one whom we will marry. Forget about yesterday and focus on today and tomorrow. Both men and women must stop – cold turkey – abusing and misusing one another for sexual pleasure without committing to marriage.

The Honorable Minister Louis Farrakhan said, *"Sex before marriage is forbidden: the beauty of its expression and the pleasure derived from it can cloud our ability to make the proper discovery to aid us in making a proper choice. This is why the Law of Allah (God) is so harsh on fornication. Since Allah (God) hates divorce but will permit it, His Law is very hard on that which clouds the mind disallowing us to make a proper selection of a mate. This alone should teach us the power of sex and its extraordinary effect on our hearts and minds. It can absolutely interfere with our ability to make a good decision."*

Allah (God) has ordained that we marry and that we marry first before we conceive. Women can only give their virtue once and we can only truly love once – unless God intervenes through another man. So, we must make sure that the man we have decided to give our virtue to, is devoted to us for life. It is not only important that we decide not to willingly partake in premarital sex, but we must also take all necessary precautions to keep ourselves as safe as we can from predators. We live in a society where men literally prey upon women like savages. Women are raped every day in every city in America. This heinous abuse of women should be punished by death.

One simple, yet powerful change we can make towards the reduction of rape in our society is for women to dress modestly. Yes, a man *should* be able to control himself regardless of what a woman is wearing; but clearly, that is not our reality. And since we know this, we must protect ourselves. The fact is – women are seen in the streets, in clubs, in office buildings, in our religious houses of worship, etc. with breasts exposed, legs bare up to the crotch, and buttocks revealed. Sometimes we could be covered from head to toe, but our clothing is so tight that it leaves nothing to the imagination.

Now, one may ask, *'Why do I have to change my attire – it's not my fault that men are weak?'* You are correct; however, we should help our brothers to think and act better in order to protect our girls and ourselves. Let me paint this picture: If you are at an intersection in your vehicle and you have the right-of-way, but you see a big truck ready to barrel through the intersection – do you (a) leave your foot on the break and allow the truck to pass or do you (b) foolishly say, *'Well, I have the right-of-way, so I'm going to accelerate regardless'* – ultimately causing a serious injury or losing your life? Being a defensive driver gives us added protection.

The Honorable Minister Louis Farrakhan said that a man's nature is not to exercise control in the presence of a naked woman. Yes, he should do so, but it is unnatural. Our improper dress encourages men to respond and behave badly. Going out alone at night and hanging around crude place also puts us at risk. We can no longer be all talk about eliminating rape – our actions must reflect our desire. The Most Honorable Elijah Muhammad said, *"Where there are no decent women, there are no decent men; for the woman is the Mother of Civilization."*

ARRANGED COURTSHIPS:

Do you remember the 1988 hit movie, *Coming to America*, starring Eddie Murphy as Prince Akeem and Arsenio Hall as his annoying, but hilarious sidekick, Semmi? The premise which propels the plot of this movie centers around the notion that arranged marriages are antiquated and everyone should be free to choose with whom they will spend the rest of their lives. Based on that belief, Prince Akeem and Semmi make their journey to America on a quest to find a bride of the Prince's own choosing, rather than agreeing to marry the woman his family had arranged for him. Of course, Prince Akeem did not want his future bride to know that he was the wealthy heir to the throne of the kingdom of Zamunda. He preferred a woman who would genuinely love him for who he was on the "inside." I will stop right there for the sake of that one person who has not seen this movie.

Arranged marriages are now far removed from being commonplace in most American families; though the practice was widespread through the early 1900s. An arranged marriage is defined as, *"a marriage planned and agreed to by the families or guardians of the bride and groom, who have little or no say in the matter themselves."* Today the term ignites negative visceral reactions because it is now associated with the horrors of child trafficking, child brides and the abuse of women and girls around the world. In its inception; however, it was nothing of the sort. At present, there are many cultures who continue this practice around the world. Those who maintain righteous intentions and actions at the core are finding the practice to be mutually beneficial for the families; boasting countless successful marriages.

However, we do agree with Prince Akeem, in that everyone should be free to choose and decide with whom they will commit to spend the rest of their lives in holy matrimony. Both parties should definitely have the final say in such a personal and consequential life decision, and no one should ever be forced to marry anyone for any reason. **What needs to be arranged is not the marriage, but the courtship.** America's exceedingly high divorce rate dictates a need for a radical change in how we are choosing our mates. We need HELP!

Courtship is not marriage. Courtship is also not dating. There is one intention during courtship: to determine whether or not the two individuals are compatible with having a successful marriage. As with court – questions are asked, discovery is permitted, and witnesses are called, before the final judgment. There is no physical contact during courtship because no commitment has been made. If both individuals prove compatible, then there is an engagement followed by a wedding; if not, the courtship ends with everyone's reputation and character still intact.

Who knows us better than our parents, our grandparents, close relatives and respected elders who were involved in our rearing and watched us mature from childhood into adulthood? It seems that in-laws; particularly mother-in-law, gets a bad rap. Why is that? What causes a mother to become seemingly unhinged and intolerable to the in-laws when she believes that her daughter or son has married the wrong person? Though disguised, her true motivation is sincere. After the love of God, there is no greater love to be found, anywhere, that can equal the love that a mother has for her child. This is not to excuse the bad behavior that some in-laws inflict on others in the name of wanting what's best for their child, but only to highlight the root; which is love.

Children are the greatest investment that parents make. Good parents are constantly investing in their children, and we are not talking about stocks and bonds. We invest in their future by making daily sacrifices to ensure that they will have a good home, a solid spiritual base, quality education, opportunities to travel and to have experiences that will benefit them considerably. Not to mention the mental, emotional and physical sacrifices that only another parent can begin to understand. So, after decade's worth of investment, the hope of every parent is for their child to make a good choice for a spouse and to build a family that is greater than the one they were born into. What seems to be happening, particularly in the Black community, is that every generation is starting over from scratch; instead of building upon what was established. The choices made can set the whole family back for generations, or they can propel us towards a limitless future.

In an interview conducted by Brother Jabril Muhammad, the Honorable Minister Louis Farrakhan discusses the three sciences that the slave master did not want the slave to ever learn. Regarding the science of mating, the Minister said, *"The third science is the science of mating: to know how to properly marry this or that in order to produce a better future. They learned how to produce great horses, pedigreed dogs and how to do this with other life in the animal kingdom. This same science is applicable in the human sphere. (He touched an example where Caucasians used this knowledge among themselves in Europe). They did not wish for us to learn that science because that would mean that through proper mating, we might produce those that would free us from their grip, ultimately and challenge their ruler-ship over us and over the planet."* Great and powerful families

36

whose influence crosses regions and extends for generations are not produced accidentally.

The Most Honorable Elijah Muhammad was taught the science of mating and wanted his followers to practice it as well. There were many arranged courtships by the Most Honorable Elijah Muhammad – couples that he wanted to get married because he knew they would produce great offspring and their families would contribute to the future of our great Nation. Wise parents are ideal for this role. They know the strengths and weaknesses of their children better than anyone. This information helps them to know who may be compatible. In the game of basketball, sometimes the player can make the shot by simply going one-on-one against a defender. But often, they need an assist; the right pass at the right time before they can score. Parents and other close relatives are great at making the assist. An assist does not guarantee a made basket, but it sure helps. Believers in our mosques and churches are also ideal. These houses of worship should arrange the proper social settings and circumstances where single Brothers and Sisters can meet each other. Keeping in mind that while the courtship may be arranged, the decision to marry should exclusively be made and agreed to by the courting couple.

Although Prince Akeem wanted his wife to love him purely for who he was internal, we are the sum total of our life experiences. So, it was the family that he was born into, his way of life and the education and culture that he was exposed to that ultimately made him such a good man. If we are going to establish a strong Nation that will make perpetual progress, we have to look beyond our personal superficial desires. In a recent lecture, The Honorable Minister Louis Farrakhan said to the sisters, *"The man that God made for you may not be very handsome."* Allah (God) never intended marriage to be just about you and me, that's why it is referred to as the institution of marriage. If marriage were just about the couple, then its success or failure would have no impact on anyone beyond the two; but it does. The strength of our Nation is directly proportional to the strength of our marriages and our families. Let's provide a righteous assist by arranging courtships among those whom we love in an effort to strengthen our Nation through strong marriages.

WE ATTRACT WHO WE ARE:

Prophet Muhammad (PBUH) of 1,400 years ago said that marriage is one-half of faith. The greatest of all struggles is to become one with Allah (God) and second to that is the struggle to become one with your spouse. Therefore, if you can make your marriage work; it is a sign that you can become one with Allah (God). Remember that the male and female are not only completely different on the physical plane, but both male and female reflect the two opposite natures of Allah (God). This is why all male/female relationships bring about a necessary difficulty factor. However, we can try to avert much *unnecessary* difficulty by being very careful in our choice of a mate.

One of the biggest errors both men and women make is basing our choice for a mate solely on physical appearance – HUGE mistake. Now, please do not misunderstand. Being physically attracted to someone is certainly necessary since you have to be with them every day for the rest of your life – but it is only a minor requirement to making sure he or she is the one. Another mistake made particularly by women is choosing someone based on financial wealth and/or elite status. You may have heard some women say, *'I don't care what he looks like or what he does, as long as he has money.'* This is insanity. We are neglecting the one essential quality that must be present when making this most serious commitment to be married – the presence of the spirit of Allah (God) in the man and in the woman.

It is a fact that the woman has no resistance to God. If our desire is strong about giving birth to a god, we will call into existence and choose a spouse that complements our will. We call all of our experiences both good and bad into existence by the energy and vibrations we emit, which are produced from our thoughts and actions – this is a universal truth. Negative energies attract negative energies and positive energies attract positive energies. The Honorable Minister Louis Farrakhan teaches us that we will have a spouse in direct proportion to the type of husband or wife we are – no more, no less. Take a look couples you know very well and see if this is not true.

We pray that women will come to the realization that they do not have to "settle" for *whomever they can get*. Do not listen to people who say that you will never find a husband because you expect too much. Our problem has been that we have not expected enough from our men and this is why we have become unhappy, unfulfilled women who are stuck in a marriage that is going nowhere, but down. Choose a good man. Examine him thoroughly during courtship; make sure he understands your sacredness and then make a lucid determination as to whether or not he is worthy of you. Remember – almost always, what you see is what you get. If he is 'the one,' you will know it in the depth of your being. But if there is any doubt…do not get married. Be patient because Allah (God) is still preparing someone for you and preparing you for him.

In order for sisters to attract great men, we must become great women. Here are some qualities shared by the Honorable Minister Louis Farrakhan of a great woman: (1) She loves deeply and unselfishly, (2) she serves with joy, (3) she feels good as a sweetheart, a good wife, a good mother, a good grandmother, and a real companion to her husband, and (4) above all, her greatest quality is love. Love is not an intense feeling or emotion. To truly love is to be like God {more on this later in the book}.

Brothers: You too must desire to produce a god. Be careful of your choice for a wife. Choose a good, righteous woman. Remember, she is the one who is going to reproduce you into the future. The Honorable Minister Louis Farrakhan stated that the greatest gift to any man is a virtuous woman. The Holy Qur'an reads, *"And they who say, Our Lord, grant us in our wives and our offspring the joy of our eye, and make us leaders for those who guard against evil. These are rewarded with high places and salutation, Abiding therein. Goodly the abode and the resting-place"* (25: 74-75).

Men cannot see God except through the woman because the secret of God lies in her. Minister Farrakhan said every time you handle a woman right, you are handling your future right. Every time you tell her that you love her, you are saying you love your future. The Black woman is not man's woman, but she is the woman of God. We will never become a great people or Nation disrespecting the woman because she is the most important element in Nation building.

The Holy Qur'an states that we should reverence the womb that bore us. This not only refers to the womb of our biological mother, but the womb of every woman should be reverenced. To reverence something is to hold it in awe and high esteem. The Honorable Minister Louis Farrakhan said, *"Allah (God) will punish us severely for violation of these principles of conduct concerning the treatment of the woman. Where there is disrespect for the woman, there is disrespect for Allah (God), for the secret of the womb is the secret of His Work that is taking place within the womb. When this reverence is displayed, only then will the Kingdom of God be established."*

So, before a man gets married, he should study and pray for understanding and guidance on how to properly maintain the woman spiritually. Pray that Allah (God) keeps fresh in your mind her importance. If the only value one sees in the female is access to sexual gratification or making her a personal slave; then please do all of humanity a favor and leave women alone until Allah (God) blesses you with understanding. Allah (God) hates divorce, and a marriage based on sex and selfish desires is guaranteed to be unsuccessful. We must make Allah (God) the only reality and the true center of our marriages.

The Honorable Minister Louis Farrakhan said, *"Heaven lies at the foot of mother...In order for heaven to be at the woman's foot or mother's foot, the mother has to be in complete submission or surrender of her life to the Will of Almighty (God) Allah. This becomes exceedingly difficult if the woman is not in the charge of or in the company of a righteous man. Mary was blessed to be this kind of virtuous woman because she was prepared from the womb, but she was also under the authority of a righteous male figure...If the female is unprotected, disrespected, and devalued, then, what comes from her womb is the same."*

PROPER COURTSHIP WORKS:

Let's be honest: When we hear that a couple is getting divorced, 9 times out of 10 we are not the least bit surprised. Why is that? How could we have anticipated the end was coming long before the pronouncement? The Honorable Minister Louis Farrakhan said that how something comes into existence often determines how long it will last. This universal law is as true for the origin of a country as it is for each of our marriages. Everything has a beginning – every plant has a root; every building starts with a foundation, and every marriage was initiated by a pursuit. The composition and quality inherent in every beginning will determine its strength, health, and longevity. So, if we want to determine why something ended or how long it will last, examine the beginning.

According to the U.S. Census Bureau, in 1890, just 25 years post chattel slavery – Black women were more likely to be married than white women; and Black men were more likely to be married than white men. However, the trend began to reverse in the 1960s for men and in the 1970s for women. In 1890, 80% of Black households were comprised of two parents. Over one hundred years later, only 40% of Black children live in a household with married parents. As it stands today, according to the National Healthy Marriage Resource Center, *"African Americans are significantly less likely than other racial/ethnic groups to ever marry, less likely to remarry, more likely to divorce, separate and cohabit and bear and rear children out-of-wedlock (and in mother-only households)."*

There are many factors contributing to these sad statistics, but one variable remains unchanged. Instead of engaging in a careful, thoughtful and deliberate courtship process, we are replacing courtship with dating, premarital sex, and cohabiting. This is the way of the world, not Allah's (God's) way. Allah (God) forbids premarital sex and He hates divorce. Therefore, in the Nation of Islam to increase our likelihood of success, we do not date. We do not have boyfriends or girlfriends; in fact, this concept is completely foreign to both Bible and Holy Qur'an. We will not find a reference or equivalency to "boyfriend" or "girlfriend" in the scriptures. Today, we can no longer lip profess about God being the center of our lives and our marriages, our actions and choices must bear witness that we prefer His way.

When a young man believes he is ready for marriage and sees a young lady he would like to pursue, he should never share his intentions directly with her without first approaching her father. Regardless of her age, if the father is living; any honorable man will seek permission from the father and mother first. There can be no shortcuts during the courtship process because a proper courtship has one purpose: *to determine whether or not the couple is compatible to have a successful marriage*. This must be approached with all seriousness and righteous intention, we cannot allow our physical attraction to one another to cloud our critical discovery.

The Honorable Minister Louis Farrakhan shared these words, which give us a snapshot of a proper courtship process: *"Among the righteous, courtship is chaperoned. This is done to keep the parties who are attracted to each other from entering into premarital sex, which then stops the process of courtship. In the word courtship is the word court. By definition, we mean a place where justice is administered and a place where the process of finding the truth which forms the basis of justice and judgment. When two people are courting they are bringing evidence to either support their intention to be engaged, or evidence that they should look in other directions. This process of finding out as much as we can about each other is necessary for forming good and proper judgment. The individuals are the jury that must render a decision and the individuals must become the judges that ultimately make the decision that he or she is the right one for me. Cross examination is a part of court procedure, which allows direct testimony to be challenged to see if the persons are telling the truth, for it is only truth that will permit us to make good judgment. The more truth we know about each other, our characteristics, ways, strengths, and weaknesses, it is the more right we can be in making a decision if we should become engaged to be married or not."*

Our conversations during courtship should begin with a focus on spirituality, our personal backgrounds, career ambitions, and family goals. If we find compatibility in those areas, we must then deal with and not shy away from practical areas. For example, in the N.O.I. if either has been previously married, proof of divorce must be provided. Before marriage we must also be willing to share our medical history and provide proof of health screenings; particularly for HIV and other STDs. Finances must also be discussed – some couples actually request to see credit reports before walking down the aisle (not a bad idea). In addition, it is mandatory that all couples receive counseling before they are married.

All courtships do not lead to engagement and marriage. If a couple determines they are not compatible, the courtship should end immediately. There are no commitments made during courtship and no intimate contact; so, this allows both to part with reputations intact and no ill feelings toward each other. The courtship process is far more in-depth than can be shared in this book; therefore, we strongly recommend that before entering into a courtship everyone read the Nation of Islam's ***Comprehensive Courtship Manual*** compiled by The Healthy Relationship Initiative Team. We also recommend reading the book, ***Before You Say I Do*** by Brother Nuri Muhammad; and ***Real Love*** by Minister Ava Muhammad. Most importantly, please invest in your future by taking the time to listen to as many lectures on marriage and family by The Honorable Minister Louis Farrakhan as possible. He has given dozens of lectures on this profound topic that must be parsed. Not to mention he is a living example of a happily married man for now 65 years!

In a lecture, The Honorable Minister Louis Farrakhan said to the Sisters, *"There are good men around. Don't look for them. Let God bring one to you."* We need to stay out of God's way and remain steadfast and patient. He is preparing someone for everyone. Do not circumvent the courtship process out of fear of losing out on someone. What Allah (God) has for you, no one can take from you; and what He does not intend for you to have, no one can give to you. We know that insanity is doing the same thing over and over, expecting different results. It's time to try God's way and submit to a righteous courtship process – His way works!

PREPARING THE BODY TO CONCEIVE IN ONE YEAR:

If we were to poll a large group of parents and ask if they believed they were one-hundred percent ready for parenthood – or even 80-90% ready, most would say, *"Absolutely not!"* If Allah (God) required us to be one-hundred percent ready before reproducing, the human population would have faced extinction eons ago. This is not to say that the application and preparation to become parents should not be taken seriously – it certainly should. But if we waited until every aspect of our lives was perfect, we may never become parents. The purpose of this section is to share a few areas of focus that will help future and current parents reach a level of comfort and confidence before conceiving; whether it's their first or fourth child. Knowing that we have actively prepared by making sure crucial elements have been achieved, allows us some level of peace and readiness for parenthood.

There are seven primary areas of focus we should be aware of that will prepare the body to conceive new life. Though our primary focus is on the body, we should approach this with an understanding that there are other areas that should be settled before deciding to become parents. The two biggest areas are marriage and finances. If we are not married to someone with whom we are equally yoked, mentally and spiritually, then we are not yet ready to reproduce. Our spouse does not have to be perfect, but they do need to be perfect for us. If our finances are nonexistent, we are not ready. Again, we do not have to be wealthy, but we should definitely be financially stable. Once these two areas are cemented, it's time to prepare the body.

CHILDREN OF THE MOST HIGH

AREA 1:   The Honorable Minister Louis Farrakhan said that we should take at least one year to clean up our bodies before conceiving. The intention of both husband and wife has to be to purify their physical vessels before conceiving. Each must desire to have optimum cleanliness of mind, body, and spirit. This must be discussed and planned together. There is nothing more powerful than a made-up mind. Our mind has to be made-up to produce children who will make a tangible impact on the world – we have to desire to give birth to gods. Great children are desired long before they exist. If the desire is absent, the will cannot be fed and if the will is not fed, we will not make the necessary sacrifices to transform desire into reality.

AREA 2:   Women should schedule a preconception visit with their midwife or OB-GYN and get a complete gynecological exam and overall physical, including bloodwork. This should be done at least one year before trying to conceive, and then again one month prior to conception. This is the best way to know what health issues are specific to you. Men should do the same with a family practice physician. Our health is paramount; including good oral hygiene – so see the dentist! We may be surprised at the regularity at which health issues begin in the mouth. Do not be discouraged by any health challenges uncovered – be grateful for such knowledge. Almost every negative condition can be reversed by changing our diet, daily habits and making different lifestyle choices.

AREA 3:   We must cast away all harmful, foreign chemicals and substances. This includes drugs (crack, cocaine, heroin, marijuana, inhalants, synthetics, etc.); over-the-counter and prescription medications (most of which have natural and much healthier alternatives); alcohol; cigarettes and all tobacco or nicotine products; caffeine; and all forms of hormonal birth control. All of these vices quickly enter the bloodstream and therefore will become a part of the genetic make-up of a woman's eggs and a man's sperm.

AREA 4: Invest in a copy of *How to Eat to Live: Book I & II* by The Most Honorable Elijah Muhammad and practice the diet he describes as a prescription for our ills and to give us an abundance of life. Our healthcare practitioners will tell us to begin taking folic acid and prenatal vitamins prior to conceiving. However, if we are strict in our discipline and practice of the principles detailed in these two books, not only will we not need additional vitamins and supplements, but we will be able to prevent and reverse illness and disease.

AREA 5: Both men and women have to establish a regular exercise pattern and routine. Stagnation is death – we have to get moving. Women, in particular, need to prepare their bodies to be fit for pregnancy. Conception can be difficult if we are extremely underweight or overweight. During pregnancy, this can lead to unhealthy birth weight and/or complication during labor and delivery. So, we should strive to be at a healthy weight prior to conception. If one has not been exercising, start slowly then gradually increase the duration and level of intensity every couple of weeks. We should focus on cardiovascular exercises, increasing muscle strength and flexibility during this preparation year.

AREA 6: As women, we should use the months before trying to conceive to get an understanding of the dynamics of our personal monthly cycles – menstruation and ovulation. This is solely the woman's responsibility, but what she discovers must be shared and discussed with her husband so that conception does not take place prematurely. When a woman is about to ovulate, the increase of LH (luteinizing hormone) can be detected in her urine by using ovulation kits. There are also clear changes in her basal body temperature and cervical mucus. However, in order to determine one's personal pattern, these changes must be charted and recorded over a period of several months. This makes it possible to pinpoint ovulation, so conception can take place when desired. {More specifics later in the book}

AREA 7: Humans do not exist on the physical plane alone. The body is affected by the mind and the spirit, and how we feel about ourselves physically has a bearing on our willingness to strive to achieve mental and spiritual greatness. The Honorable Minister Louis Farrakhan said that prior to conceiving, women should say a prayer, *"O Allah (God), help me to produce from my womb, a son or a daughter that will glorify you and change the reality of the world's condition – bless my womb…"* He went on to say that if this is said over and over again, it will be in our blood, in the cells of our brain and in our eggs. A thought is a chemical substance. It permeates from the mind and travels throughout the body, affecting every cell – from the brain to the heel. Every action is first preceded by a thought, so we must work to rid ourselves of internal vices which are affecting our mental, spiritual and physical health.

The Honorable Minister Louis Farrakhan said, *"So as you get yourself ready…the first thing you [have] to do is weed out your garden. Pluck up the things from yourself that you know will not be good for your child to feed on in your mind: Bitterness, envy, jealousy, hatred, vile behavior, that comes from vile thoughts; you [have] got to make a sacrifice and get rid of that, if you want to produce a child for God… Get your womb together. Get this womb (mind) and this womb (body). Both wombs work together, co-operating with God; for the resuscitation, reformation, regeneration, and procreation of human life."*

WE REPEAT: OUR PHYSICAL HEALTH IS CRUCIAL:

In preparation before conception, we cannot say enough about the physical body. Our physical health is crucial. Start immediately cleaning up the body, even if we are not yet married. Time is the only commodity that we can never get back; so, the sooner or earlier in life we begin, the better for ourselves and for our future children. As we stated, take at least one full year to clean up the body physically. Eliminate all alcoholic beverages, cigarettes, marijuana, illegal drugs, and medications. Stop using hormonal birth control. And absolutely stop eating the awful swine (pork and all its by-products). Remember what we said earlier – it is going to take sacrifice! Alcohol, cigarettes, drugs, medications, etc. go directly into our bloodstream. Our blood feeds every cell in the body including the female's eggs and the male's sperm. If we indulge in these poisons, then we have sentenced our babies to death before they are even born. Our children will be born genetically weakened and their bodies will have become what the Honorable Minister Louis Farrakhan has called a *'toxic waste dump.'* We have now made it close to impossible for them to reach their God-given potential, which is their birthright. Whatever we consume becomes the make-up of our eggs and the same for the male sperm.

We mentioned swine, but there are other horrible foods that we must eliminate from our diet. We must change our eating habits drastically; particularly in the Black community. We love so-called soul food – pig, fried foods, black-eyed peas, collard greens, and corn bread – all of which are harmful. Swine is so bad for us that Allah (God) forbids us from touching it, smelling it and definitely eating it. Allah (God) blessed us with this most precious gift of life and if we want to remain healthy, we must obey His prescription for a long life.

We repeat: Two books that are mandatory for our personal library are: *How to Eat to Live – Book One* and *How to Eat to Live – Book Two*; written by the Most Honorable Elijah Muhammad. In these books, he lists several foods that we should stay away from and also those foods that we should partake. What we eat keeps us here, but it also takes us away. Every item we put in our mouth is either going to prolong our life or shorten our life – there is no grey area. Therefore, we should give serious thought when it comes to our food choices.

We must live a natural life in order for future generations to live as long as the old patriarchs. In the Bible, we read of people such as Noah, who lived 950 years and Methuselah who also lived nearly 1,000 years. These are not fairytales. We look very foolish getting excited to hear that someone lived to be 100-years-old before passing away; when the human body has the capacity to live a maximum of 1,000 years and still look young, be healthy, active and still be able to reproduce. Now, we are not saying that anyone alive today or even our children are going to live 1,000 years. But, if we start, today, cleaning-up physically, mentally, and spiritually, our children will live significantly longer and healthier than you or I and our grandchildren will live longer than our children, etc. A few generations from now we will once again live as long as the old patriarchs. *All praise is due to Allah (God)!*

All of this means coming away from McDonald's, KFC, Burger King, and other fast food merchants of death, who sell so-called food, filled with chemicals and dangerous preservatives. We must get back into the kitchen and make our own meals. The Most Honorable Elijah Muhammad teaches us to eat fresh foods, not canned, frozen or boxed meals. Fresh foods contain life in them and if we learn to cook them properly, we can preserve the life in them, which will sustain our own life. A vegetarian diet is best.

An additional mandatory sacrifice is to cut down the number of meals we eat per day, gradually, until we are eating only one complete meal per day. What??? Yes. We have to change our thinking about food. We have been taught to eat three meals a day, which is absurd because it takes the body at least 24 hours to completely digest a meal, distribute the nutrients and expel the waste from our system. The Most Honorable Elijah Muhammad teaches that some food even takes 36 hours to digest. So, one meal a day is all we need. We promise it will not kill you. On the contrary, you will be healthier, have more energy and lengthen your time on this earth. What ultimately kills us is the over working of our stomach and digestive system by constantly putting food in it without adequate rest. This wears down our stomach and intestinal lining. If our stomach could talk, it would beg us for a break. How often we eat is even more important than what we eat (with the exception of the pig).

The ultimate sacrifice for the physical body is FASTING. Fasting 72 hours (3 days) every month will keep us protected from most illnesses. By fasting, we mean eating no food at all and only drinking water or coffee (tea, if you do not drink coffee). Again, you will not die. Fasting regularly is necessary because all food has some poison in it regardless of its origin or how clean it appears. The Most Honorable Elijah Muhammad wrote, *"Every meal we put in our bodies has some poison in it. And, some of our food, as I have said in this book (How to Eat to Live – Book Two), takes 36 hours to digest. If we do not wait until our previous meal has been digested and we add a new meal to the previous meal we have new poison, in its full strength, to aid the dying poison of the previous meal or help it revive in strength; and we will continue to be sick."* Fasting is the cure for 90 percent of our ills. However, it is difficult and takes mental and spiritual preparation – the fact is, we are denying ourselves one of the body's most natural functions – to eat. However, the benefit far outweighs the sacrifice.

And of course, we must reemphasize exercise in the preparation of our physical body. Master Fard Muhammad said the best form of exercise is walking. We must exercise our bodies in preparation for pregnancy, which we know adds several pounds of additional weight; and there is no question about the physical strength and endurance we will need to actually withstand labor and then deliver the baby. Walking does not take much effort. So walk briskly at least three or four times a week for a minimum of 30 minutes each time. This goes for brothers also. Exercise gives us natural energy, strength and promotes good health. Sweating is also good for the skin – it removes toxins, which will, in turn, purify the skin and keep it smooth and clear. Weight lifting, aerobics, running, dancing, and playing sports (basketball, tennis, volleyball, swimming, etc.) are all excellent forms of exercise. Whichever we choose to do, we should make sure that we remain consistent.

New studies are now showing that men have to begin cleaning up their physical bodies at least five years prior to conception. This makes sense because it is the male sperm that carries the genetic make-up for the child. Sperm poisoned by drugs, alcohol, smoke and bad food is harmful to the child both mentally and physically. The Black woman, however, is so powerful that if she is in-tuned with God, she can take a weak sperm and still produce a giant – so imagine what she could do with healthy sperm. The man's role is crucial to our future. The Honorable Minister Louis Farrakhan said that the man carries the ideals and the vision of the future, not the woman. So, when the man's ideals are crushed it can sometimes destroy the man. But what type of vision and ideals can a man conceive if he is dependent on chemical agents instead of Allah (God)?

IS DOUCHING HARMFUL OR ESSENTIAL?

Sisters, we've got to talk about it! Allah (God) blessed us with two wombs – one physical of course, and the other mental – our mind. Both must be protected and properly maintained. This section's focus is on the woman's physical womb (uterus) and her sacred vaginal tract, the path of entry to God's laboratory. The womb must be guarded from predatory men and those who "appear" well-intentioned but have not yet committed to marriage. Our sacred chamber must also be protected from those who profit from our ignorance or are simply malicious and desire to see our birth rate significantly reduced. The womb should not be tampered with, so we have to be wise about how we cleanse ourselves.

The Holy Qur'an reads, *"And they ask thee about menstruation. Say: It is harmful; so keep aloof from women during menstrual discharge and go not near them until they are clean. But when they have cleansed themselves, go in to them as Allah has commanded you. Surely Allah loves those who turn much (to Him), and He loves those who purify themselves"* (2: 222). It is important to put this scripture into proper context. Menstruation is a part of the woman's natural reproductive function, designed by Allah (God), so it is not the process of menstruation that is harmful. However, this scripture is an answer to men who are inquiring about having sexual relations with their wives during menstruation, which is indeed harmful; so, husbands are told that they should not be sexually intimate with their wives during this time of the month. This same guidance is given in the Bible (Leviticus 18:19).

Moreover, we want to highlight another aspect of this same scripture where it reads, *"But when they [women] have cleansed themselves…"* This indicates that after menstruation there is a process of cleansing that should take place. And here is where we have to be careful. There are many over-the-counter commercial products that claim to be safe for vaginal douching (vaginal washing). These products contain a liquid solution, but often the chemical combination can be more hazardous than beneficial. Women douche for several reasons: to cleanse after menstruation or sexual intercourse, personal hygiene, to eliminate odor, prevent an infection, treat an infection, and because they believe it will prevent pregnancy – it does NOT. With the exception of the latter, all of this can be achieved by using natural methods for cleansing.

The female vaginal tract is considered a hostile environment due to its natural acidic nature. When we use commercial products to douche, we can disrupt the vaginal pH levels by weakening or reducing acidity levels. The acid produced in the vaginal tract allow healthy bacteria to thrive while protecting it from dangerous bacteria and disease. If our body chemistry is altered and our vaginal tract is weakened, it is left vulnerable. Studies now warn that traditional methods of douching can actually increase the risk of infections, STIs, pregnancy complications, and other health problems. The National Institutes of Health states, *"Douching has been associated with many adverse outcomes including pelvic inflammatory disease (PID), bacterial vaginosis, cervical cancer, low birth weight, preterm birth, human immunodeficiency virus (HIV) transmission, sexually transmitted diseases, ectopic pregnancy, recurrent vulvovaginal candidiasis, and infertility."* The chemicals and fragrances found in many commercial products seem to be doing more harm than good.

It is important to emphasize that douching with the wrong products can lead to problems getting pregnant and staying pregnant. These chemical combinations are destroying our physical womb by breaking down the lining of our uterine wall. Once conception takes place, the embryo has to latch on to the uterine wall and remain there until delivery in order to survive. This attachment is not strong or secure until the third month of pregnancy. This is why so many miscarriages take place before the pregnancy completes its first trimester. A history of douching can increase the likelihood that the embryo will not properly latch on to the uterine wall, causing a miscarriage.

In addition, the Honorable Minister Louis Farrakhan teaches that the acidic nature of the vaginal tract gives sperm a necessary difficulty factor, in the form of a hostile environment, where it must struggle to navigate before reaching the egg. This allows for only one sperm, the most intelligent one, that can endure such an environment to make it to the egg. It is the most intelligent because not only did it conquer the hostile environment, but it did so by traveling upstream against the pull of gravity and winning the competition against tens of millions of other sperm.

So, let's be careful not to upset God's handiwork. There are natural and safe ways to go about cleansing without altering nature. First, it is important to understand that not every woman needs to "douche" in the traditional sense; but every woman does need to go through a process of cleansing. For some, bathing thoroughly or soaking regularly is sufficient; particularly if she is healthy, has a strict diet, and disciplined exercise routine. In addition, those who need to douche may not need to douche every time. We must become masters of our unique body chemistry, so that we are able to note and manage any fluctuations. If women find that they do need to douche or formally cleanse themselves on a regular basis, please choose a natural alternative. Each woman has to decide what works best for her, but some suggestions include: adding a little distilled white vinegar to a warm bath and soaking; or adding baking soda to a warm bath. Also, try drinking apple cider vinegar (slightly diluted); and adding garlic to your daily diet. There are many additional healthy and safe alternatives. We strongly recommend consulting with a naturopathic or holistic healthcare practitioner for more guidance.

THE SECOND WOMB:

Both men and women possess a mental womb. Today is the day to begin to change our attitudes and thoughts because our thinking has a direct bearing on the child growing in the womb [more on this in the next section]. The Book of Proverbs reads, *"Wisdom is the principal thing; therefore get wisdom: and with all thy getting get understand"* (4:7).

The saying: *'Everything you need to know is found in a book,'* is very true. We cannot wait until we are pregnant to start exercising the brain. Minister Farrakhan said that our life depends on our willingness to read. And he did not mean silly fairy tales, romance novels or tabloid magazines. We must read and study material that informs, educates and elevates our thinking to a higher level. It does not matter if we have a Ph.D.; none of us have arrived. Knowledge is infinite and as long as we believe that we are "learned" individuals, we will stop the process of learning, which leads to mental and spiritual stagnation.

The more knowledge, understanding, and wisdom we have as women, the more our children will have. Again, in the Book of Proverbs, it reads, *"A wise man maketh a glad father: but a foolish man despiseth his mother"* (15:20). The hard truth is that we cannot be dumb women and think that we will produce mental giants. We must constantly be on a quest for more and more knowledge. The brain is composed of approximately 75% water, which makes it a transmitter. It can be stimulated by thinking over and over on righteousness until it is in the cells, the blood, our eggs and every fiber of our being.

The Honorable Minister Louis Farrakhan said, *"In order for the female to produce a great future for us, she must be filled with the desire for knowledge, specifically the knowledge of Allah (God) and His Word. Any society that deprives the female of the deepest aspect of the study of the Word of Allah (God) is a society that will not approach the potential of its greatness. For, only when we have a highly spiritual and moral woman, educated, cultivated, cultured and refined will she be able to bring into existence a civilization bearing these same fine qualities and characteristics."*

Our spirituality must also be advanced through prayer and meditation. Prayer is the greatest force to keep us away from evil and indecency. There is nothing more humbling than direct communication with the Source of Life, Allah (God). Several times each day, we should commune with the Supreme Being to thank Him for all of the blessings He has bestowed upon us and to ask Him for His guidance and protection as things seem dark and unsure. We cannot emphasize enough the importance of praying for and about everything and anything. The more we pray and have conversations with Allah (God), the more His Reality will be made known to us. We must build a personal relationship with Allah (God) and learn to turn to Him for help. Allah (God) says in the Holy Qur'an, *"I, Allah, am the Best Knower."* He also says that He would not care for us were it not for our prayers. We turn to everyone and everything else for assistance except for the One Who controls every atom in the Universe. This is insanity. Prayer will also begin to change our physiological chemistry as Allah (God) begins to dwell within, making us one with Him.

In addition to prayer, meditation is very calming and helps us to focus on maintaining inner peace. It helps us attract to ourselves those people and things in life that are authentic. Every morning after prayer, we should take at least ten minutes of quiet time to ourselves before the rest of our personal world awakens. Choose a relaxed position and close your eyes – practice breathing deeply, then exhaling slowly. Relax the entire body from head to toe, one section at a time until the body becomes limp. Allow the chaos to leave the mind and peace to enter. Remember, two things cannot occupy the same space at the same time. Use this opportunity to not only relax but regain focus before the busyness of the day begins. This time can also be used to concentrate on future or current goals and desires.

Prayer and meditation will help rid us of all negatives such as fear, vanity, pride, envy, lust, anger, greed and the list goes on. Prayer cleanses us of vile thoughts, which lead to vile behavior. Remember, every action is first preceded by a thought. It is a daily struggle to become like our Creator – but it is not impossible, in fact, it is natural to strive to be like the Father.

Prayer, meditation and a thirst for knowledge will naturally lead us to actions, which will reveal our greatness. Make goals, small and large, which will allow a way to measure personal growth and progress. An idle mind is indeed the devil's workshop. When we have nothing to do and no vision to fulfill, we will find ourselves stuck in a daily or weekly rut. Our routine pattern of behavior will go no further than watching television all day; playing video games, partying or clubbing, eating anything and everything; or getting stuck in a job we hate for no other reason than to pay bills. If this sounds recognizable, we must make a change today.

THE ACT OF PROCREATION:

The ultimate goal of every sensible parent is to produce children who will one day become exceptionally greater than they are, in every aspect of life – health, spiritually, mentally, financially, relationships, etc. We want to see our offspring in a continuous state of onward progression. Growing to become *just* like the parents is unsatisfactory and regression can be completely devastating to loving parents. One key component that seems to be absent when it comes to realizing this ultimate goal, is a lack of respect for the power of planning.

The Most Honorable Elijah Muhammad said that there were three scientific fields of knowledge that the slave master did not want the slave to ever learn: (1) the science of business, (2) the science of warfare and (3) the science of mating. Notice that we did not say: how to make money, how to shoot a gun and how to have intercourse. To know the science of something goes far beyond the surface. One who sciences something uncovers the very nature of the thing because he/she has observed, researched, tested and proven it several times over. If we know the science of something, we can master it. For the purpose of this book, we will focus on the science of mating.

What is the special formula to mating that wise white people have held in secrecy; but by the permission of God has been exposed? The science of mating covers a broad spectrum; which begins with how we are reared and educated during childhood and continues throughout courtship and marriage. There is one aspect of the science of mating that we tend to shy away from, which is the actual act of procreation – this too is scientific.

There are several instances in the Holy Qur'an where Allah (God) makes clear that He is continuously planning. He also declares at least twice in the Holy Qur'an, that He is the BEST of Planners (3:53, 8:30) – disabusing us of any thought to the contrary. One of the many Glorious names of Allah (God) is Al-Khāliq, which is most often translated to mean The Creator. But in addition to meaning, The Creator, other scholars translate it to mean, The Planner. If we are direct descendants of The Creator and Planner; then we are imbued with His essence and should manifest His attributes. The fact that Allah (God) plans is an indication that we, too, should plan – understanding that we will <u>never</u> become the Best of Planners. However, we do have the potential to become exceptional at planning. Is there any greater aspect of our lives that should be planned with thoughtful consideration and detail, than the moment we decide to procreate?

Allah (God) created the act of sex for the divine purpose of procreation, not recreation. Let's rewind…The number one purpose of sex is to reproduce! We are not saying that we <u>only</u> have sex for that purpose, but the fact that Allah (God) allowed sex to be pleasurable is a nice bonus that helps to keep our marriages vibrant and passionate. To be clear, sexual intercourse outside of the sanctity of marriage is misuse and abuse of this most profound and sacred act. Each generation is falling further and further away from understanding that sex was not meant to be a cheap, low down, dirty act; but an act of responsibility and glory. The Honorable Minister Louis Farrakhan stated, *"These (sexual) pleasure centers in the human being, used properly in accord with the Will of Allah (God), brings comfort, ease, consolation, rest, reward and joy to the souls that are working hard to fulfill their divine duty and obligation."* If sex comes before natural love has been established and sanctioned by marriage, then that becomes the base of our relationship. A relationship based on physical desires will be short-lived.

The hard truth is that most of us were conceived accidentally, not planned. Our parents most likely did not say to each other, *'Sweetheart, let's try to conceive a baby tonight.'* We were likely the product of a lustful encounter. Many of us may even have been the product of a one-night stand – our mother hardly knowing the man; or the unthinkable, a product of rape or incest. With proper planning, current and future generations can break this destructive cycle. It's imperative that we learn the science of mating because what goes on while something is being fashioned becomes a part of the nature of the thing.

Once we get ourselves together morally, physically, mentally and spiritually; it is strongly recommended that husband and wife take at least two to three years to adjust to marriage and enjoy quality and quantity time together before the tremendous demands of parenthood enter into the picture. Get to know one another and start to build a strong foundation by strengthening your relationship with God and with each other. Learn what makes each other happy and what annoys. Talking on the phone and going out to dinner once in a while during courtship is one thing. But as the cliché goes, *'You never really know a person until you have lived with them.'* In the second month of pregnancy is not the time to first discover that your husband has the world's worst snoring problem or that your wife refuses to clean up after herself. This sounds petty, but it seems that everything is magnified when a woman is pregnant. Our children will enjoy a more loving and peaceful household if these small issues are worked out before conception.

Unlike the man who is constantly producing sperm; women are born with all of the eggs they will ever have. Women release one egg every month, so she must be careful of the foods, drinks and outside influences that she consumes; this will all affect that specific egg. Maintaining a healthy and regular diet, exercise routine and lifestyle increases the ability of a woman to know, with precision, her fertile days (before, during & after ovulation). This information is necessary in order to plan the very moment that intimacy with her husband will lead to conception. Spontaneity certainly has its rewards and benefits, but it must be temporarily deferred when the intention is to procreate. Once the glorious decision has been made – there is nothing left to do but conceive. When a couple anticipates and desires for a specific moment of intimacy to result in pregnancy, then they must both become mentally and spiritually involved; not just physically. It is especially important for the woman to elevate her thoughts. How and why we were conceived has much to do with the type of person we are today.

The Honorable Minister Louis Farrakhan said, *"Plan the very minute you want to conceive. Conceive at dawn as the sun is rising in the east and you are both well rested and full of energy from a night of sleep. Do not conceive in the middle of the night or before bed when both of you are tired and sleepy. Be sure that you are prayerful at this moment repeating the attributes of Allah...Bismillahir Rahman nir-Raheem (In the Name of Allah, the Beneficent, the Merciful). Lay down with your husband/wife in the Name of Allah. The woman lies prone looking to the heavens and the man is looking to the earth. You become one, head to head and chest to chest, not filled with lust and passion alone, but filled with the spirit of God. Have Allah (God) on your mind, woman, and the type of child you wish to conceive."*

A man and woman who have Allah (God) as the center of their relationship learn to see one another as Allah (God) sees them. The Honorable Minister Louis Farrakhan said that a woman who truly loves you wants to produce you over again. She will not be upset but will be overcome with joy when she learns of the life that is growing inside of her. The most sacred thing a woman can do above any profession is to bear a child. This sacred act demands that we take it seriously and place the uppermost importance on it. The Book of Psalms reads, *"Ye are all gods, children of the Most High God."* Let us give our children a proper start and ensure them the best opportunity of living up to that declaration.

CHOOSING THE SEX OF OUR BABIES NATURALLY:

If you were told that you could choose the sex of your baby before conception, would you do it? If so, why? If not, why not? Is it ethical? Is it in harmony with your moral ethos and principles to predetermine the sex of your baby? If we answer, "yes," to choosing the sex of our children but our reason is superficial – girls have cuter clothes or boys are so much easier – then, we would argue that the motive is without substance and therefore could be considered unethical or at a minimum misguided. However, if the intention is farseeing and the decision is made to produce future eventualities that will have a consequential impact on the family, community, and Nation; then it is not only ethical but worth our serious consideration.

The birth of Master W. Fard Muhammad, founder of The Nation of Islam – long awaited Saviour of the Black man and woman, and Teacher of the Most Honorable Elijah Muhammad was not by happenstance. His Father (in addition to other wise scientists), having Supreme knowledge of both history and prophecy knew that it was time for such a Deliverer to be born for the purpose of redeeming the Black man and woman of America. Before our incredible fall, we wrote history thousands of years in advance and then walked into it. Did gender have any significance in our writings? Of course, it did. The coming of Master W. Fard Muhammad and His work was written in the scriptures thousands of years before His birth.

Brother Jabril Muhammad writes, *"He (Master Fard Muhammad) took the Honorable Elijah Muhammad back to what led His (Master Fard Muhammad's) Father to produce Him in the first place. That which led to His birth was rooted in prophecy (the foresight and insight of the Gods) written in the Bible and Holy Qur'an concerning a lost people that needed finding, and of the new world that He would produce through them...This Father was a real Black man. He knew, therefore, that it would not have been wise for Him to come Himself. He knew He had to have a Son Who looked like the wicked infidels among whom He would have to go (and there were other factors in His reasoning). So, He went up into the mountains and got a*

CHILDREN OF THE MOST HIGH

White woman: a Caucasian. He prepared her to give birth to this special Son. This is hinted at in the Bible in the mentioning of a woman out of whom was drawn seven devils in the 'gospels.' You can also find her mentioned in Revelation and elsewhere. The preachers and theologians used to ponder and argue over the coming of this special Son. He is referred to in the New Testament as the Son of Man."

So, Master W. Fard Muhammad's father knew He needed a **son** for this special mission, not a daughter. How was He able to guarantee that the woman would bear a son, fulfilling the prophecy? We cannot be one-hundred percent certain; but we now have a level of knowledge in the fields of science, biology, and reproduction which allows us to make an intelligent exploration as to how we can determine the sex of our own children.

It is the man that determines the biological sex of the baby, not the woman. We know that the female or X-sperm is slower; yet slightly bigger, stronger, and lives longer than the male or Y-sperm. The male (Y) sperm has a smaller head, it is weaker, dies sooner, but is much faster than its counterpart. With that in mind, consider that a man can emit anywhere from tens of millions to hundreds of millions of sperm at a time; most of which will die within minutes. However, those that remain can live inside of the woman for up to five days (3 days on average). Now, ovulation takes place when a woman's egg is released. Women have one ovulation day per cycle. The egg only has 12-24 hours to be fertilized once it is released. But since sperm can live up to five days inside of a woman, she can have up to six fertile days per cycle. This means she can get pregnant from sperm that was emitted within the five days leading up to ovulation and up to 24 hours after ovulation.

This information is important if a couple is trying to increase the chances of having one sex over another. If a boy is desired, then based on what we know about the characteristics of the male (Y) sperm; intercourse

64

should take place on the day of ovulation, not before. Theoretically, the faster male (Y) sperm will make it to the egg first. If a girl is desired, then intercourse should take place a few days before ovulation; because based on the characteristics of the female (X) sperm; it will outlive the male (Y) sperm and still be around to fertilize the egg once it is released days later. This natural method for choosing the sex of our babies is called the Shettles Method, named after Dr. Landrum Shettles – studies confirms that it is effective 85% of the time. The Shettles Method makes a few other suggestions that factor into its high accuracy rate, but they are far too intimate for this book. You and your spouse are free to do the research if you so choose.

As is the case with many scientific theories, there are those who dispute this method. They argue that though there are differences between the male (Y) sperm and the female (X) sperm that those differences are microscopic, which makes them moot. However, sperm itself is microscopic and the natural biological differences that later manifest in the man and woman appear to support the differences in the male (Y) and female (X) sperm. For example: Generally speaking, women live longer than men; their bodies are rounder and fuller; nine times out of ten she will lose in a sprint (everything else being equal), and we can argue over who is stronger, but she does bear human life – smile!

It is true that there is probably only a small selection of us who are looking beyond the superficial and can see the actual future benefit of having one sex over the other, but those people do exist. And we believe that soon, more and more will exist. For the rest of us, we should probably stick to being surprised. It goes without saying that Allah (God) is the Best Knower. And although 85% is a good percentage, there are no guarantees. Once conception has taken place, the mother-to-be should not focus on any specific gender.

CHILDREN OF THE MOST HIGH

The couple should pray for a healthy child, who will contribute to the upliftment of the family, community, and Nation. If we are of the righteous, then what pleases Allah (God) pleases us.

It is against the law of Allah (God) to kill a living fetus or embryo simply because it is not the desired sex. This happens far too often through abortions. But it also happens by some couples who use artificial insemination or in vitro fertilization. They will often request genetic testing before implantation of the embryo, which among other things determines the sex. The desired sex is then selected and sometimes if the pregnancy is successful, the other embryos are destroyed. This destruction is considered unethical to most people of faith.

It is no secret that worldwide, boys are desired above girls. Even in Islam, Prophet Muhammad (PBUH) had to admonish the people for burying their female children alive. We conclude this section with a warning for Brothers. It is every man's wish to have a male child; this is completely natural. But, once it is confirmed that you have been blessed with a girl, you should rejoice in her birth just as you would the birth of a son. The Holy Qur'an puts it like this, *"And when the birth of a daughter is announced to one of them, his face becomes black and he is full of wrath. He hides himself from the people because of the evil of what is announced to him. Shall he keep it with disgrace or bury it (alive) in the dust? Now surely evil is what they judge!"* (16: 58-59). This should never be in our thoughts or actions. Remember that the father is the first adult male that the daughter will know. He must be her example of a righteous, honorable man from the start. This requires that he love her unconditionally. If she receives pure, genuine love, then she will not settle for anything less when it is time for her to marry. She will have made her first critical step to one day also give birth to a god.

66

In an address to the women of the Nation of Islam, The Honorable Minister Louis Farrakhan said, *"I don't know why they call you miss. You know, miss so and so. Maybe it's because the father missed because he was after a boy and when you got here, he missed. So, they call you miss. That's a hell of a thing. How in the world could somebody have missed when they produced you? See the language of the world is against the female. Miss. He missed. Usually, all men want to see themselves first. So usually if it's a girl, you see this look of, oh. In some societies, they literally go off. He never missed when you were born. That was a hit if ever there was one because God has come to make Himself known to you and through you, to the entire world, but you got to give Him a chance to make Himself known."*

SECTION 2: DURING PREGNANCY

"Read in the name of thy Lord who creates – Creates man from a clot, Read and thy Lord is most Generous, Who taught by the pen, Taught man what he knew not."

Holy Qur'an 96:1-5

GOD'S CO-CREATOR:

This is perhaps the most important section in this book. What we think, feel, see, do, eat and drink during pregnancy can potentially have a marvelous or damaging effect on our child's entire life. In this section, we will learn how to become actively and consciously involved in our pregnancies. As the Honorable Minister Louis Farrakhan said, *"Any woman with a womb can allow a baby to be made – because all that takes is breathing and the intake of food – but how many of us know how to make a baby?"* Most of us do not and that is okay because we may have never been taught, but the future of our Nation depends on our willingness to learn.

The woman's womb is fashioned after the womb of the Universe. The Holy Qur'an 39:6 reads, *"...He (Allah) creates you in the wombs of your mothers – creation after creation – in triple darkness..."* The Honorable Minister Louis Farrakhan said, *"Every life is a witness of the self-creation of God."* So, to understand our own creation is to understand Allah's (God's) self-creation from the triple darkness of the womb of the Universe. If we were to sit in a small closet located in a cabin in the middle of the woods, during the dead of the night with our eyes closed; we would not be experiencing triple darkness – not even close. During the night hours, the sun is simply hidden from our direct view and we are in her shadow. But triple darkness refers to the absence of the sun, which is the source of light for the entire Universe. Triple darkness is so dark this it is actual substance. Allah (God) loves the female so much, that the only place in His vast Universe where He replicated the womb of His origin was within her – giving her the perfect environment and ability to produce another being like Himself.

The Most Honorable Elijah Muhammad teaches that Allah (God) created this entire Universe from nothing – just as we start out as nothing.

The Holy Qur'an verifies this as the man's sperm is referred to as *'worthless water.'* Seeing nothing, He (Allah) then had a thought to produce what we now know to be the Universe. He said, *"Be,"* and it was. The word, *'be,'* does not mean abracadabra or hocus-pocus. *'Be,'* activates the process of arranging atoms and molecules, which over a period of time will eventually form, Universe. The children of God have that same ability. The type of child that we wish to produce must become a thought in our mind first; then we too can say, *"Be,"* which will start the process. We must then actively engage and continue this process by making those vital changes which will ultimately result in our initial thought. The way the Universe was created was no accident; Allah (God) created exactly what He envisioned, and we can too.

The Most Honorable Elijah Muhammad teaches – after creating **Him**self, Allah's (God's) first act of creation was the female. She was here before the sun, the stars and the additional planets. He (Allah) studied Himself and produced the female from the cream or the Best part of Himself. She is the woman of God and not the woman of man. Therefore, her essence is truly divine.

The woman's womb is God's laboratory and the woman is God's assistant as she co-creates with Almighty God, Allah. This wonderfully divine gift cannot be viewed casually. The fact that Allah (God) would give the woman this kind of power is proof of His inexhaustible love for the female.

We begin by emphasizing what makes human beings Allah's (God's) greatest creation. What separates us from the sun, moon, stars, mountains, the ocean and every other living creature is knowledge. Our ability to learn and to make decisions based on rationale instead of natural instincts separates us from the insects and animals. Allah (God) referred to man and woman as 'His Glory.' If our ability to think and reason is what separates us from all other creation in this awesome Universe, then herein lies the key to giving birth to a god.

Our thoughts are so powerful that they can affect our physical make-up and call into existence our immediate reality. The type of friends we attract; our choice for a mate; the conflict and trials in our life; and our overall lifestyle, all materialized from both our conscious and subconscious thoughts. We must understand that our thoughts are not independent of our body. Emerging from our mind is who we truly are. This is why when someone is considered 'brain dead,' families agonize over allowing the person to live by artificial means or to discontinue life support. Our definition of living does not stop at breathing or having a heartbeat. If our brain, which houses the mind, does not function; we are NOT living.

A thought is not abstract – something immaterial floating through space or the air. A thought is a substance; it is liquid, and it causes chemical reactions all throughout our body. To repeat…THOUGHT IS LIQUID.

In her book, *The Force and Power of Being: Lift Yourself to a Higher State of Energy and Expression*, Minister Ava Muhammad explains 'thought,' as she received it in a lecture by Dr. Jewel Pookrum, who among other things, studies the process of mind-body interaction. The following is quoted from Minister Ava's book: *"The form of thought is liquid, it is manufactured by the brain, and that liquid is carried by the blood and nerves to every cell in the physical body. When a thought, which is liquid, starts traveling around in a body it visits all of your cells. It penetrates right through the cell membrane into the nucleus of that cell. In that nucleus is a chemistry lab. You have six trillion tissue cells in your body, and inside each one is a whole laboratory. This is how wonderful your God is. And when that thought breaks in through that membrane, and comes into that laboratory and looks around, that thought takes charge over that lab, and that thought starts stimulating the*

74

creation of enzymes, chemicals, and other substances to direct the intelligence of that cell to do what it wants."

So, what is the point? We should be careful of what we think, especially during pregnancy. Our ability to produce a god, a mental giant every time we bear a child, without missing, is largely dependent on our thoughts. We can just as easily give birth to a potential devil.

Once we learn that we are pregnant, whether that pregnancy was planned or accidental – if we sincerely want the baby – our initial thoughts are joyous. We are happy and excited. But if this is an unwanted pregnancy, then the first thoughts our baby receives stem from disappointment, fear, anger, frustration and perhaps denial. We will explain how these thoughts and feelings can directly affect our babies later in this section.

The baby's brain is the first part of his body to form. Think of the child's brain like a blank sheet of paper and the mother has the pen. A blank sheet of paper has no importance without words, diagrams, symbols or pictures. Our thoughts and actions as an expectant mother are the means by which we write those words and images, our desires, on our baby's brain. And whatever we write is written with permanent ink that cannot be removed unless Allah (God) actively intervenes, for He is the only One with a strong enough solution to erase what we have impressed on the baby's developing brain.

The remainder of this section has two key parts. The first part will explain how some specific thoughts and actions can have a negatively powerful effect on our children; which should also help us to understand the current state of our world. And of course, we will close this section discussing in detail what MUST be done during pregnancy to give birth to a god. *[Please note: more often than not, we will continue to refer to the baby in the masculine tense, but we are always meaning both male and female; unless we specifically make an obvious distinction.]*

Let us go back to the mother's initial thought when she finds out that she is pregnant. Many women pray that the positive pregnancy test was wrong. They may become angry or experience shock and denial. She just does not want to be pregnant, but she is. That liquid thought that we are sending to our child – if we could see it in writing – would read: *"I don't want you; I don't love you; I wish you were not a part of me; you are an awful mistake; I want to get rid of you."* Just imagine, our own mother saying these dreadful words to our face. Many of us would be devastated emotionally to the point of self-destruction. When we channel these thoughts to the womb, particularly if they are very intense and long-lived, they then become a part of the baby's brain and overall being. The baby will be born severely insecure with a predisposition towards self-hatred.

What is even worse, is that some of us take our feelings a step further. The idea of bringing a child into this world is so overwhelming that we decide to do what should be unthinkable – have an abortion. Now, the thought that travels to our baby is, *"I am going to kill you!"* Let me stop here for a moment and take up this very important issue of abortion.

KILLING THE FRUIT OF THE WOMB:

"And kill not your children for fear of poverty – We provide for them and for you. Surely the killing of them is a great wrong" (Holy Qur'an 17:31).

In his book, **A Torchlight for America**, the Honorable Minister Louis Farrakhan clearly states our position when it comes to abortion. He writes, *"Some of us are pro-life and others are pro-choice. I am both. I'm* *pro-choice in that women should have the right to choose to whom they will commit their lives. So, don't regret bearing life from that one to whom you have made a commitment. I'm not for any woman or man having the luxury of pleasure without responsibility. There is a procreational aspect to sex, and it's the neglect of this aspect that gains us disapproval in the sight of God. No one should be free to kill the fruit of the womb not understanding that what you are producing could be the answer to your own prayers and those of your forebears."*

In addition, the Minister writes, *"However, I am not in favor of letting the product of rape or incest come to term. Abortion is justified in these cases, along with those instances where the mother's health is at risk."*

Unfortunately, in the United States of America, the legalization and promotion of abortions for any reason have led to an exceptionally high number of abortions every year. According to recent data from the Center for Disease Control and Prevention (CDC): *"In 2014, 652,639 legal induced abortions were reported to CDC from 49 reporting areas. The abortion rate for 2014 was 12.1 abortions per 1,000 women aged 15–44 years, and the abortion ratio was 186 abortions per 1,000 live births."* It is important to highlight that these are only the number of 'legal' abortions 'reported' in just one year from only 49 areas in the entire country. Therefore, we can reasonably presume that as staggering as this number (652,639) is – we know that the actual number of abortions is likely so much higher. Well over half a million lives are not coming to term every single year in the United States…this is a serious problem. But even more horrific is that Black women have the highest abortion rate and ratio according to the CDC.

The womb of every woman is sacred. But Black women, in particular, are direct descendants from God and therefore what we produce from our womb is genetically coded with the essence of the Originator of the heavens and the earth. To kill the fruit of our womb is to kill a potential god and the answer to someone's prayer.

The intent of this section is not to make any woman feel guilty over past mistakes, but to serve as a reminder to some and a warning to others that Allah (God) in not pleased with us for committing an act of murder because we fear the consequences of an unplanned pregnancy or simply do not want the responsibility of parenthood. Anytime man's law conflicts with the higher law of God, we must follow God if we want to be in line to receive His blessings and His favors.

We know that the killing of our children is not a new practice because Allah (God) had to correct this abhorrent behavior in both the Bible and Holy Qur'an. The difference is that centuries ago, children were primarily killed **after** they were born due to their gender (mostly females) or because of fear of poverty. This certainly could not be openly practiced in America today because it goes against both man's law and God's law. But the enemy of God and the righteous, has wickedly devised a plan to continue to kill babies by arrogantly determining when "life" begins based on man's definition; thereby justifying the annual mass murder of hundreds of thousands of babies. This would be called genocide if it were not "lawfully" permitted by the Supreme Court.

It is no coincidence that the rate and ratio of abortions are highest amongst Black women when we trace the origin of the promotion of "birth control," which eventually graduated to abortions, back to Margaret Sanger. She was an advocate for the population control of Black and poor people, whom she felt were genetically inferior. In 1939, Sanger sought to enlist the help of Black ministers and doctors in a letter to a member of the Birth Control Federation of America, where she wrote (in particular) about Black ministers, *"We do not want word to go out that we want to exterminate the Negro population and the minister is the man who can straighten out that idea if it ever occurs to any of their more rebellious members."*

Extermination of the Black population was the plan then and remains the plan today. The prevalence of abortions is just one way to achieve this end. Unfortunately, the freedoms afforded in this country extend beyond all morality. We are free in this country to do practically anything that opposes God's Will and the U.S. government will sanction our rebellion.

We were all created with the nature of righteousness, except the rebellious devil. So, our appeal is to the Righteous. We must consider the hand of God in ALL circumstances. Nothing happens without His permissive or active will. A pregnancy may have been unintended or unplanned by the mother or father, but Allah (God) is the Best of all planners. His universe is ample to support **every** new life. When He declares that He will provide for them and for you, we can take that to the bank! This does not mean, we should sit on our hands – but after we pray, we must go to work and draw from the mammary gland of His universe. It is Allah (God) who declares that the killing of our children is a great wrong; so, if we are striving to be righteous, then there is simply no rationale for aborting a new life – outside of the aforementioned exceptions.

Let's now explore the personal and societal consequences of just having the thought of abortion while pregnant and why killing the fruit of our womb due to perceived fears of poverty, responsibility, disappointment, or any other fear can have irrevocable consequences.

"They are losers indeed who kill their children foolishly without knowledge, and forbid that which Allah has provided for them, forging a lie against Allah. They indeed go astray, and are not guided" (Holy Qur'an 6:141).

At some point, we are going to have to see the bigger picture. Do not get distracted by so-called liberals and pro-choice advocates who claim to have an agenda that champions the rights of women and social equality. They are so hypocritical when they advocate that a woman, regardless of her reasoning, should have the right to kill the fruit of her womb – while at the same time holding other positions that encourage community and reject individualism. When we choose to end a pregnancy that was a result of consensual sex and our health is not at risk – this is an individual, self-serving action. It does not take into consideration the community and the future of our people as a whole. It does not take into consideration that this life could be the answer to someone's prayer. Perhaps a child whose life was aborted today could have discovered the cure for a disease that will plague the lives of others in the future. Our fear of immediate personal inconvenience, unfortunately, cripples our willingness to see the god-potential of this new life beyond the moment.

We know that in America over 600,000 babies are killed every *year* from abortions. However, there is also an untold number of babies that are born every day from mothers that never wanted them. The most potentially destructive thought is one that garners intense negative emotion and is prolonged. The agony, stress, fear, and uncertainty that a woman experiences when she is pregnant and DOES NOT want to be – can lead to unthinkable thoughts and actions. What type of mental and spiritual predisposition could these children inherit? What burden do they unknowingly bear at birth? Which way of life will they naturally incline, if environmental factors do not intervene and reverse their course? The Honorable Minister Louis Farrakhan said, *"What you see is the result of somebody's thinking…your presence is the result of somebody's thinking…"*

We all understand the definition of "kill" in terms of the physical. Going through with abortion will physically end the life of a baby forever, thus; the baby has been 'killed.' But, to *kill* someone spiritually and mentally can also have irrevocable consequences. Imagine a pregnant woman having murderous thoughts and plans – thoughts of rejection and hatred – being deceptive and telling lies – experiencing agonizing sadness and mental torment. All of these powerful thoughts and emotions are helping to form the brain of the baby and *if* these thoughts are prolonged, the child could be born predisposed to act out on many of these impressions.

In the scripture mentioned previously, Allah (God) calls those of us who kill our children foolishly, without knowledge – "losers." If we do not kill them physically, but we kill their god-potential, are we still losers? Let's take a look: Is our community rampant with behavior that could qualify us as being "losers" in the sight of Allah (God)? Unfortunately, from our womb, we have produced too many who have become liars, thieves, robbers, rapists, destroyers, and murderers. We have produced an untold number of individuals who are born emotionally and psychologically insecure – children who are born with self-rejection, self-hatred, and self-negation baked into their genetic make-up.

Certainly, we cannot and should not deny the fact that there are external systems and individuals that benefit from contributing to the perpetuation of our condition. However, it is also true that we greatly increase the likelihood that our children will become victims by setting them up at a great disadvantage right from birth. The brain of the baby is fashioned by the thoughts, desires, and blood of the mother. The woman can produce children from her womb that are more inclined to righteousness or more inclined to evil.

CHILDREN OF THE MOST HIGH

In his lecture, ***How to Give Birth to a God: Part 5***, the Honorable Minister Louis Farrakhan said – *"We are not what our mothers are pleased with. But, mothers, your children are yours. Society has to take its part, but I'm sorry – you have to take the full weight, because the scripture says, '**Train the child up in the way it should go: and when it is old, it will not depart from that way.**' If you put the right stuff in the children, then society can't take it out. But the right stuff has been absent from the mind of the Black woman and the Black man. And so, from generation to generation, we keep on repeating history. We don't make a new step."*

As women, we should not see our responsibility as an overwhelming burden, but as a BLESSING! Yes – to be able to co-operate and co-create with a magnificent God is a powerful and sacred gift. It is time for a new thought, a new way, and a new woman. Just as easy as we can transfer wicked thoughts to our children, we can also transfer righteous thoughts and characteristics to our children. It all starts with the woman coming back to God. We must bathe in the reality of His presence in our daily lives and believe in His sufficiency to intervene and improve every aspect of our condition. Only then, can we begin to understand that all of our fears are irrational because God is in control!

We must not *"forge a lie against Allah."* If God says that He **will** provide for us and our children, then we must have faith in Him. Our fear of poverty will be erased; along with our fear for the future and the responsibility that parenting demands. Allah (God) would never allow us to reproduce without providing us with the means to care for and maintain the life we produced. The Most Honorable Elijah Muhammad wrote, *"If you accept Allah (God) and follow me and if you give birth to 100 children, each of you girls and women is considered more blessed and right in the eyes of Allah (God) than those who try to kill the birth seed."*

82

For anyone who may think that it is too late, know that Allah (God) would be unjust if He left us hopeless. Fortunately, the human being is the only one of God's creations blessed with free will. We have the will to submit to righteousness and reject wickedness or oppose righteous behavior and indulge in the debauchery of this world. Understanding the science and the circumstances involved during our personal gestational period is critical to our ability to reverse any damage done. The only time being born with a negative predisposition is irrevocable is if we are not aware of why we are the way we are and do not seek a way to rebel against our natural negative inclinations. So, rebellion in this sense is a blessing.

NOTE: The way to counter those who encourage abortions is for us to make difference life choices and to educate our children and anyone else within our sphere of influence about the value of human life. We should NEVER destroy abortion clinics or harm doctors that perform this procedure – that is not the answer.

A LIAR FROM THE BEGINNING:

During Part IV of his historic 1987 lecture series, ***How to Give Birth to a God***, The Honorable Minister Louis Farrakhan said, *"You do not know how to make a baby. You know how to let one be made, but you don't know how to properly make one. You're making one whether you know it or not – your thoughts are being projected onto the womb…You are so powerful, Sisters. When you get into the right frame of mind, you can produce mental giants from your womb with a predisposition to master this life – any phase of it, you can produce that. Do you doubt that? We have done it accidentally. Now, what about if we did it with purpose?"*

Most of us have seen images or footage of a surgeon operating on his patient? The surgeon could be the hospital's chief surgeon, but he is NEVER in the operating room alone. There is always a surgical team or unit assigned to assist any head surgeon. If he had no other choice, there is a chance that left unassisted, he could manage to still save his patient's life; but it would be very difficult, and complications would likely ensue. So, the role of additional doctors, nurses, and technicians is critical. They make sure that the head surgeon's work is safe, unimpaired, and produces optimal results for the patient. Every person assisting in that operating room is very clear of his or her role and responsibilities. And although they are "co-operating" and assisting the head surgeon; it is also very clear that they work under his direct guidance and supervision.

So, it is with the expectant mother and Allah (God)! In order for a woman to actively co-operate and co-create with Allah (God) as life is forming in her womb; she must be knowledgeable of her role and how she can best assist The Creator. One of many things a woman can actively do to serve Allah (God) is to remain mindful of His attributes – one of which is, The Truth. We all know that we should always speak the truth. But there is added importance for a woman to do so during pregnancy. Lying can be a particularly dangerous act to engage in while the baby's brain is developing in the womb.

Have you ever witnessed a two or three-year-old lie to you or to someone else? The child is asked, *"J.J., did you spill powder all over the floor?"* And little J.J. lies right to his mother's face when there is no one else in the house except for the two of them. Then the mother wonders, *"Where did this child learn to lie like that?"* We know that no parent in their right mind consciously trains or teaches their child *how* to lie. So, the question is, how did they learn? A two-year-old has likely not been influenced much by society; so, we must travel back to the womb to find the answer.

Let's revisit that profound description of thought we highlighted earlier. In her book, *The Force and Power of Being: Lift Yourself to a Higher State of Energy and Expression*, Student Minister Ava Muhammad explains 'thought,' as she received it in a lecture by Dr. Jewel Pookrum, Minister Ava writes: *"The form of thought is liquid, it is manufactured by the brain, and that liquid is carried by the blood and nerves to every cell in the physical body. When a thought, which is liquid, starts traveling around in a body it visits all of your cells. It penetrates right through the cell membrane into the nucleus of that cell. In that nucleus is a chemistry lab. You have six trillion tissue cells in your body, and inside each one is a whole laboratory. This is how wonderful your God is. And when that thought breaks in through that membrane, and comes into that laboratory and looks around, that thought takes charge over that lab, and that thought starts stimulating the creation of enzymes, chemicals, and other substances to direct the intelligence of that cell to do what it wants."*

Every action is first preceded by a thought. We have to think about lying before we act on it since the objective is for our deception to be effective. The process of thinking produces a chemical reaction in the body. Evidence to prove this is found in the use of sodium pentothal or "truth serum." Scientists have crafted a chemical that can force a person whose lying has become second nature, to tell the truth. Regardless of how strongly they may wish to keep the truth hidden; a chemical can break them down. So, if a chemical can make us tell the truth regardless of our desire to lie; then a lie is a chemical and the truth is also a chemical. The significance in pregnancy should be obvious. When we tell lies while we are pregnant, we generate a chemical reaction that permeates from the brain, then penetrates our cells, our blood, the placenta and ultimately our baby. Right from the womb, we are birthing into the world children with a propensity for lying.

Children who have no respect for truth and will lie at the drop of a dime – without hesitation. We are creating liars from the beginning.

If we examine our own experience with liars, we can bear witness that Allah (God) formed everything with Truth because lying brings with it an unsettling aura. Have you ever instinctively felt that someone was lying to you without any actual facts to confirm the feeling? It was just something about the way they said it – the words vibrated unnaturally off of their lips – their mannerisms and demeanor just didn't jive. Our body is constantly sending vibrations into the atmosphere and we are constantly picking up and responding to the vibrations that we receive from others. Polygraphs or lie detector tests rely heavily on vibrations. Vibrations in the form of a faster heart rate, higher blood pressure, and increased perspiration are some of the indicators used to prove that a person is lying.

In the Book of John, Jesus is speaking to the powerful Jews and says, *"Ye are of your father the devil, and the lusts of your father ye will do. He was a murderer from the beginning, and abode not in the truth, because there is no truth in him. When he speaketh a lie, he speaketh of his own: for he is a liar, and the father of it"* (John 8:44, KJV). The devil is not the devil only because he was physically grafted from the original. What makes him evil and wicked are the teachings he received in the beginning; while he was being fashioned into shape. Whatever is going on while something is being made goes directly into the thing that is being made. This means it was in the very nature of the devil to be a deceitful liar.

Conversely, it is in the nature of the original man and woman to be righteous truth-tellers. But if we give our babies different teachings based on lies and falsehoods, we too can bake into their genetic make-up a tendency for lying. During one of his lectures, The Honorable Minister Louis Farrakhan asked the audience why it was so difficult to remember the good things we have done in our lifetime, but we can easily and quickly list every low-down rotten thing we have ever done since childhood. He answered for the audience; saying, doing 'good' comes naturally so we don't think about it – it is not necessarily a big deal to us. But doing evil goes against the grain of our nature, so it constantly agitates the psyche.

Let's take a closer look at the scope of lying. One of the 99-plus attributes of Allah (God) is The Truth, which means that His Universe is formed with the truth. Anything other than truth is not in harmony with the Universe. The nature of the Original man and woman is that of righteousness and honesty; anything contrary to that forces the Universe to call out for correction. We have all heard that whatever we do in the dark will come to light. The Bible declares that the truth will make us free.

The Holy Qur'an states, *"We hurl truth at falsehood till it knocks out its brains."* The Most Honorable Elijah Muhammad gave us a law: No lying regardless of circumstances – reminding us that there is NEVER a good reason to lie. Why? Because for every lie we tell, we are moved farther and farther away from Allah (God). Just look at our language. We usually refer to the truth with the definite article, 'the.' So, it is 'the truth' as opposed to 'a truth,' but the word 'lie' goes either way. 'The' refers to one, singular, only – just as Allah (God) and His Universe are One.

The Most Honorable Elijah Muhammad teaches, *"The brain cells are created to think rightly. To think rightly means to perceive reality properly, and to think on the basis of truth. Since falsehood has created nothing, falsehood then has a negative effect on the cells of the brain."* We can physically damage the brain cells of our babies while they are in utero. This means that before they are born, we have placed them at a significant disadvantage. But just as easily, we can give them a proper start by keeping our focus on Allah (God), who is The Truth. Our desires, our thoughts, our actions, and our entire being can align with Allah (God); and this will be projected on the womb, helping us to produce gods from the beginning.

The Honorable Minister Louis Farrakhan admonishes us to take a good look at what this generation, particularly of Black people, is producing. He highlights that the children have no natural love for their parents or others; we are producing a generation of liars and murderers. We cannot blame the schools and societal institutions alone for this condition – this is what our wombs have produced.

THE PAIN OF EVE:

Sexism can be as insidious as racism. Although it is pervasive in every culture and every religion; it is not always immediately recognized for what it is. Like racism, it is systemic and shelved as just being a part of the fabric of our society. Sexism is defined as, *"discrimination against a group of persons because of the fact or character of being male or female."* Sexism is a vice whose root must be exposed to the light in order to be destroyed. The demographics for the United States of America claim a population that is only 13.3% Black or African-American; but 50.8% female – yet somehow, we all knew that this country would see its first Black male president in office before there would be a white female president; not that we're complaining. However, it is something to ponder…If Black people are only 13.3% of the population, then we did not put Barack Obama in a position to hold the country's highest office; white people did. They chose a Black man over a white woman.

During a lecture at Mosque Maryam on May 27, 2018, The Honorable Minister Louis Farrakhan discussed the pervasive disrespect and outright abuse of Black and Gentile women. He said, *"The #MeToo*

Movement is real, women are tired of being misused by men in power." Allah (God) is not the Originator of racism nor sexism. Racism and sexism are two great impediments – along with nationalism and materialism – that are the byproduct of the madness of this world. Sexism ironically has its root in this world's most prominent religious doctrine. Unlike racism, which many justify by misinterpreting the scriptures; the language of the Bible was intentionally tampered with to condone sexism in order to relegate women to a status of lesser beings.

The Bible reads, *"So the Lord God caused the man to fall into a deep sleep; and while he was sleeping, he took one of man's ribs and then closed up the place with flesh. Then the Lord God made a woman from the rib he had taken out of the man, and he brought her to the man"* (Genesis 2:21-22, NIV). The Honorable Minister Louis Farrakhan said that if the woman was made from the rib of man, this would make her inferior and she is not. Not to mention that according to Biblical doctrine, the woman was not only made subsequent to God making the man, but she was His last creation. Supposedly she was created after all of the lower animals, the streams and rivers, celestial bodies and all plant life. Not so! According to the Teachings of the Most Honorable Elijah Muhammad, *"Before there was Sun, there was a Woman. Allah came out of the womb of darkness with a womb within Himself. Every man has a woman in him. If you notice, the male has the X and Y chromosome, which has the male and female part. The female has the X chromosome. As Allah came out of the womb – the Holy Qur'an calls it 'triple darkness' – He had a womb within Himself. He studied Himself and from Himself He fashioned Woman. She is His First Act of Creation. This is why you don't understand the woman and you cannot deal with a woman; you think she is a man's woman. She is the Woman of God"* (Self-Improvement: The Basis for Community Development). Obviously, this knowledge would cause a huge shift in the psyche of both men and women since there is a tremendous difference between being first on the planet (after the Supreme Being) and being dead last.

To add insult to injury, the first woman, who the Bible calls Eve, is then blamed for all that is wrong in the world and as a result, she must suffer. "To the woman He said, *'I will make your pains in childbearing very severe; with painful labor you will give birth to children. Your desire will be for your husband, and he will rule over you'"* (Genesis 3:16, NIV). There it is – the go-to scripture used to explain menstruation and pain during childbirth as well as to keep women in "their place." The Bible has been diluted, mixed and tampered with to such a degree that even the scholars cannot seem to find consensus as to the authenticity and correct interpretation of such a verse because contradictions run rampant throughout.

So, what is the pain of Eve? It cannot be childbirth, because the pain of childbirth is a natural pain; it's a demonstration of the universal difficulty factor attached to everything of value. Nothing is more valuable than producing human life; hence the high degree of difficulty? It also cannot be menstruation. Menstruation is actually a blessing from God – it gives women the capability to detox and expel impurities from their bodies every single month, keeping them salubrious and in a state of balance. According to the Bible, Adam named his wife Eve because she would become the mother of all the living. The Black woman is indeed the mother of all the living, all of civilization; therefore, Allah (God) provided a process for her temple to be in a continual cycle of purification.

Within the woman lies the secret of God. A replica of the womb out of which the Originator created Himself is found in the woman. The fact that God would place His secret in her is a demonstration of His immense love for women. However, there is a serious responsibility that comes with being

God's co-creator; and there is also a serious consequence when we are negligent or rebellious against instructions from Allah (God). The Honorable Minister Louis Farrakhan explained the true interpretation of the pain of Eve in his lecture, How to Give Birth to a God. He first asked the Sisters, *"What burden do you bear in producing children that are a scourge to you and to the earth? How do feel, mother, when you behold your son, your flesh, your blood – a thief, a liar, a rapist, a murderer, a drug addict, a prostitute, a low-life, a degenerate?"*

The Minister goes on further to explain, *"The pain is that you bring forth children into the world that will one day curse you and give you, the mother – pain. Your own children make your life burdensome and miserable and you die in pain because you have left behind you, children that cannot cope with the realities of this life. Sons who are still waiting for you to give them something though they're 20, 30 and 40 years old. Your children are born, and they die giving their parents pain...If something new and better is to come about, this must come about through men and women who are careful of the way they think, careful of the way they live, careful of the foods that they eat, careful of their obedience to the laws of God."*

For this to be our new reality, we must elevate women. She is the second-self of God. Through her womb, He can create His likeness. The feminine side of the expression of God must also be encouraged to contribute to humanity in every field of endeavor. The world is in a state of imbalance and chaos because the feminine side of God, which brings the equilibrium to politics, religion, science, education, health, defense, and justice is absent. Men who see home as the woman's place and not her base, do not desire to include her. Deep-seeded misogyny is alive and well today, but it is the Will of Allah (God) that this terrible perversion in society is destroyed. Allah (God) desires that His divine intention for women be firmly established throughout the earth. And we are now seeing evidence that anyone who interferes with His Will is being eliminated expeditiously.

THE DEVIL IN OUR LIVING ROOMS:

In *Self-Improvement: The Basis for Community Development* [Study Guide 20: Closing the Gap], The Honorable Minister Louis Farrakhan wrote, *"One day Master Fard Muhammad told the Sisters that a time would come when they would let the devil into their living rooms and entertain him. Little did we know that when the television was made, and we put it in our living rooms that the wicked ideas of a satanic mind that governs this world would come into our homes and spoil our women and children."*

An expectant mother whose greatest desire is to give birth to a god must make tremendous sacrifices. She must walk her post in a perfect manner, keeping always on the alert. She must be vigilant; observing and protecting herself and her child from wicked ideas and images coming from a satanic mind. Casual, everyday activities that usually seem mundane and nonconsequential are anything but; especially when life is forming in the womb. Most pregnant women are naturally more careful about what they consume during this delicate stage – they are conscious of food, drinks, medications, caffeine intake, etc. Women are also very careful when deciding which physical activities are safe to participate in while pregnant. But what is often overlooked is what we consume mentally, such as our entertainment choices.

During his *How to Give Birth to a God* lecture series, The Honorable Minister Louis Farrakhan said to the Sisters, *"The trainer and the teacher, the shaper and the molder is you. So, what is in you, mother, is what's going to be in your child. And since you make his brain, then what does your brain*

92

constantly think about? Is it the soap opera? You're making a baby, 'Hold it baby, hold it now...let's put on the General Hospital; All My Children, that's on.' Now you call your friend: 'Yes honey and that woman murdered that man!' See you're thinking about murder; you're thinking about all these negative things while you're producing a new life. It's better to turn off the TV while you're pregnant. Don't go to no movies and hear somebody saying, 'm-f' and 'f-you' and 'You S-O-B' – and you're looking at death and murder, and mayhem, and you're bringing your pregnant wife and little babies that you're nursing..."

Violence, sex, profanity, madness, and lies are laced in every form of entertainment – television, movies, music, video games, etc. All of which are now easily accessible on our mobile devices. So, today the devil is not only in our living rooms; but we are now able to entertain him everywhere we go. Soap operas may not be as popular in 2019, but they have been replaced with foolish reality shows that are becoming more and more outrageous.

Why should we sacrifice going to the movies while pregnant? Let's look at what happens at the movie theatre. Our unborn child cannot distinguish which thoughts are being directed towards him or towards someone or something else. This is because thoughts do not instantly compartmentalize. So, when we are in the theatre watching a movie filled with mayhem, murder, death, pandemonium, and filth – on a mega screen with thunderous acoustics – we become consumed and at one with that environment in an instant. We become increasingly excited as the plot thickens and the movie reaches its climax. The creepy music begins, which warns us that someone is about to die in a brutal manner; but we cannot take our eyes off the screen – so we watch, then wish we hadn't. We cannot un-see or un-hear anything. Our heartrate increases, and we realize that we, too, are out of breath as if we were the actual victim. The grotesque image and environment stay with us sometimes for hours after the movie has ended. Are we getting the picture? Profanity, lying and scheming in the plot of a movie works the same way. Our eyes are watching; our ears are listening, and our brain is processing and recording everything coming off the screen. And since thought is liquid, the brain of our unborn baby is easily absorbing the same sensations.

Since the pregnant mother is asked not to go to the movies, her husband should do the same. The Honorable Minister Louis Farrakhan said, *"You should stay with her because she'll be quick to think that you're rejecting her because her shape is changing and you're running out; you're always with the boys. When she's pregnant, you need to be with her…You don't do crazy things with a woman while she's carrying your life. You give her good things to look at."*

Television is not as magnified as movies, but it has a similar effect because it is continuous. We must turn off the television for most of the day. In our society, it seems that we have an unwritten rule that states, *'If I am in the same room as a television set, then it must be turned on.'* Many of us fall asleep watching television and then wake up and start the process all over again. What are our brains constantly soaking up? Silly reality shows or sitcoms – watch them once and you're addicted. Ridiculous dramas that depict Black people, in particular, in the most degenerating roles; but we think that it's harmless entertainment. We consume music videos filled with filthy lyrics about sex and debauchery; not to mention the barrage of images showing our scantily dressed sisters parading about. We fill our heads with so much foolishness on a daily basis and then wonder why our children are so heavily inclined to sex, violence, and profanity. It's time to stop the madness and break the cycle.

Our poor choices for movies, television shows, and music while pregnant are evidence that there is no reverence for the womb; nor is there reverence for the mind. Righteous women and men should be focused on producing children that are going the put an end to the filth that is being promoted through these mediums. Women must desire to co-operate with God in the procreation of human life. She should be feeding on wisdom, feeding on the Word of God and showering nothing but love on the womb. It's interesting that Master Fard Muhammad said that we would entertain the devil; **not** *the devil will entertain us.* The devil is killing us, but we are handing him the knife. The enemy only exists because we feed and nourish him constantly. *"Resist the devil, and he will flee from you!"*

NO FUNERALS DURING PREGNANCY:

People who are devoutly religious can also be the spookiest, most superstitious people on the planet. A superstitious Believer in God is an oxymoron – both cannot be true. You either believe that God is Possessor of power over all things or you do not! We cannot profess that God controls every atom in the heavens and the earth but remain equally convinced in the power of 'good-luck' charms and bad omens. A common belief found across a broad spectrum of religions and cultures is that pregnant women should not attend funerals. This belief is found in Native American, Asian, South American, and Central American cultures. It is also a strongly held belief amongst practicing Jews and some Christians; particularly Black Christians. Unfortunately, upon examination of the justification for their belief and practice, we find that its source comes squarely from a superstitious doctrine.

The Holy Qur'an reads, *"Surely Allah is He with Whom is the knowledge of the Hour, and He sends down the rain, and He knows what is in the wombs. And no one knows what he will earn on the morrow. And no one knows in what land he will die. Surely Allah is Knowing, Aware"* (31:34). The Most Honorable Elijah Muhammad also taught the women of the Nation of Islam not to attend funerals while they were pregnant. However, the Nation of Islam is NOT superstitious. Islam, as taught by the Most Honorable Elijah Muhammad, dignifies, *"it destroys superstition and removes the veil of falsehood."* So, why give this directive? The reason is based solely in science, not superstition; and today researchers and scientists are bearing witness to the potential negative impact that prolonged sadness, grief, and depression can have on the brain of a growing fetus.

We do not believe in coincidences. For every effect, there was a cause and for every action, there will be a consequence. There was a time not too long ago when it was not abnormal to see a pregnant woman smoking a cigarette or drinking alcohol. Today, this is frowned upon because we are now aware of the damaging effects these poisons have on the developing brain and body of a baby in utero. Tobacco contains nicotine, arsenic, tar and carbon monoxide – all of which is absorbed by the mother's body and therefore, her baby. Alcohol goes straight to the baby's bloodstream through the placenta. Nicotine, alcohol, caffeine, and drugs (illegal & otherwise) are all dangerously potent chemicals that can cause low birth weight, SIDS (sudden infant death syndrome), stillbirths, miscarriages, physical disfigurement and abnormalities, intellectual disabilities, heart defects, brain damage, weakened immunity, behavioral problems and more. Thoughts are also powerful chemicals – and depending on the intensity and span of certain thoughts, they can be just as harmful.

When addressing the environment of a pregnant woman, the Honorable Minister Louis Farrakhan said to the Brothers, *"Make sure that all harmful influences are kept from her mind. Don't let her go to funerals because she shouldn't be thinking on death when she's making life. Even if it's funerals of dear ones...Don't bring the pregnant woman around death and grieving people. This is what the Messenger taught. Say, 'Sweetheart you stay at home and think on good things. Think on the good things of the life that has just gone by.' But don't go where people are screaming and hollering and falling out and acting a fool; because all of us got to die. Don't go around people that just play games with death to pacify themselves and their mistreatment of the one that is departed. 'Stay home baby, you [are] making new life...I want you to see good things, so you can bring forth a good child.'"*

It is natural to mourn the death of a loved one and if the person was particularly close to us, it cannot be helped since their physical presence will be missed. However, when we attend the funeral, we invite our unborn child into an intensely sad environment where there could be those who are so overcome with grief and sadness that crying is continuous and they are inconsolable. The emotions of others trigger our own emotions and it is likely that the expectant mother, who is already emotionally vulnerable, will find herself grief-stricken; not only because she is sad, but because she is enveloped by overwhelming grief. Our attendance at the funeral is not the yardstick used to measure our sincere love for the deceased. Life and death are two polar opposites. So, when life is forming in the womb it should be far removed from death. To be sad and pregnant is just not a good combination. Pregnancy should be the most joyous time in our life.

Studies now bear witness to the physiological effects of sadness. Research states that prolonged sadness lowers the body temperature and weakens the immune system, which increases the mother's risk of disease. Sadness affects cortisol levels, which controls blood sugar and blood pressure. Intense sadness can lead to stress, which is bad for the heart, lungs and the liver. Being overcome with sadness and grief also decreases serotonin levels which can lead to depression, obsessive compulsive disorders, and violent outbreaks. Depression can even influence the onset of cancer. According to researchers, the brain works harder when we are sad because we are *"remembering, thinking, suffering, and looking for reasons, solutions, and alternatives."* This takes an enormous amount of energy resulting in an elevated need for glucose to feed the brain, causing the pregnant mother to crave more sweets, another toxin. Everything the mother consumes, her baby consumes. Everything the mother experiences, her baby experiences.

Unfortunately, we face an inordinate amount of death in the Black community primarily as a result of violence and disease; so, to have a loved one pass during the span of nine months is not improbable. However, we must remember that no soul dies, but with the permission of Allah (God) and to grieve for an extended period of time is a sign that we are not at peace with God's decision. As mothers, we cannot be one-dimensional creatures – we must rise above our emotions and protect the fruit of our womb. Every day of our pregnancy, Allah (God) is creating new brain cells for a new life. Our role is to co-operate with Him and provide a happy, nurturing environment to the best of our ability.

THE CHEMISTRY OF THOUGHT, HOMOSEXUALITY & THE WOMB:

There is an adage in the Book of Proverbs that is often quoted but rarely analyzed or transposed into all facets of life, giving it the proper weight that it deserves. The Scripture reads, *"For as he thinketh in his heart, so is he…"* (Proverbs 23:7, KJV). These words are particularly relevant to lay a base when we attempt to get to the root of understanding how individuals can reconcile engaging in a lifestyle that can easily be proven to be contrary to God's law, science and nature. There are many angles and players to consider when answering the question of why homosexuality is more prevalent at this time than it has ever been in the annals of human civilization.

It is not possible nor is it our intent to cover the entire scope of this issue in one section of a book. We state from the onset that we will never exonerate Satan and his wicked scientists of evil, who are working feverishly; using the science of chemistry to alter food, medications, hygiene products, household goods and especially marijuana to accelerate abominable behavior. It is the enemy's research, study, and mastery of the chemistry of thinking and neurology that allows him to now manipulate the behavior of millions. [Please read more about this in Dr. Wesley Muhammad's book, *Understanding the Assault on The Black Man, Black Manhood and Black Masculinity*]. The purpose of this section is to convey how we, as mothers, may be unknowing conspirators in the enemy's destructive operation.

To know that there is life growing inside of us is nothing short of amazing. Our mind goes into overdrive planning out the baby's future. But even before that, we quite naturally wonder, *'What am I having; a boy or a girl?'* We imagine what it would be like to have a little girl and then what it would be like to have a little boy. Then our heart may settle on one or the other. There is nothing wrong with having a gender preference for our child, but make sure it stops right there! To prefer one gender over the other means: If I could choose, then I would choose *A* over *B*, but if I get *B* instead of *A*, then I am perfectly fine with that too. Preference is natural. However, there could be a problem if preference becomes an obsession – our mind gets fixated on a particular gender and there is a complete denial of the possibility that the baby could be the alternate gender.

Here is an example: *You tell everyone you are having a girl without knowing for sure. Every time you talk to the baby or rub your stomach, you call the baby by the female name you have chosen. You purchase clothes, beddings, decorations, and toys all fit for a little girl. And lastly, anyone who even slightly suggests that the baby could be a boy quickly becomes persona non grata.* This may sound extreme, but I have heard of a case where a woman decided to get an abortion in the second trimester because her baby was not the "right" gender – that's horrendous! Obsessing over one gender over the other can be very dangerous, especially if we are wrong!

What happens if we are obsessed with having a girl but are unknowingly carrying a boy? Our thoughts for a beautiful little girl are being thoroughly impressed on the brain of the baby. Without realizing our own tangible power of influence, a male child is forming with the feminine attributes of Allah (God) becoming predominant. Yes, Allah (God) has both masculine and feminine attributes. Attributes such as *The Beneficent, The Merciful, The Forgiver, The Nourisher, The Giver of Life and The Most Patient* are all attributes that females exude more prominently than males. Whereas some of the masculine attributes include: *The Protector, The Provider, The Mighty, The Strong, The Powerful, etc.*

What could happen is that the male child (that we wanted so desperately to be a female) will begin to exhibit feminine inclinations. Our feminine-focused thoughts can even affect our child's physical appearance. Have you ever seen a little boy that could pass for a girl? A boy that is very soft spoken, sweet and sensitive? He may also enjoy artistic expressions: dance, theatre, music, or fashion.

Strong thoughts permeate matter – affecting every atom, cell, tissue, organ and body system. They each respond accordingly, reacting to the tangible energy from one's thinking. The impact of intense thoughts is demonstrated most consequentially from a mother to her unborn baby. Consider this; during his lecture series, **How to Give Birth to a God – Part 5**, the Honorable Minister Louis Farrakhan said: *"It's not good to say, 'I want* *a boy, or I want a girl.' [Just] say, 'I want a healthy child, I want one that I vow to give to God.' You may have your preference, but don't impress that on the womb. My mother wanted a girl, so I was born into the world, Brother, with very small hands; very small feet; very small stature – very strong, but very small. If you saw me before I was converted to Islam, my features were very soft and beautiful; feminine-like, if you will. It's true."*

In addition, the Minister has also expressed that his mother's desire for a girl gave him inclinations towards the feminine attributes of the Nature of Allah (God): Mercy, Compassion, Forgiveness, and Long-suffering. The chemistry of his mother's thinking affecting him both physically and mentally while he was forming in her womb. However, though her desires gave him a physical and mental leaning towards the feminine side, she did NOT produce a homosexual. So, what is happening with so many of the rest of us?

In another lecture, **The Problem of Suicide and the Causes of Homosexuality**, the Minister explains it like this [addressing the Brothers], *"Suppose, then, mother wanted a girl. Now, the feminine side of our nature is accentuated. Then you want to dance, or you want to go into music or you want to be an artist. Artistic nature calls for the beauty side of the characteristics of God – still minus the power side. So, the more you keep feeding the feminine side of the man, you're beginning to make an effeminate...He's not a female, but he's tender; soft; sweet – but, NOT homosexual. Some older person sees these soft qualities – beauty...handsome, nicely formed and they tap you out...After a while, if the male side of you rejects the advances then they stop. If you're a child, you can't reject; they overpower you, and put you in a circumstance now that has you going in life toward homosexuality."*

We must emphasize that there is nothing wrong with a male that possesses feminine attributes in and of itself. But we have a serious problem in our society, which not only accepts homosexuality; but also encourages it and makes it popular. There is no such thing as being born homosexual – Allah (God) does not make mistakes. If He meant for you to be sexually attracted to men, you would be born female; and if He meant for you to be sexually attracted to women, you would be born male. So, understand that our son who may possess feminine attributes and inclinations is not a homosexual. However, having this type of predisposition makes it easier for him to be tapped out by someone who is homosexual when we are not paying attention. Unfortunately, we live in a world that labels men as gay if they show any signs of sensitivity, neatness, lack of interest in sports, an interest in fashion, or a love for the arts. We give our young boys these messages and they begin to believe that they are in-fact this, which can lead them to experiment with homosexual behavior. Now, we have a problem.

It can be just as harmful to obsess over having a boy and all the while we are carrying a girl. Now, she is born with the masculine attributes of Allah (God) more dominant than the feminine. We will notice our innocent little girl becoming aggressive, rough and quick to anger. She likes to fight, wrestle and plays every sport. Our daughter, as she gets older, may have more male friends than female; she dislikes dresses and refuses to carry a handbag or wear jewelry. She has become what we used to call a *tomboy*. Again, there is really nothing wrong with these characteristics outside of the context of America's labels. But we must be scientifically aware of why she is how she is; so that we can protect her from society's interpretation of her and any attempt to guide her away from the straight path of God.

Though the advances of science and medicine are making it so that expectant mothers can determine the gender of their babies earlier and earlier; there is yet no safe and accurate way to determine the gender before the brain begins to form. The thoughts, desires, and blood of the mother form the brain of her baby. The Minister said, *"The stronger your thoughts are and the more continuous your thoughts are, they resemble a printing press. And you stamp out an impression on the mind of the forming fetus. So, the body and the mind are like a blank piece of paper that you, mother, are the first one to write on. And whatever you write is permanent…The life led by the pregnant woman is the preparation of the paper; the mind. Her thoughts and desires stamp the mind; write on the paper. Unseen – what you are making, but oh after it is writ, you cannot take back what you have produced. Only God can put His hand over your destructive work and bring something good out of something that is prepared for death"* (**How to Give Birth to a God – Part 1**).

Faster than the speed of light is the average speed of thought, traveling at 24 billion miles per second. This is why it takes the direct intervention of God through our environment to liquidate the chemistry of our mother's negative impressions on our brain by her thinking. Heredity is baked into our genes, but the environment can be more powerful than heredity. This means that with assistance from Allah (God) and the right environment, we can submit to – or rebel against the natural inclinations we were born with.

Environment is so powerful that in 1961, after the Most Honorable Elijah Muhammad watched a performance produced by the Honorable Minister Louis Farrakhan, in which a brother was playing the role of a homosexual and a sister was a prostitute; he said to the Minister, *"Brother, when you catch a fish you don't leave it on the banks, as it will continue to flop around until it falls back in the water…They (the actors) have to go back into that life in their mind in order to play and portray such part and it could lead them back into such life."*

This contrary lifestyle is a problem because Allah (God) called this behavior an abomination in His Sight and destroyed entire cities – Sodom and

Gomorrah – because homosexuality was prevalent. We all instinctively know that homosexuality is wrong. We know that two of the same gender cannot reproduce, but we are so afraid of being called homophobic and told that we are not accepting of others. So instead of standing on God's Truth; we just pretend as if we accept it.

We should NEVER engage or encourage others to engage in any acts of violence or abuse towards any gay man or woman – we have all fallen short of the Glory of God. None of us are sinless, so we are in no position to judge or condemn. But it is just as abhorrent to become so cowardly and disrespectful of the Laws of our Creator, who permitted us to exist, that we no longer follow His direct instructions and guidance. Allah (God) is the Best Knower and He deems what is righteous and unrighteous conduct. If we only care about being socially acceptable; then we cannot claim to be of the righteous – we are deviants. The righteous cannot support the homosexual lifestyle and agenda – not because some Reverend, Minister, Imam or Rabbi says so; but because it is displeasing to Allah (God).

However, today we have an entire society accepting, promoting, encouraging and manufacturing homosexual and transgender lifestyles. Being "born this way" only means being born with strong feminine inclinations if male and strong masculine inclinations if female. No one is born homosexual from the womb; that would imply that there is nothing at all that could be done to counterbalance those inclinations and tendencies. For example, everyone is born of a particular race – Black, Brown, White, etc. We can artificially lighten or darken our skin complexion, but there is nothing we can do to change our race, our biology. But there is something we can do to correct homosexual inclinations.

We have shared previously that an expectant mother, through the chemistry of her thinking, also has the ability to impress on the mind of her baby an inclination towards lying, cheating, murder, etc. But with the help of Allah (God), this too can be counterbalanced if we rebel against it. Although different sins bring about varying degrees of consequences; a sin is a sin. We have all fallen short of the Glory of God. The difference is that we all agree that murder, stealing, rape, cheating, and lying is deviant behavior. But there has been an orchestrated effort in place for decades to make us accept homosexuality as natural and normal. It is not.

During his recent press conference (November 16, 2017) in Washington, D.C., the Honorable Minister Louis Farrakhan stated, *"Do you know that homosexuality can be produced through chemistry? Don't be mad at me. Think! You can be turned into something through chemistry and the misuse of biology."* As mothers, we do not want to be in any way complicit by making it easier for the enemy to turn our children towards behavior that Allah (God) is not pleased with. This is not to burden us, but to wake us up to accepting our awesome power!

Thoughts are so powerful and potentially dangerous because they become our reality. We should take a good look at ourselves and examine our personal history. If possible, we should ask our mother to be honest about her pregnancy. Perhaps we can draw parallels with our personality, preferences, and lifestyle. This may help us to understand why we are the way we are.

During that same press conference, the Minister said to the Muslims, *"Do you know that we are the only thing that stands in between their wicked plan of the demasculinization of the Black Man?"* We love our people, all of them, regardless of their lifestyle. We are not condemning or judging because we have all been victims of Satan's wicked machinations. But Black families are being destroyed by the droves; and this is threatening to keep us from benefiting from the Promise of God. We each have a personal duty to examine and analyze our deviation from the straight path of God, so that we may correct it and be restored to what Allah (God) originally intended.

A BUN IN THE OVEN:

Going back to Maryam, we need to examine the sacrifice she had to make in order to give birth to Jesus, a perfect example of a man who was one with Allah (God). We have already mentioned and will continue to mention again that we must be willing to sacrifice. According to the dictionary, to 'sacrifice' means, *"to forfeit something for something else considered of greater value."* Maryam withdrew herself to a remote place away from her family and friends because she considered her child to be of *"greater value"* for the entire world and could not risk anyone interfering with his life. So, what are we saying?

As we mentioned in Section One, we must take an honest assessment of our family and friends and those with whom we interact and ask ourselves if they create an environment contrary to the type of child we are trying to produce. Are they supportive of our desires? Are they conscious of our pregnancy and willing to refrain from profanity or vulgarity in our presence? Do they encourage us when sometimes we get weak and the sacrifice seems too much? If our answer to these questions is, 'No,' then our circle of family and friends are creating a contrary and harmful environment for our unborn baby. We must make the sacrifice of keeping our distance from those negative influencers for the duration of our pregnancy or until we see evidence that they will respect our wishes.

This is a huge sacrifice, but our babies are more than worth it. The Honorable Minister Louis Farrakhan said, *"How we relate to circumstances surrounding our pregnancy determines certain character traits in the child which is known as your prenatal influence."* We must do whatever it takes to see that our prenatal influence is uplifting.

As soon as we find out that we are pregnant, we should inform our spouse and over time we should tell those who need to know. Pregnancy is not a disease or a defect that we should hide or be ashamed. The Holy Qur'an says that it is unlawful for us to conceal what Allah (God) has created in our wombs. That is not to say that the whole world should know, just those within your sphere. The time will eventually come when we will not be able to hide our condition no matter how hard we try. The reason we want people who will have regular contact with us to know that we are pregnant is that we expect them to be mindful of how they behave when they are around an expectant mother. If one is not aware of the pregnancy, it is difficult to hold them accountable when they constantly ask us to accompany them to view the latest horror flick, *smile*!

The Honorable Minister Louis Farrakhan gave a simple yet descriptive analogy comparing pregnancy to a cake baking in the oven. He shared that we often hear women who are pregnant say, *"I've got one (or a bun) in the oven."* When we are baking a cake or bread in the oven, we are careful of how we handle the oven because if we bump the oven or open the door too soon; our cake may fall and be ruined beyond repair. A pregnant woman is like this. She must be handled gently, with the utmost care; so that the baby she is making will not fall from a potential god to a devil. We must be careful of everything we see and hear because all can have an effect on us in one way or another.

Just take a look at the story of Cain and Abel. Cain and Abel were brothers that were completely opposite in terms of disposition; but yet, they both came from the same womb – Eve's. Eve bore a righteous son, Abel, and another son, Cain, who was filled with so much hatred and envy that he killed his own brother. The explanation that is not evident is as to why Cain was capable of executing such an unspeakable act and why Abel could never even imagine taking the life of his own brother. The Minister shared that it may have been that Cain was conceived at a time when Adam and Eve were not in harmony with Allah's (God's) Will and actually had a suspicion in their hearts regarding the truthfulness of His instructions. Abel, on the other hand, may have been born during a time when Adam and Eve were back in harmony with their Creator and obeyed His Laws. We could say so much on this particular Biblical narrative, but the point is clear.

Unfortunately, we have been just like Eve in that when we have children, one is bad and the other is good, or the first one is good, but the next two are bad; or the last one is the only good one – you get the idea. Since we have never been taught *How to Give Birth to a God*, we hit sometimes (usually by accident) and miss the other times. The Honorable Minister Louis Farrakhan teaches that every time we bear a child, we can make that child a god and never miss! The world is filled with too many devils; so, from now on, every time a child comes forth, let him be a god.

Heaven and hell are not places we go after death, but they are two conditions of life. Heaven and hell are established on earth; depending on the condition of the individuals that inhabit this space. The Honorable Minister Louis Farrakhan wrote, *"Heaven represents a state of peace where the citizens of heaven live in accordance with the laws, rules, statutes or commandments of Allah (God). This is also called in the scripture, the Kingdom of God. Again, it is also called the hereafter. The Honorable Elijah Muhammad taught us that the hereafter means 'here' on the earth 'after' the works of Satan are destroyed. Some Islamic scholars say that the hereafter is a continuation of this life. Only it is lived on a higher plane."*

The woman's mind is one of the laboratories that produce the new world. Our children must be conceived in righteousness. The consequences of conception in the back seat of a car filled with thoughts of lust and filth have led to a generation motivated by lust and filth.

We do not have to allow this hellish condition to continue for one more day. Whatever our mind can conceive, if we are a Believer, it can become reality. The 23rd Psalms reads, *"The Lord is my shepherd; I shall not want."* The Most Honorable Elijah Muhammad said that this means that we will never want for anything that we cannot have; the only condition is that we believe that we can have it. In her book, *The Women in Islam Educational Series: Part 3*, Mother Tynnetta Muhammad wrote, *"Whatever our brains are capable of thinking, we can bring into existence."*

Most of us have heard of people who claim that they can heal the sick with only the use of their mental and spiritual gifts. We may have also heard of those who claim to be able to see the future or can see what is happening in the present in another place. I once heard of a woman who claimed to have the ability to detect the root of someone's illness by simply asking specific questions about them – without having physically examined them. This all may sound like a bunch of jive or abilities that could only be possessed by the Supreme Being, and often these instances are scams with money at the root. However, there are some cases that are as real as the sun and the moon. Babies are born every day that will grow to have these special abilities – though accidental. Allah (God) has blessed special women to unknowingly produce these gods as an example to the rest of us of our true human potential.

MAKING THE WORD FLESH:

The moment we find out that we are pregnant, we should focus all of our energy on the womb. Our physical womb and our mental womb are connected; so, our feelings for our child are helping to fashion his brain and overall being. In her book, *Queen of the Planet Earth: The Rebirth and Rise of the Original Woman*, Minister Ava Muhammad writes the following: *"It is a proven fact that by the sixth month of pregnancy and often earlier, the unborn child is living an active emotional life. He can see, hear, taste, experience and even learn. Most importantly, he has feelings. And what he feels and perceives begins to shape his attitudes and expectations for himself for life."*

Our sincere feelings for our child can easily be expressed to him with words. Therefore, we should start talking to our baby as soon as we know life is there. Though our child is not able to look at us and see our smiling face as we are speaking, he can hear every word we are saying as well as absorb the joy and love being expressed. Sound travels through water. Our baby is immersed and protected by water while in utero; so, talking to our baby every day is extremely advantageous.

As we talk to our baby, we should tell him about Allah (God) and his potential to be like Him. We should be specific when we share what we desire him to become. Take a look at the condition of the world – greatness is required to make a significant impact. This is the direction we should guide our child. Talk to him about everything positive that comes to mind – behavior, discipline, having a good attitude, working hard and most importantly, obedience to the divine laws of Allah (God).

I can almost see many of your faces as you read these words. If this is a new concept to you, it may sound ridiculous to speak to a growing fetus as if he were a fully developed human, but just stay with me. If our desires for our child are concretized through verbal expressions and energy, they will make an indelible impression on the forming brain, increasing our baby's intellectual acuity and spiritual inclination toward God and righteousness.

110

Of course, talking alone is not enough. We must connect our sincere desires for our child to the only Being who can turn all desires into reality. Allah (God) desires for us to give birth to gods. He did not come to make us followers or simply to make us really smart people. He came to make us gods, exercising both force and power. It is not pleasing to Him to see us continue to produce liars, freaks, murderers, and devils. Therefore, when we turn to Him and pray for a righteous child, it is a prayer He answers with delight. During pregnancy, our prayers MUST increase – there is just no way around it. Pray, pray, pray, pray, pray and then pray some more. Our prayers impress themselves on the womb more than anything.

Pregnancy is a time in our life when we can bear witness without any shred of doubt that Allah (God) is actively with us. How do we know this? As women, we only possess the laboratory, but we do not call the baby's eyes, ears, limbs, cells, organs, and blood into existence. The umbilical cord and placenta seem to come from nowhere. Everything our baby needs to survive outside of the womb is being formed without our direction or consent. Only Allah (God) could call into existence such a perfect creation, evolving seamlessly from an amphibian state to a human. We should be grateful. Perhaps if it were up to us, our children would be born with three heads and eight legs; looking like something better suited to live in the depth of the sea – *smile*.

The Holy Qur'an reads, *"And certainly We create man of an extract of clay, Then We make him a small life-germ in a firm resting-place, Then We make the life-germ a clot, then We make the clot a lump of flesh, then We make (in) the lump of flesh bones, then We clothe the bones with flesh, then We cause it to grow into another creation. So, blessed be Allah, the Best of creators!"* God is indeed the Greatest!

Allah (God) gave the woman the ability to not only assist Him in calling a child into existence who is a god internally; but externally as well. Do not get this confused with vanity. Beauty is indeed in the eye of the beholder. But desiring a child physically appealing and beautiful to most beholders, is not wrong. The Honorable Minister Louis Farrakhan said that being happy during pregnancy and thinking righteous thoughts can affect our baby's physical appearance. Have you ever seen someone and said to yourself, *'She would be so pretty if she just wasn't so angry and nasty all of the time?'* A foul attitude combined with bad food and drink will rob us of our natural beauty appearance and can mar our baby. There are many who have made themselves ill and have even died early due to living troubled, angry, and bitter lives. Anger is physically toxic to the mind and body – it negatively impacts the developing baby.

Allah (God) must be uppermost in our mind and heart; above our husband, other family members and even ourselves. Recite His beautiful attributes over and over again: *Bismillah ir Rahman ir Rahim (In the Name of Allah, the Beneficent, the Merciful)*. Allah (God) is *The Peace, The Majestic, The Forgiver, The All-Knowing, The Loving, The Truth*, and so much more. The more we reflect on these attributes, the more our child will be like his Creator. He will not be *'The' Beneficent*, but he will be beneficent. He will not be *'The' Forgiver*, but he will have a forgiving spirit. The more we pray and think on something, Allah (God) begins to arrange the forces in the atmosphere to give us exactly what we want – another divine law. It is important to be mindful that anything we ask Allah (God) regarding our child; we must also ask that it be a blessing. Have you ever heard of the expression, *'Be careful what you wish for because you just might get it?'* Sometimes we pray for something and when we receive it, instead of it being a blessing, it becomes a burden – or worse, a curse.

Remember that one of the most powerful prayers to say while pregnant is found in the Holy Qur'an, embedded in the words spoken by the mother of Maryam (Mary). It is found in Chapter 3, Verse 34; it reads, *"When a woman of Amran said: My Lord, I vow to Thee what is in my womb, to be devoted (to Thy service), so accept (it) from me; surely Thou, only Thou, art the Hearing, the Knowing."* These words are so profoundly beautiful if carefully understood. To know that you are bringing a child into this world and to then immediately have the presence of mind to first and foremost declare a righteous intention for that child is glorious.

In an article titled, *The Most Honored Woman in History; Mary, the Mother of Jesus*, the Honorable Minister Louis Farrakhan wrote, *"When the female finds that she is expecting, immediately, as it was with the mother of Mary, a vow should be made in the form of a prayer…It is most important that the vow is made as soon as the female discovers that she is with child. This vow sets the stage for the forming of this new life, for, it sets up the precondition or orientation of the mind of the expectant mother. All during her pregnancy, her mind is staid on Allah (God), since it is Allah (God) working with the expectant mother, forming that which is in the womb. This vow connects what is in the womb to the Originator of Life. This vow helps the expectant mother to know that she must observe clean habits in her eating, drinking and daily life because now she is forming something that she desires to be accepted by Allah (God) for His Service."*

The more we pray, the more our supplications are forming a child who loves Allah (God) more than anything. We are forming a child that will want to serve Allah (God) and will find tremendous joy in being obedient to Him. Though there is much within our realm of influence and control, only Allah (God) can make a righteous child. So, He cannot be absent from the equation. We must beg Him to intervene so that we may be blessed to experience the privilege of giving birth to gods.

IQRA (READ):

"In the name of Allah, the Beneficent, the Merciful. Read in the name of thy Lord Who creates — Creates man from a clot, Read and thy Lord is most Generous, Who taught by the pen, Taught man what he knew not" (Holy Qur'an 96:1-5).

The Holy Qur'an was not arranged in chronological order, the order in which the revelations came to Prophet Muhammad (Peace Be Upon Him). Centuries have passed, and its divine compilation remains a conundrum. However, we do know that in this Book of 114 surahs (chapters), we find the first revelation given to Prophet Muhammad (PBUH) near the end of the Qur'an in the 96th surah, *The Clot*. This surah opens with the first direct instruction ever given to Prophet Muhammad (PBUH) from the Most High through the angel, Jabril. His instructions were: Read – or "Iqra" in Arabic. Interestingly, Allah (God) was well aware that His Prophet was illiterate; nevertheless, He commands the Prophet to, read. Why is reading so important? And why does this divine command come to us in a chapter titled, *The Clot?*

A blood clot is a coagulating or congealed blood that forms a semi-solid lump or mass in the body. This is the physical make-up of every new life in the womb of a woman during its initial stage of development – just after conception. As the cells and tissues of this new life begin to multiply and take shape, the first and most essential organ of the body also begins to form – the brain.

The Honorable Minister Louis Farrakhan teaches – just as the brain is the first part of the new life to develop, we should synchronize this development with the first instruction given by Allah (God) – read. While the baby is a clot – *read*. While the brain is developing – *read*. During each trimester of pregnancy – *read*. READ to our baby every day.

In his lecture, **How to Give Birth to a God**, the Minister said, *"Talk to the child while it is in the womb. Teach it, read to it; not silly fairy tales. Read to it and read to it the most beautiful narratives, the most beautiful stories, the most beautiful attributes; read it into the child. Write on the paper of the child's mind. Stamp his mind with your heart-felt desires for God and bring forth a child in the image and likeness of God."*

As a student of literacy, I was taught that there are five essential components of reading: phonemic awareness, phonics, vocabulary, fluency, and comprehension. Once a student achieves basic comprehension, they are considered a good reader because reading is not just the recitation of words, but the ability to comprehend the meaning behind those words. In short, reading is understanding. An advanced reader is always involved in comprehensive reading – the ability to understand and connect to the material by purposely absorbing the meaning of each word, phrase, sentence, and paragraph throughout the entirety of the text.

If a pregnant mother is truly reading, she is also thinking because thinking is required if our objective is to comprehend or understand what we are reading. Thinking is the result of stimulated thoughts, which are not abstract formless things. A thought is substance; it's tangible; it's real. Thought permeates from the mind and travels throughout the body, affecting every cell in the body – from the brain to the heel. How can this be easily proven? When one gets nervous or frightened; anxious or stressed…These are feelings from thoughts that in-turn cause a physical reaction in the body:

The heartbeat increases, palms get sweaty, the stomach is nauseated – the mouth is dry. These are all physical reactions in different parts of the body from thoughts. If these symptoms of thought are not quelled, it could lead to a more serious condition; perhaps even nerve, tissue or organ damage. Well, what if these same thoughts or similar ones persisted and increased in intensity from the mind of a pregnant mother? How would the baby, who is completely reliant on the mother, be affected? What if, instead, those thoughts were positive?

Consider the Honorable Minister Louis Farrakhan's words to Brother Jabril Muhammad: "The Honorable Elijah Muhammad told me once that, *'It takes 500 seconds—eight minutes and 20 seconds for the light, traveling at 186,000 miles per second, to travel from the sun to the Earth.' Likewise, he said, 'It takes 500 seconds—eight minutes and 20 seconds for the blood to make a complete circuit between the heel and the brain and back.' He said, 'When you go to visit a person that is sick, if you put the right word in their ear, within eight minutes and 20 seconds you will see a change in the spirit of such person.'* What that told me was that the level of energy, light, spiritual power that is contained in right words communicated from the right motivation energizes the brain of the recipient of such word. That energy is delivered to every part of the body, thereby increasing the energy level of that person."

Regardless to circumstances, no expectant mother is so busy that she cannot devote a minimum of 500 seconds – eight minutes and 20 seconds – every day to communicating the right words to her baby; energizing the brain of her baby. The Honorable Minister Louis Farrakhan stated, *"There is no other book more valuable to read, than that which God reveals for the destiny of human beings. The Word of God, whether you find it in the Bible or Qur'an is valuable if understood."* The Holy Qur'an, in particular, covers every aspect of life. It informs us of how best to live the life that Allah (God) gifted to us. These divine instructions should be passed on to our baby – imprinting them on the developing brain so that Allah's (God's) words become a part of the nature and character of the child. It may sound incredible, but the woman is in-fact blessed with this magnificent ability when she actively co-operates and co-creates with God.

Along with spiritual readings, we must emphasize mathematics and science. No matter what career or endeavor our child eventually pursues, he will undoubtedly have to know math and science in order to become a master in that field. The mother should focus on mathematics and science. But we can also give our baby his/her purpose right from the womb. Ask yourself: What does our Nation need? EVERYTHING. How would you like your child to contribute to the upliftment of our people and Nation – through what field of endeavor: Health & Human Services, Agriculture, Education, Defense, Art & Culture, Trade & Commerce, Justice, Information or Science & Technology? We should choose a field and find books about that particular field and immerse ourselves in reading those books to our baby. With the help of Allah (God), we will produce a child with an inclination – a natural leaning – towards its purpose in science or health or agriculture or any of the aforementioned ministries.

So, our baby's mental foundation is being established – we are writing scripture on the brain; we are writing math and science on the brain, and we are writing knowledge of a specific field on the brain. At the same time, we are showering our love, joy, and gratitude for this new life on the womb. During these wonderful bonding moments, we should allow NOTHING to distract us from the goal or bring us down. Mental giants or geniuses are continually made accidentally; let us now make them on purpose and with purpose.

CHILDREN OF THE MOST HIGH

The Honorable Minister Louis Farrakhan has taught us that the brain of the child is fashioned by the thoughts, desires, and blood of the mother. In his lectures, Minister Farrakhan spoke of a Japanese woman who discovered that reading to her children while they were still in the womb made them highly intelligent. This woman gave birth to four geniuses. According to scientists, by the time the baby is born, it already has almost all of the neurons it will ever have; given to it by the mother. The brain of the child grows at an astounding rate in the first years of life. From birth to age three, the brain develops 700 new neural connections every **second**. The brain doubles in size in the first year and by the age of three, it has reached 80 percent of its adult volume. Our babies are capable of learning almost anything during this critical period of brain development.

If we read to our baby consistently while in the womb, we will find that as we continue to teach our baby from infancy and beyond; he/she will learn with ease. Not only have we laid a foundation of divine and purposeful knowledge as a base for our child; but in addition, a desire and a natural inclination in him/her to read and to continue to learn.

Student Minister Ava Muhammad, National Spokesperson for the Honorable Minister Louis Farrakhan and the Nation of Islam, is a brilliant scholar. She wrote these words: *"You do not select your child; your child selects you."* When we are careful of how we think, eat, live – striving to be obedient to the laws of God, our child will select our way of life right from the womb. Our children are born equivalent to the effort we put toward our pregnancies. They select us. Whether we are good or bad – they cannot become much better than we have made them, unless Allah (God) intervenes. We can only have righteous, powerful giants with the direct assistance and intervention of Almighty God, Allah.

FATHER'S INFLUENCE ON PREGNANCY:

You can determine the true character of a man by how he treats the women and girls in his life, especially his wife. It is reported that Prophet Muhammad (PBUH) said, *"The best among you is the best towards his wife."* A key element that cannot be overlooked during pregnancy is the relationship between the mother and the baby's father; ideally also her husband. If our desire is to give birth to a god, there is no denying that the mother must have a strong connection with the baby growing inside of her; but the quality of that relationship oftentimes is dependent upon how she feels about the baby's father and how he feels about her.

How a man treats his wife while she is pregnant with his future is critical to both the mother and the child's sense of peace and security. It is essential to the child's willingness or even ability to bond with the father once he or she is born. Naturally, it is difficult for most men to even imagine what their wife is going through physically and emotionally as the baby grows within. But consider that a pregnant woman should be handled with the same care that one would give to a million-dollar crystal vase as it is being prepared to be packed for a long-distance journey. She is infinitely more valuable and must be protected as such; mentally and physically at all times. After all, it is her thoughts and desires that are forming the brain of her child. So, every effort must be made to keep her happy, peaceful and secure throughout the duration of her pregnancy.

While every woman is different; therefore, every pregnancy is different – there is a high probability that the most demanding time during her pregnancy will be during the first trimester and again during the final trimester. Remember that during the first couple of months of pregnancy, her body is adjusting to what it initially interprets to be an intruder. The body naturally goes into overdrive trying to expel the foreign object. This causes many women to become nauseated to the point of vomiting. Some experience extreme exhaustion, have serious food cravings and aversions without warning, urinate frequently and have big emotional swings. In addition, first-time mothers are usually nervous about labor and delivery and may even question whether or not they will be good parents.

Great consideration must be given to the physical changes that occur during pregnancy. The second trimester is typically a lot smoother for many women. But as mothers begin to near the last couple of months of pregnancy some of the same symptoms may reoccur but in addition, the mother is now carrying extra weight which makes her move slower. Her feet and ankles may swell, and nights may be uncomfortable and restless. Her lower back may ache and the only thing on her mind will be getting that baby out of her as soon as possible. A father's patience will definitely be tried, but she will need him to rise to the occasion. A test of a man's true love, discipline, and understanding of the sacredness of the female is how he handles his wife during this most trying time.

The absolute worst thing that a man can ever do is to abuse a woman. But to abuse her while she is pregnant is ten times as heinous and potentially irreparable. The Honorable Minister Louis Farrakhan asked: *"How can you live in fear in a home and produce the right kind of offspring? How can you live under that kind of tyranny and produce children who recognize what love is and what justice is and what mercy is and what tenderness is? You are producing wicked children because you live under environmental circumstances that make you able to produce a devil."*

Remember that a crime against a woman is a crime against humanity and it is almost an unpardonable sin. Physically abusing a woman in any condition is intolerable, but when a man abuses a pregnant woman physically or verbally (which sometimes can be worse), he may have sealed his fate when it comes to his children. The woman's fear turns into an indescribable hatred for him. She can easily give birth to a child born hating the father. The abandonment, disrespect, harsh words, abuse, the tears shed, and overall mistreatment she had to endure from him throughout the pregnancy will result in the father having an improbable relationship with the child. The father will wonder why his child distances himself; why he/she cries when left alone with him; and why the last thing he or she wants when older is anything to do with the father. The woman has the power to pass on love as well as hate from the womb, based on what she is experiencing.

Therefore, the Honorable Minister Louis Farrakhan reminded us why the Most Honorable Elijah Muhammad made it against the law for a Brother to strike his wife: *"He put us out of the society for ninety days for the first offense, six months for the second offense. Because it is wrong, wrong, wrong for a man to beat a woman. I say it again, it is wrong, wrong, wrong for a man to beat a woman. Why is it wrong for you to beat a woman? The Honorable Elijah Muhammad says when you teach a man you teach an individual; when you teach a woman, you teach a Nation. When you beat a man, you beat an individual. When you beat a woman, fool, you beat a Nation. You must think about your actions and the consequences thereof. The beating of our wives, the abusing of ourselves, is forbidden by God."*

Needless to say, the last thing a pregnant woman who is trying to give birth to a god needs is a weak, insensitive husband. Though the woman is the one who has to carry the child in her womb, she should not go through the joys and struggles of pregnancy alone. Her husband should be right there with her letting her know how much she is loved and what an honor it is that she is the mother of his child. Every day ask her how she feels and what can be done for her. Rub her swollen feet and massage her aching back. Walk next to her proudly, hand-in-hand; because as Minister Farrakhan put it, she is in the most beautiful stage of her life.

The Honorable Minister Louis Farrakhan also reminds the brothers: As your wife is losing shape, you must now build up her mind and protect her from harmful influences – this takes a strong, loving man. She needs to be encouraged (not forced) to do right. As the maintainer of his wife, the man should care about his wife doing the proper things during pregnancy. He should make sure his wife is praying, talking to the baby, reading to the baby, eating right, exercising and staying away from negativity. Since she should not go to the movies, then he shouldn't either; since she should not watch violence and foolishness on the television, he should make sure that it is not on the screen when she is home. The father should also talk to the baby every day and shower love on him or her while gently rubbing his wife's stomach. If there are other children, they too should shower love on the new life before he or she is born; building closeness between the siblings from the onset.

If we had a happy and enjoyable pregnancy, we are likely to have a happy baby. The baby will appear to come out of the womb smiling. Returning smiles after just a few weeks of life is definitely possible. And laughing out loud by two months can also be our reality.

Arguing with your wife once or twice; causing her to have a couple of bad thoughts may not doom your future entirely. But what is being stressed here is the duration and magnitude of each instance. The father's influence on the natural inclinations of his newborn baby will be impactful in the most positive way if he masters how to handle the woman's mind, not just her body. Brothers: Love your wife and take good care of her and your child will love and honor you immeasurably.

EATING TO LIVE – WHILE PREGNANT OR NURSING:

The Most Honorable Elijah Muhammad wrote, *"There is no way of prolonging the life of human beings – or any other life – unless it begins with restrictions of the foods which sustain life: the right kinds of food and the proper time when it should be taken into our bodies."* These words are taken from the first page of the first of two books he wrote titled, **How to Eat to Live**. The main purpose of teaching us how to eat to live is to *"prolong our lives."* Having an abundant life is a promise made to us from God through His Servant: *"I am come that they might have life, and that they might have it more abundantly"* (John 10:10, KJV). Allah (God) will not fail in His promise to us, but the Most Honorable Elijah Muhammad said that He demands strict obedience to His Will.

There is no substitute or shortcut for acquiring and reading every single word of **How to Eat to Live, Books I & II** – several times – and then personally implementing this dietary law so that we may begin to benefit from a Teaching that was given to the Most Honorable Elijah Muhammad from God in Person. The Holy Qur'an declares that Allah (God) will send us a Messenger who will inform us of what we should eat and what we should store in our houses (3:48). The Most Honorable Elijah Muhammad fulfills this prophetic scripture.

Those who are familiar with the Teachings of the Most Honorable Elijah Muhammad know that his followers follow a strict diet. Many are aware that we only eat one meal a day; we fast regularly, and we do not eat swine or scavengers. By simply practicing these minimal restrictions, one will begin to experience immediate health benefits. However, in order to reach the level that Allah (God) desires for us, which is our god-potential, we must apply and master the comprehensive scope of the wisdom found in **How to Eat to Live.**

In this world, when women are pregnant or nursing, their doctors or midwives will advise them to eliminate certain foods and beverages from their diet and tell them to increase their intake of healthier foods which contain higher levels of rich vitamins, minerals, and nutrients. Expectant or nursing mothers are typically asked to avoid large fish that are high in mercury such as tuna and swordfish. They are also asked to avoid eating raw and undercooked fish; raw eggs; organ meats; caffeine; alcohol; nicotine; junk foods; and microwaved meals – just to name a few. Have you ever wondered why it is okay for a woman to consume such things when she is **not** pregnant, but the same foods or activities are considered harmful when she is? The truth is: It is not okay! Ninety percent of the time, if your diet and lifestyle are not good for your baby; then it was never good for you in the first place.

How to Eat to Live, Books I & II do not offer an alternative diet in terms of "what" a pregnant or nursing mother should eat. It does, however, make exceptions for pregnant and nursing mothers, as well as for children on "how" they should eat. The Most Honorable Elijah Muhammad wrote, *"EAT GOOD FOOD so that you will be able to give your baby good, pure milk. You can drink cows' milk; your own milk glands will put it into the right stage for your child. Be careful as to what kind of drugs you take while nursing your baby. And do not take fasts while you are breast-feeding an infant or even while you are pregnant. If you like, you may eat once a day while pregnant or breast-feeding your baby, but you are not forced to do so. You should not go for two or three days without eating"* (Book II, page 90).

We emphasize that the Most Honorable Elijah Muhammad said that if you are pregnant or breast-feeding an infant, you should NOT fast and you are NOT forced to eat one meal a day. Several studies have indicated that there has been a dramatic decline in the nutritional value of most fruits, vegetables, grains and other crops over the decades. Most notable was a landmark study by Donald Davis and his team of researchers from the University of Texas at Austin's Department of Chemistry and Biochemistry – published in the December 2004 *Journal of the American College of Nutrition.* According to this and numerous studies, the primary culprit is the depletion of the soil, overuse of fertilizers and overall poor agricultural practices that seek to produce bigger crops, much faster – in essence, profit over health. The result is that today's crops are not as rich in vitamins and minerals as the fruits and vegetables decades ago. For example, it was determined in a similar study that one would have to eat eight oranges to equal the nutritional value of one orange from several decades ago. On the other hand, we must also be careful not to use pregnancy as an excuse to overeat or to eat poorly.

It is no secret that pregnant and nursing mothers have heightened sensitivities, which are not just reflected emotionally, but also physically. All senses are at their optimum during this period of maternity; including intense food cravings and aversions. It is important that we are conscious of our cravings because more often than not, it may be that our body is signaling to us that we are lacking some nutrient contained in that food. Meaning, it is not so much that the food we crave is what we need, but we need the nutrients found in that particular food. So, if what we crave is not a healthy choice, then we should determine which nutrients the food contains and choose a healthier alternative. Many women take vitamin supplements (prenatal pills) while they are pregnant to ensure that they get sufficient nutrition. This is a decision that the mother must make in consultation with her midwife or doctor; together they can best determine what the mother is lacking and if additional supplements are needed.

The Holy Qur'an guides mothers to breast-feed their babies for two whole years. For the first few months, the infant is one-hundred percent exclusively reliant on mother's milk for all of his or her nutritional needs. Therefore, it is just as important to eat an adequate amount of the best foods while breast-feeding as it was when we were pregnant. Our food should be organic, Non-GMO, fresh (not canned or frozen) and prepared properly.

Beware of the MICROWAVE. Zapping our food not only destroys the life that is in it; it also replaces it with death. Standing near a microwave that is turned on gives the mother and her baby direct contact with active radiation. This can lead to permanent mental damage, cancers and other abnormalities from the womb. The microwave is a horrible invention. It is best not to buy one, lest you be tempted to use it. It is quite simple – radiated food leads to an early death.

According to **How to Eat to Live**, our fruits should be eaten raw and our vegetables should be cooked – but not overly cooked and robbed of their nutritional value. We should eat whole wheat bread that is at least 24-hours old (never freshly-baked, right out of the oven). We should beware of starchy foods and sweets, and we should drink pure fresh whole milk. Though many foods contain calcium, milk is one of the best and least expensive sources of calcium. If the mother does not consume enough calcium for herself, she will begin to notice rotting teeth and weakening joints and bones – the baby will get all of the calcium he needs first, and the mother will get what is left.

The best food, solid food is the navy bean. The Most Honorable Elijah Muhammad wrote, *"No bean did He advise, except the small navy – the small size and not the larger size – the little brown pink ones, and the white ones. This bean He valued to be very high in protein, fats and starches, and it is a safe food for prolonging life"* (Book I, page 5). The Most Honorable Elijah Muhammad also taught that no meat is good for us; he said,

126

"TO EAT MEAT is against our life and shortens the span of our life" (Book II, page 63).

In his lecture, **How to Give Birth to a God: Part Two**, the Honorable Minister Louis Farrakhan said, *"Put the best food in yourself...Eat fresh food, not canned food; not frozen food. Go where there are fresh vegetables, fresh fruit – eat it while there's life in it. Cook it and know how to cook it, that you don't cook the life out of it; so that when you feed yourself, you're feeding life into yourself. Because you're going to make tissues and flesh and a pump and cylinders and veins; you know, almost six miles of veins – nerves. This is what you're going to make from what you eat. You're going to fashion a brain."* All praise is due to Allah (God)!

Diet and exercise go hand-in-hand not just before pregnancy; but during. Exercise should not be abandoned during pregnancy – again, walking is the best form of exercise. Walking 30 minutes a day, three to five days a week will produce beneficial results. Exercise and a proper diet prevent unnecessary weight gain during pregnancy and gives the mother the strength, endurance, and flexibility she will need to make her labor and delivery as smooth as possible.

As we near the end of our pregnancies, the biggest challenge will be to maintain our discipline. However, if we see it through and follow the guidelines contained in *How to Give Birth to a God*, we will soon hear those unaware of these Teachings tell us how "lucky" we are to have such beautiful, well-behaved and intelligent children. Tell them that "luck" had nothing to do with it. Our children are not born in a vacuum. With the help of Allah (God), if we strive to be obedient to these restrictions and suggestions, we will all be blessed. Our children are proportional to the effort we give as an active, conscious co-creator with God – no more and no less.

A GOOD NAME IS BETTER THAN GOLD:

"A good name is more desirable than great riches; to be esteemed is better than silver or gold" (Proverbs 22:1 NIV).

I remember when my sister was pregnant with my nephew, she chose a respectable Biblical name for her son and enthusiastically shared it with our strong African grandmother. Our grandmother (may Allah be pleased with her) was a devout Christian and an impassioned student of the Word. So, it came as a complete surprise when she forbade my sister from naming her son after this particular man in the scriptures. Although he was a good man, my grandmother explained that he was "crippled" and lived a life of hardship. She was convinced that if my sister named her son after him, she would be sentencing her son to a similar life. Being obedient, my sister submitted and chose a more agreeable Biblical name for her son.

Now, one may say that our grandmother was a little extreme and clearly overcome by superstition. You could be right. But there was a bigger message that she was trying to communicate to us. It is the same strongly held belief that remains till this day in many African and Eastern cultures – *'you become your name.'* Believing this, great care is always given when naming children.

What encompasses a name? Our name is certainly that word that we are referred to as, identified with, and referenced by – it distinguishes us from all others in a particular space and time. When someone mentions our name, we become especially attentive and alert because we are being specifically addressed and whatever comes next will likely be of particular importance to us. Our name is the distinction that signifies our presence. But even bigger than that, our name is the label attached to our work, our character, our history, and our reputation.

The title of this section, *A Good Name is Better than Gold*, comes directly from the name of a chapter in the book, *Message to the Blackman in America*, written by the Most Honorable Elijah Muhammad. He opens this chapter by stating, *"One of the first and most important truths that must be established in this day is our identity."* He also writes, *"First, you must be given the names of your forefathers, whose names are the most Holy and Righteous Names of Allah."*

The Book of Isaiah 65:15 bears witness – it reads, *"And ye shall leave your name for a curse unto my chosen: for the Lord GOD shall slay thee, and call his servants by another name"* (KJV). In reference to this scripture, the Most Honorable Elijah Muhammad writes, *"Here, we are warned that God will not accept us in the name of the white race, because He has another name that He will call us by, and He mentions this throughout Isaiah and the New Testament. We must have a name of God and not the name of an enemy of God"* (How to Eat to Live: Book I).

The Black man and woman are direct descendants of God. And just as children resemble their parents, God's descendants also resemble Him in likeness and in image. Similarly, children wear the name of their parents and we too should also wear the name of Our Father. His names illuminate His divine attributes, His characteristics, His works, His history, and His reputation.

Allah (God) has at least 99 distinctive attributes which are manifested in both the feminine and masculine expression. We argue that the energy from these attributes is best absorbed if spoken in the original Mother tongue of the planet – Arabic. We know this is the original language because every other language spoken on Earth has derivatives from Arabic. This language is mathematically precise and absolutely perfect. So, by choosing a name in the Arabic language we are reconnecting to our origin as the Mothers and Fathers of civilization – synchronizing our being and our identification and aligning it with the universe.

If we study the 99 attributes and the countless other names of Allah (God), we will discover that the names are all describing human characteristics because a good name illustrates our god-potential. For example: Al Qadir – *the Powerful*; Al Halim – *the Patient, Tolerant, Forbearing, Generous*; Ash Shahid – *the Witness*; Al Jalil – *the Great, Exalted, Magnificent*; or Ar Rashid – *the Wise, Right-minded, One of Good Council.* Each of these beautiful names and meanings is also found in the feminine expression of God: Qadira, Halimah, Shahidah, Jalilah, and Rashidah. According to the Holy Qur'an and the Bible, both the male and the female were created from the same divine essence of God; therefore, both can exemplify His attributes to the fullest.

Contrast that to continuing to wear the names of our enemy and former slave masters, which connects us to them and identifies us as still belonging to them. The Original man has no beginning nor end – we are as old as God Himself. The enemy of God – on the other hand – had a beginning and will certainly have an ending. We must refuse to allow another generation to walk in the enemy's finite names – his newness to the planet compels him to choose names after God's lower creations: River, Wolfgang, Apple, Stone, Colt, Rose, etc. These things are subordinate to the human being and are unworthy to be assigned to our divine identity.

So as parents, we may not be able to choose the gender of our children or the shade of their skin; nor do we determine how tall they will become or their final shoe size – it is Allah (God) who shapes us in the wombs as He pleases. BUT we do have the ability and responsibility of choosing the name they will carry during their sojourn on this earth. Yes – it is true that our children are not born into the world exemplifying these attributes, but like Grandma believed, *'You become your name.'* The scriptures verify, *"In the beginning was the Word, and the Word was with God, and the Word was God"* (John 1:1 KJV). Later it reads, *"And the Word was made flesh, and dwelt among us..."* (John 1:14 KJV).

So, let's take the naming of our children a little more seriously. Together, with our spouse, agree on a male or female name for the child. A name, after-all is **not** *just* a name. There is actual palpable energy – universal transformative rhythms – that are attached to *all* words. Imagine everyday being called; *Powerful, Magnificent, Wise, or Generous.* Every time we say his or her name, we will be reminding them and ourselves of the righteousness of the meaning. Could a meaningful name increase the likelihood that our children will raise their standards and behavior to exemplify God? Could a righteous name improve their self-concept? Could they grow to one day become worthy of their name? Well – it certainly gives them something noble to strive for. Gold is very valuable, indeed; but a good name is PRICELESS!

SECTION 3: LABOR & DELIVERY

"Surely with difficulty is ease, with difficulty is surely ease. So when thou art free (from anxiety), work hard, And make thy Lord thy exclusive object."
Holy Qur'an 94:5-8

A RETURN TO NATURAL CHILDBIRTH:

"A woman giving birth to a child has pain because her time has come; but when her baby is born she forgets the anguish because of her joy that a child is born into the world" (John 16:21 NIV).

No right-minded person willingly and eagerly seeks out pain and discomfort. However, it is a fact of life that none of us can escape. To live is to struggle and experience pain – this is part of our growth and development ordained by Allah (God), for our benefit. Sometimes the pain exists on the mental or spiritual plane, and other times the pain is undeniably physical – such is the pain of childbirth. The Most Honorable Elijah Muhammad said that the pain of birth is equal to the pain of death. The Honorable Minister Louis Farrakhan said that this means, *"every time mom has a baby, she dies a little to give life."* These two statements are understandably enough to make any woman welcome a way to circumvent the natural process and find an alternative to avoid this degree of pain. This provides an opening for wicked manipulators in the health and pharmaceutical industries to take full advantage, by systematically guiding women away from what is natural.

Childbirth is natural – just as death is natural. The fact that we now have to qualify the "type" of birth lets us know that we have moved from what is natural into what is normal. The techno-medical model of birth is the new norm and Cesarean sections or C-sections (delivery by surgically cutting the abdomen) are a strong second – leaving natural childbirth for the so-called kooky and eccentric. Natural childbirth is comprised of two fundamental features: (1) a non-invasive vaginal birth and (2) little to no medical intervention, including medication. The disturbing new normal in U.S. obstetrics is that only about 8% of deliveries meet this definition of natural childbirth. Whereas, 32% of deliveries are now by C-section and 60% of women opt for an epidural and spinal anesthesia for pain relief during vaginal deliveries (CDC). These numbers are staggering, particularly when you consider that in 1965 the U.S. C-section birth rate was only 4.5% and epidurals only became a common labor and delivery practice in the 1980s. An epidural is powerful anesthesia that comes with consequences. Medical professionals know that any medication administered during labor will enter the bloodstream and will reach the baby – regardless of the percentage, no amount is good.

Today, it is nearly impossible to witness a hospital labor and delivery that does not include one or more of the following: an epidural, forceps, a vacuum, an episiotomy (a surgical cut to enlarge the vaginal opening), intravenous needles and tubes, fetal monitors, administration of Pitocin (drug used to induce labor), a catheter, amniotic hook, etc. Childbirth is treated like an illness or medical trauma, rather than a natural occurrence. And if the delivery is by C-section, we can include a host of other supplies, equipment, and procedures. Though C-sections are one of the most common major surgeries in the U.S.; it is still major surgery and therefore includes all of the dangerous possible complications that come with any major surgery.

There are certainly valid reasons that would require a mother to have to rely on a C-section in order to delivery her baby safely. We are not opposed to medical advancements and are grateful that there are options for mothers who have high risk pregnancies due to medical complications or physical disabilities. We also recognize that unforeseen crises can arise during labor that would require an emergency C-section. If C-sections were only reserved for the aforementioned circumstances, we could return to a 4.5% rate.

Taking the Hippocratic Oath is required by medical students in most medical schools. The Oath is very noble, and the practice of healing is a noble profession. But the Oath is now just a theory that has been nullified by the lack of diligent application to uphold its intent. According to the Hippocratic Oath, doctors should avoid overtreatment; they should be conscious that a patient's illness may affect their economic stability; they should bear witness that prevention is preferred over cure; they should be mindful that there is an art to medicine, and they are not to play God! Hmm. If obedience to the Oath were the standard, what grade does the U.S. healthcare industry deserve?

Prevention and healing in the healthcare industry have been replaced with a corporate model that now boasts a profit of billions of dollars (annually). Contrary to God's way, things that are natural like childbirth and the burial of our deceased have exorbitant fees. According to Kaiser Health News (KHN), *"A surgical birth can bring in twice the revenue of a vaginal delivery."* KHN reports that obstetricians are not above pressuring women to preschedule a C-section; encouraging inductions that increase the likelihood of a C-section; or inventing emergencies. All of this constitutes medical malpractice. Today, it is dangerous for women to put their complete faith in their physicians.

So, try to avoid C-sections. We want to be in control of our body during birth. On a personal note: I witnessed the C-section of a very close relative and will never forget it. Unfortunately, I saw much more than I was supposed to. The process was very violent: The doctor had to literally saw through layers of flesh, which caused the bed to rock back and forth. I could hear the sound of skin and flesh tearing. It was brutal. The Caucasian doctor reminded me of the slave-master barbarically slicing open the womb of a pregnant Black woman, then ripping out her baby. My nerves were only quelled by the sight of a beautiful baby boy.

It is difficult to be restored completely after a C-section. The immediate recovery is longer and more difficult than vaginal birth, and endurance is required to care for our newborn. Not to mention that the heavy pain medications required after surgery will affect the chemistry of our breastmilk.

Why is natural childbirth so critical? Anytime we partake of anything unnatural, there are consequences. Electing to determine when your child will be born through a planned C-section may now be normal, but it certainly isn't natural. The Holy Qur'an reads, *"Allah knows what every female bears, and that of which the wombs fall short of completion and that which they grow. And everything with Him has a measure"* (13:8). It also states, *"And Allah brought you forth from the wombs of your mothers – you knew nothing – and He gave you hearing and sight and hearts that you might give thanks"* (16:78). Allah (God) knows our condition, it is all measured (calculated). Based on His science and mathematics, if He sees fit, He will determine when our babies come forth.

Yes, natural labor and delivery are painful. But the pain of childbirth is a natural pain – it is NOT a punishment for the transgressions of Eve. The pain is so intense that many analogies are given throughout the scriptures that compare the chastisement of God to the pain of childbirth. The Holy Qur'an describes the experience of birth as *"faintings upon faintings."* Even the Mother of Jesus was stunned by the throes of childbirth and wished for death rather than to endure the pain. But look at what she produced!

The Holy Qur'an 19:23 describes Maryam's pain while giving birth to Jesus, *"And the throes of childbirth drove her to the trunk of a palm-tree. She said: Oh, would that I had died before this, and had been a thing quite forgotten!"* Any mother can bear witness to Maryam's agony. As mentioned previously, the Most Honorable Elijah Muhammad said that the pain of childbirth is equal to the pain of death. During death, the shutting down of the body causes pain to the victim; so, the righteous pray for ease and peace as they die. The pain of birth and death are equivalent because, during birth, a part of the woman must die in order to bring forth life. So, therefore, life and death exist at the same time. If the woman holds on not allowing her baby to come forth, then both she and her baby will die.

To every physical law, there is a spiritual counterpart. The baby receives a spiritual impression by physically travelling through the birth canal. This process is not only painful for the mother, but for the baby as well. It is Allah (God) who determined that the head will physically forge the way to freedom for the body; just as the mind spiritually exercises control over our lower desires. All of our life experiences, whether conscious or subconscious, are recorded in our memory banks. We do not want to deny our children the natural struggle, ordained by Allah (God), which sets them up with their first foundational victory.

Mother Tynnetta Muhammad, the wife of the Most Honorable Elijah Muhammad, said that there would be no pain during childbirth in the Hereafter. Remember, the hereafter is not a place we go after death, but the hereafter will be right here on earth after the power of wicked to rule has been broken. However, the hereafter is not something we should simply be waiting for, but a world that we must actively be working every day to establish.

After difficulty comes ease. So, remember the opening scripture to this section. The difficulty of childbirth is immediately rewarded with a beautiful new life. The intensity of the emotions we experience at that moment is so overwhelming that we forget the pain. This is because Allah (God), in His Mercy, never gives us more than we can handle.

FUDIA MUHAMMAD

WHY CHOOSE A MIDWIFE?

In 1997, my husband and I were blessed with the birth of our first child. To say the least, it was intense, emotional and beautiful all at the same time. We have since been blessed with three more equally intense, emotional and beautiful experiences with the birth of our next three children. All four of our children were delivered with the aid of a midwife instead of an OB-GYN. Our first two children were hospital births and the last two were born at birthing centers. Having a midwife for each birth always offered a sense of peace because we knew we had a measure of control. It is a decision that we do not regret and an option we wish more Black women would choose.

The person who oversees our pregnancy, labor, delivery and postpartum cannot be chosen haphazardly. Today, for Black women and their babies, it could be the difference between life and death. The benefit of choosing a midwife over a traditional physician is that midwives allow and encourage the mother to be squarely in the driver's seat when it comes to her body and the details surrounding her birth experience. Women who desire to have a natural delivery and a low-tech birth experience should opt for a midwife because this philosophy aligns with that of all midwives.

Midwives are typically not an option for women whose pregnancies are complicated or considered very high risk (multiple births, VBACs, etc.), though it depends on the specific issue and the level of training and experience the midwife has acquired. Understand, midwives are not doctors – they are not trained or equipped to perform surgery.

There are different types of midwives: A Certified Nurse-Midwife (CNM) is a licensed registered nurse who has completed an accredited graduate program in midwifery and has also been certified by the American College of Nurse-Midwives. A Certified Midwife (CM) receives the same training, education, and certification in midwifery as a CNM but does not have a nursing background. A Certified Professional Midwife (CPM) is educated and completes her apprenticeship through The North American Registry of Midwives. In addition, there are Traditional (or Lay) Midwives who receive informal training and are not licensed or certified through an accredited organization. If considering a midwife, it is important to check the laws in your specific state particularly if you want to deliver in a hospital or birthing center. Whoever is chosen we must exercise due diligence and research their education, training, experience, and background.

Why choose a midwife instead of a traditional physician or obstetrician-gynecologist (OB-GYN)? A midwife has more flexibility than a doctor who is restricted by hospital policies and regulations. Midwives give you options galore! There are a handful of doctors who put individual patient care first; but the reality is that most doctors have far too many patients (more money), making it impossible to spend the quality time necessary to offer patient-specific alternatives. A midwife, on the other hand, is not just a healthcare practitioner, she is also an educator and a counselor.

When it is time to be admitted to the hospital, it is not uncommon for expectant mothers who have traditional doctors, to spend the majority of their time with nurses instead of their doctor? She may only see nurses coming in and out of her room to examine her until she is about seven or eight centimeters dilated – then the doctor appears. Women often do not see their OB-GYN much during the laboring process, but she is there for the delivery and then gone again soon after – her primary role is to be present for the delivery only. A Sister once shared with me that when she was in labor with her first baby, fully dilated and ready to push – the nurses told her NOT to push because her doctor had not arrived. They kept her laboring until her doctor arrived. He did nothing except receive the baby in his hands as she delivered. Any one of those nurses could have delivered her baby, but the doctor does not get paid unless he/she is the one to actually deliver the baby. I'm certain that this was not an isolated incident.

Due to a high number of patients, as well as inordinate greed, many doctors like to plan exactly when their patients will deliver. This is done by either scheduling a cesarean section (C-section) or an induction. C-sections and inductions are on the rise. Scheduling the delivery of their patients means it will not conflict with the personal lives of the doctors. Those doctors who are motivated by greed know that any time surgery or cutting is involved; so is more money. Inducing labor greatly increases the mother's chance of needing a C-section. During induction, the woman is given a chemical (usually Pitocin), which causes her womb to begin to contract, initiating labor. Often, during inductions, the sac of water (amniotic fluid), which protects the baby, is broken. The nurse or doctor will use a tool to break the water instead of allowing the water to break naturally. As soon as the baby's water is broken, it is vulnerable and must be born within the next several hours (24-hour maximum). However; if the mother does not dilate (widening of the cervix) fast enough, a C-section must be performed to retrieve the baby alive.

Birth should be natural, not artificial. The Holy Qur'an reads, *"Did We not create you from ordinary water? Then We placed it in a secure resting-place, Till an appointed term, So We determined – how well are We at determining!"* Midwives have been delivering babies long before a hospital was a concept in the mind of the new man. Midwives pride themselves in specializing in the care of the mother before, during and after labor/delivery. The laboring mother has her midwife with her the entire time, providing her with both physical, emotional and spiritual support. She patiently assists and guides the mother as she gives birth; providing her with low-tech comfort measures to relieve pain and help labor to progress. Midwives take a limited number of patients with due dates spaced in order to ensure each woman receives individualized care throughout her pregnancy.

According to research, women who have a midwife working with them throughout their pregnancies have fewer recovery complications after delivery. Midwives are also reported to have lower chances of preterm birth, fewer epidurals, episiotomies or assisted births. Midwives know how to induce labor naturally when necessary. Her goal is for the entire birth process to be natural; from the mother's delivery position to anything she ingests.

Good midwives are committed to close personal rapport, ongoing client and family education, and promotion of individual responsibility for health. Through research, nurse-midwifery care has been shown to have good mother and baby outcomes, low incidence of cesarean sections (the cutting of the abdomen to retrieve the baby) and high levels of satisfaction by the patients and their families.

Some midwives administer home deliveries only; others deliver in birthing centers and depending on the state, some midwives deliver in hospitals. A midwife can also be a cost benefit for families. The actual cost is far cheaper than a typical delivery; they offer monthly payment plans throughout the duration of the pregnancy, accept health insurance and many also accept Medicaid. This will vary from state to state, city to city, and midwife to midwife. Sometimes the type of insurance one has, or lack thereof will limit options. It is truly a shame that something as natural as childbirth costs so much! Quality healthcare is a human right and should be afforded to everyone regardless of income level. If for whatever reason a midwife is not an option where you are; make sure the doctor selected is well vetted and meets high standards and expectations.

Whoever is chosen as our healthcare practitioner; it should also definitely be a woman. No man, except our husband, should be permitted to see us in such an intimate manner. In addition, another woman is more likely to know exactly what the expectant mother is experiencing and what she needs to get her through. Allah (God) created the female naturally compassionate, patient and long-suffering; which gives her the prerequisite attributes to care for a woman in travail.

The Holy Qur'an reads *"And Allah brought you forth from the wombs of your mothers – you knew nothing – and He gave you hearing and sight and hearts that you might give thanks"* (16:78).

BLACK DOULAS:

While *doulas* may simply be an added luxury for some who desire personalized care and tutelage in natural birth management; Black doulas, in particular, have become a necessity for Black mothers whose maternal mortality rate has reached an all-time high – rivaling that of 'third-world' countries. Black mothers are nearly four times more likely to die from complications surrounding childbirth than their white counterparts. Black babies in America are also dying unnecessarily during pregnancy and delivery, or shortly thereafter. According to Linda Villarosa, New York Times, *"Black infants in America are now more than twice as likely to die as white infants…a racial disparity that is actually wider than in 1850, 15 years before the end of slavery, when most Black women were considered chattel…Education and income offer little protection. In fact, a Black woman with an advanced degree is more likely to lose her baby than a white woman with less than an eighth-grade education."* Yet, there is no national outcry – no public health emergency declaration – no nationwide investigation!

Black people have always had good reason not to trust the medical industry, which historically has been rampant with discriminatory and racist practices. It is clear that Black mothers are not receiving the same quality of care during and after pregnancy as others. However, Black women are not rolling over – Black women have responded by exploding onto the scene and becoming their own advocates and caregivers. Black women are receiving training and certifications as doulas and are actually saving lives by providing options and alternatives for their Sisters! They are filling the void that often manifests during the Black childbirth experience – a void that is no different from the Black experience in America's educational system, the judicial system, and business industry; where there is an overwhelming lack of empathy, equity and sense of community.

According to DONA International, the world's first, largest and leading doula certifying organization, a Doula is *"a trained professional who provides continuous physical, emotional and informational support to a mother before, during and shortly after childbirth to help her achieve the healthiest, most satisfying experience possible."* The word 'doula' is of Greek origin which means, *"a woman who serves."* And serving Black mothers is exactly what is happening in several pockets throughout the country. There is a wide range of specialized Doula services, but the three most common are; childbirth doulas, postpartum doulas, and full spectrum doulas.

The impact doulas are making is remarkable; but not surprising – traditionally, communal care was always the Black way. The relationship between an expectant mother and her doula is personal and intimate. Though she is a professional, Black doulas, in particular, believe it their foremost responsibility to invest in the future of their community by providing a safe, healthy and natural birthing experience for both mother and baby. According to Jasmine Roussell, a postpartum doula in Austin, Texas – doulas provide both physical and emotional support for the mother by assisting her throughout her entire pregnancy, birth, and postpartum journey. The doula maintains a constant presence. However, she also stressed that postpartum doulas actually serve the entire family – the first six-weeks (or more) after birth is completely planned out – everything from breastfeeding, arrangements for housekeeping, cooking, medical appointments, and errands are all organized in advance.

Though doulas do not provide any direct medical or clinical care, they are well trained in natural techniques and remedies that can provide additional assistance and support beyond what a midwife or doctor may offer. Just over a century ago, Black women comprised the vast majority of midwives in America and these midwives always had an assistant to provide direct care and comfort for the mother. The term doula was coined in 1969; and doula, as a profession began shortly thereafter – however, Black women have been serving their Sisters during pregnancy, childbirth and postpartum since time immemorial. Somehow, the use of midwives and doulas was co-opted and is now seen as belonging exclusively to a class of posh, elite, white women. Yet, as more and more Black women receive the proper education concerning the benefits of having a doula-assisted pregnancy and birth, we will continue to see improved Black childbirth outcomes.

According to a published study in the Journal of Perinatal Education, *"Expectant mothers matched with a doula had better birth outcomes. Doula-assisted mothers were four times less likely to have a low birth weight (LBW) baby, two times less likely to experience a birth complication involving themselves or their baby, and significantly more likely to initiate breastfeeding."* This study was done with mothers of color and showed that Black and Brown women specifically benefited from the assistance of a doula. Premature births and cesarean rates are also much lower with a doula's assistance. The wonderful birth outcomes are so significant that there are now many organizations that provide low-cost and even free doula services for expectant mothers. At the same time, there is a strong push for insurance companies to begin to cover the cost of doula services.

Black women no longer have to suffer in silence, bear their burden alone and have their complaints dismissed. There are a host of organizations and services devoted to connecting Black mothers with Black doulas; they also guide potential doulas who desire to receive proper training and certification. Some of these organizations include but are not limited to – *National Black Doula Association, Black Mamas Matter Alliance, Mamas on Bedrest & Beyond, Black Women Birthing Justice, RouCares, Radical Doula and Blackdoulas.org.* Not to mention a host of Facebook pages and groups devoted to Black doulas and mothers.

The Honorable Minister Louis Farrakhan said, *"The world is in trouble because the world has no respect for woman. And if the world has no respect for woman, the world has no respect for God. When you respect God, you must respect woman, because the womb of the woman is a place of sacredness. A woman should be held in awe, because of the majesty of her womb…"*

10-POINT BIRTH PLAN:

Every expectant mother should prepare a Birth Plan several months prior to her due date. A Birth Plan is a written document given to her midwife or doctor that briefly expresses her unique preferences for her labor and delivery experience. The assumption for any Birth Plan is that the mother expects all of her wishes fulfilled unless there are unforeseen complications or emergencies that prevent her medical team from adhering to her desires. If the mother does not have a Birth Plan, her midwife or doctor will proceed at their own volition.

It is advisable that every point included on the Birth Plan be thoroughly discussed with the medical team in order to confirm whether or not specific requests can be accommodated. It is particularly important to do this if the delivery will take place in a hospital – hospital policies and procedures may override the Birth Plan (i.e. photographs, video recordings). Anyone the mother desires to witness her labor and delivery should also be aware of what is stated on the Birth Plan. Whether discussed in advance or not, the Birth Plan should be physically present (digital or hardcopy) and easily accessible for the midwife or doctor when admitted.

Labor and delivery are very intimate and personal. There are not many hard and fast rules when it comes to trying to create the optimum experience and environment, only suggestions. Some Birth Plans deal strictly with the medical and health concerns for mother and baby; whereas others include everything from music being played during delivery to the lighting of the room. The latter does not need to be included in the Birth Plan – it is always good to verify, but patients are generally free to play music, dim the lights (as long as the attendants can see), and eat or drink. Over the decades, the advantages of a calm and soothing birthing environment and experience has been accepted by both medical professionals and patients. So, there should not be any concern over allowing a mother to create this type of atmosphere in a hospital or birthing center.

The following is a sample 10-Point Birth Plan. Certainly, Birth Plans can be longer or shorter and list different preferences; but this plan includes a few critical points that we believe will be beneficial to both mother and baby. An explanation for each point is listed for the purposes of this book only, but it is not necessary to give the explanation in one's personal plan if the points were discussed in advance with the attending midwife or doctor…

1.   **Drug-free natural vaginal delivery**: *Specify your delivery plan. Health permitting, a natural vaginal delivery is recommended, with no artificial means of induction or prematurely breaking the water. Also indicate the preferred delivery position (birthing stool, birthing chair, or water). Avoid an epidural. We do not want to risk any amount of medication interacting with our baby. Sometimes the effect of drugs and medication is not immediately apparent. Some side effects take months or even years to manifest. The mother or baby can have internal adverse reactions to medication without midwives or doctors immediately noticing. Talk with your midwife or doula; she is trained with natural techniques that will ease some of the pain and make it more tolerable. Nothing she can do will remove all of the pain, but she can definitely help. Something as small as changing the mother's position, a massage, a shower, or a tub of warm water does wonders. Delivering in a sitting or squatting position instead of laying on your back allows gravity to assist in delivery.*

2.   **List the family/friends who have permission to be in attendance during labor and delivery:** *Labor and delivery are very private, it is not a party. The mother is at her most vulnerable, so the room should not be packed full of spectators. It is exclusively the mother's decision as to who she wants in the delivery room. Outside of her husband, midwife or doctor; she may not want anyone else to witness. Or, she may want her mother or sisters to be present. Certainly, no other men or very young children should be in the room. When the baby arrives, a peaceful environment should await; not the chaos of several people cheering or clapping. Her desires should be communicated in advance so someone other than the mother can ensure her privacy is respected.*

3.   **Limit medical intervention – no routine episiotomies or use of suctions or forceps:** *Plan for the ideal delivery. The ideal delivery is*

a vaginal birth with no complications and no medical interventions. Midwives and doctors know what must be done in an emergency, so the mother's job is to communicate what she does and does not want to be done if all is well. We need to return to natural childbirth. Most women do not need episiotomies. And to increase the chances of not needing one, request perineal support (a warm compress) during delivery. There are also prenatal exercises and massages that can be done during pregnancy to increase elasticity. Working with your midwife, doula or physician to discuss gentle pushing techniques and delivery positions will eliminate the need for episiotomies, suctions and forceps. A natural tear heals better than an artificial cut with scissors. If the mother tears (unless the tear is severe), she need not bother with stitches. That area of the body will heal just like the skin on any other part of our body that sustains a cut or tear. Again, ask the midwife about exercises and oils that can be used throughout pregnancy and also the proper pushing and muscle control techniques, which can lead to zero tearing during delivery.

4.   **Allow my husband (baby's father) to receive the baby during delivery:** *What??? Yes, that is actually a very important role for the father. He should be guided to receive his baby from the birth canal, not the midwife or doctor. This is our way and it is becoming more and more acceptable. There should be no objections as long as notification is given in advance. [More specifics later in this section.]*

5.   **Do not clamp or cut the umbilical cord until it stops pulsating:** *There are documented benefits for waiting to cut the umbilical cord. The placenta continuously passes blood and nutrients to the baby. This process does not immediately stop at birth. For up to five minutes, the placenta could still be passing blood and nutrients to the baby, which is*

indicated by the fact that it is still pulsating. Insufficient blood transfer can lead to anemia and other health challenges.

6. **Allow time and privacy for a prayer after the baby (and placenta) is born:** *After the placenta has been expelled, there should be a few minutes of privacy for the parents to say a prayer to demonstrate their immense gratitude to Allah (God) for their blessing and asking for His unequalled Guidance and Protection over the new life. The Holy Qur'an 7:189 reads, "He it is Who created you from a single soul, and of the same did He make his mate, that he might find comfort in her. So, when he covers her she bears a light burden, then moves about with it. Then when it grows heavy, they both call upon Allah, their Lord: If Thou givest us a good one, we shall certainly be of the grateful."*

7. **I plan to breastfeed exclusively and bond with my baby:** *Give the baby God's formula, breastmilk. There is no substitute that comes close. Be clear that the baby should not be given any formulas, supplements, glucose water, artificial nipples or pacifiers. Bring a breast pump, should the baby need to be separated due to an emergency, so he/she can still be fed mother's milk. [More specifics in the next section.]*

8. **My baby should not be removed from my room; all exams should be performed in my presence:** *If delivering in a hospital, put a big sign on the door and bassinet – "DO NOT REMOVE BABY FROM ROOM." Nurses change shifts regularly, so it needs to be clear to all who will have access to the baby that he/she is not to be removed. Short of being premature or being born with a serious complication, there is NO need to remove the baby from mother's sight. If the baby is healthy, everything that is done in the nursery can be done right there in the room, do not let anyone convince otherwise. The mother can even give the baby its first bath if she chooses. The purpose of keeping the baby with the mother is not only for protection,*

but also to transfer peace and security to the baby. Immediately, the baby knows his/her mother and only wants her. If the couple has a boy and chooses to circumcise at the hospital; either the mother or father should go with the baby for his circumcision. [More on circumcisions later in this section.]

9.   **No immunizations/vaccinations, Vitamin K shot, or eye treatment should be given to my baby:** *Just say NO! See more details in an upcoming section, "Vaccine Deception" for reasons to abstain from these deadly artificial vaccines. The Vitamin K shot is supposed to help blood clotting, but the form of Vitamin K that babies are receiving is synthetic. There is an assumption made that all babies are born deficient in Vitamin K without even checking. Any synthetic drug is dangerous particularly for a newborn. Mothers who eat a diet rich in Vitamin K can naturally transfer it to their babies in the womb and while nursing. As for eye drops and eye ointments – this is for mothers with an STD. If the mother does not have an STD, her baby should not arbitrarily be given treatment.*

10.   **Leave the hospital/birthing center as soon as possible:** *Get out of there! Recovery is faster at home. Birthing centers and midwives seem to understand this more than traditional doctors. Staying in the hospital for two or three days is just not necessary; not to mention, it's costly. Most birthing centers allow mother and baby to return home 6-8 hours after delivery.*

We pray that readers will find this 10-Point Birth Plan useful as a guide in creating their own or helping a loved one. Starting several months in advance allows time to adjust the plan. Just keep it brief and easy to follow. The birth of a baby is sacred, and the experience should reflect its majesty. Planning is a divine attribute of God that we should exercise during pregnancy. Let's not give away our power and right to have the labor and delivery experience that we absolutely deserve.

FATHER'S ROLE IN THE DELIVERY ROOM:

The Honorable Minister Louis Farrakhan stated, *"Prophet Muhammad said, 'Heaven lies at the foot of mother.' Prophet Muhammad was asked, 'After Allah (God) and His Messenger whom should we honor most?' The Prophet answered, 'Your mother.' The companion asked who next? The Prophet answered, 'Your mother.' The companion asked again, and, the Prophet answered, 'Your mother.' The companion asked a fourth time, and, the Prophet answered, 'Your father.' These two sayings of Prophet Muhammad (Peace Be Upon Him), teach us the importance of the female in building a heavenly society, and the level of honor that should be accorded to our mothers right after honor to Allah (God) and to His Messenger."*

These statements were made by Prophet Muhammad (PBUH) of Arabia, over 1,400 years ago. He bore witness then and it stands true today, that the honor we give to our mothers should be three times the honor we give to our fathers. Why? In order for a woman to give birth, she must go through death's door. The Most Honorable Elijah Muhammad said that the pain of childbirth is equal to the pain of death. Though it is a natural pain; nonetheless, it is horrendous to endure. There is no debate about whom has the most important role during pregnancy, labor, and delivery – mother has no equal in this divine stage. However, a father's role is very significant and has a direct bearing on the mother and her baby during every phase of pregnancy and childbirth.

Fathers were not allowed in any hospital delivery rooms until the 1970s and as late as the 1980s in certain hospitals until advocacy and undeniable research proved the benefits. The role of the father during labor and delivery is not only to support and comfort his wife; his role is more than helping her to push and stay focused; his role even extends beyond being her protector and advocate at the birthing center or hospital. During natural childbirth, the role of the father is also to deliver ("catch") his baby. He should be the first and only person to touch the baby before the mother. As the baby transitions from one world to the next, this is a very critical time for the baby, so father must be ready. He should be taught and prepared well in advance to receive his baby from the birth canal and gently place him or her on his wife's chest. The role of the midwife (or doctor) at the moment of delivery is to be right at the father's side guiding him with precision and specific instructions.

The Honorable Minister Louis Farrakhan said that this is our way; the way of the righteous, the Original man and woman – and it is becoming more acceptable and encouraged. This should be included in the mother's birth plan and as long as it is discussed several weeks prior to delivery, there should be no objections. It is a father's duty and his right to be the first to receive and greet the life he produced.

Science supports the value of this special practice. Mothers are not the only ones who are physiologically, hormonally and neurologically connected to their children. Fathers who immediately connect by physically touching their babies at the earliest possible moment experience notable hormonal changes. There is an elevation of oxytocin levels similar to (but not as intense as) a new mother who just delivered or is breastfeeding her baby. MRI imaging also shows heightened brain activity in these same fathers when they hear the cry of their own babies. Fathers strengthen both their biological and emotional connection to their children by bonding with them immediately.

This immediate contact is also critical for the newborn. We may have witnessed babies instantly recognize the scent, touch, and voice of their mothers at birth. But according to research, nearing the end of pregnancy (32 weeks in utero), babies are also able to recognize the voice of their fathers. Remember that everything is energy; so, not only his voice but especially the father-to-baby touch carries with it an exchange of energy which is transmitted at a higher vibratory rate that cannot be achieved by a stranger (midwife or doctor) and the baby. Passing a newborn from doctor to doctor, nurse to nurse, and person to person all before reinforcing the natural parental bond abruptly disrupts the baby's physical and metaphysical transition. Unknowingly we are injecting foreign and potentially harmful energy exchanges; which could affect everything from the baby's ability to latch onto his mother to nurse – to newborn sleep apnea.

A father's role during delivery cannot be overstated; so, every potential father should prepare to be present and fully participate. If one is particularly squeamish and believes he may become faint, he should remember what his wife will endure; then prepare psychologically far in advance. Attend all prenatal visits and childbirth classes. Study and learn exactly what's happening with the female anatomy during childbirth to remove the mystique – we fear what we don't know. Ultimately safety is the most important element. In order for the father to be helpful and not harmful to his wife and newborn, he must be ready for this divine assignment – physically, mentally and spiritually. God-willing, the couple will be blessed with successful labor and delivery. Afterwards, the father should lead a prayer thanking Allah (God) for the new life and asking for His Guidance, Protection, and Mercy.

Men can never fully understand the pain of childbirth and the undertaking that the female body must sustain, but to be able to witness the process and to be willing to receive the product of their seed is honorable and a great privilege. For a father to remain by his wife's side, providing solace and protection on the birth-day and everyday will ensure that the love she has for her husband will be transferred to her children and passed on to future generations.

VACCINE DECEPTION:

The greatest of all knowledge that one could have is the knowledge of self, the knowledge of God and the knowledge of the devil. We can find a myriad of self-help books, seminars, and experts that attempt to bring enlightenment to others through self-awareness, introspection, and whatnot. In that same vein, there are countless religious and spiritual books, seminars, ministers and motivational speakers who seek to bring us closer to God. No doubt that many have good intentions, though most lack the ability to truly reform since they do not see the intersection between self and God. Most also fail because they teach the coming of God, rather than the **presence** of God. However, there is a noticeable absence from the "wise" to attempt to teach the knowledge of the devil – because to teach about him is to admit that the devil is not a spook, spirit or a ghost. The devil is a man. To expose the devil and the maker of devils, Satan, is to expose individuals; and few have the courage to do so. Therefore; we remain vulnerable to constant deception by our open enemy, who does not let up an inch!

The promotional verbiage encouraging vaccinations from doctors, pharmacies, school administrators, politicians, and even television personalities is relentless. They all echo the U.S. Department of Health and Human Services (HHS), the Centers for Disease Control and Prevention (CDC), as well as the Food and Drug Administration (FDA); these agencies are all tools of Satan. The CDC states, *"Vaccination is one of the best ways parents can protect infants, children and teens from 16 potentially harmful diseases. Vaccine-preventable diseases can be very serious, may require*

hospitalization, or even be deadly – especially in infants and young children."
Sounds scary, right?

Let's be clear: The idea of preventing men, women, and children from getting a disease by building up their immunity to be able to fight against a potentially harmful or deadly disease is honestly noble and wonderful! It's not the concept of vaccinating that is a problem; it's the wicked manufacturers and distributors that we do not trust. What parent would not want to prevent their child from getting a disease? If there is 100% proof of safety and effectiveness, sign me up. But the fact is that vaccinations produced in and distributed by the United States are NOT safe! The risks and side effects far outweigh the chance of ever getting one of those 16 very **curable** diseases.

On their website, The Department of Health and Human Services admits, *"Any vaccine can cause side effects."* They then proceed to list the potential side effects of all 25 approved CDC vaccines; listed in categories: mild, moderate and severe. Some possible side effects include (but are not limited to): fever, headache, muscle aches, rash, fainting, abdominal pain, respiratory infections, seizures, internal bleeding, permanent brain damage, deafness, coma, organ failure, and on and on. ALL vaccines have the potential risk of severe injury and DEATH. It is all right there on the HHS website in plain sight for everyone to read for themselves.

It goes against our natural protective instincts as parents and all common sense to willingly expose our children to all of these colossal risks, knowing that the chance of them getting any of these rare diseases is miniscule. And should they get one of these diseases, the treatment is readily available. We appeal to parents: We must stand our ground and refuse to give our children vaccinations and immunizations. The contents in that syringe could be DEADLY.

It is wholly absurd to require, encourage or even suggest that a mother or father subject their newborn baby to an immediate injection of a foreign substance (Hepatitis B vaccine) into their pure bloodstream. No one could possibly have any idea what the likely immediate reaction could be – not to mention long term. The recommended vaccination schedule for a baby from birth to 24-months is excessive and dangerous – *overdose* by definition. Do not do it! Do not be intimidated by doctors who are knowingly or unknowingly drug pushers for the greedy pharmaceutical companies, who only exist to create more and more illnesses to further our demise. These pharmaceutical companies are so rich and powerful that they have bought off members of Congress and the media – so they all spew the same lies about the need for vaccines for our collective public health and safety.

In layman's terms, to immunize through vaccination is to essentially give the body the disease in a weakened state via a live or "inactivated" microbe, virus or bacteria. Then the recipient is supposed to just wait and hope that the body responds by fighting off the disease; thereby building immunity towards it. We have already mentioned many of the adverse immediate side effects. But there are tremendous long-term side effects as well; particularly for Black boys. For years, advocates have been sounding the alarm that vaccines cause autism. The alarm reached a crescendo when a whistle-blower at the CDC revealed that Black boys had a 240 percent higher chance of getting autism from the MMR vaccine than their white counterparts. This information came to the attention of the Honorable Minister Louis Farrakhan and the Nation of Islam from Robert F. Kennedy, Jr., son of the late Robert F. Kennedy. [Please read more about this at http://hurt2healingmag.com/exclusive-the-hidden-enemy-and-the-plot-to-kill-all-black-boys/.]

CHILDREN OF THE MOST HIGH

The United States has never been above sacrificing Black bodies for experimentation and money: Dr. James Marion Sims experimented on Black female slaves (1845-1849); Tuskegee Study of Untreated Syphilis in the Negro Male (1932-1972); Sterilization of Black women in Mississippi (1933-1963); Ebb Cade plutonium experiment (1945); Avon Park mosquitoes experiment (1950s); Holmesburg prison experiments (1951-1974); irradiation of Black cancer patients (1960-1971); and fenfluramine experiment (1990s) – just to name a few. Vaccinations continue this tradition – not only in the U.S. but throughout Africa and "third-world" countries.

Efforts to force vaccinations on all children regardless of a parent's desire to abstain are reaching tyrannical intensity. As of 2018, there are three states that do not allow any non-medical (religious or personal) exemptions from school required immunizations – California, Mississippi and West Virginia. All other states (as of now) permit parents to submit an affidavit to exempt their children from receiving immunizations due to religious and/or personal beliefs. However; in all states, many pediatricians and health clinics are now refusing to accept children as patients, who are not being vaccinated. New mothers have reported how aggressive the nurses are in pushing them to immediately vaccinate their newborns; many babies are vaccinated without the mother's consent or knowledge. If an expectant mother cannot deliver at a Birthing Center or at home and must rely on a hospital delivery, it is strongly recommended that a loved-one be present with her and her new baby at ALL TIMES, to watch and protect.

Allah (God) never leaves us in want. He provided every mother with a natural immunization for her new baby, when He provided her with a special chemical produced from her breasts called *colostrum*. Colostrum is so rich in antibodies that it protects the newborn against disease! It is the first substance produced by the mammary glands of almost every mammal. The baby nurses

160

the colostrum from his or her mother for the first two to three days, building the immune system before the actual milk comes in. This is the real boost our babies need at birth, not poison manufactured in a lab.

It was Hippocrates, the so-called founder of medicine that said, *"Let food be thy medicine and let medicine be thy food."* The Honorable Minister Louis Farrakhan said, *"Every illness can be cured with the proper intake of **properly** raised food."* So, for those of us who have already been immunized, let the detox begin! And for those who are still skeptical, study everything you can on both sides of the issue. We believe you will discover enough information to be wary of vaccinations. Allah (God) is forcing us to separate from our enemy's institutions – his schools, hospitals, and government – or we will continue to suffer the consequences. May He give us all the strength to resist Satan and unite like minds for the sake of our people, our Nation, and our future.

WHY WE CIRCUMCISE:

The definition for a medical circumcision is – *"Surgery that removes the foreskin (the loose tissue) covering the glans of the penis."* According to the Scriptures, the history of circumcisions predates Muhammad, Jesus, and Moses. 'To circumcise' was a directive from God to Abraham – a physical sacrifice that was to be made, in order to secure a covenant with God for Abraham and all generations after him.

Genesis 17: 9-10 reads, *"And God said unto Abraham, Thou shalt keep my covenant therefore, thou, and thy seed after thee in their generations. This is my covenant, which ye shall keep, between me and you and thy seed after thee; Every man child among you shall be circumcised. And ye shall circumcise the flesh of your foreskin; and it shall be a token of the covenant betwixt me and you. And he that is eight days old shall be circumcised among*

161

you, every man child in your generations, he that is born in the house, or bought with money of any stranger, which is not of thy seed. He that is born in thy house, and he that is bought with thy money, must needs be circumcised: and my covenant shall be in your flesh for an everlasting covenant. And the uncircumcised man child whose flesh of his foreskin is not circumcised, that soul shall be cut off from his people; he hath broken my covenant" (KJV).

The three predominate monotheistic religions – Judaism, Christianity, and Islam – all claim Abraham as the Father of their faith traditions. So, it is no coincidence that the practice of circumcising has continued by those who consider themselves to be true followers. However, today it is practiced considerably less by those who consider themselves Christians; but still very prevalent among Jews; and most Muslims are overwhelming strict in obedience to this rite for all males. The latter is notable since there is no mention of circumcision in the Holy Qur'an. However, the Qur'an does clearly command Prophet Muhammad (PBUH) to *"Follow the faith of Abraham, the upright one."* Hence, it is reported that Prophet Muhammad (PBUH) said that circumcision was a "law for men." According to many sections from the Hadith (a collection of the reported words and actions of The Prophet), Prophet Muhammad (PBUH) practiced and suggested male circumcisions. However, Islamic scholars continue to debate as to whether it is obligatory for Muslims to continue the practice today.

The Pentateuch (first five books of the Old Testament) or Torah, is one of the Jewish Holy Books. Here is where we find the Book of Genesis and those clear directives from God to Abraham; so, in Judaism, there is not much debate at all about the observance of this rite. In the Jewish tradition, circumcisions are far more ritualistic and rigid; involving many rules and customs that are simply not performed in either Christianity or Islam.

It is true that in accordance with Mosaic Law, Jesus was in-fact circumcised (Luke 2:21). However, present-day Christians have veered from the practice principally because of the words of Paul in the New Testament. He states, *"Circumcision has value if you observe the law, but if you break the law, you have become as though you had not been circumcised. So then, if those who are not circumcised keep the law's requirements, will they not be regarded as though they were circumcised? The one who is not circumcised physically and yet obeys the law will condemn you who, even though you have the written code and circumcision, are a lawbreaker"* (Romans 2: 25-27, NIV). In other words, it's going to take a lot more than being circumcised to claim righteousness – our deeds far outweigh our physical appearance.

Circumcision is not compulsory in Islam, but it is strongly recommended. The primary reason for circumcision in Islam is for "tahara," – purification or cleanliness. Yes, one must be physically clean in order to make salāt (prayers), pilgrimage or even to handle the Holy Qur'an. But going much further than that, cleanliness and exceptional hygiene support good health. Removing the foreskin allows for the male instrument to be easily cleaned, keeping it free of bacteria buildup. This greatly reduces the risk of a urinary tract infection whereby severe cases can lead to kidney trouble. Circumcised males also have a lower risk of contracting sexually transmitted infections, including HIV and herpes. The risk of penile cancer is considerably lower than for uncircumcised males. It is also less common for the female partner of a circumcised male to have cervical cancer. Other health benefits include prevention of penile problems like phimosis (inability to retract the foreskin); paraphimosis (inability to return the foreskin to its original location); balanitis (inflammation of the glans); and balanoposthitis (inflammation of the glans and foreskin).

There are considerations on the other side as well. Though local anesthesia is used, circumcision is a painful surgical procedure. It takes about 5 to 10 minutes to complete, and a week to heal. But circumcisions are no exception to the reality that all surgical procedures have risks: bleeding and infection could occur; irritation of the glans; the foreskin might be cut too short or long; there is risk of injury; failure to heal; the remaining foreskin may reattach to the end, and there is an increased risk of meatitis (inflammation at the opening). Parents who are considering circumcision must carefully weigh the potential benefits and risks in advance. If a decision is made to proceed; the credentials, experience and success rate of the physician performing the procedure should be thoroughly scrutinized.

While Jews circumcise by the eight day of birth; for Christians and Muslims, the age for circumcision does not seem to be clearly established. Many do choose to circumcise their newborns, just days after birth; not only for Biblical reasons but also because healing tends to be faster and an infant cannot disturb the affected region, which could lengthen recovery time. However, others believe, it is barbaric to strap down a newborn and cut them. Ultimately, it is a parental choice. If the choice is made to circumcise when the child is older, he should be much older – old enough to know better than to agitate that region of the body while healing. So circumcising toddlers is not recommended.

We conclude with words from The Honorable Minister Louis Farrakhan on this subject. His words bear witness to a universal truth: **For every physical law, there is a spiritual counterpart.** The Minister said, *"– And Paul comes back so beautifully, saying the Jew is not the Jew outwardly by the circumcision of the flesh, the Jew is the Jew inwardly by the circumcision of the heart. Now, what is needed to perform the circumcision of the heart? It takes a sharp instrument to cut away the foreskin of the male* *instrument. Why do you want the male instrument circumcised? Because, as that skin, folds over the head of the penis, it becomes a depository for bacteria. You know I have to stop, you know and give praises to God – [very tearful and pausing] because see when you hear it, you know it's the truth. The Word starts cutting away the flesh of the heart. Because the heart, the core of your thinking, is where all the issues of man and woman are hidden."* All praise is due to Allah (God)!

NOTE: This section intentionally dealt only with male circumcision. The Nation of Islam does not perform, nor do we agree with the practice of female circumcisions or "female genital cutting" (FGC). This practice takes place in many parts of the world. It has nothing to do with religion, spirituality or cleanliness – it is primarily cultural.

BABY SHOWER DILEMMA:

Most modern traditions, customs, and rituals did not manifest out of the blue – they originated from a specific need, intention or belief. However, after a period of time, many traditions, customs, and rituals gradually move away from their original intent and become no more than established routines, which have become accepted as normal. The true purpose often gets buried in the time-honored tradition. Baby showers are no different. A baby shower is typically a party thrown for a mother-to-be by her family and friends, who "shower" the expectant mother with gifts to be used primarily for her baby and occasionally for herself. Modern baby showers are held several weeks BEFORE the baby is born. Though, many women are now having baby showers AFTER the baby is born for various reasons. Herein lies the dilemma?

When one studies the evolution of what we now call "baby showers," over different historical periods and regions – Ancient Egypt, Ancient Greece,

Middle Ages, Renaissance, and Victorian Era – they all have one thing in common…the "baby showers" all took place after childbirth. It is only when we enter the modern era that we see a shift towards having baby showers before the birth of the baby. According to Alison J. Clarke's book, ***Maternity and Materiality: Becoming a Mother in Consumer Culture***, *"The modern baby shower started after WWII during the baby boom era and evolved with the consumer ideology of 1950s and 1960s. In other words, baby showers in the mid-twentieth century not only served an economic function by providing the mother-to-be and her home with material goods that lessened the financial burden of infant care, but purchased "things" also emerged as the principle whereby women make themselves into mothers."*

Today this concept has exploded. What we see with many baby showers is that they have become less about the needs of a new mother and her baby and more about a status symbol, which indirectly links motherhood with materialism and social inclusion. As with any party, "attendance" at the baby shower is of the utmost importance. The mother-to-be is burdened with who came; who didn't come; why didn't they come, how many attended, etc.? Then – what gifts did I receive? Were they of the highest quality? Can I exchange them? Typically, the mother-to-be will open each gift individually and recognize the giver of the gift publicly. This can be an added burden to those in attendance because there WILL be comparisons and silly conclusions drawn – the more extravagant the gift, the more "love" the giver has for the mother-to-be. What about the Sister who brings diapers, baby wipes or nursing pads – very practical gifts, but she is overshadowed by the Sister who brings the $200 designer outfit that the baby may wear once?

There are some strong arguments for having the baby shower before birth – the mother will ideally have everything she needs ahead of time, she can plan and get organized, and it will help her out financially. However,

166

there are also important reasons to consider having a baby shower after the baby is born. Historically, the primary focus was always on the successful birth of the baby and the health of the mother. Ceremonies, prayers, and devotions were held to celebrate and bless the new life. Sadly, the reality has always been that not all pregnancies result in a live healthy birth. In addition, having a baby shower after the baby is born (approximately six weeks) allows the shower to be far more celebratory and practical at the same time. There is a brand-new life to welcome and the mother knows exactly what she needs the most. She is also likely to be more engaged in the festivities.

The actual duration of pregnancy used to be (and should return to) a private personal time; it was never viewed as a social experience. Mothers would often keep the pregnancy a secret until approaching the due date. When a baby shower is held before the baby is born, this is typically the last time the expectant mother sees or hears from most friends and relatives until the next special event or occasion. But women need help and assistance when the baby is born; particularly if the pregnancy was difficult. Everything from buying diapers to helping with errands to cooking a few meals is far more appreciated post childbirth. Feeling alone can lead to depression and anxiety. Women who have baby showers or gatherings after the baby is born are also not as impressed with superficial gifts – they have had a reality check and tend to request very practical gifts or assistance.

At the prompting of one of my MGT Sisters, I began to inquire about the history of baby showers in the Nation of Islam. I was already aware that a few years ago, the Sisters in the Nation of Islam were asked not to host baby showers unless we could commit to giving every single Sister a shower, so no one is left out. But at present, the Sisters no longer include baby showers as a formal part of our class affairs. *"If they are done, they are done privately* with close friends and family." (MGT and GCC – A Look at the Feminine Side of the Culture of Islam).

However, many Sisters also recall that some time ago, the Sisters in the Nation of Islam were given instructions to have our baby showers AFTER the baby is born. We can all take it upon ourselves to search further into this if we so choose, but here is what we were able to confirm. After reading these statements, we can all decide for ourselves:

Sister Ati Hamid Cushmeer (daughter of Brother Jabril Muhammad, author of Closing the Gap) said, *"I am 99% sure Mother Evelyn said this (we should have baby showers after the baby is born) to us in M.G.T. (Muslim Girls' Training) when I lived in Phoenix. I texted her daughter, Marie, to verify it…"* Later, Sister Ati shared the following from Sister Marie: *"My mom does not remember when I asked her. She said that sounds right, but I can't give you a definite answer because she's forgetful now, but she said that makes sense. But of course, to quote what the Honorable Elijah Muhammad said on that subject, I can't do."* Sister Ati then shared with me, *"My mother-in-law said that back then they didn't really have baby showers. She said first there was no way of knowing the baby's gender and that if a Sister needed something, the M.G.T. would come together to help her get whatever she needed."*

Sister Callie from Detroit added, *"I always heard that we should wait until the baby was born to have a shower. When the Minister (Honorable Minister Louis Farrakhan) got the Nation back, we did not have showers with Sisters outside the M.G.T. because it was done after class when Sisters returned from having babies…We did not have a need for showers as we understand them today, we all helped each other because we only had each other."*

In summation, after asking additional Sisters, Sister Ati said, *"I believe it varies from Mosque to Mosque prior to 1975, but the consensus seems to be that after the baby was born if a Sister needed items, the M.G.T. would band together and get her what she needed. Some of it sounded informal and sometimes it was done more formally as in a 'shower' after M.G.T. class."*

Who would have thought that something as common-practice as a baby shower could be far more layered when we consider the history? The moral of this lesson is that we should all probably get back to focusing on the mother and what she truly needs to take better care of her baby. Parties, fancy gifts, games, and decorations are not the true expressions of our love for her or her baby.

In the Bible, Jesus says: *"Whoever welcomes one of these little children in my name welcomes me; and whoever welcomes me does not welcome me but the One who sent me"* (Mark 9:37, NIV). Whether the baby shower takes place before or after the baby is born; or if we forgo a baby shower altogether, we must return to genuine intentions and sincere motives. Helping to care for a child is honoring the Source of his or her existence – Allah (God). Our goal is to come together to serve our Sister in a period of need and provide her with our company, our assistance, and our resources. We should come to her aid, in a timely manner, so she is free to completely focus on caring for her precious new life and regaining her strength. That's LOVE!

[A special thanks to Sister Ebony Safiyyah for bringing this subject to my attention and being the inspiration behind this section. My deepest gratitude to Sis. Ati Hamid Cushmeer, Mother Evelyn Muhammad, Sister Marie Farrakhan, Sis. Bobbie Muhammad, and Sister Callie for their valuable insight.]

SECTION 4: BREASTFEEDING IS A MUST

"And We have enjoined on man concerning his parents – his mother bears him with faintings upon faintings and his weaning takes two years – say: Give thanks to Me and to thy parents. To Me is the eventual coming."
Holy Qur'an 31:14

THE DIVINE VALUE OF MOTHER'S MILK:

One would be hard pressed in 2019 to find anyone who would attempt to argue against the overwhelming health and nutritional benefits of breastfeeding for both mother and baby when compared to any of the most popular manufactured baby formulas. Most reputable organizations in the health industry including the Centers for Disease Control and Prevention, the American Academy of Pediatrics, La Leche League and the Surgeon General all advocate and promote human milk as the best source of nutrition for infants. In fact, the companies that produce baby formulas also bear witness to this truth! Similac ®, for instance, states on its website, *"We believe that breast milk is the best nutrition for babies."* Nestlé, the parent company of Gerber, states on Gerber's website – *"Nestlé believes breastfeeding offers the best possible start for babies, followed by inclusion of developmental, stage-appropriate feeding choices."*

The list of health benefits for both mother and baby from breastfeeding is extensive – it includes everything from better cognitive development to fewer allergies. Breastfeeding lowers the risk of SIDS (Sudden Infant Death Syndrome), cancers and other chronic illnesses. The list of advantages is vast; but even more amazing is that these are only the benefits we are aware of – there are many more yet to be realized! And still, we would argue that the many health benefits discovered by doctors, chemists, nutritionists, and researchers are yet just a portion of the overall picture.

The Honorable Minister Louis Farrakhan said, *"Anyone who takes a baby from the breast of its mother is committing a crime against humanity."* He also stated, *"When baby nurses from mother's breast, there is satisfaction for the child, not only in the stomach but in the mind. As the baby is physically fed, the act of nursing produces a chemical reaction in the brain of the child, resulting in contentment...When the mother has peace of mind, this is transferred to the child through the milk...Milk is capable of being the conduit of security or fear, due to the mental condition of the giver"* (Building the Will, Part IV).

One of the definitions of the word 'divine' is ***"of, relating to, or proceeding directly from God or a god"*** (Merriam-Webster). Mother's milk is indeed divine. It is not just the best source of nutrition for the baby, but it is the PERFECT food for the baby; created, formulated and designed by Him who is Perfect, Allah (God).

More than once in the Holy Qur'an Allah (God) guides the woman to suckle (nurse) her baby for two whole years. He is the Best Knower and with His infinite wisdom, He has created a different combination of ingredients in each mother's milk that is absolutely perfect for her child. Though similar, no mother has the same breastmilk as the next. And no mother produces the exact same milk pregnancy after pregnancy. That's right; breastmilk is different for each baby that comes from the same mother. It is formulated and designed by Allah (God) perfectly for that specific baby, providing him/her with the specific recipe he/she needs to develop – not only the body but the mind and spirit. This gives the baby the best start on the road to health and toward finding and fulfilling his/her divine purpose in life.

Breastmilk changes DAILY, along with the rapidly developing body and brain of the baby. This simply cannot be replicated in baby formulas; some of which cover a span of birth to twelve months using the same ingredients. Now, you do not have to be a mother to know that there is a huge difference between a newborn baby and a twelve-month old. This can result in nutritional deficiencies and vulnerability to sickness and disease. It can also lead to spiritual and mental deficits.

In *How to Eat to Live*, The Most Honorable Elijah Muhammad stated that the reason we have such a great percentage of delinquency among minors is that the child is not fed from his mother's breast. He also wrote, *"A baby nursed from its mother's breast will love its mother more than the baby fed from the bottle. He loves the bottle…"* (How to Eat to Live, Book Two). So sometimes, the baby does not even care if the mother is around as long as the bottle is there since he is bonded to the bottle and not human life. At the earliest age, we are in-fact bonding our children to things instead of life when we deprive them of mother's divine milk. Our natural love, reverence, and respect for humanity can be reinforced through mother's milk and the bond of nursing. This makes it difficult, as we get older, to harm another human being because from infancy we are bonded to life and not material possessions.

Unfortunately, as mothers, we have to accept responsibility for our own deviance. There was a time not too long ago when the most natural thing to see was a mother and child bonding through the gift of nursing. This is still the way of life in most countries and cultures but has become unusual in America particularly in the Black community. This is yet another sign of our deviation from the path of God. Giving birth to a god does not refer to what is done in the womb alone. It makes no sense to do everything correctly up to this point and then skip over breastfeeding. Breastfeeding reinforces what we put in the mind of our baby while he was in the womb. When we give our baby man-made formula, we stop passing on the *"chemistry of our thinking."*

Taking on the responsibility of motherhood means being willing to sacrifice and put our child's needs above our own wants. A good mother only desires what is best for her children and she does everything possible, without deviating from God, to give her children every advantage for a much better life than she may have had. To deny our children the advantages which come

176

with being breastfed is thoughtless. We must stop making excuses…'*I work; I don't have time; it's gross; no one else will be able to feed the baby; it will cramp my style'*…Please stop it! For mothers who work, there are breast pumps. This allows the caretaker to bottle-feed breastmilk to the baby while the mother is at work. But it is important for the mother to physically breastfeed her baby when they are together.

Food and drink keep us here, but they also take us away. Before putting anything in our baby's mouth, we should ask ourselves: *Is this going to lengthen my child's life or shorten it?* Because it is one or the other; no grey areas. We demonstrate our love for our children by giving them the best. Similac, Enfamil, Gerber Good Start, cow's milk, soymilk and whatever else is out there is not the best and some are poison to the baby. A cow cannot rear a human baby. And to put our baby on the enemy's formula instead of Allah's (God's) formula is to say that we trust in man more than God. Every time we put a bottle to our baby's mouth instead of our breast, we should know that we are not offering the BEST. Allah (God) has created each mother's breastmilk so potent and powerful that even a sick mother's milk is better than anything a man can create.

Our babies come through us, but they are not from us; they are from Allah (God). They are His creation. And Allah (God) has already predetermined and prepared the proper substance with which He wants His children to be reared. The Honorable Minister Louis Farrakhan teaches us that there is a difficulty factor attached to everything of value; the greater the value, the greater the difficulty. How valuable are our children? Yes, making the decision to breastfeed can be a challenge and requires the mother to make certain sacrifices, but every time we follow God, the reward is immeasurable!

BREASTFEED IN THE FIRST HOUR:

In his book, ***This Is The One***, Brother Jabril Muhammad quotes the following words from The Most Honorable Elijah Muhammad, *"If your religion's roots are not found in the universal order of things, it is not from Allah (God)…Almighty Allah has taught me that if we study the universe and the nature of the earth: its plants, animals and insect life; if we study this part of Allah's creation and the natural laws working among them, we will have the key to the understanding of the way of life intended by God for you and me."*

Let's look at mammals, the most advanced and intelligent of the animal species. Their unique characteristics distinguish them from all other species – mammals are warm-blooded, they breathe air, they have hair (or fur), they give birth to 'live' young, and all mothers feed their babies milk produced by mammary glands – hence the name '*mammal.*' This phenomenal ability to produce a substance from the body to immediately feed the newborn offers a superior advantage, eliminating the need to hunt or search for food. The milk produced by mammals is specially designed to meet the immediate needs of the baby right from birth. This has been the physiology of all mammals since the beginning of time, including humans.

Increasingly, there is worldwide awareness and advocacy to educate and encourage mothers to breastfeed their babies immediately after birth, within the first hour of life postpartum. This promotion is known as the *"early initiation of breastfeeding"* and is proven critical for saving the lives of newborn babies by ensuring that they receive all of the health, nutritional and protective advantages provided by mother's first milk, called ***colostrum***. According to the World Health Organization (WHO) and UNICEF, *"Three in five babies are not breastfed within the first hour of life, putting them at* *higher risk of death and disease and making them less likely to continue breastfeeding."* WHO and UNICEF maintain that delaying breastfeeding for even a few hours after birth could pose life-threatening consequences. This is because mother-to-baby, skin-to-skin contact along with the act of suckling at the breast instantly stimulates the mother's production of colostrum.

All mammals produce colostrum. Colostrum is the mammary glands first secretion after giving birth. Colostrum is so rich in nutrients, antibodies, white blood cells, cell-defending antioxidants, and immunoglobulins that it primes the baby's immune system. This is why colostrum is considered the baby's first vaccine; it prevents infections by not allowing germs and bacteria to enter the baby's bloodstream – so, no artificial injections are required. During the first 2-5 days after giving birth, the female body *only* produces colostrum, which is thicker and more yellow in color than milk. She then produces "transitional milk" for the next 10-14 days, which is a mixture of colostrum and breastmilk before her regular supply of thinner, whiter milk is established.

As soon as the baby is born, the baby should be placed on his mother's chest (ideally by the father). This skin-to-skin contact with mother regulates the baby's body temperature and heartrate. This contact also comforts the baby who instinctively recognizes and interacts with his mother's scent, voice, and vibrations, causing him to be soothed and to cry less. Mothers who have natural deliveries without an epidural will find that their babies are usually very alert after birth. If left undisturbed, the baby will detect and naturally gravitate toward the scent of colostrum secreting from his mother's breast and initiate breastfeeding. It is ideal that breastfeeding start soon after the baby is born since a large amount of colostrum can be expressed in the first hour after birth.

Colostrum has properties that **cannot** be found in baby formula or any other food source. Not only does it help the baby's body to grow; but it allows the body to immediately begin to repair itself after the stress and trauma of the delivery process. Colostrum helps to regulate all bodily functions as well as metabolism. Whereas, nonhuman milk or supplements can lead to constipation, colostrum aids digestion. It flushes out the digestive tract by rapidly expelling meconium (the tar-like substance that makes up the baby's first stool) from the baby's system. Colostrum also seals the holes in the gut, decreasing the likelihood of having food allergies and other issues that stem from a leaky gut like colic, asthma, ADD, eczema and more.

Colostrum is the original superfood! Not only for what it does for the body but for how it benefits the brain! There are special fats in colostrum and breastmilk which allow for brain development and growth. Humans are unique from other mammals in that we have the largest brain of all other mammals, yet at birth, our brains and bodies are very immature; which makes human babies the most dependent mammals at birth. Human colostrum unlike the colostrum of other mammals allows for the human brain to grow rapidly, while the body grows moderately. Conversely, large four-legged mammals need rapid growth of the body, but not so much the brain because they need to be able to walk, run and fight soon after birth in order to survive independently of their mothers.

The Honorable Minister Louis Farrakhan also shared the benefits of breastfeeding for the human mind and brain. He stated, *"When baby nurses from mother's breast, there is satisfaction for the child, not only in the stomach but in the mind. As the baby is physically fed, the act of nursing produces a chemical reaction in the brain of the child, resulting in contentment. This is manifested in the peaceful countenance you see on a nursing child as it drinks. There is also a chemical reaction in the mother's brain and satisfaction for her as she obtains both relief and pleasure as the milk that fills her breasts is drawn out. When the mother has peace of mind, this is transferred to the child through the milk."*

Breastfeeding saves lives! It is a fact that the longer breastfeeding is delayed, the more likely complications will ensue and the less likely the mother is to continue to nurse successfully. For mothers who have premature births, or cesarean births, or have to be separated from their babies, they may not be able to nurse within the first hour. However, their colostrum can be manually expressed and stored for later feedings.

The World Health Organization recommends that mothers exclusively breastfeed their babies for the first six months of life and then to continue to breastfeed with supplemental foods for two years or longer. This is right in line with the Holy Qur'an, which encourages mothers to suckle their babies for two whole years.

The Book of Luke reads, *"Blessed is the womb that bore you, and the breasts at which you nursed."* We pray that those who read this book will encourage all expectant mothers they know to initiate breastfeeding within the first hour after giving birth, in order to give their new babies, the best possible start at a healthy life.

HOW BREASTFEEDING BENEFITS MOTHER:

Whether we admit it or not, we all know instinctively that breastmilk is best for babies; but we may not realize how beneficial breastfeeding is for nursing mothers. First, it is a tremendous bonus economically. Similac ® and other formulas are very expensive compared to breastmilk which is absolutely free. All we have to do is eat properly and our baby will eat. According to the Most Honorable Elijah Muhammad, we do not have to eat any more than we were eating while pregnant to produce good milk for our baby. We may eat one meal a day but are not forced to do so. He said we should drink pure whole milk because our milk glands will put the milk in the right stage for the baby.

Another benefit for mothers is that breastfeeding saves time and is convenient. The baby does not have to wait for us to measure, mix and warm his bottle before he is fed. When the baby wakes up at 2:30 am during the best part of our sleep, all we have to do is bring him to our breast instead of preparing a bottle – so much easier.

However, the greatest benefits are the physical health benefits for the nursing mother. Some women are under the impression that breastfeeding ruins their physical form, but the opposite is true. According to the American College of Obstetricians and Gynecologists, as a woman is breastfeeding, her womb contracts and is restored to its original size faster. We lose our form by not being obedient to nature.

The act of breastfeeding also suppresses ovulation and menstruation in most women – for some, it is suppressed for the duration of breastfeeding. This helps to ensure that if we nurse for two years, as recommended, we will not become pregnant during that time. The Most Honorable Elijah Muhammad said that it takes a woman's body two years to completely heal after giving birth; so, breastfeeding for some women is a natural way to give the body time to recover before conceiving again.

Other health benefits are more serious when it comes to breastfeeding such as prevention of breast cancer. By breastfeeding, we significantly reduce our chances of ever getting breast cancer. If we were breastfed as babies and then we breastfeed our own babies, we virtually eliminate the possibility of ever getting breast cancer – outside of toxic environmental factors. There is a direct relationship between the increase of breast cancer in our society and the decrease of breastfeeding. According to Debra Denmark Elza, RN in a

1996 publication by The Learning Curve, nursing for a lifetime total of two years lowers the risk of breast cancer before menopause by 40%; six years of breastfeeding lowers the risk before menopause by 66%; and nursing for seven years or more lowers the risk of breast cancer throughout a woman's lifetime to almost zero. She also states that breastfeeding provides protection from cancer of the ovaries as well as osteoporosis (the thinning of the bones).

As stated previously, refusing to breastfeed is a violation of nature. The Honorable Minister Louis Farrakhan said that we attract diseases and other female disorders then eventually die young because we violate nature. We die physically young and also by the ovarian perspective because we can no longer have children. To say that it is natural to not be able to have children anymore at the age of 40 or 45 is absurd. Our violation of nature generation after generation is what has called into existence the 'biological clock' syndrome. Women can have healthy children naturally, without artificial intervention, as long as they have vital eggs.

Last, but certainly not least – breastfeeding produces a closeness, a sacred bond that connects mother and baby. Breastfeeding should be a beautiful experience for both mother and baby. Some mothers find that after their child is born, they actually miss being pregnant because, after nine long months, they are suddenly no longer one unit. But when we nurse, we are once again attached, and both are comforted by the physical bond. Both are also content because there is truly a spiritual and cognitive peace gained by both mother and baby through nursing.

In the Study Guide, *Self-Improvement: The Basis for Community Development – The Struggle for Balance*, The Honorable Minister Louis Farrakhan wrote, *"Allah (God) placed in male and female, a natural inclination towards one another (biologically, physiologically, spiritually). He also placed this inclination, in another way, between mother and child.*

The power or force that is the source of inclination is a need in the two for one another. The need causes us to incline toward that which will fulfill the need. The baby needs the milk in the breast of the mother and she needs to give the baby the milk, in order for each of them to be in a balanced state of health."

HOW BREASTMILK BENEFITS BABY:

Let's first examine the benefit of breastfeeding for the baby in a rational manner. When we go to the grocery store to purchase Similac ® or other formulas for our baby, there are millions of other women giving their baby the exact same formula. Sure, it is full of vitamins and minerals that will sustain our baby's physical life; but what kind of life? Allah (God) has created every human being different. Humans have inhabited the Earth for trillions of years and during all of that time, He has never made two beings exactly alike – not even twins. So, if we are all different, then the same formula will react to us all differently.

Allah (God) in His infinite Wisdom has created a different combination of ingredients in each mother's milk that is absolutely perfect for her baby. As stated previously, no mother has the same breastmilk as the next. And no mother produces the exact same milk pregnancy after pregnancy. Breastmilk is different for each baby that comes from the same mother's womb. It is formulated and designed by Allah (God) so perfectly for that child that the child is provided with the necessary chemical combination he needs to develop not only his body but his mind and his spirit; which will enable him to better achieve his purpose in life.

Every person was born with a divine aim and purpose in life or else they would have never been born. Our purpose in life goes far beyond going to school, getting a job, having a family and attaining a few material possessions. What Allah (God) has ordained specifically for you can only be perfectly expressed by you. When our baby is born, his brain is still growing and continues to grow significantly for the first three years of life. When we refuse to breastfeed, we detach our child's growing brain not only from his mother but also from his Creator. We allow the enemy to nourish his growing brain instead of Allah (God) who put the brain there and gave it its purpose. At the same time, the baby is growing in our womb, the formula is coming together in our body to produce perfect food (milk) for our baby. Breastmilk is food for the mind, not just the body.

Studies show that children who are breastfed have higher IQs than those who were not breastfed. Several other studies were done comparing breastfed babies from the same family as formula-fed babies have similar results. They found that decades later, the breastfed babies have grown to become more intelligent and led happier, healthier, more fulfilled lives than their non-breastfed siblings. This is no coincidence. Again, according to Debra Denmark Elza, RN, as adults, people who were breastfed have less asthma, less diabetes, fewer skin problems (including dermatitis and eczema), fewer allergies, lower risk of heart attack and stroke due to lower cholesterol levels, less ulcerative colitis (ulcers in the large intestine), less Crohn's disease, and greater protection from certain chronic liver diseases.

Now, one may say, *'I formula-fed my children and they grew up to be just fine.'* This may be true by your standards, but what about the standard Allah (God) set for our children when they were conceived. No matter how wonderful our children or we may have grown up to be without being breastfed, consider that we and our children could have been even greater if we were reared on mother's divine milk.

CHILDREN OF THE MOST HIGH

We stated previously that The Most Honorable Elijah Muhammad said that the reason we have such a great percentage of delinquency among minors is that our children are not fed from their mother's breasts. In many households, when the baby is hungry or simply wants to be comforted, instead of the baby finding nourishment and comfort from his mother, he finds it in the bottle. The baby does not care if the mother is around, just as long as he has his bottle or his pacifier, he is happy. The baby is no longer bonded to human life, but he is bonded to things. He has more respect and love for material things than he has for human life.

We allow bottles, pacifiers, toys, and television to rear our children, so we do not have to. Now, if we give our child any one of these things instead of the mother he will be satisfied. As he becomes a teenager, it is now easier for him to rob someone, kill another for his shoes or jacket, and be quick to get into a fight or disrespect authority because his forming brain did not experience the value of human life. The baby naturally loves whoever or whatever feeds him and takes care of him. Sometimes the baby loves his caretaker or babysitter more than his mother because she is the one who feeds and cares for him most of the time. Let us do our duty as mothers and rear our children instead of leaving them in the hands of inanimate objects.

Another benefit of breastfeeding for the baby is that breastmilk changes with the child as he grows and his needs change. Some formulas are not formulated by stages of growth and development and those that do have too great a range. For example, we may find a brand of formula that reads: *'For infants 0 to 4 months.'* Well, again there is a huge difference between a two-week-old baby and a four-month-old baby. This leads to nutritional deficiencies, whereas breastmilk changes daily, some even say from feeding to feeding, with our rapidly growing babies. This also means that breastmilk is always physically satisfying for the baby. There are well over 300 ingredients (that we know of) in breastmilk, most of which chemists cannot identify and are therefore unable to duplicate in formulas.

Breastmilk contains absolutely everything the baby needs including water. Giving a breastfed baby too much additional water can lead to overhydration. In fact, many breastfed babies need no water, juice or solid foods for six months. However, some babies do require supplemental foods. But DO NOT introduce any solid foods (including cereal) before three months of age. Waiting until six months of age is encouraged. The baby's stomach and digestive system are not mature enough to handle anything stronger than milk. The introduction of solid foods too early can lead to complications including allergies, stomach ulcers, digestive difficulties, and even cancer.

Our breastfed baby will grow healthier and stronger than he would if he were formula-fed. And because he is exclusively breastfed, being overweight or extremely underweight will be less likely. As stated previously, for the first few days of life, our baby receives the substance, colostrum, from mother's breast before her milk comes in; this aids in building the baby's immunity. This is why breastfed babies are less susceptible to illness during their first year of life.

Here are a few additional little-known facts about breastfeeding: According to the book, *What to Expect When You're Expecting*, breastmilk is more digestible than formula or any other milk, so babies who are solely breastfed spit up less often, are never constipated and rarely have diarrhea. Another nice bonus is that their bowl movements will not produce as strong an odor as it would if the baby were formula-fed; particularly before the introduction of solid foods. No baby is allergic to breastmilk and every baby loves the taste because it was formulated specifically for him. There is no risk of contamination or spoilage for breastmilk, so we eliminate the possibility of ever giving our baby bad milk. Also, since nursing at the breast requires more effort from the baby than sucking on the bottle, it encourages the greatest development of his jaws, teeth, and palate.

Do not give the baby soymilk because it is worse than cow's milk. Both soymilk and cow's milk contain a substance called Beta lactoglobulin, which doctors are now saying triggers Sudden Infant Death Syndrome (SIDS). For every 87 bottle-fed babies who die of SIDS, only 3 breastfed babies do. Additionally, babies who are breastfed for at least six months have three times fewer ear infections, five times fewer serious illnesses and seven times fewer allergies. Breastfeeding for at least 26 weeks makes our babies six times less likely to develop lymphoma (a type of cancer) in childhood. And breastfeeding for at least one year makes our baby only half as likely to develop diabetes.

Breastmilk and breastfeeding are both divine. The baby demonstrates and exercises his faith through the very act of nursing. The only God an infant or toddler knows is his mother. As far as the baby is concerned, Mommy is the Supreme Being in his small world. The baby knows – she has the power to feed me, to clean me, change me, comfort me, play with me and she responds to my cries each and every time. When we observe babies, we will concede that they exemplify faith from the day they are born. We are all born believers.

Any nursing mother knows that when you put a baby on the breast, the heavier milk does not let down until after the baby has pulled on the breast for a while. The baby only continues to draw on the breast because he has faith that the milk will eventually come. His faith is strengthened every time he receives the gift of milk while nursing or the blessing of having his cry answered by his mother. Though our baby does not yet know Allah (God); he bears witness that he is born in need of someone greater than himself. How highly must Allah (God) think of the woman to permit her to sit in His seat and be allowed to be recognized as the Supreme Being in the eyes of little babies that may come through her, but are in fact from Him? It is a blessing and a vivid reminder of our responsibility. Mothers have a duty to be good stewards and examples of righteousness for their children.

What more can be said about the endless benefits of breastfeeding? If our babies could speak and were aware of these benefits, what do you think their vote would be? Breastfeed your baby and in the future, he will thank you in more ways than you could imagine.

LOGISTICS & CONSIDERATIONS:

Our health and nutrition as a nursing mother are critical to producing good milk for our baby. Remember, we are not forced to eat one meal a day while nursing. Absolutely do not go without food for more than 24 hours at any time while you are still breastfeeding. Be sure to drink plenty of water and milk. It is also important to be mindful of both prescription and over-the-counter drugs – whatever goes into our system goes into the body of our baby.

Many women have minor complications when they first begin to nurse especially after the milk comes in and breasts may become sore and engorged. To help prevent soreness, during pregnancy apply natural oils/creams on the nipples and areola a couple of times daily. Initially, nursing may also be uncomfortable because the baby has not learned how to latch on properly and we may not know how to help him. Do not panic and do not stress because there is plenty of help available. Contact your midwife or doctor who will be able to directly assist or refer you to a lactation consultant, who specializes in assisting struggling breastfeeding mothers. Experience is a wonderful teacher, so do not be too proud to contact other women who have overcome the challenges that come with breastfeeding – they will be happy to help. In the meantime, try to keep calm as our babies are super sensitive to our feelings and will react to our stress.

When women experience complications while trying to breastfeed, the biggest mistake made is to give up, even temporarily. If we attempt to try to wait to nurse, our baby will get used to the bottle nipple, which will make it more difficult (not impossible) to re-introduce breastfeeding. Also, the longer we wait, the more likely we are to lose our milk production. The mother will notice that after only a couple of days of not nursing, her milk supply has dramatically decreased.

Another mistake made is that the mother may think that her baby is not getting enough milk because he wants to nurse so frequently and therefore, the mother will supplement his breastfeeding with formula – BIG MISTAKE. Yes, it is true that there is no way of measuring the amount of milk our baby is getting per feeding, but as long as there is steady weight gain and progressive physical development; then he is getting what he needs. Another indication that he is getting enough is the regularity of urination and bowel movements.

It is absolutely normal for a newborn baby to want to nurse every hour to hour-and-a-half. A dramatic increase in nursing is also likely a sign of a growth spurt. Refrain from scheduling the baby's feedings, especially a newborn. Infants cannot lie. If the baby motions hunger, then please feed him – do not wait until a scheduled time. The more the baby nurses, the more milk the mother will produce and when he begins to nurse less, the milk production will decrease. Allah (God) has this thing worked out! Be patient for the first two weeks because, after that, both mother and baby will have mastered breastfeeding.

Synthetic formulas are a relatively new invention when we consider the scope of human existence and realize that women have been exclusively breastfeeding their babies since time immemorial. The only reasons not to breastfeed in this modern age is if the mother suffers from an illness or ailment, which makes breastfeeding impossible or would adversely affect the health of the mother. According to the Holy Qur'an, women are not forced to suffer harm on account of their children. Also, mothers who must take medication regularly which could be harmful to the baby may be advised against breastfeeding.

We, as mothers can make excuses and try to convince others and ourselves as long as we want about why we did not breastfeed our children, but Allah (God) knows the truth. If our reasons are legitimate or if we did not know any better, God is Aware, so we should not feel guilty for something beyond our control. However, to not breastfeed just because we do not want to or to breastfeed for a week or two and stop, has its consequences. And unfortunately, many times the children suffer for the sins and iniquities of their parents. Keep in mind, however, that if breastfeeding is not an option, the next best thing in NOT formula or other store-bought milk.

Several months after I had my first child, a Sister asked me what I would feed my son if I could not breastfeed him. I honestly had no immediate answer for her because I never considered the possibility of not being able to breastfeed. After a day or two, I gave the Sister my answer. I will share it shortly. But we would be remiss if we did not reemphasize the importance of a mother's desire to breastfeed. Breastfeeding should not be our first option, but it should be our only option. When we begin to think about all of the other formulas and supplemental options available, we will give up breastfeeding much faster with the first sign of difficulty. We should not enter breastfeeding with any thought in mind that if this does not happen easily, there is always Similac ®. Remember, desire feeds the will – be and it is.

I finally told, the Sister that if I could not breastfeed, then I would do my best to do what the Holy Qur'an says, which is to pay a wet nurse to feed my baby. A woman who is currently lactating and nurses another mother's baby is considered a wet nurse. If it is not logistically feasible for her to physically nurse the baby, then she can be asked to express her milk so that the mother can feed her baby the wet nurse's breastmilk by bottle.

WET NURSE RESURGENCE:

Just a few decades ago, couples who struggled with infertility did not have many options available for them. Today, the advances in science and medicine allow couples who cannot conceive on their own, due to medical or physical reasons, to go on to have healthy children and build wonderful families. There are always moral and ethical dilemmas to wrangle with, particularly if considering surrogacy; but nonetheless, this is one of the many options available. There are different types of surrogacies, but in all instances, a third party is brought into the picture for the purpose of physically carrying the baby to term. Usually, the female partner is either unable or unwilling to carry the baby. The surrogate mother's medical expenses are all paid for by the couple – and unless she is a relative or close friend who is availing herself for purely altruistic reasons, the surrogate is generously compensated beyond her medical expenses.

In many respects, a wet nurse is similar to a surrogate mother – she is a third party that is brought into the picture to fulfill a role that the natural mother is either unable or unwilling to do and she is compensated for her service. However, instead of carrying the baby in her womb, the role of a wet nurse is to "nurse" or breastfeed another woman's baby. Today, in addition to the term wet nurse, many refer to this as "cross-nursing" or "shared-nursing."

It is intriguing that many of us, particularly in the United States, have come to accept surrogacy (another woman giving birth to a couple's baby) as an acceptable solution to infertility, but find another woman nursing a couple's baby as weird or even disgusting. This is odd since surrogacy is relatively new, but wet nurses have been used for centuries.

Occasionally in the Bible, the term "nurse" is used, but its use is not referring to a medical nurse by today's definition; the nurses were those who breastfed babies that were not their own. We may recall that according to the scriptures, when Pharaoh's daughter found Moses, she sent for a woman to nurse him and paid her wages for the service. Of course, unbeknownst to her, the woman she paid to nurse Moses was his biological mother. Likewise, the Holy Qur'an states – if a couple so chooses, they may engage a wet nurse for their baby, *"...so long as you pay what you promised according to usage"* (2: 233).

To be clear, there is no longer **any** debate about the tremendous health benefits and advantages of breastfeeding for both the mother and the baby, so EVERY **able** mother should make it a priority to breastfeed her own baby. But for those who cannot breastfeed or simply choose not to, why should man-made manufactured formula be the next option when there is a much healthier alternative for our babies? We all spend money on the things that are important to us. For many of us, when it comes to something we deem beneficial for our children, we will **FIND** the money – education, private lessons, sports, travel, braces, entertainment; you name it. So, what about nutrition and health?

In **How to Eat to Live: Book Two**, the Most Honorable Elijah Muhammad wrote, *"A SICK mother's milk is better for her baby than a*

193

healthy cow's milk or any animal's milk." This does not mean that we should not consider the health and lifestyle of the woman when choosing a wet nurse for our baby – we absolutely should. But it does highlight the infinite value and profound superiority of breastmilk; after all, it was designed by God Himself.

We may ask: Is hiring a wet nurse practical in 2019? Believe it or not, there are professional wet nurses and they are not hard to find. Costs vary, but it is a great investment in the health of our baby. Ideally, we should choose someone we know personally. There was a time when it was very common in the mosque or church to see a sister nursing another sister's baby. All mothers know that when you are lactating if you hear another baby cry, your milk will involuntarily letdown – perhaps that's a sign (smile). I have also witnessed (not in this country) a woman who was not lactating, put another woman's crying baby on her breast to soothe and console the baby until the mother returned. There was no milk coming out, but just like a pacifier, the baby was content and comforted at that moment.

As Black people in America, when we think of wet nurses, the image that often races to the forefront of our consciousness is that of the "mammy" figure during slavery – our Black mothers being forced to nurse and be the primary caretakers of the slave master's children. The fact that we were forced to nurture, nourish, comfort and strengthen our future tormentors is reprehensible. At that time, some wet nurses only saw their biological children once every two weeks if at all, since she had to be at the behest of the mistress who was inept to care for her own children. If we were paid anything at all, it was inadequate, and we had no rights and no recourse. Some argue that the trauma experienced from someone owning our bodies and dictating how it should be used has been passed down through the generations – "post-traumatic slave syndrome." The effect is that today, many Black women do not choose to breastfeed their own children much less someone else's.

It was primarily Black women who were aghast when images and video surfaced of the actress, Salma Hayek, breastfeeding a Black woman's baby in Sierra Leone in 2009. I was not there, so I cannot speak to the context and circumstances surrounding her decision; but according to what was reported, the baby was hungry, and the mother could not provide milk, so Hayek instinctively went to nurse the baby. Salma Hayek is of Mexican descent and shared that her own great-grandmother did something similar to help a woman and her baby in a Mexican village decades prior. We do not know Mrs. Hayek personally; but we should be able to appreciate her intentions as well as the fact that she had no aversions toward nursing someone else's baby.

Breastmilk is life. It is a living substance that not only provides food but also medicine for the baby. Studies show that "baby saliva stimulates an immune response." This means that if a baby is ill, the mother's milk can provide the cure. Scientists say that the retrograde milk flow (backwash) sends pathogens to the mother triggering an immune response in her, which she returns to the baby in the form of a healing remedy. Babies are completely dependent on the mother's immune system, while they strengthen their own. This does not work with adult saliva, but the same results are found if the nursing woman is not the biological mother. Would you believe that the saliva from another baby can trigger the nursing mother's brain to produce a different chemical combination in her milk better suited for that specific baby? Wow!

Allah (God) is The Master Scientist and has provided everything that we need to get the most out of this life. The fact is that breastmilk from almost any woman is several times better for our baby than anything manufactured in a factory or anything we can get from the cleanest plant or animal. Somehow, over time, breastfeeding has become undesirable and using a wet nurse, unthinkable. This may not be feasible for every mother, but thankfully a slow and steady resurgence of wet nurses is taking place; providing a healthier and better alternative for the mother who desires to give her baby nature's best.

BREASTFEEDING – FATHER'S ROLE:

For our wonderful brothers, yes, even in breastfeeding there is a role for you. In this world, a woman who desires to breastfeed needs a lot of support and encouragement, particularly at the beginning. The best source of this support is her husband. The last thing she needs is a husband that says, *"Well Babe, if you don't want to breastfeed that's your choice, do you."* That sounds really nice, but it is all she needed to hear to give up instantly. Our duty is to encourage one another to follow Allah's (God's) instructions and do what is best for our children. Do not promote disobedience. Encourage her and get her the help that she may need. Do not get angry with her or try to force her to breastfeed; a gentle word and reminders will be more effective.

Though it is the mother's responsibility to provide milk for the baby; it is not her baby alone. A woman who desires to give birth to a god needs a strong man to pick her up when she gets weak. Her obligations should be centered on Allah (God) and her baby. A spiritually weak Brother who does not include himself in this journey is of no use to her when difficulty comes. Be clear on the specifics of her difficulty and if you cannot help her, seek the assistance from others. If she still does not breastfeed; only then should you have a measure of calm knowing that you did all that you could do.

The Honorable Minister Louis Farrakhan gives men another warning when it comes to their nursing wives. He stated that a man must be careful how he handles his wife during her nursing years. If an argument arises, the chemistry of the woman's mind changes and this affects the blood and then the milk. When she goes to feed her baby, the baby is feeding on this milk and feels the rejection of his father. Everything a woman feels for her husband, good and bad, is received by the child. A husband should make sure that his wife is calm, relaxed and in good spirits when she goes to nurse her baby.

During a lecture, Student Minister Ava Muhammad discussed an article she read about a woman in an airport who was nursing her baby as she awaited the arrival of her husband. While this woman was nursing, she received news that the plane her husband was on crashed. The extraordinary grief, anxiety, and trauma immediately consumed this woman's mind and produced a toxic, poisonous reaction that instantly affected her blood, changing the chemistry of her breastmilk dramatically. The milk was so toxic that it killed her nursing baby. This is the power of thought. The woman can transfer peace, love, and life; or anxiety, hatred, and death to her baby.

Everything that Allah (God) has created is obedient to His laws except for man and woman. The sun, the moon, the trees, the birds and the planets are all submissive to their nature – they have no other choice. Allah (God) only gave the gift of reason and the freedom of choice to His greatest creation, the human being. Collectively, we have abused our gifts and put the human family in this miserable condition by choosing to follow everyone and everything else except for Allah (God). We must use our gift of reason and choice wisely and live our life in a way that would be pleasing to Allah (God), which will restore us back to our rightful status – The Glory of God!

SECTION 5: REARING THE CHILD OF GOD

*"And Allah brought you forth from the wombs of your mothers –
you knew nothing – and He gave you hearing and sight and hearts that you
might give thanks."*

Holy Qur'an 16:78

HOW TO REAR OUR CHILDREN:

As parents we understandably comfort ourselves by saying, *"We did the best we could – children don't come with any instructions, you know."* Many parents **are** doing the best they can; making daily decisions based on what they know. Some parents know better, yet for one reason or another refuse to do better. But we would argue, that **most** parents have simply never been taught how to rear their children, so they begin at a great disadvantage. Childrearing can be a very sensitive topic because no mother or father wants to be charged with being a "bad" parent. However, the art and science of childrearing are far too important not to speak straight words. So, here we go…

Unfortunately, there are in fact a lot of really bad parents out there – but for the most part, it is not their fault. Our hope is that if parents and potential parents become aware of the presence of a Master Teacher, God in Person; and know that He generously shared how to **best** live this life and how to rear future generations, then we will take advantage of such knowledge and seek to become better parents.

The Honorable Minister Louis Farrakhan said, *"There are no parents who are free of mistakes or errors in the rearing of their children. It is sad that we can go to colleges and universities to receive degrees that tell us that we are qualified to work in our various fields of endeavor, but, the most important endeavor, which is the building of human life through the skill of parenting does not seem to matter in our quest for the acquisition of knowledge. There are no courses offered in high school or college that will allow us to become proficient in this skill. Yet, all of us will eventually become parents. Doctors who make mistakes or errors can leave their patients permanently wounded or even dead. Lawyers who make mistakes can cause their clients to suffer great loss, even the loss of life. Builders who make mistakes can cause what they build to crumble and fall. What happens when we make errors or mistakes in the rearing of our children?"*

The Women's class in the Nation of Islam is called, Muslim Girls' Training and General Civilization Class (M.G.T. & G.C.C.). Why "girls" if it is a class for women? Our biological maturity may indicate that we are women; but when we enroll in the classroom of God, we must come as a little child. We must come humble and eager to learn; bearing witness that we know very little compared to all there is to know. Yes, we are women; but to Allah (God), we are His little girls. We are given seven major training units in this class. One of which is: ***How to Rear Our Children!*** Wise people seek teaching and training in areas they have not yet mastered. The condition of this world bears witness that few, if any, have mastered this most important subject of parenting.

A curriculum, which teaches both men and women how to give birth to gods and how to properly rear their children, must be implemented in every school in America and the world over. It cannot be just any parenting curriculum; it must be a god-centered curriculum. As parents, our ultimate goal should not be to simply reproduce academically trained robots and good employees; we should want to produce gods! We have to bear witness that we have not been taught how to do that. A curriculum this demanding must be introduced before becoming a parent. This means mandating course curricula beginning at the high school or even middle school level.

In every other endeavor or walk of life, preparation precedes the profession or practice and the preparation begins early. We cannot buy a car without knowing how to drive. The proof that one knows how to drive is by the issuance of a driver's license. Young teenaged drivers are not only required to pass written tests; but they have to log several hours of supervised driving in all conditions – inclement weather, nighttime, highways, rural, residential areas, parking lots, etc. One must meet a certain degree of mastery before being allowed to operate an automobile unsupervised. Yet, absolutely NOTHING is required to become a parent! No teaching, no training, no license, no degree, no proof of income, no spouse, no babysitting experience, no CPR/first-aid training – no requirements at all. We are all free to reproduce human life without any preparation whatsoever. That is a problem!

Every creator or manufacturer of a product provides a manual or instructions on how to use and maintain the product. The manufacturer does not leave us to our own understanding. Even Q-tips have instructions for safe usage! The Bible states that God gave men dominion; and similarly, the Holy Qur'an refers to men as Allah's (God's) khalifah or successor. If this is the case, are we to actually believe that the Supreme Being anointed us with rulership, but did not leave us any instructions on how to care for His most precious gift – human life? Of course not, Allah (God) would never give us power and influence without guidance.

We know that perfection does not exist in parenting. Most of us as parents fall into one of two categories. We are either too hard on ourselves or we are not hard enough. Unfortunately, today's modern parents may need to lean toward the latter. Parents are allowing children to rear themselves and encouraging children to make adult decisions – in the name of "allowing them to be their own person." How can our children be themselves if they are not seeking understanding of the God who gave them their aim and purpose? Sorry, hands-off parenting is just lazy and reckless. Only wealthy, well-connected parents can afford to experiment on their children. If these parents mess-up, no problem – money, and connections can give almost anyone a do-over. The rest of us need God's way the first time.

We also may have heard some parents say, *'Oh I would never tell another person how to parent their child; they have to do what works for them.'* This sounds good, but at the root of this statement is, *'I do not want anyone else to tell me how to rear my children.'* It exposes a bit of arrogance as a parent to say that we do not need any direction, guidance, teaching or training with our most sacred endeavor, the rearing of our children. And it is also equally selfish not to share with others our successes and our failures, so they may learn.

After all, God Himself established childrearing as a training unit in conjunction with other units. Isn't it interesting how we do not hesitate to seek additional knowledge about our other training units? We seek recipes and cooking techniques from great chefs; we will learn how to sew from premier seamstresses; we will buy books or attend workshops to strengthen our marriages; there is no resistance to a Sister sharing her DIY cleaning agents or how to be a good hostess; and we will tune-in to hear about the best travel tips and etiquette before we take that overseas vacation. But, how to rear our children – *'I'll figure that out on my own.'*

The scripture reads, *"My thoughts are not your thoughts. My ways are not your ways. I am from above while you are from beneath."* The Honorable Minister Louis Farrakhan stated, *"This teaches us that our thoughts and our ways are far beneath what Allah (God) desires for us. Therefore, what we have produced as the man, the woman, and the family by our thoughts, and, our ways are far beneath the man, the woman and the family that Allah (God) desires for us. So, in order for us to make a new family, we have to return to Him who created the man, the woman, and the family and we must be willing to accept His Thought and His Ways."*

We are not saying that if we enroll in the M.G.T. & G.C.C. that there will be an answer to every possible circumstance or situation that may arise with our children. But we will learn enough to be very well prepared to handle 90% of the challenges which will come our way. Mistakes will happen, but they do not have to exist – meaning, the parent will move swiftly to correct those mistakes once it comes to his or her attention. And where someone's specific circumstance does not have a clear answer, this is when we turn inward and listen to our intuition. Intuition is never wrong because it is directly from God. The Most Honorable Elijah Muhammad said, *"You and I were reared by the devil, in his hell. Since we were reared by the devil, it takes an awful powerful teacher to get him out of you."* That awful powerful Teacher is God in Person. We do not teach the coming of God, we teach His Presence and He has invited us all to enroll in His classroom.

There are three major areas of childrearing. The first two, which are often neglected, have already been discussed – *Preparation before Conception and During Pregnancy.* The final major stage of childrearing comes after the child is born. It would be impossible for me or anyone else to share ALL there is to know about childrearing, simply because no one knows ALL there is to know and if we did, it would take volumes upon volumes of books. So, we hope to share the condensed version in this book or some of the most important topics as we understand it from the Teachings of the Most Honorable Elijah Muhammad under the guidance of the Honorable Minister Louis Farrakhan.

MATERNITY LEAVE IS ESSENTIAL:

In December 2017, my daughter and I visited the country of my birth, Sierra Leone; a small country on the west coast of Africa whose entire population is less than New York City's. Like most developing countries, there is a struggle to find the balance between making modern advancements to improve the quality of life for its citizens, while at the same time preserving the cultural norms and mores that make a country and its people cohesive and unique. We were able to witness examples of this delicate balancing act in many realms, including childrearing.

Since my sister and I were both reared in the United States, my mother never hesitated to share as much as she could about life in Sierra Leone. Her reflections and stories were primarily about the years of her youth. After I had my first child; she reminded me of a tradition that I recalled her mentioning many times prior, but it never meant as much to me as it did when I became a new mother. She said that when she was young, whenever a woman had a baby; a family member – usually a young woman, sometimes in her teens, would move into the home to assist the new mother with her household chores, cooking, and tending to the other children so that the mother could focus exclusively on bonding, nursing and caring for her new baby. This helper would remain in the home for at least three months. What a remarkable custom! Now, we may be able to get similar assistance in the United States, but we are definitely going to have to pay for it.

The United States remains far behind both developing and advanced countries when it comes to demonstrating in a tangible way that motherhood is sacred, and family is a priority. Not only do we not expect ANY additional help after having a baby, but if we were working prior to, we are rushed to get back. According to the Family and Medical Leave Act, which DOES NOT cover every American (only around 60%); new parents are entitled to twelve weeks leave, but often it is a combination of unpaid and paid leave. Juxtapose this to Denmark, Belgium, Japan, Norway, Sweden, and most other countries who not only offer paid leave but for a substantially longer period – some up to 52 weeks and beyond. In fact, the United States is the **only** industrialized nation not to mandate paid maternity leave and it is one of only four countries in the world (Papua New Guinea, Lesotho, and Swaziland) not to guarantee paid maternity leave.

Mothers must have adequate time to heal, adjust and bond with their babies. This is necessary for the overall health of both mother and baby; but also, the overall strength of our families. There is no question about the immediate physical health benefits of maternity leave, but studies of European countries also show that there are long term mental health benefits for mothers who receive "paid" maternity leave. Governmental policies are a clear reflection of the values and priorities that prevail in cities, states, and nations.

According to the Teachings of the Most Honorable Elijah Muhammad, the majority of an expectant mother's maternity leave should actually take place during pregnancy. The Sisters are expected to take maternity leave from the mosque beginning at the third month of pregnancy and ending no sooner than three months after the baby's birth. This is a total of nine months; six during pregnancy and three after. Why is that? When asked this question via Twitter, the Honorable Minister Louis Farrakhan responded, *"Women who are pregnant, as they grow in their pregnancy it becomes uncomfortable for them to sit and the Honorable Elijah Muhammad did not want the sisters to be spectacles of the brothers. It is wise that she's in an environment where her husband sees her evolving, where her husband loves and nurtures and cares for her – where her friends in the M.G.T. Class come and visit her! And where she's constantly feeding on The Word without others 'feeding their eyes' on her. After birth: That's a critical time for the mother and the child to begin bonding."*

After all, maternity is defined as *"the period during pregnancy and shortly after childbirth."* In this book, we regularly emphasize the significance of a woman's mental and physical state, as well as her environment during pregnancy; and how all of these elements directly impact the baby. If being away from the mosque for two-thirds of the pregnancy is good for the mother and her new baby; then what about time away from work? Unfortunately, the enemy has made it so that it is very difficult (though not impossible) for any household to have adequate income with one salary – many women have to work, sometimes for the entire duration of their pregnancy. This is insane and proof that we do not live in a society that believes family should be prioritized. Nor does this way of life show the proper reverence and respect for the gift of life.

Allah (God) is Al-Muhyi, *The Giver of Life*. We are NOT self-created. No soul comes into existence without the express knowledge and permission of Allah (God). The gift of life is the single most precious gift that we could ever receive. Our children are from Him – He is The Source. The Holy Qur'an reads, *"Allah's is the kingdom of the heavens and the earth. He creates what He pleases. He grants females to whom He pleases and grants males to whom He pleases, Or He grants them both males and females, and He makes whom He pleases, barren. Surely He is Knower, Powerful"* (42: 49-50).

Great care must be taken during pregnancy to protect the sacred life of the baby. We would have to rack our brains in order to imagine any work environment outside of the home that is conducive for pregnancy; physically and mentally. Stress agitates the mind and the body, which alters our behavior. Stress unchecked contributes to a myriad of health problems including high blood pressure and heart disease. Every woman who does not have the benefit of maternity leave during and after pregnancy is vulnerable to health risks – the level of that vulnerability depends on the demands of her job. Naturally, the woman's body has endured the ultimate undertaking that the body can naturally experience; she needs to heal and to rest. She has to refrain from strenuous physical activities, so she will not impede the process of healing. Allowing our mothers to be exposed to any such risk should be unacceptable.

There can also be risks for the baby after birth. Our newborns should remain at home more often than not. First-time mothers, in particular, have to be careful not to parade all over town with their infant. Keep in mind that the baby is no longer in the womb where he was protected from pollution, germs and harmful bacteria. His tiny body is still fragile and sensitive to foreign antigens. We dramatically increase the likelihood that our baby will become sick by taking him outdoors where he will be exposed to hundreds of others. Or, being forced to put him into daycare because we lack adequate maternity leave. During the first four weeks, it is best to remain in the house with the exception of visits to the pediatrician or other appointments that cannot be avoided. After this stage, we can gradually increase exposure to people outside of the home; but continue to stay home as much as possible until the baby reaches three months of age.

It is very likely that a first-time father may become jealous of the new baby. The baby demands a tremendous amount of the mother's time and attention, which reduces the amount of time she can give to her husband. It is natural to be jealous initially, but a good father will mature and understand that all babies are born selfish, not just his. The baby's needs must be put before our own. The time for the father to become a more dominant and influential figure in the child's life is when the male child is nearing adolescence (preteen years). But every baby and young child needs his or her mother more than anyone else during his or her first several years of life. Allah (God) put essential qualities in the woman that the baby can only get from her. She knows instinctively what the baby needs and wants. The fact is that the responsibility of the mother weighs heavier than that of the father. This is one of the reasons why the Most Honorable Elijah Muhammad said that 75% of his work was with the woman; only 25% was with the man. *'The hand that rocks the cradle rules the world.'* And how she rocks that cradle will determine how the world will be ruled.

The Book of Proverbs reads, *"Train up a child in the way he should go and, when he is old, he will not depart from it."* Minister Farrakhan wrote, *"The baby is secured in its mother's womb, but when it comes into its new environment it cries because it is insecure. The baby is secured by the love and warmth from the mother's body; it is secured by the milk that flows from its mother's breast; it is also secured by the loving care of a mother who makes sure that the needs of a baby to be fed, to be changed, to be in a clean and safe environment are met. All of this must be provided by the mother, with the help of the father."*

With that being said, we would be foolish to expect the United States government to be a moral example for the rest of the world and implement a policy that is fair and just. Therefore, it is up to us to prepare and plan as best we can so that we can implement what the Most Honorable Elijah Muhammad desired for expectant mothers. Studies show that *"women with unintended pregnancies return to work sooner than those with intended pregnancies."* Therefore, planning and saving are crucial. It is a small sacrifice to be able to offer our mothers-to-be a proper sanctuary where she can co-operate and co-create with The Giver of Life – giving her added serenity and stability; and the best opportunity to give birth to a god.

PACIFIER WOES:

For a first-time young mother, the cries of her newborn can stir a range of emotions. She may experience moments of excitement followed by stress; happiness coupled with anxiety; elation deflated by a nagging concern, *"Will I be able to interpret my baby's cry?"* The role of a mother is extraordinary and those new to motherhood can easily be overwhelmed. Motherhood can be an emotional rollercoaster for all new moms, but some are just better at managing it than others. One thing a new mother knows for certain – a crying baby means something is wrong! Therefore, she may believe that a pacifier is the best invention ever known to man since it appears to satisfy the baby and buys her some time.

Unfortunately, the momentary comfort and peace of mind gained by the use of a pacifier pales in comparison to its lengthy drawbacks and potential health risks. These negatives can be exacerbated by a mother who lacks experience as well as discipline and overuses the pacifier. The baby's cry is instinctive, and it forces the mother to respond. The sound and intensity of the cry will determine the speed of her response. The misuse of a pacifier can interfere with a mother's ability to decipher and interpret the specific needs of her baby if she is quick to reach for it at the first whimper.

The Honorable Minister Louis Farrakhan has taught on the universality of a baby's cry and how the cry is evidence that we are all born with faith. A baby's cry is a prayer. It is an indication of the baby's innate faith at birth. The baby cries because he has faith that his cry will be answered. When the mother answers the cry (prayer) of her baby by feeding him, changing him, holding him, burping him or soothing him to sleep, his faith is rewarded and strengthened by her actions. This is proof that mothers are God's representatives in the lives of their young children. As children mature, they eventually grow to no longer cry for mommy; but instead, pray to Allah (God) for aid.

In England and Australia, a baby's pacifier is commonly referred to as a "dummy." In the United States, a dummy refers to a mannequin or

212

human-like doll. It is also an offensive synonym for the equally offensive term, stupid. But the root word 'dumb,' was commonly used to refer to someone who is mute or cannot speak; unable to communicate verbally. So, the "dummy" or pacifier is given to stop the baby from crying; which is his way of communicating his needs to the mother or caretaker. So, why would we want to render our babies dumb, mute or even pacify them?

Allah (God) does not silence us when we call on Him. In fact, it is His nature to respond. The Holy Qur'an reads, *"And when My servants ask thee concerning Me, surely I am nigh.* ***I answer the prayer of the suppliant when he calls on Me***, *so they should hear My call and believe in Me that they may walk in the right way"* (2: 186). He wants us to know He answered our prayer, so that our faith in Him may be strengthened, which will encourage us to continue on the right path. Allah (God) declares that He cares for those of us who pray to Him.

The Honorable Minister Louis Farrakhan said, *"Babies have a bigger faith sometimes than grown-ups."* As God's representative in the lives of our babies, we should never allow the cry of a baby to go unanswered. We should also not get in the habit of silencing their cries without addressing their specific need. Babies do not have the competence to deceive or connive. They cry because a need is not being met and we are obligated to satisfy it. You cannot spoil an infant, so we should never reject a baby's attempt to be comforted. In extreme cases of abandonment, studies have shown that babies whose cries go unanswered, eventually stop crying. Faith unrewarded leads to disbelief. We want our children to grow in faith, not grow out of faith.

We must also consider that pacifiers can pose potential health risks for our babies. Pacifiers are made out of latex, silicone, plastic or rubber. Synthetic latex pacifiers can contain nitrosamines, a known carcinogen. Silicone pacifiers often use chemical softeners, and both silicone and plastic pacifiers often use colorants. Even 100% natural rubber pacifiers can contain carcinogenic chemical compounds if they have not been baked in a special oven for days and thoroughly washed multiple times, then sealed. If a pacifier must be used, do it sparingly, but first, do your homework. Be sure they are free of Bisphenol-A (BPA), polyvinyl chloride (PVC), phthalates, parabens, allergens, artificial colors, endocrine disruptors, chemical softeners, and carcinogens.

While there is some debate about the potential for a breastfeeding baby to suffer from nipple confusion if a pacifier is introduced, there is no doubt that introducing a pacifier too early can affect the mother's milk supply. The more the baby nurses, the more the mother's milk supply increases. If the baby is offered the pacifier too often, the mother will be inadequately stimulated and will not produce as much milk; thereby making breastfeeding difficult.

Additional issues may develop if pacifiers are used extensively into toddlerhood. They can increase the risk of ear infections because the continuous sucking and swallowing motion changes pressure behind the ear, which leads to fluid build-up in the middle ear. Pacifier overuse can also lead to serious dental issues, thrush, facial rashes, gas and delayed or distorted speech.

The Most Honorable Elijah Muhammad stated that the reason we have such a great percentage of delinquency among minors is that our children are not fed from their mother's breasts. He also wrote, *"A baby nursed from its mother's breast will love its mother more than the baby fed from the bottle. He loves the bottle."* The baby's attachment and longing should be for its mother, not for a bottle, a toy or a pacifier. The baby's brain is still developing during infancy and toddlerhood at a rapid rate – we should take advantage of this time by securing his connection and bond to human life and not to things.

214

Otherwise, he may grow up to have more love for material objects than for humanity.

Parents who know they are not disciplined, should not even buy a pacifier. We may convince ourselves that we will only use it occasionally, but it is terribly habit-forming for the parents and the baby. If we have one available, we will use it and when most parents use it once, they will use it a hundred times. Pacifier woes can be agonizing and unforgiving. So, it may be better to take the cry of a baby over the tantrums of a toddler.

BABY'S FIRST FOOD AFTER MILK:

We cannot overemphasize the profound value and wisdom contained in two monumental books written by the Most Honorable Elijah Muhammad, *How to Eat to Live (HTETL) – Book I and Book II*. He gives his readers the diet prescribed by Allah (God) that will prolong our life and keep illness and disease at bay. The Most Honorable Elijah Muhammad provides a list of foods that will sustain human life and also the foods that are harmful to our health; giving a clear explanation of both. In addition, he teaches us how our food should be prepared, the best times to eat, how often we should eat, the benefits of fasting, and so much more.

If we study nature, read the scriptures, ask doctors or nutritionists – all will confirm that the Most Honorable Elijah Muhammad is correct when he wrote, *"Mothers should feed their babies from their breast milk if they possibly can, as this is the best"* (HTETL – Book I p. 67). This is no longer being debated – there is simply no man-made synthetic formula, manufactured in a lab that can come close to God's chemistry. However, even though it is perfect and nutritionally beneficial, breastmilk will not be sufficient indefinitely. A child's primary need is the need for food. Therefore, throughout both books, the Most Honorable Elijah Muhammad describes how to transition to a sustainable diet for our babies and children.

He writes, *"When you are able to start feeding them on solid food, give them weak [navy] bean soup – not the highly seasoned, strong soup that you eat. You also can start them out with orange juice and mashed apples. This is done whenever you think the baby is able – after he is about three months old. This depends on the health of the baby and its age"* (HTETL – Book I p. 67). Mothers often make the mistake of introducing solid foods to their babies too soon. Those who use formula will often thicken the milk with processed cereals, causing illness. The stomach and digestive system of an infant are not the same as an adult; it is very sensitive and cannot handle much more than milk. We should bear in mind that during infancy, solid food should be a supplement to breastmilk, not the staple.

As the baby gets older and stronger it will be necessary to increase the intake of solid foods, but the baby should continue to nurse from his mother's breast until the age of two. All solid food should be mashed or pureed until the baby has teeth and can sufficiently chew the food well enough to be easily digested. This should be done by hand or with a kitchen appliance, as we are warned not to feed our babies (chewed) food out of our own mouth (HTETL – Book II p. 89).

It is important when transitioning our babies from a breastmilk-only diet to adding solid foods, that we do not allow them to dictate their own diet. We must choose the best foods available and be an example. There is no need for a lot of variety; keep the food simple and remain consistent. Babies and children will eat whatever they are given to eat, which is as it should be. Once we begin to allow them to pick and choose their meals; then their diet will quickly decline followed by their health. The Most Honorable Elijah Muhammad said, *"Some mothers are very careless. The baby can act as if he wants what mother is eating, and even if it is a beef steak, she will cut him a piece. We create sickness right in our homes, from the cradle to the grave"* (HTETL – Book I p. 67).

After being completely weaned from breastmilk, the diet of parents and children in terms of "what" should be eaten is the same. If it is not good for our children, it is not good for us and vice-versa. Our children should continue to consume good, pure whole milk daily. The only time we are cautioned against too much milk is if our children suffer from bronchial-asthma (HTETL – Book II p. 90). But generally, we are taught to feed our babies and children good navy beans, good milk, and thoroughly cooked wheat bread.

The Most Honorable Elijah Muhammad states that meat is against life! It is very difficult to insist on a vegetarian diet for our children and have it sustained if we are not vegetarian ourselves. We must become what we want to produce. Our children will not desire any meat, including fish if the family as a whole does not consume it. A vegetarian (not vegan) diet is the best diet prescribed for us and our children by God Himself. So, we should begin our children on a vegetarian diet from the womb. They will be healthier, stronger, more intelligent, and it will prolong their lives. Fruits, vegetables, and grains are from the earth and contain the seed of life even when harvested. On the contrary, meat is against life – the animal must be killed in order to be consumed. We are what we eat. So, consuming a carcass is consuming death, which can only lead to the grave at an increased pace.

Promoting a diet of three meals a day is probably the biggest nutritional falsehood out there. No human being, not even children require three meals a day. In fact, eating too often is worse than eating the food of lesser quality. Three meals a day and snacking in between is death for us. The Most Honorable Elijah Muhammad said that you cannot replace the stomach, *"When it wears out, you are gone"* (HTETL – Book II p. 151). It is the overworking of the stomach and digestive system that eventually kills us.

How to Eat to Live – Book II, he writes, *"Children should not be forced to fast or to eat once a day or once every other day. Children and babies should eat at least twice a day"* (p. 31). In the same book, he later emphasizes this point by adding, *"Adults should try to eat one meal a day. If you eat one meal every two days, three days or five days it is okay, but do not force children under 16 years of age to do the same. They are growing and most of them need two meals a day"* (p. 90). The Most Honorable Elijah Muhammad does not state when these two meals should take place, but The Honorable Minister Louis Farrakhan has told us that we should not send our children to school on an empty stomach; they should eat breakfast before going to school. The Most Honorable Elijah Muhammad then states that we (adults) should have our one meal between 4:00 to 6:00 pm if possible; if not, it should be at the same time each day.

Again, our children should eat at least twice a day. Two healthy meals a day without overindulging is sufficient. We should refrain from snacking because snacking interrupts the period of rest that we want to give our stomach before the next meal – so we should not get our children into the habit of snacking. Not to mention that most of us resort to processed or sugar-filled snacks. The Most Honorable Elijah Muhammad said that there is enough sugar in fruits, vegetables, and bread for us (HTETL – Book II p. 64). So, let us strive to reserve snacks for long distance travel or instances when food will not be readily available.

Sugar is toxic. When white sugar hits the bloodstream, it solidifies and instantly causes a chain reaction that causes illness, disease and an early demise. For the first three or four years of age, we should strive to completely refrain from giving our children any sweets with refined processed sugars – cookies, cakes, candies, ice cream, etc. Sugar is highly addictive – some say it is only one molecule from cocaine – so we will find that our child will have to have sugar in his diet otherwise he will give his parents difficulty at meal time. A habit has now started that is very hard to break. After the age of three or four, our children will have a regulated palate and will not desire sugar. Several weeks should pass in between each serving of high sugar content foods. Ideally, we should learn how to make our own sweet treats for our family so that we have full control of the ingredients.

For our girls, their diet has added importance. Currently, our young girls are developing far too quickly because we allow them to eat fast foods and other processed meals, which are filled with preservatives and other toxins. Eight and nine-year-old girls should not have started their menstrual cycles, but this is exactly what is happening. If we study the dietary habits of other cultures, we will find that their girls begin menstruating at a much older age – this is a direct result of their diet. We are what we eat.

Disciplining ourselves and our children to follow this prescribed diet will reap benefits for future generations that we cannot fathom today. Remaining on this strict diet will enable our children to live far beyond 100 years of age and still look and feel young – each generation will live longer than the previous. The long life of the prophets and others in the scriptures are not fairy tales. Master Fard Muhammad said that we could enable our children to live to an age of 240 years. In addition, The Most Honorable Elijah Muhammad wrote, *"Your children may be able to eat two meals a week which will put them into centuries as Noah and Methuselah (Noah lived 950 years and Methuselah lived close to 1000 years)."* We may not be physically around to witness this reality; but how we eat, think and live our lives today will give us peace of mind, knowing that our descendants will experience the promised abundance of life tomorrow.

We will begin to notice that our properly nourished, breastfed baby may also learn to reach physical milestones far sooner than the average baby. He will learn to make cooing sounds, sit-up, crawl, pull-up, walk and talk weeks or months before expected.

Our children will rarely become ill if we keep their diet consistent and practice the prescription found in *How to Eat to Live*. However, this does not mean that we should avoid taking our children to the doctor. Regular visits to a pediatrician and dentist for nothing more than physical well-checks will help to prevent any surprises from sneaking up on you. We must study our children and be wise when it comes to their health. Children are going to get an occasional fever, cold, upset stomach or allergic reaction. If these cases are not severe, then do not be too quick to take them to the emergency room or doctor's office. There, they will likely be given drug after drug; which helps the pharmaceutical companies, but not our baby in the long term. Holistic health practitioners will tell you that in cases of mild illness, it is better to allow the child to fight through the sickness, while using natural remedies to calm side effects because it will strengthen their immunity. There are countless natural ways to aid in a child's recovery from mild illnesses – seek them out by consulting an expert.

WARNING: *Do not deny a child the benefits of modern medicine and technology if his symptoms persist or appear life threatening.*

FUDIA MUHAMMAD

GIVE THAT BABY SOME WATER!

We cannot survive outside the earth's atmosphere unless we are confined in a special contraption. And those who make it out of the earth's atmosphere can only survive for a little over one year – maximum. Earth will forever and always be our home planet. There are countless similarities between the physical composition of the earth and the physical make-up of the human body, which bears witness that we came from the earth and must maintain a similar compositional balance as earth if we want our existence on this planet to be optimal and abundant. The Most Honorable Elijah Muhammad wrote, *"Our bodies are made of the earth and contain a little of every matter of the earth's chemicals, stone, gold and silver."*

One of those chemicals is water. Approximately 75% of the earth's surface is water. This means that the vast majority of the earth is water. Where there is water, there is life. Water allows for the procreation of all life and it is second only to oxygen in its importance to sustaining life. The body of the human being, which came from the earth, has a high proportion of water similar to the earths. Water is absorbed in our cells, tissues, organs, blood, muscles and even our bones. Every part of our body has a high-water content. For example, 92% of blood plasma is water; 79% of our kidneys is water; 79% of our muscles is water; 83% of our lungs is water; the brain and heart are both 73% water; our skin is 64% water; and even our bones contain 31% water. No water, no life!

We know that we are what we eat, but we are also what we drink. Good or bad drinking habits are instilled very early in childhood; as early as infancy and toddlerhood. Remarkably, breastmilk consists of 88% water – so an exclusively breastfed baby does not require any additional water. Allah (God) formulated the milk in a way that bears witness to the essential quality

221

of water. Unfortunately, many seem to believe that children and juice are a great match. We have all seen young children with "sippy" cups and could fairly speculate that nine times out of ten, they are not drinking water. If we start our children drinking water before their toddler years, they are more likely to continue to desire to drink water regularly throughout childhood – and beyond.

Water (along with milk) has to become the staple beverage in our homes. Many households consist of children (and adults for that matter) drinking orange juice for breakfast; fruit juices with school lunches; soda with a late afternoon snack; and more juice or soda with dinner. To make matters worse, the juice is rarely, if ever, fresh or natural. So why do our children need to drink water? As stated previously – water is life. Water sustains life by balancing the body. It improves digestion, absorption, and circulation. Water also naturally cleanses the body by flushing out toxins. In addition, it regulates body temperature and boosts our immune system.

There are no magic tricks required to get children to drink water; just start immediately, so it becomes a part of their regular drinking habit. Water should accompany the introduction of solid foods. Babies and toddlers who are introduced to water early, have no problem drinking water with every meal because this is all they know. The only time they will desire anything other than water to drink is if they see others with something sweeter. This is not rocket science – if a child is given a choice between juice and water, they will almost always go with the sweeter option. So, eliminate the option and watch them submit. We will also find that our children will complete their meals easier with water. If we give our children juices and other beverages with their meals, they will likely fill-up on the sweet beverage instead of the nutritious meal.

In his book, *How to Eat to Live: Book II*, The Most Honorable Elijah Muhammad wrote, *"There are many doctors who will not agree with you on drinking a lot of raw juices – not even a lot of raw grape juice, orange juice, or any kind of fresh juice. It is too much for our stomachs. The vitamins in it are good for us but there are other enemies in raw vegetables and fruit juices from the land where they were grown and from the insects that fed upon them."*

If you must – as children get older, offer an alternative every once in a long while, but definitely not every day and absolutely not with each meal. These options should be limited to 100% natural juices (Non-GMO, organic, no added sugar) – ingredients listed should be whole foods only. Water can be used to dilute these juices as well. To be honest, if our children are eating fruit daily, the juice is not necessary. Sugar is toxic and highly addictive. The concentration of sugar in one cup of juice is much higher than in a piece of fruit because it takes more fruit to equal a cup of juice. For example, 3 medium apples yield one cup of apple juice; 3 medium oranges yield one cup of orange juice, and 3 cups of strawberries yield one cup of strawberry juice.

No sodas at all – ever! Public health advocates call sodas and other sweet drinks "liquid candy." Sweetened beverages are one of the leading causes of childhood obesity. They are also linked to childhood diabetes, high blood pressure, low HDL (good cholesterol), tooth enamel erosion and anemia (when replacing meals) – just to name a few.

This does not mean we should go to the extreme and risk overhydrating our children. Those who eat three meals a day should, in fact, drink eight glasses of water per day. But those who subscribe to the dietary law of the Most Honorable Elijah Muhammad – one meal a day and two meals a day for our children – do not require nearly that much water. Also, if we follow a plant-based diet, much of our water intake will be found in the foods we eat. Most fruits and vegetables have an astounding water content of 75% to 96%.

The Holy Qur'an mentions the value of water several times. Two such verses read, *"And He it is Who sends the winds as good news before His mercy; and We send down pure water from the clouds, That We may give life thereby to a dead land, and give it for drink to cattle and many people that We have created"* (25: 48-49). As with everything we take into our bodies and provide for our children, we should always seek the best that is available. Allah's (God's) water is pure, but our open enemy has tampered with it. The Most Honorable Elijah Muhammad wrote, *"Water should be at least 99 percent pure in order for it to be good for humans to drink."* Tap or fountain water is not pure. This water is filled with fluoride and other harmful chemicals that are not fit for human consumption. Therefore, we must do our due diligence to not only give our children water to drink as often as we can but to see to it that it is clean and pure.

NATURE MUST BE NURTURED:

One of the all-time great psychological debates is *Nature vs. Nurture.* The purpose of this debate is to identify the root of one's behavior traits and characteristics. Do we behave the way we do as a result of our genetic make-up, meaning it's inherited so it can't *really* be helped *(Nature)*? Or, are behavior and characteristics acquired from environmental factors and influences *(Nurture)*? This description is admittedly oversimplified, but this is the crux of the argument. There are very strong points and counterpoints for each position. However, it should not be so much an either-or debate as it should be a debate over the strength of one to overcome the other.

The Holy Qur'an states that all human beings are made in the nature of Islam (entire submission to the will of God) except the rebellious devil.

224

Our nature, our inherited genetic make-up, was fashioned and designed to submit to do the will of Allah (God). This means that the nature of the Black man and woman is that of righteousness, as a result of being direct descendants of God. But something happened. At present, the mental and spiritual condition of the Black man and woman in America and throughout the earth is evidence that our nature has been compromised. We have been nurtured – *reared, supported, raised, fostered, parented, mothered, fed,* and *nourished* – by our enemy, the rebellious devil. So, what we have been taught by the Honorable Minister Louis Farrakhan stands true – *environment is more powerful than heredity.* But today, the weight of responsibility is primarily on parents, but when parents work in tandem with the village to nurture what nature has begotten, we have the best of both worlds and can produce gods.

The peak period for brain growth is when the baby is still in utero, mother's womb. Mothers must take advantage of their divine position as God's assistant, by feeding on His words and righteous thoughts, in order to have maximal influence on the brain. From the womb, a mother can give her child a strong inclination and predisposition to submit to do the will of Allah (God). But nature must then be nurtured. During the first three years after birth, our child's brain is continuing to grow rapidly, then it slows dramatically, but is still growing. If we charted the growth of a child's brain on a graph, the growth from utero to age three would be indicated by a nearly vertical line, which would gradually taper off after three years of age. The child's brain must be fed with the right information during this tremendous growth spurt. This is why talking to our baby and reading to him is just as important once the baby is born as it was during pregnancy.

Since many of us have been unaware of the high level of intelligence possessed by our children a birth, we have been inadvertently diminishing their innate potential instead of building upon it. There was intelligence found in the human being when we were worthless water (sperm). If we look at sperm under a microscope, it looks simple – a large head followed by a tail. But intelligence is found in the head. There are tens of millions to hundreds of millions of sperm emitted at one time, but only one can fertilize the egg. Each sperm is placed in the same acidic hostile environment, competing with many, and traveling upstream against gravity. But the fastest or strongest sperm is not always the one to fertilize the egg. The scripture bears witness – *"The race is not to the swift nor to the strong, but to the one who can endure to the end."* So, we are taught that the most intelligent sperm is the one that makes it to the egg – that was you; that was me; that is our children!

The only way to be absolutely positive that this intelligence is being nurtured and that our children are being reared in the manner that we desire is to do the rearing ourselves. It is necessary that the mother be home with her children until they reach school age. In 1996, during a Women's Conference in Houston, Texas, Mother Tynnetta Muhammad (wife of the Most Honorable Elijah Muhammad), was asked a question regarding balancing motherhood with pursuing a career or going back to school. She told the Sisters that we should stay at home with our children until they reached the age of six. After which, we can go after those aspirations. Parenting is a very demanding responsibility that must be planned in advance before we decide to bring children into this world – that is, if our goal is to produce and nurture gods.

This world has given us its own timespan of when things should take place in our lives. According to "society," we are supposed to go to college, get married, have children and have a successful career all before the age of thirty – PLEASE! Sisters, if you want college and a career, you can have it and you can have a family. But if you want the best out of each, you cannot have them conflict with each other or something will get missed. Our children are not going to be young forever. We should sacrifice to lay a solid foundation during those first six years. We will not be too old to pursue additional aspirations, not the original woman – *smile*.

The fact is, no one will take care of our children as we will. Not necessarily because they do not want to, but because by nature, they are incapable of it. Allah (God) made you the perfect parent for that child and fashioned that child in the womb perfectly for you to nurture. If the natural mother is balanced – mind, body, and spirit – no one can draw out of the child his or her greatness better than she; otherwise, Allah (God) would have made another person the child's mother and not you. Let's just accept our role as it was intended. This is why it is important for couples to make the necessary preparations before the baby comes, which will enable the mother to stay home with her children. It is not fair to our children to bring them into this world only to turn them over to someone else when all they really want is us. From birth to the age of six is a crucial time to reinforce security, stability, and structure. Very young children are not interested in spending quality time with us; they just want quantity time.

If this is not our reality and we are a single parent or must work for whatever reason, then be very careful about who cares for the children. Daycares and babysitters must be vetted thoroughly and have a clear understanding of our expectations. Every day, when our child returns to us, we must examine them physically and emotionally for any injury. Some of the nicest, most respectful persons have committed the most egregious and unthinkable acts against children. We hope for the best, but the only way to get the best 100% of the time is if we are doing the rearing and nurturing ourselves. If nature is not properly nurtured, environment will overpower heredity and we may look up one day and not be able to recognize what we produced.

6-MONTHS OLD & POTTY-TRAINED!

I remember listening to a lecture by Student Minister Dr. Ava Muhammad, National Spokesperson for the Honorable Minister Louis Farrakhan and the Nation of Islam, where she said emphatically that the Original, natural inhabitants of the planet earth, the Black man and woman, were capable of being potty-trained by six-months of age; yes, that's right, during infancy. I have to admit, when I first heard this, I was extremely skeptical and thought that she must have been referring to a time trillions of years ago when our supernatural abilities were at an apex and we were immersed in the opulence and grandeur of life on Atlantis. Nope. She was referring to the present-day little gods that we are giving birth to right now!

But, before I lose you, I should mention that potty-training, just like most of our childhood milestone timetables has been set by others; usually White pediatricians, scientists, and doctors who base these achievements on, what else…the abilities of their own kind. The Caucasian is a new man on this planet. He has only been here for 6,000 years; so of course, his natural abilities are limited. This is not racism, just a fact – they are different.

Parents have been conditioned for so long to begin potty-training at two or even three years of age. This is because the Caucasian child took this long before he was capable of being toilet-trained and therefore this was where the standard was set for all children. But there was a time when Original children were clearly indicating the need to relieve themselves by six months of age and sooner. Potty-training, however, is a learned behavior so while it may take a little more effort for others, most babies regardless of race can be potty-trained by six-months of age. Why wait until our child is two or three years old if perhaps this can be accomplished at 18-months, 12-months,

9-months or even 6-months. Societal common practices tell us to wait even though our child is capable – he's just waiting for us to train him.

So, let's be clear on what is meant by an infant being potty-trained or toilet-trained. Obviously, we are not saying that an infant can get up independently, walk to the toilet, use the bathroom, clean himself, adjust his clothing, flush and wash his hands. Of course, not! Being fully potty-trained definitely cannot take place until toddlerhood. But infants are able to accomplish the first two critical steps of potty training. The first step is to be able to recognize the urge to go and communicate it; the second step is to then wait until you're at the designated location for relief. To draw the distinction, the process just described is often referred to as, "communication elimination."

So how does this work? How is an infant able to communicate their need to eliminate waste? There are many books available if you want lengthy specifics, but here's the short version: Some parents start immediately introducing their newborn to the toilet, but others wait until the baby is two or three months old because at this age urination is more routine and bowel movements are less frequent. Parents are able to determine when their babies need to go by paying very close attention to the baby's subtle cues or body signals that come with each urge to go. Babies may get squirmy or shake, change their breathing patterns, or begin to make faces as a sign. Whatever the cue, it can only be identified if the baby remains close to his mother for long periods of time throughout the day. And it is also helpful if the baby's bottom is partially or completely uncovered for long periods of time throughout the day. Once the cue is identified, the baby is held over the toilet or receptacle to relieve himself. Like most learned behavior, potty training is mastered through the art of repetition. So, there must be a commitment to remain disciplined. Some parents will then make up a special sound or say a special word while the baby is going; so that sooner rather than later – after bladder control is established – the infant will be able to go when prompted.

Non-Western countries have a much easier time at infant potty training because babies are carried around all day, sometimes swaddled to their mothers; disposable diapers are considered too much of a hassle and even gross. In that sense, the United States is behind the curve when compared to other parts of the world. Toilet training infants is considered a very normal aspect of parenting in parts of Africa, Latin American, Southeast Asia, India, China, the arctic and Eastern Europe; basically, mostly non-Western countries. Only recently is it growing in popularity in the United States and other Western countries.

Choosing to infant potty train is extremely time consuming and can get quite messy, but truth be told, it does not matter if we choose to toilet train at three months or three years, it will be time consuming, messy and will require patience and consistency. As with many parenting choices, there are advantages and disadvantages. But believe it or not, many find infant potty training very advantageous.

There are others, however, who are faithful subscribers to the philosophies of T. Berry Brazelton and Benjamin Spock, who both had remnants of Sigmund Freud's school of thought weaved into their logic. By the way, Freud was a man who clearly had sick impulses and tried to excuse and normalize them by trying to convince the world that everyone else had these same sick impulses. I digress. Brazelton and Spock were renown pediatricians who believed in a child-directed approach, where parents waited for "readiness cues." They believed that potty training too early led to low self-esteem. Huh? What? Well, they were convincing because many parents ran with this philosophy and so today there are three, four and five-year-old's who have not yet mastered toilet training – something that could have been achieved during infancy.

There is no magical perfect age to potty train; but the sooner the better. Children will submit to the training at any age, including infancy. There is ample evidence and studies that prove this can be accomplished. However, we have been so conditioned to certain practices and habits which require dedicated weaning. So, do not fret if it takes a bit longer, it just may take a generation or two before we can easily achieve our original standard again. Early potty-training is just another ability of ours, which has laid dormant and needs to be resurrected.

"And Allah's is the unseen of the heavens and the earth. And the matter of the Hour is but as a twinkling of the eye or it is nigher still. Surely Allah is Possessor of power over all things" (Holy Qur'an 16: 77).

IS QUALITY TIME A HOAX?

"Time is the only commodity you can never get back." These profound words were shared by Brother Jabril Muhammad in the late 1990s with the Believers in Austin, Texas – and likely with so many others. Whenever we catch ourselves procrastinating or being frivolous with time, we can check ourselves by reflecting on those words. We should all be keenly aware that time is precious since no one has been promised an infinite amount of it. The Holy Qur'an warns, *"And say not of anything: I will do that tomorrow, Unless Allah please. And remember thy Lord when thou forgettest and say: Maybe my Lord will guide me to a nearer course to the right than this"* (18: 23-24). So, in Arabic (our original language) we say, Insha'Allah – if God wills, it will happen or God willing…I will do such and such tomorrow.

As we approach the end of each day, most parents want more time – "just a couple of more hours" we say, is all we need. In order to incorporate the way of life promoted in America, most families require that both parents forfeit time with their children in order to be available to work at a job for an unnatural amount of time each week. Parents are then sold the lie that quality time is more important than quantity time, and we gladly gobble up this deception in order to console ourselves and keep from feeling additional guilt over being more absent than present with our children.

Quality time is defined as, *"time spent in giving another person one's undivided attention in order to strengthen a relationship, especially with reference to working parents and their child or children."* According to some counselors, psychologists, and parenting "experts," quality time trumps quantity time; which is defined as, *"the amount of time a parent is physically present with their child."*

We argue that unless the parent is abusive or in any way dangerous to the child; then every child actually needs more quantity time over so-called 'quality time.' When quality time is our primary focus, what tends to happen is that the experiences we have with our children are manufactured, not organic. We will plan 30-minutes here or an hour there. That *deep* conversation is planned; we plan the outing, the book readings, we plan the shopping spree, the laughter and the excitement is all planned. We consider these prearranged moments of time as being valuable and they can be, but they are also fleeting. So, while the intention is to have a profound and lasting impact – most of our children cannot easily recall the details of many of those moments without the aid of pictures, videos or paraphernalia. However, they can instantaneously recall whether or not their parents were present during critical milestones; since feelings of neglect tend to linger.

232

From the perspective of a child, above all, they want our physical presence – they desire quantity time over quality time with their parents – they do not categorize or rank our time with them based on the type of activity. First and foremost, the primary need of any child is to feel secure. Nothing compares to the physical presence of a parent to make a child feel instantly safe and secure. It does not matter what type of chaos may be surrounding them; a parent's physical presence quells those fears.

Children also often equate love with time and attention. Those who were present around the Most Honorable Elijah Muhammad have said that he was very attentive when children were around. It has been shared that he would stop in the middle of a meeting or dinner if a child entered the room and give his full attention to that child. It has also been reported that when his grandchildren would visit, he would kneel right on the floor and play with them. It is a beautiful image and reminder to those of us who think we are too busy. Here is a man who was given the hardest job of any man who ever lived; but in an instant, he could see the value of renegotiating the time that he knew he would never get back. He did so for the benefit of the children who came around him.

Those of us who lack quantity time with our children may try to substitute material things to express our love. While every child loves a gift, it is a brief enjoyment. The greatest thing we could ever spend on our children is our time. Quantity time is actually a quality gift. If time is the only commodity we can never get back, then there is nothing that is of higher value or quality than our time. Quantity time creates the capacity for quality moments to naturally emerge. In other words, we cannot capture genuine quality moments with any regularity, without having large quantities of time. So, in essence, quantity time is quality time.

CHILDREN OF THE MOST HIGH

There are many other lasting benefits to quantity time with our children. According to Focus on the Family, *"The more involved parents are with their children – and the word 'more' here is used with direct reference to the concept of quantity – the less likely they are to have social, emotional, or academic problems, use drugs or alcohol, become involved in crime, or engage in premarital sex."* The nature of a child is to explore and to be curious. But the presence of any authority figure is going to reduce and can even eliminate attempts at harmful experimentation by our children. Also, the more time we spend with our children, the more we get to know them. There are countless examples that prove that giving birth to someone and living with them does not mean we fully know them. In addition, quantity time allows children to enjoy their childhood and not compel them to grow up too soon.

While the details of the basketball game, recital, science fair, or fieldtrips may be fuzzy – our children will remember if we were available; not just for the special events, but every time they needed us. It's no wonder why long-distance relationships fail. A special moment here and there can never compare with the connection and bond that is created through everyday activities and spontaneous interactions.

We are taught that every human need is a human right. Children not only need affection from parents, but they need validation. The Honorable Minister Louis Farrakhan said that no matter what the child does, children desire validation from their parents and those who mean most to it. The Minister has warned us about being too busy that we neglect our children, *"When we do not get sufficient attention as a child, we act in a manner to get attention and sometimes this results in anti-social conduct or behavior. When the need for attention and validation is not supplied in the home or in the school, and we find that we have a gift or talent, that sets us apart and gives*

234

us attention, we have a tendency to focus on that talent and give all of our time to the talent, gift, or profession because it has given us the attention, acceptance, and validation that we missed coming up as children."

Ultimately, children need both quality and quantity time with their parents. But perhaps our definition of quality time needs to meet a higher standard, so we will not settle for staged snapshots, but will meet the expectation and right of our children to know that their parents see the value in spending much of their time with them. Not only do children want us to be present (quantity), but as the Minister said, *"The child wants to know that we are aware of its presence"* (quality).

BABY LANGUAGE:

The Honorable Minister Louis Farrakhan stated, *"We must remember that the Honorable Elijah Muhammad said that baby language should not be used by us. Now, we thought at one time that baby language meant profanity and certainly, that is baby language. But baby language means an immature understanding of the word that Master Fard Muhammad brought."*

Parents do not have to teach their babies the mechanics of speech any more than we have to teach them how to suck, how to crawl or how to walk. Allah (God) took care of this for us. Some may call these milestones, innate instincts; but bigger than that, it is an indication and confirmation that we are all born with God-given natural intelligence. Having intelligence and knowledge are not the same thing. The Holy Qur'an reads, *"And Allah brought you forth from the wombs of your mothers – you knew nothing – and He gave you hearing and sight and hearts that you might give thanks"* (16:78). So, we are born without knowledge – knowing nothing and yet intelligent. Intelligence is *"the ability to acquire and apply knowledge and skills."* It's brainpower!

It is worth mentioning the lesson taught by The Honorable Minister Louis Farrakhan on divine intelligence once again. He teaches that there is intelligence found in the human being when we were nothing more than sperm. Remember, if we look at sperm under a microscope, it basically consists of only two parts – a large head followed by a long thin tail. As simple as it appears, there is a superior intelligence found in the head of each sperm. One emission can consist of tens of millions to hundreds of millions of sperm. And all must face the same three obstacles in order to achieve the ultimate goal – conception!   The first obstacle is the hostile acidic environment of the vaginal tract that immediately works to eliminate the sperm, which is perceived as a foreign object and potentially harmful. The second obstacle is that each sperm must travel upstream against the natural pull of gravity, which means it must not only move swiftly but strategically. The final obstacle is competition with many – **millions** of sperm all competing to accomplish the exact same goal. But in the end, only **one** can fertilize the egg. The most intelligent one wins every time! That was you! That was me! That is our children!

The fact that we exist and were able to overcome tremendous difficulties is proof of our supreme intelligence and our divine relationship with our Creator. We must keep this at the forefront of our mind when we handle our children. Just because they are small, does not mean that we should treat them like imbeciles. At birth, babies are in-fact more intelligent than we are because they are closer to God. However, we know more. So, while we do not have to teach our babies the mechanics of how to talk – we do have to introduce them to language by modeling and demonstrating proper speech for them. I'll be honest, educated white women seem to understand the value of talking to their babies far more than any other group. We need to disabuse ourselves of any notion that talking intelligently to babies and toddlers is silly. A significant amount of research has been conducted which corroborates the power of talking to our babies.

Children are ready to learn as soon as we are ready to teach them. Knowing this, we should begin talking to our babies when they are in the womb. Sound travels at the rate of 1,120 feet per second. But according to scientists, sound travels about four times faster in water than in air. A baby in utero is living in a sack of water for the duration of the pregnancy. The baby can feed on the mother's thoughts, energy and spirit immediately after conception. But later, the baby can also literally hear the sound of the mother's voice during the second trimester of pregnancy and will physically respond to additional sounds near the end of the second trimester. So, we should talk to our babies everyday while in the womb. But DO NOT stop when the baby is born!

In the Supreme Wisdom Lessons given to the followers of the Most Honorable Elijah Muhammad, we are admonished not to use baby language at any time. We are also taught in our Lessons that everyone – young, old, men, women and children – are all equipped physically and mentally to accomplish our given assignments. How does this relate to the type of language that we should use when rearing our children?

Master Fard Muhammad made no exceptions with regards to age and our ability to learn. Speech and language run a close second only to sight when it comes to stimulating the brain receptors and overall development. Since babies are able to understand language far sooner than they are able to speak – we must be careful to model the proper speech and proper use of language for them. Master Fard Muhammad said, *"Baby language will not be tolerated."* As noted earlier, this has multiple meanings. But what we do know is that the Lessons given to us by Master Fard Muhammad do not consist of any made-up or childish speech. What people call baby talk should only come from babies, not from adults addressing babies. It is a part of the developmental process towards understandable speech for a baby to '*coo*' and '*goo-goo-ga-ga*.' Babies use high-pitched squeaky nonsensical sounds in their attempt to imitate what they hear others say – we are not to reciprocate in a like manner.

For example (with a high-pitch), '*Good morning my little chubby wubby, Mommy wuvs you, choochie choochie choo.*' Why do we do this? Also, speak to babies and toddlers without misusing or abusing the language, this includes slang. So, always correct children when they speak improperly. Do not allow them to say, '*I ain't got no more,*' without correcting them each and every time until they get it right. The only difference between how we speak to our children and how we would speak to another adult is, when speaking to a child we should speak slower and use simple, yet real words. They will understand every word we are saying long before they are able to speak.

Let's not forget those made-up names. Make sure that if your son's name is Hakeem that you call him, Hakeem. Sure, it's okay to call our children Beloved or Son or Sweetheart; or any variety of pet names; but do not turn Hakeem into Hakeemee. This is particularly offensive when our child has a name of Allah (God). The Holy Qur'an warns us against the use of nicknames.

As parents, we can be funny and actively playful with our babies and toddlers without making up words and misusing the language. The reason this is not encouraged is that this starts the process of dumbing down these highly intelligent beings; instead of strengthening their intelligence by exposing them to the proper use and articulation of language and communication. We do not want to be responsible for making a child who could have potentially learned five languages before Kindergarten to now barely being able to speak English. Yes, our word choice should be age-appropriate, but that does not mean it can't be dignified, refined and correct. For example, when our children have an injury, do not refer to it as a '*boo-boo*' – call it what it is – a bruise, a scrape, a cut, a burn, etc. Most of us are guilty of this, but then we send our children to school and expect them to use the language correctly.

The baby recognizes the voice of his/her mother instantly from hearing her in the womb. Allah (God) says that everything in His creation is a word. As mothers, we are the first teacher of our babies. So, we should expose them to as many of God's words as possible. Note: God's words do not include profanity because this is also baby language. The language of God is never profane. There is no level of anger, frustration or pain that does not have a word to describe it. So, for most of us, the use of profanity exposes our slackness and immaturity. But as we mature in our own understanding of the Word that God brought, we will perfect our expression of that Word so that even a baby can understand. After all, Jesus is our example and he spoke wisdom from the cradle to old age…*smile*!

START WHERE YOU INTEND TO FINISH:

In his monumental book, *A Torchlight for America*, The Honorable Minister Louis Farrakhan explained that what we deem to be an education in America is contrary to the true purpose of education. He writes, *"Education is supposed to be the proper cultivation of the gifts and talents of the individual through the acquisition of knowledge. Knowledge satisfies our natural thirst for gaining that which will make us one with our Maker. So true education cultivates – mind, body and spirit – by bringing us closer to fulfilling our purpose for being, which is to reflect Allah (God). The second purpose for education, after self-cultivation, is to teach us how to give proper service to self, family, community, nation and then to the world"* (p. 47)

We are taught that everything that Allah (God) created has an aim and purpose – and anything without aim and purpose is considered nothing. We are born into the world with an innate aim and purpose that drives us to know more about ourselves; and as a result, know more about God. True education will allow us to justify our existence by understanding the aim and purpose for our being. Conventional education is deeply flawed because it focuses on superimposing external information, masked as preeminent knowledge and wisdom, which allows us to be better suited for this world; not the Kingdom of God.

The word *'education'* comes from the Latin word, *'educere,'* which means, *"to bring out what is within."* The Honorable Minister Louis Farrakhan said that children today are born with the intelligence for their era of time in history; so, every generation is genetically capable of solving the problems of its time. Therefore, our children are more advanced than we are; however, we can unknowingly limit them based on our own limitations – forcing them to ingest outdated information and data. We must bring out what God has already put in. Student Minister Ava Muhammad, National Spokesperson for the Honorable Minister Louis Farrakhan and the Nation of Islam, stated that at the age of three, our children are more intelligent than we are at the age of thirty. They are more intelligent, but we know more – there is a difference. This gives us the awesome responsibility of helping them to utilize their intelligence.

In the book, *Closing the Gap: Inner Views of the Heart, Mind & Soul of The Honorable Minister Louis Farrakhan*, the Minister gives the following response to a question by Brother Jabril Muhammad concerning education:

"The Honorable Elijah Muhammad said to me, 'As in geometry, the shortest distance between two points is a straight line. So, it is in education.' He said, 'Why don't you start the course where you intend to finish. You'll be surprised how quickly the children are able to grasp the end of the course. And you are wasting valuable time leading up to something that they could grasp if you had the mind to teach.' He said that, 'At six years old, we should know what we want to do with our life'" (p. 393-394). The concept of 'starting where you intend to finish,' is applicable at every level of education – primary school through graduate school. But if understood, it can also be applied at the genesis of learning – infancy.

If we ask younger children what they want to become when they grow up, what do they typically say? They want to become a firefighter, a police officer, a doctor, or a teacher. Why do they choose these types of professions? Could it be that they have experienced or witnessed the end of the course – someone in their life or on television who is already working in that field makes it look appealing? They have no idea how much time is spent studying or training; how much money it costs to acquire the requisite skills or education; how much they need to grasp about physics, geography, chemistry or psychology. There is likely no tangible evidence that verifies that this child, in fact, wants to become a doctor, but they say it anyway because they have a visual of where they intend to finish. That's powerful!

The Most Honorable Elijah Muhammad said, *"You can have a university under a tree, as long as you are teaching subjects pertaining to the universe."* He said that children can learn as soon as we are able to teach them. We are taught to begin teaching our children while they are yet in the womb. So, it is puzzling that so many of us take a twelve-month break from teaching our babies after they are born. We wait until they are one, two or three-years-old before we expose them to the fundamentals of literacy and arithmetic. Some parents even wait to send them to Kindergarten and leave it up to the teacher. If the baby can learn while in the womb – and he can – then the baby can certainly learn at six-weeks-old or at three months old.

In order to bring out what is within, our children must have basic training and fundamental tools; one of which is literacy. So how can we apply the concept of *'starting the course where you intend to finish,'* with our infants while having literacy at the forefront? We must begin with the end in mind. For example, babies (infants) learn primarily through rote learning, which is memorization through repetition. We know that ultimately, we want to understand; but there is great value in memorizing as an early learner. The method of rote learning is used primarily to learn alphabets, numbers, colors, and basic shapes. Later, we continue to use it to learn our multiplication facts and sight words (particularly those that do not conform to phonetic rules). But our babies can begin learning their alphabets, numbers, colors, shapes, body parts, action words, names of people, and more when they are just a couple of months old! They will not be able to show us what they have learned until a little later; but all the while, if we remain consistent, their brain will record and memorize everything. In time, they will be able to speak or physically demonstrate what they know.

So, if the goal is reading; then we should start **infants** with reading whole-words, as this is where we intend to finish. Purchase or create large flashcards (wait until the child is older to introduce screen time). Remember, they are born ready to learn. If we wait until they are four or five, then we **must** start with phonemic awareness and phonics. But, if we teach them in infancy, then we can use the whole-word method. Show them the card and simultaneously say the alphabet or the word. The print should be neat and large, and our pronunciation should be clear. Their brains are like sponges at this age, so take full advantage and stimulate their brain activity during this rapid season of growth. Gradually increase to more words and stay consistent; even if it is only for 15-minutes a day. It is most effective to do short 5-minute intervals a few times a day. The same can be done with learning action words, names of people, body parts, etc.

Remember, an infant is only going to look at the cards and listen to his mother's voice; but all the while, his brain is recording. You will find that the baby is increasingly attentive. He will not take his attention away from the cards as long as his mother is teaching him. Better than that, the baby is beginning to love to learn. Studying will become a natural part of his life, as natural as eating and sleeping. Keep in mind that the infant or toddler is likely only memorizing, so it is our responsibility to instill understanding at the appropriate time. However, if we can get the basics memorized and out of the way, there is no limit to what they can learn. No child should be five years old, ready to attend Kindergarten and cannot recognize nor write the letter 'A' or the number '2.'

Our babies will amaze us as they playback everything that has been recorded. As the baby gets older, he will be able to express what he knows even before he can speak – by using gestures and other indicators. When we ask for a letter or word, he will grab the card. When he sees the word, '*stomach*,' he will touch his stomach. When he sees the word '*clap*,' he will clap. When he sees the name, '*Farrakhan*,' he will point to his picture. By the time they are ready to speak, they will already know how to read. It sounds counterintuitive but having this foundation will make the introduction of phonics and decoding easier. And more importantly, the mechanics of learning will not be a struggle because it is not a foreign concept, having done it since infancy.

Take advantage of every opportunity to teach. It can be done during bath time, before bedtime, during meals, etc. These opportunities can be used to repeat numbers, alphabets and also prayers to the baby. What this world calls a genius will be developing before our eyes.

Remember, the first revelation and instruction given to Prophet Muhammad (PBUH) were to read. *"Read in the name of thy Lord who creates – Creates man from a clot, Read and thy Lord is most Generous, Who taught by the pen, Taught man what he knew not"* (Holy Qur'an 96: 1-5). The Honorable Minister Louis Farrakhan said that our life depends on our willingness to read. With so much that needs to be accomplished, let's not waste time. Start the course where you intend to finish. We can give our children an amazing head-start and help them to cross that finish line in record time!

TOYS, TELEVISION & BOOKS:

During his 1991 lecture titled, **Who is God**, The Honorable Minister Louis Farrakhan said, *"Today, they start your little children in school at six; but if you train them right from the cradle, at six they will know exactly what they are born to do. You train your children all wrong, feeding them lies instead of truth. Feeding them foolish fairytales; making them think bunnies talk, that rats and pigs and wolves talk. You are killing your babies' minds with fairytales. Feed your baby on truth and one day your baby will become a master of truth."*

We know that every mother needs a break every now and then. We also know that while older children and teenagers bring their own plethora of worries, drama, stress and trials to their parents – there is no denying that the most *physically* taxing period of childrearing is

244

when children are in their sensorimotor and preoperational stages of development (birth through age 7). However, this is precisely the time when parents must be the most careful about what is used to "babysit" our children when we need a break.

According to Jean Piaget, who is best known for his work in the field of psychology, specifically the cognitive development and early education of children – during the sensorimotor stage of development (birth to age 2), children are *"discovering the relationships between their bodies and the environment."* And during the preoperational stage (ages 2 to 7) children are beginning to *"engage in symbolic play and learning to manipulate symbols."* This is a crucial span for progressive brain development.

It is almost impossible to keep our children away from toys, television, books and other images or programming that is not based in fantasy, fairytales and impossibilities for the entire span of their childhood. However, it is possible to accomplish the above said during those critical developmental years. The Most Honorable Elijah Muhammad said that the enemy has our brains a little rusty, but the brain has no limit of power. We are taught that the brain of man is infinite; therefore, we have to do our due diligence to keep falsehood and foolishness from our children particularly before they reach that critical cognitive milestone that enables them the ability to differentiate between reality and fantasy. According to what we are taught, falsehood causes a spiritual and chemical imbalance in our brains. Therefore, a three-year-old will believe that *"bunnies talk; that rats and pigs and wolves talk,"* if that is what they are regularly fed through their toys, television or books.

Playing and learning are not mutually exclusive. Learning should be fun. And playtime is an opportunity to learn. As the Honorable Minister Louis Farrakhan stated, we want our children to become masters of truth; so, mothers in particular must resist taking the path of least resistance. It is very easy to sit our children in front of a television screen to watch unrealistic cartoons or other foolish entertainment programs. It is also easy to give them a silly toy, so they will not bother us when we are busy or just want a break. The problem is that toys and television (or electronic devices), just like that pacifier, can be habit-forming for parents and children if we are not careful. We have to be mindful and not allow these objects and devices to rear our children.

Children need toys; but we should be careful of the types of toys we choose for our children and how often they play with them. Toys that stimulate learning by challenging the thought and creative processes should be the vast majority of our children's toys. Infants and toddlers also benefit from toys that allow them to develop dexterity and their fine motor skills. We should seek out toys or games that offer these dynamics.

Toys based on specific television or movie characters are intentionally targeted to toddlers and very young children, but this is the exact group that should not have them. These toys should be minimal or absent from our homes until our children are old enough not to associate the toy with having the same 'magical' abilities as the fictional character. Often, these fictional characters are animals or inanimate objects that have been personified; making our small children believe they are real. After all, they see it on screen walking, talking and accomplishing supernatural feats.

The same discipline must be practiced when it comes to our children and television, especially when very young. *SpongeBob SquarePants* and other foolishness keep our children in a constant fairytale mindset, not to mention the suggestive subliminal messages. In the age of the internet, there is really no excuse for settling for poor programming. There are wonderful child-friendly and age-appropriate shows and movies with great lessons and relatable characters that we can offer our children. We just have to do a little research and be willing to make the small financial investment that may be required to have access.

Now, what should our children be reading? First, don't skip over spiritual reading from the Bible and Holy Qur'an because we *think* our children will not understand. We should not hesitate to read to our children from these great books until they can read for themselves. For the registered members of the Nation of Islam, we should also read English Lesson No. C1, found in the Supreme Wisdom Lessons, to our children as a bedtime story. Infants and toddlers are easy to please. We could read a chemistry book to them and they will not care because they just love to watch and listen to mommy's voice as she reads. But we should try to find children's books that are considered realistic fiction.

Make reading a staple in the home. We will discover as our children get older that we have instilled within them a profound enjoyment for reading and learning. Take full advantage of this gift by giving them stimulating materials to read. Silly fairytales and fantasies go against the grain of the brain which was created to think right. Anything that goes against the grain of the brain damages the power of it. Books that make children believe that bears, birds, and rabbits can talk; or that carpets can fly, and wishes come true by simply snapping our fingers, alters a young child's developing brain – it's mental confusion. Our children are either subconsciously believing this is reality or reconfiguring their natural reasoning processes to figure out how in the world an elephant can fly by flapping his ears – after all, seeing is believing.

Yes, when our children get a little older, they will still be able to distinguish reality from fantasy; but look at how much time and mental energy may have been wasted, never to return. This time could have been used feeding on truth and laying a foundation to master truth and universal laws that govern the forces within our sphere. God is man and man is god. The Most Honorable Elijah Muhammad said, *"we just cannot make Him other than man, lest we make Him an inferior one; for man's intelligence has no equal in other than man. His wisdom is infinite; capable of accomplishing anything that his brain can conceive."*

BEDTIME STORIES

According to demographers, the majority of the world's population believes in God, a Supreme Being; or at least recognizes that there is a Power greater than themselves. Those believers choose to connect to that Source through some form of prayer, supplication or meditation. While rituals and practices vary, from religion to religion and culture to culture, there is a unique commonality – praying or connecting to that Source before going to sleep. Our head – thoughts and mental state – guide the body. So, praying before bed soothes the mind and spirit which calms the body making it easier to settle into rest. Those who pray before bed not only sleep better; but they suffer less from anxiety, depression, stress, anger, and even physical pain. Studies show that people who pray before bed are generally happier individuals. While there is no substitute for prayer, similar effects are found in children who have consistent nighttime routines that include bedtime stories.

Children need reliable structures and practices, which include a sound sleep pattern. As much as they may try to delay bedtime, if children do not get adequate sleep they will not function well. Establishing a bedtime routine that includes a bedtime story does not only give children a reason to look forward to getting ready for bed, but it provides an opportunity for parents to bond with their children while simultaneously cementing a love for reading and imparting jewels of wisdom. Children absolutely love it when their parents read to them aloud! It's best to begin this bedtime tradition in early infancy and not to abandon it too soon. It has proven beneficial for parents to continue reading aloud to their children up to age 10 or 11. At this age, the benefit goes beyond preparing for sleep, but the parent is also modeling reading with prosody (rhythm/intonation) and fluency for their child.

Planning to read ten to fifteen minutes before bedtime goes a long way. It is a wonderful opportunity for our children to wind down while learning at the same time. A little study at bedtime is so important that Our Saviour, W. D. Fard Muhammad mentioned it in one of the 13 instructions given to the laborers. In His 8th instruction, it reads, *"ENGLISH LESSON NO. C1: Spelling must be used by all Muslim girls and mothers to their children for Bedtime Study; also, in regular Courses. Muslim girls must get away from reading that Devil's Bedtime Story to their children."*

Mother Tynnetta Muhammad said that English Lesson No. C1 should be read to our children as a bedtime story, helping them to separate truth from falsehood in everything they see and do. She wrote, *"Our true bedtime story, as contained in English Lesson Number C1, reveals the identity of Christ as manifested in the Person of Master W. Fard Muhammad coming under a disguise in His Divine Mission of the Resurrection of His dead people. So, our bedtime story is to awaken our children and our families from a deep sleep that has lasted thousands of years on our planet under the dominion of the White man's rule."*

English Lesson No. C1 consists of 36 lines – these sentences are written in the form of a conversation or dialogue. The lesson is a series of questions and answers which explain the plight of the Black man and woman in North America. It opens with an introduction by the Saviour and continues on to discuss how long we have been in North America and who brought us here. This lesson reveals our divine nature of righteousness and explains our insane attachment to our open enemy. It goes on to give our population count (at the time of the writing) and that of others. It also explains how the enemy managed to trick us by offering false promises and then kept us separated from our brothers and sisters in Africa. All of that and more is written in simple rhythmic language that our babies can easily absorb, read, memorize and understand.

English Lesson No. C1 is part of a larger body of knowledge that if understood provides a level of immunity against the madness our children encounter daily in the form of white supremacy. In *Closing the Gap*, the Honorable Minister Louis Farrakhan said, *"We live in America. We have no other nation to go to. We live in the world leader. We pull whatever we can and filter it through the placenta, or the blood of The Teachings of the Honorable Elijah Muhammad, that forms around us as a protection for us. What we draw from this satanic mother is filtered through this screening system called Actual Facts; Student Enrollment; Lesson No. 1; Lesson No. 2; the Problem Book and English Lesson #C1. The wisdom in these Lessons is the filter, so that through this filter we can take what we need from the larger system, as we develop our own system, hopefully somewhat free of that which is corrupting and destroying the larger system or body."*

We are instructed to get away from reading the Devil's bedtime stories to our children. The Devil is God's natural enemy; they are polar opposites. How can our children grow to become like God if they are nursing and feeding on the Devil's diet? His bedtime stories and nursery rhymes are filled with lies, fantasy, fairy tales, fabrications, impossibilities, and falsehoods. Falsehood destroys the beauty of a brain that was created to think rightly. God's bedtime story is 100% truth – supreme wisdom from the Supreme Being. Our children should fall asleep while having God and truth on the mind so that one day they will become masters of truth.

IT'S PLAYTIME!

Children need to play. Adults need to play. The benefits of play, recreation and participating in fun activities can easily be overlooked since

251

Black people, in particular, seem to constantly be in survival mode. Self-preservation is the first law of nature, so the primary purpose of every cell in our body is to survive. For most of us, this means that the vast majority of our time is spent finding a way to sustain life; which usually translates to providing food, clothing, and shelter for ourselves and our families – the basic essentials. However, we would argue that play is also essential for survival, maintenance, and fulfillment. Being overly stressed can lead to burnout, health complications, and early death.

Everyone needs to make time for play, but especially our children. Striving to be righteous and having fun are not mutually exclusive – we can do both. Our children have to be exposed to what we CAN do for enjoyment, instead of always focusing on the things that we cannot do. As parents, if we constantly harp on what we are not permitted to do, children begin to feel limited and restricted; and find it difficult to enjoy being righteous. We never want our children to believe that they have to be rigid soldiers 24/7. There is a time and place for order, structure, and regulation; and then there's a time to just run around freely. Children need opportunities to engage in both free play and organized play, like team sports and athletics.

The Honorable Minister Louis Farrakhan once expressed a bit of regret that when his children were young, he did not make the time to do the fun things with them that most parents do, like trips to amusement parks. He reminded us that The Most Honorable Elijah Muhammad told him to focus on the mission and not to worry about his family because Allah (God) would take care of them. The Minister said he took those instructions literally and sacrificed his time, money, musical ambitions and his family in order to focus entirely on the mission of the resurrection of our mentally dead brothers and sisters. To be clear, Allah (God) did take care of his family in the process; but The Honorable Minister Louis Farrakhan sacrificed his family so that we would not have to sacrifice ours. So today, he stresses that Allah (God) must be first in our lives, then family – then Nation.

So what activities should our children be encouraged to do for fun? Of course, there is the obvious – play outside with friends and siblings, go to the park and play at the playgrounds or just enjoy a leisure game of catch, frisbee, jumping rope, soccer, football, volleyball or basketball. Children should ride bicycles, skateboards, go swimming, bowling and roller-skating. But children should also experience and be exposed to museums, stage performances, the beach, concerts, fairs, and carnivals. Families should prioritize saving money to plan vacations away from home and truly experience their state, this country, and the world. There are actually wonderful tourist attractions right in the cities where we live that we take for granted. An occasional movie and playing video games are fine; but there is nothing wrong with planning trips to amusement parks, professional sporting events, camping, hiking or fishing.

In addition, extracurricular activities like organized team sports are great for our youth. Not only are sports great for their health, challenging them to stay physically active and to eat properly on a regular basis; but team sports reinforce basic fundamental life skills. Children learn self-discipline, teamwork, endurance, fair play, hard work, communication, limiting excuses, perseverance, competitiveness, comradery, leadership, time management, resilience, and self-esteem. All of these skills go beyond the court and the field, serving them socially and academically.

As parents, we must, however, keep sport and play right where it belongs. It is irrational to make team sports and athletic competitions more than what they are. Even if our children exhibit exceptional athletic abilities, they have a miniscule chance of becoming a professional athlete. And if they should become a professional athlete, the average age of retirement is 33 years! Then what? If retirement is at age 33, then their purpose in life cannot be to become a professional athlete. They must continue to focus on their aim and purpose for existence.

We must also, respect the fragility of human life. We have to show respect to the God who gave us this precious gift of life by not being careless with it. We were not granted life to be daredevils and reckless thrill seekers. So, as we attempt to restore balance and find things to do for "fun," recreation, and relaxation; we should avoid participating in activities that are exceedingly risky to life and limb.

There is so much to do and plenty to experience. We should work hard and play hard. The key is a balance. The toys we purchase for our children and the activities they engage in should not be trifling, foolish or mindless. We can have fun and learn at the same time. We can exercise and learn at the same time. We can be creative while learning. And we can explore and learn concurrently. In all we do, we should engage the mind, body, and soul. The Honorable Minister Louis Farrakhan said, *"What is fun? Fun is watching intelligence develop. Fun is feeding intelligence to create the creative mind that the child will be able to say like God, 'Be' and it is. That's fun!"*

FIXING THE PUBLIC-SCHOOL SYSTEM:

There is no denying the importance of a good home and educational environment to reinforce everything we have done up to this point. To put our children – no matter how physically, mentally or spiritually advanced they may be – in an environment contrary to their potential will make it increasingly difficult, if not improbable that they will continue on this path.

The subject of education really needs to be addressed since it has failed us terribly. The Honorable Minister Louis Farrakhan details this serious issue in his book, *A Torchlight for America*. He highlights nine key principles that must be inculcated into the public-school system in order to dramatically improve education outcomes. Before we risk our child's mental acuity and potential to reach their God-given purpose in life by placing him in just any school, we should use this check list to measure how close or distant the school is from meeting the following standard:

1. **PUT GOD FIRST**: This is a country that has the phrase, *"In God We Trust"* on its currency and makes everyone who testifies in court place his or her hand on the Bible and swear to tell the truth. Yet, there is no mention of God in the public-school system due to the so-called separation of church and state. This is hypocritical madness. The school day should begin and end with prayer, giving glory and praise to the One God who blessed men and women with the ability to receive and offer knowledge, wisdom, and understanding. The Honorable Minister Louis Farrakhan wrote, *"The knowledge of God is infinite. I would argue that leaving God out of our schools limits our education and confines the scope of what we are equipped to do and achieve."*

2. **TEACH THE TRUE KNOWLEDGE OF SELF AND OTHERS**: It is no secret that Latinos, Native Americans, and especially Black people are not taught the true knowledge of themselves in school and therefore have difficulty relating to the subjects being taught. If you are a Black child in a public school in America, you probably believe that your history began in 1619 because this is when we are introduced into the history books. Our accomplishments are portrayed as beginning when we were forced to these shores, which would mean that we haven't accomplished much

of anything compared to White people. The Most Honorable Elijah Muhammad said, *"If a man won't treat you right, he won't teach you right."* Minister Farrakhan writes, *"Every human being requires a knowledge of self as part of the proper cultivation of the divinity that is in them. Additionally, and if we hope to live together in peace with others in society, we must know something of the cultures that make up this so-called melting pot."*

3.   **HONOR THE PROFESSION OF TEACHING**: It is because of teachers that we have doctors, engineers, politicians, construction workers, lawyers, architects, etc. However, all are monetarily compensated more than teachers. And let's not forget athletes and entertainers who are honored far more because of what they can do physically than mentally. So why work on the mind when we can make millions in this country for dunking a basketball? We cannot express it any clearer than our teacher, The Honorable Minister Louis Farrakhan who wrote, *"Teachers must be compensated commensurate with their role in society. We have to restore honor among those who choose and are employed in this noble profession. Better compensation of education professionals at the public-school level can help us attract and retain those whose talent is otherwise channeled into corporate America and other endeavors that pay more and provide lifestyles that are treated with respect and honor. In so doing, the school system can be more selective and use only those teachers who have a genuine love for people and a desire to bring the best out of children."*

4.   **FOCUS   ON   RAISING   STANDARDS, PARTICULARLY IN MATH AND SCIENCE**: In the Nation of Islam, we are taught that *"Mathematics is Islam and Islam is Mathematics."* Well, what is Islam? Islam is, entire submission to do the Will of Allah (God). The

Originator of the Heavens and the Earth had to master science and mathematics in order to create all that we see and don't see. Any profession or way of life we choose will require us to use science and mathematics because it is a part of our nature and the Universe out of which we came. American students rank at the bottom in science and mathematics compared to other industrialized nations. More emphasis needs to be placed on these universal subjects if we intend to compete with the rest of the world.

5.　　**HOLD CLASSES YEAR-ROUND**:　The question is: When our child is not in school or studying, where is he and what is he doing? An idle mind is the devil's workshop. In most public schools, children are given three months out of the year to do absolutely nothing academically. When they return to the next grade level, much is forgotten from what was learned the prior school year. All public and private schools should hold classes year-round to encourage our youth to never stop learning and advancing.

6.　　**SEPARATE SCHOOLS FOR BOYS AND GIRLS**: The male and female are not somewhat different, but they are completely different. Each gender must be taught and trained according to his or her nature. Because we are so unalike, we naturally have a strong attraction to one another, which causes unnecessary distractions in the classroom. An extra effort must be made to ensure that the school for girls is equal to the boys with respect to the level of knowledge acquired and eventual pursuits of God-given potential. The Honorable Minister Louis Farrakhan wrote, *"You can't deprive women of higher learning and produce a great nation."*

7.　　**HAVE A DRESS CODE**: Every school should have a uniform that each student must conform to. There is so much unnecessary pressure put on children to have name-brand clothes or expensive shoes. Added pressure is on young girls to have the latest hairstyles, expensive jewelry, flawless make-up, and manicured nails. School has become a fashion show where one is ridiculed for not wearing high-end clothes and hurt or robbed for having it all. The focus has moved from receiving a good education to just trying to fit in socially. That type of environment is completely changed when everyone is required to look the same, right down to the fabric and color. The Honorable Minister Louis Farrakhan wrote, *"A dress code is a protection for you in that you gain the peace of mind from knowing that others have to conform to a code as well as yourself."*

8.   **ESTABLISH DISCIPLINE VIA A PARENT-TEACHER PARTNERSHIP**: Parents – we must get to know our child's teacher and educators, then become actively involved in what they are learning, so that what our children learn in school can be reinforced at home. Do not wait for a report card to find out their status – by then it may be too late. The teacher should be informing the parent on a regular basis about the student's progress or lack thereof – both academically and behaviorally. If the teacher is not diligent, then as parents, we must seek them out at every opportunity. We should be aware when our child is due to have a test, a fieldtrip, a presentation and even the details of daily assignments. The student should also be fully aware that the parent and the teacher are working together for his or her benefit.

9.   **CREATE SCHOOL SAFETY**: It is an absolute shame that our children have to go through metal detectors before entering the school building. Students and teachers should never have to go to school fearful of losing their lives. But metal detectors and armed security do not solve the

real problem. We have a lack of avenues available to our young brothers, in particular, to channel their natural aggression and their need to assert their manhood. The Black community just does not have adequate athletic facilities, league sports and camps like those found in wealthy communities. This leaves violence as the number one way to exert backed-up energy.

Depending on where we live, these nine prerequisites for our child's school may seem years away from becoming a reality. This helps us to understand one of the reasons why education reform advocates say, *"Education should begin twenty years before the child is born."*

The Honorable Minister Louis Farrakhan stated – once you have a mental giant, you should not take that mental giant and put him or her in the enemy's school. It really makes no sense to put a god in the hands of a devil to be educated. We can no longer permit this and must be willing to make the required sacrifices. Until a proper school is established, it may be better that our children are homeschooled; rather than to have to be deprogrammed every time they come home. Unfortunately, the curriculum is often tainted with lies, which are used to maintain the status quo. Children need truth in order to work towards establishing the Kingdom of God.

Homeschooling is not the ideal nor the goal, but it is a good temporary fix if we do not have a quality school in our area. Homeschooling must be well structured. A few hours a day should be devoted to learning – assignments, tests, projects, exploration, presentations, etc. Children must be taught math and science; geography, history, literacy, foreign languages, etc. The home should be organized around education. Homeschooling is no longer a phenomenon in the United States. There is so much information at our fingertips that can be accessed online to both instruct our children and/or guide the parents. For those parents who just do not have the time, resources, energy, discipline, education or willingness to put towards becoming their child's instructor; then find someone who does, until a suitable school is established in your community.

The Honorable Minister Louis Farrakhan wrote, *"Education must teach us to master the sciences. If education does not prepare the human being to do what Allah (God) intended for us to do, then, it is not the proper education for us."*

SINGLE-SEX SCHOOLS:

According to a recent study (August 2018) published by the *Proceedings of the National Academy of Sciences of the United States of America (PNAS)*, entitled "Patient-Physician Gender Concordance and Increased Mortality Among Female Heart Attack Patients" – female heart attack patients had a significantly higher survival rate when a woman physician treated them in the ER. This study covered a span of 19 years and 582,000 heart attack cases. Male patients faired relatively the same whether the physician was a man or a woman, but there was a stark increase in survival for female patients who had women doctors instead of men. As one writer put it, *"If you're having a heart attack and you're a woman, hope a female doctor greets you in the emergency room."*

This study is particularly relevant in a time when society is on an accelerated pace to all but eliminate any differences between the sexes – the prevailing message being that one's biology does not have to align with one's identity. However, according to this research, during a life and death emergency trauma; the one factor that could make all the difference is, biology. There are similar studies in medicine that prove the benefit of patient-physician concordance in gender as well as race. We also find this benefit experienced in other social institutions – employment, law enforcement, housing, politics, and **education**.

According to **The Muslim Program: What the Muslims Want**, Point No. 9 reads, *"We want equal education – but separate schools up to 16 for boys and 18 for girls on the condition that the girls be sent to women's colleges and universities. We want all Black children educated, taught and trained by their own teachers. Under such schooling system we believe we will make a better nation of people. The United States government should provide, free, all necessary textbooks and equipment, school and college buildings. The Muslim teachers shall be left free to teach and train their people in the way of righteousness, decency and self-respect."*

The Most Honorable Elijah Muhammad mentions separate schools, and in addition, he emphasizes a special condition that the girls attend women's colleges and universities. He does not include this condition for the boys. As with healthcare, gender concordance in education leads to a special advantage and benefit experienced by girls at a higher rate than boys. The Most Honorable Elijah Muhammad wanted our women and girls respected and protected, but he also wanted them highly educated. He envisioned women flying planes, navigating ships and serving as ambassadors. All endeavors are available for women to pursue; he only did not want women to participate in those fields that would degrade them.

America's legacy of slavery, racism, bigotry, white supremacy and sexism has not spared anyone – all have been affected. This makes the ideal learning environment for our children to be one that reflects their individual history, experiences, and their nature.

In his book, *A Torchlight for America*, The Honorable Minister Louis Farrakhan outlines several key components that must be implemented to fix the public-school system. One such component is to have separate schools for boys and girls. He writes, *"We must understand that the natures of men and women are different, and that therefore we need separate schools for boys and girls through high school. In my view, it's intellectual cowardice not to recognize and act wisely concerning the differences between the sexes...We can all see that the female is not like the male. But it's deeper than that. Because of the difference between the sexes, if we hope to truly develop the person, the school has to train him according to the nature that God gave him and train her according to the nature that God gave her."*

When single-sex schools function properly, not only are our children free from the distractions that come with too much intermingling with the opposite sex; but the students significantly outperform their coed peers in all subject areas. Students are also far more confident, so girls find it easier to gravitate towards math and sciences in single-sex schools, while boys are not intimidated by literature. The learning style differences between boys and girls have long been researched and documented, right down to the difference in response to classroom temperature and discipline. One's learning environment is directly related to their academic performance. Girls and boys, particularly in primary school, respond to subjects differently depending on the time of day the instruction takes places. According to researchers, some other notable differences are that boys generally need more individual space while learning and require an allowance for movement. Girls are documented to benefit from collaborative and cooperative activities and lessons while learning. Boys are also found to be single-task oriented while girls are natural multitaskers.

The two greatest objections to single-sex schools are that these schools make it more difficult to have positive interactions between the sexes; and secondly, separate schools will not be equally advantageous for girls. Both arguments are important, but the research finds no legitimacy to either claim. Regular daily interactions between the sexes continue whether or not children attend single-sex schools. Children must still interact with their parents, siblings, other relatives, neighborhood friends, sales clerks, coaches, restaurant employees, etc., half of whom are of the opposite sex.

As for being equally advantageous for girls: Girls thrive in single-sex schools and are not intimidated by a rigorous curriculum. The encouragement, attentiveness, and relatability from other girls make a huge difference. For this reason, single-sex schools for girls dare them to excel. It is a sin for a woman to be ignorant since a nation can rise no higher than its woman. If she is deprived of advanced learning, what kind of nation will we produce? You teach a woman, you teach a nation.

So, let's end the debate on whether boys and girls learn differently – they do! The Holy Qur'an is clear, *"And the male is not like the female..."* (3: 35). Boys and girls have distinct biological, neurological and psychological differences. So, yes girls can do anything boys can do, but they do it differently. Now what's important is that educators, particularly in coed schools, understand and accept this fact. Educators must align their curriculum and teaching styles so male and female students can reach their full God-given potential and purpose. The Most Honorable Elijah Muhammad said that after our children have been educated separately by sex, *"Then they could and should seek higher education without the danger of losing respect for self or seeking to lose their identity"* (Message to the Blackman in America).

PLUTO SIGNALS A NEW EDUCATIONAL PARADIGM:

The Most Honorable Elijah Muhammad said the whole scope of the Teachings of Master Fard Muhammad is *astronomy*. Everywhere the Most Honorable Elijah Muhammad established a mosque, he also established a school – Muhammad University of Islam (MUI). Universities typically serve students who have completed high school and are moving on to "higher" education. The Muhammad University of Islam is not a university in that sense; it educates students as young as three years old through high school. But he named it right!

Before his departure in 1975, the Most Honorable Elijah Muhammad made serious moves towards establishing the university-level of MUI. His plans were all laid out in the Muhammad Speaks newspaper. He made a down payment of one million dollars towards purchasing the land that now houses the South Shore Cultural Center (formerly the South Shore Country Club) in Chicago. The arrangement was to purchase the land for ten million dollars. Ultimately the City of Chicago rescinded and returned the million-dollar down payment. The Most Honorable Elijah Muhammad was also in negotiations to purchase Tuskegee Institute in Alabama. Why? He foresaw the critical need to establish a new educational paradigm that would emerge from these institutions – a system of education that was not based in white supremacy or even Afrocentricity; but rooted in and centered on divine revelation direct from the Source – Allah (God) Himself.

From the moment White people permitted us to read, we have been intentionally mis-educated which continues today – take it or leave it. The enemy clearly understands that two things cannot occupy the same space at the same time. So, they will never teach us the sciences that lead to rulership, lest we supplant their rule. One must be completely oblivious to societal ills or extremely arrogant to concede that we have received, and our children are receiving a preeminent education of the highest caliber. This level of knowledge and wisdom just does not exist outside of the mind of God. We applaud our diligent teachers and educators who have long declared a need to develop a curriculum that incorporates Afrocentricity, reconnecting us to our

African roots and teaching our children the truth about Black contributions to world civilizations and intellectual advancements. Teaching self-love and Black pride are absolutely necessary; but we do not have to look far to acknowledge that with all its righteous intentions, this too is simply not enough.

The Most Honorable Elijah Muhammad entered, but never completed the fourth grade of school; so, in essence, he had a third-grade education. His Teacher, Master Fard Muhammad, taught him night and day for three years and four months before departing in 1935; and what He taught him continues to confound the wise of this world. Publicly they may make a mockery of these Teachings to keep the masses away from the Most Honorable Elijah Muhammad and the Honorable Minister Louis Farrakhan, but secretly they are using everything Master Fard Muhammad taught to try to extend their time to rule.

Our Supreme Wisdom Lessons teach, *"The Universe is everything – Sun, Moon and Stars. They are planets. Planets are something grown or made from the beginning."* Master Fard Muhammad established Islam in North America in 1930, the same year that the planet, Pluto was "discovered." The Book of Habakkuk reads, *"He stood, and measured the earth: He beheld, and drove asunder the nations; and the everlasting mountains were scattered, the perpetual hills did bow: His ways are everlasting"* (3:6, KJV). Master Fard Muhammad taught the Most Honorable Elijah Muhammad the measurements of the earth and its waters; including, the oceans, the hills and mountains, the lakes and rivers, the islands and deserts, the weight of the earth, the speed of light and sound, the diameter of the sun, and so much more. These Lessons also included a brief synopsis of all nine planets. Ever since the measurements of the universe were unveiled in the early 1930s, this world's scientists have gotten closer and closer to the numbers that God revealed. The only exception is the planet, Platoon (Pluto).

If we reflect on our lessons in school about the solar system, we may recall that we were taught that Pluto was the farthest planet from the Sun and also the smallest planet in our solar system. The former is accurate, but the latter is false. Pluto is 4,600,000,000 miles from the Sun, which in-fact makes it the farthest planet from the Sun. It is so far from the Sun that only a small amount of light can strike it – yet it is just enough light to fuel it to travel (rotate) at the same rate of speed as all of the other planets – 1,037 1/3 miles per hour. However, according to what we are expected to believe from today's science teachers, Pluto is very small – smaller than the Earth's moon. These teachers are confined to the publicized research from NASA scientists, who proclaim that she is so small, that as of 2006 she was no longer worthy of a full planet classification status and has since been demoted to a dwarf planet. We emphatically disagree with this downgrade and their publicized measurements!

According to what the Master Teacher revealed to the Most Honorable Elijah Muhammad; not only is Pluto much bigger than the Earth's moon, she is bigger than every planet except Saturn and Jupiter. Yes, Pluto is actually the third largest planet in our solar system! Her diameter measures 67,000 miles, making her nearly eight-and-a-half times larger than the Earth! Let that sink in. We agree, her distance is far indeed, so it takes her 345 **years** to make one complete circle around the Sun. Whereas it only takes the Earth 365 ¼ **days** to circumambulate the Sun. So, all of those solar system models we have all seen and may have created ourselves, are clearly not drawn to scale because Pluto exceeds the Earth in size by far.

So, what is going on here? Either NASA is outright lying about Pluto, which is not a stretch because NASA has withheld many of the details surrounding the moon landing, its knowledge of UFOs, the existence of life on every planet (seven of which are inhabited), and more – Or, Allah (God) will not permit the enemy to have an unobstructed view of the planet to ascertain its precise measurements. He says in the Holy Qur'an 2:255, *"...And they encompass nothing of His knowledge except what He pleases. His knowledge extends over the heavens and the earth, and the preservation of them both tires Him not."* Either way, what is being taught concerning the measurements of Pluto is exceedingly inaccurate. So, what is the point?

In a world ruled by the enemy of God, the truth is stranger than fiction. The fact is, we could have chosen any one of dozens of aspects of the Teachings of the Most Honorable Elijah Muhammad to make the same argument: *The current system of education in the United States is incredibly inadequate and wholly ineffective to produce gods.* It is not only wrapped in white supremacy, but Pluto is one of many signs that White people are misreading the anatomy of the universe, and we are being forced to accept science based in faulty math or outright deception. God is offering us a seat in His classroom and an opportunity for us to study at His knee and learn the science of everything. We are currently nursing from an educational system that will not even be a part of the new world. We must submit to a new educational paradigm!

In his book, Education is the Key, the Honorable Minister Louis Farrakhan wrote, *"Education is the key. But the scripture says, 'How can they know except they have a teacher, and how can they have a teacher except he be sent?' The slave-master is not going to send you a teacher to free you from him. Allah (God) will send you a teacher. The question is, 'Will you be wise enough to recognize the Hand of Allah (God) moving in your midst?'"*

THE NATIONAL ANTHEM & OUR YOUTH:

Most primary and secondary schools in the United States begin the school day with the Pledge of Allegiance. Students are asked to stand and face the United States flag; put their right hand to their heart and recite the pledge. If you attend public schools in the State of Texas, the United States pledge is followed by a pledge of allegiance to the Texas flag [yep, Texas has its own pledge]. After both pledges, there is one-minute of silence. During that one-minute of silence, *"Each student may, as the student chooses, reflect, pray, meditate, or engage in any other silent activity that is not likely to interfere with or distract another student"* (Texas Education Code). In addition, most public schools also include the singing of The Star-Spangled Banner (National Anthem) at the start of school-affiliated major events like graduation ceremonies, athletic competitions, and specialty programs.

The masses of Black and Brown children in the United States are not enrolled in private schools which have the freedom of independent curriculum, expectations, and daily operations. This puts the majority of our people in a conundrum when faced with the dilemma of participating (or not) in the Pledge of Allegiance and the National Anthem. In the name of so-called patriotism and promotion of American exceptionalism, our children are being forced to listen to, recite and promote outright lies.

The U.S. pledge of allegiance has been changed over the course of time, but currently, it reads, *"I pledge allegiance to the flag of the United States of America and to the Republic for which it stands, one Nation under God, indivisible, with liberty and justice for all."* A Republic built with slave labor and undergirded by white supremacy is in no way submitting to the rule of God; its divided upon inception and is incapable of providing liberty and justice for all. It is hypocritical and absurd to require any Black, Brown or oppressed group to ever utter these words in school or at any time.

The National Anthem is worse. In his August 2016 letter to Colin Kaepernick, The Honorable Minister Louis Farrakhan wrote, *"Your stand has unearthed things about Francis Scott Key and the writing of the lyrics of the Star-Spangled Banner, that would make any person of right thinking and right mind cringe at what was in the mind of the man that wrote the words of the Star-Spangled Banner."* The Star-Spangled Banner, a.k.a. National Anthem, is blantantly racist and unapologetically hateful of Black people. Americans who choose to sing the anthem must accept that the lyrics they are belting out express America's love of slavery. Most notably, in the third stanza (of four) the lyrics read in part, *"Their blood has washed out their foul footsteps' pollution | No refuge could save the hireling and slave | From the terror of flight, or the gloom of the grave."* Francis Scott Key was a virulent racist. He wanted this specific section included so everyone would know how much he loathed the fact that Black people had the gall to fight for their personal freedom.

With this as a backdrop, if our children attend a school where the Pledge of Allegiance is recited or the National Anthem is sung, how should we, as parents guide them? First, we must make sure they have read every word of the pledge and anthem and understand the meaning behind its historical context. Secondly, they should understand that America's flag is a symbol without substance. It has never represented freedom, justice, and equality for Black, Brown and oppressed people. Provide evidence to show children how we continue to be discriminated against, brutalized, dismissed and murdered while "Old Glory" is idolized and worshiped. But ultimately, we must also follow the guidance of The Honorable Minister Louis Farrakhan.

CHILDREN OF THE MOST HIGH

During an interview on Meet the Press several years ago, the late David Broder, a Washington Post columnist, asked The Honorable Minister Louis Farrakhan to share what it was in the words of the Pledge of Allegiance that he found impossible to say. The Minister responded, *"'Liberty and justice for all' is one. As a Muslim, I cannot give my all to the symbol of a government, no matter what that government is. As a Muslim, I give my allegiance only to God. And I submit to the laws that govern this land, as long as those laws do not conflict with my religion. That is a basic principle of my belief, and there are many American citizens who subscribe to faiths other than Islam who will not pledge allegiance to the flag. I will never disrespect that flag. I don't agree with flag burnings. I don't agree with draping the flag of an independent and sovereign nation over toilets. I don't believe in anyone not respecting the flag of this sovereign nation. And whenever 'The Star-Spangled Banner' is played, even though I will not pledge allegiance, I stand in respect. That is the best that I can give to the flag, is respect..."*

As a people, we hope to one day establish an independent sovereign Nation of our own, so The Most Honorable Elijah Muhammad teaches his followers to stand, out of respect for that which we hope to one day become. This is the way we should also guide our children. We should stand when the pledge is recited, and we should stand when the anthem is played. However, we DO NOT salute the United States flag; we DO NOT place our hand over our heart to honor the flag; we DO NOT recite the words of the pledge or sing the national anthem; and we certainly DO NOT give our allegiance to ANY flag, symbol or country. We will find in the word "allegiance" the word "all." As a Believer – Muslim, Christian, or Jew, our *'all'* should only be given to Allah (God). We bow only to Allah (God). This is the way of the righteous.

We must, however, continue to stress the bigger picture. As the Honorable Minister Louis Farrakhan told Colin Kaepernick, *"I stand with you. We in the Nation of Islam stand with you.*" And we continue to stand with and support those who choose to kneel in protest of police brutality and all other racial injustices. We, more than anyone understand why so many of our people choose to kneel or sit; and can easily defend their right to do so. They are true patriots; calling attention to America's wickedness so that she may atone and correct herself. However, there will come a time sooner rather than later when we will all be forced to reckon with the reality that no matter how much we kneel, sit, protest, march or vote; America will never be good, and she must be judged accordingly by Allah (God). The Kingdom of God on earth *will* be established; Allah (God) *will* be the sole ruler; the righteous *will* inherit the earth; and the greatest and the only flag of the Universe – the Sun, Moon, and Star *will* reign supreme!

THE SIGNIFICANCE OF AGE 6:

The beauty of the Nation of Islam is that we bear witness to all universal truths wherever they may be found. It does not matter if it is found in the Torah, the Gospel or the Holy Qur'an. It could have been spoken by Abraham, Moses, Jesus or Muhammad – we just love the truth. As so-called "religious" people, we also have no conflict with any of the natural sciences, mathematics or metaphysics. We accept that we are bound by all universal laws. In fact, we are taught that Mathematics is Islam and Islam is Mathematics and *"you can always prove it at no limit of time."* The purpose of God's coming was to make us perfect representatives of Himself. The scriptures bear witness that at some point in time the human being will be perfected. Since our nature is the same as the nature of God, we know we have that potential. He came to teach us the science of EVERYTHING – so that we can become like Him – a god!

CHILDREN OF THE MOST HIGH

The Most Honorable Elijah Muhammad teaches that all of the numbers have meanings – most have multiple meanings. The Bible says that the heavens and the earth were created in six days and the Holy Qur'an says Allah (God) created the heavens and the earth in six periods. Not only is the physical composition of the human being from the earth; but our spiritual divinity and mental acuity come from the heavens.

The Honorable Minister Louis Farrakhan said, *"The Honorable Elijah Muhammad said, 'As the shortest distance between two points is a straight line.' So, it is in education. The child should know at six years old what its future is. What it wants to do with its life. If it engages in mindless foolishness and triviality it will not get in tune with itself to know at six where it wants to go. The Honorable Elijah Muhammad said, 'At eighteen years of age, we should have finished our doctorate degree, ready to go out into the world to practice that which we have learned in theory. So, if you get a doctorate degree at eighteen, how much time do you have for mindless activity? None. God does not waste time. Neither should we."* (Closing the Gap, p. 373)

So, the standard is God Himself. Being reared for centuries under the burden and trauma of white supremacy, blatant racism and systemic manipulation of our genius makes it understandably difficult to accept that we could accomplish the above said with ease. The reality is that getting a doctorate degree at the age of eighteen is actually child's play when you compare it to what we once accomplished before we were tampered with. We are taught that *The Original Man is the Asiatic Black Man; the Maker; the Owner; the Cream of the Planet Earth – God of the Universe.* Our ancestors were responsible for putting the moon into orbit along with the stars and all the planets. Allah (God) gives us many signs of our original greatness – He shows us in the scriptures; throughout nature; by the handiwork of past civilizations; and by raising brilliant ones among us.

For example: Look at the great pyramids in Egypt – we could have buried them or destroyed them, but they were left as a sign of our mastery. It's 2018 and still, the best architects, archeologists, and Egyptologists can only speculate as to how these massive structures were built – the theories are never ending. Not only did Black people construct the pyramids with stones that weighed from 2 to 30 tons each, but the pyramids were aligned with the stars. Originally, these stones were so well polished, you could see your reflection. The Most Honorable Elijah Muhammad said that Master Fard Muhammad told him how the pyramids were built, but he would not share it because, in our current condition, we would do nothing with that knowledge; however, the enemy would use that type of wisdom to remain in power forever. Even more fascinating…As mysterious as the pyramids are, they were built during the time of our fall, not at the peak of our greatness. I heard Student Minister Ava Muhammad say, *"If these were our graves; imagine what our homes looked like!"*

We are in the midst of an evolution and revolution to reclaim our greatness, so we must get back to our natural timetable and not be retarded by the enemy's developmental milestones that he put in place for himself, not for the Original Man. After all, he is very new to the earth. The Teachings of the Most Honorable Elijah Muhammad bear witness that the age of six is a powerful time for the Original child. It was at the age of six that Master Fard Muhammad saw Himself *"pushing the Fords, the DuPonts and the Rockefellers into a lake of fire. At six years of age, He came into the Knowledge of Who He was."* In the book, *Message to the Blackman in America*, we learn that Yakub, the Father of the white race, was the founder of unalike attracts and like repels. At the age of six, *"he was sitting down*

273

playing with two pieces of steel. He noticed the magnetic power in the steel attracting the other...He learned his future from playing with steel" (p.111-112). And what about Mary and Joseph, who *"promised to marry when they were going to school at the age of 6..."* (Our Saviour Has Arrived, p. 159). The rest, of course, is history.

The Honorable Minister Louis Farrakhan said, *"In the very nature of the human being is the potential to subdue the earth. This means that we have the potential to bring the earth completely under our power by mastering the laws under which the earth and all therein are created."* An elite few have discovered and achieved their true godly potential; but sadly, the masses do not have a clue. Allah (God) gives us signs of our true potential in common people. We have all heard of people with genius-level intellectual skills; or child music prodigies; perhaps a person with computer-like memory; maybe one who can read thoughts; or even a person who practices telekinesis. There are many among us who are born with these gifts as a sign to the rest of us that we all have the potential to reach these extraordinary heights. All of this can be studied, learned, practiced and mastered.

Several years ago, a Sister who had young children, was desirous of beginning a new career and asked Mother Tynnetta Muhammad when she should return to school to pursue her studies toward that goal. Mother Tynnetta Muhammad said that she should wait until her youngest child reached the age of six. Mothers, in particular, have to be around physically and emotionally to not only create the proper nurturing environment to draw out what God already put in our children; but to also be able to recognize the gift when we see it. This takes tremendous sacrifice and discipline. If we are overly consumed with accomplishing our personal goals and desires; along with the other demands of life, we may miss it.

We begin teaching our children in the womb; but when they are born, exposure is everything. The baby is born knowing nothing, but in him/her is the nature of God, which desires to know **everything** – so all types of learning are fun for the new life. We should expose our children to mathematics, languages, music, colors, textures, animals, plants, geography, etc. We should buy toys that challenge development, motor skills, dexterity, creativity, and critical thinking. The law of nature suggests, *'What you don't use (or abuse), you lose.'* The earlier our children being to stimulate and exercise their brains, the more likely they are to be able to access other realms of possibilities.

The brain of a baby through the age of six experiences rapid growth and development – almost anything can be learned during this critical period of brain development. What takes place during these years is significant for the brain to fully develop in later years. The brain was created to think right, so falsehood goes against the grain, ruining the brain's capacity to operate on the highest level. Animals and plants do not talk; and certainly, inanimate objects do not talk – but this is the falsehood that our children are continuously fed, through books, toys, television, and movies. It will take loving, determined and resourceful parents to not only provide the proper cognitive stimuli for their children but also the best physical nourishment and spiritual guidance – each influences the others.

So, by the age of six, when this world says that our children should begin the first grade, we are starting our children on the road to developing their purpose in life. An exceptional child will be able to communicate exactly what they intend to do with their life at this young age. However, most children will exhibit a special skill, talent, gift or interest. It is up to the parents to properly interpret this ability and create a conducive environment that will encourage its growth and development, eventually leading the child to fully master his or her divine purpose in life.

Well, what should we do if our children do not know or do not exhibit their purpose by the age of six; or perhaps we were not in-tuned enough to recognize it? If that's the case, we should give them a purpose. The Honorable Minister Louis Farrakhan said that we look foolish asking our small children, *'What do you want to be when you grow up?'* If they have not told us or showed us; then we tell them. We need to establish a Nation of our own. Everything that a nation has, we need – but we need God at the center of it. We are to choose a Nation-building discipline for our child and guide the direction of their life in accordance with that purpose. The goal is for them to master a particular discipline and pursue it to the fullest as they mature and use the skills acquired for the benefit of themselves and their Nation. But, either way, their journey towards fulfilling their purpose in life should begin at the great age of six. *"Blessed is the man or woman that finds their purpose in life and fulfills it."*

BLACK EXCELLENCE:

The Honorable Minister Louis Farrakhan asked the question: Do you know how to end White racism? He answered by saying, *"Black excellence destroys White racism."* For centuries, there has been a deliberate and concerted effort to maintain white supremacy by hiding, co-opting and destroying all signs of Black excellence. In *Message to the Blackman in America*, The Most Honorable Elijah Muhammad shared the words spoken by Henry Berry, while speaking in the Virginia House of Delegates in 1832 – *"We have, as far as possible, closed every avenue by which light might enter their [slaves'] minds; we have only to go one step further – to extinguish the capacity to see the light, and our work would be completed; they would then be reduced to the level of the beasts of the field and we should be safe…"*

Safe from whom and what? The enemy clearly understands that the laws of physics transcend the laboratory and are applicable in all dimensions. One such law states…***two objects cannot occupy the same space at the same time.*** Contextual translation: Black people and white people cannot both be in power in America concurrently. Therefore, in order to remain "safe" or in power, the enemy's 1832 proclamation must continue. However, the Most Honorable Elijah Muhammad emphatically declared to the enemy, *"The avenue of the light of Allah (God) you are unable to shut out from coming to us."*

Everything in nature has a natural enemy, including God. Generations of our people have been unnecessarily sacrificed due to our insistence that our natural enemy will change his natural ways. We have been foolish to hope that he can be reformed. Our steadfast pursuit to eliminate racism in this manner has proven utterly futile. The Honorable Minister Louis Farrakhan said that racism will cease when Black excellence becomes the norm. He said, *"White racism and oppression should not be used as an excuse for lack of Black achievement, in fact, it should be used as fuel to bring out the greatness that lies within."* In other words, *"White oppression should make Black genius."*

The standard in every Black home should be excellence. The expectation of excellence in everything that we do must be inculcated in our children from the womb. Weaved within every fiber of our way of life should be the highest level of excellence, mastery, and distinction. We should never get comfortable with just being average. We should never settle for mediocrity or for that matter, second place. It is counterintuitive to be a direct descendant of God and at the same time believe yourself inferior to other people.

Black children should be taught from birth that they are the Righteous, the Best and the Powerful. We should train them to be the top students at the school – whether it's kindergarten penmanship or high school Calculus. C-students are average, B-students are good, but an A-student is excellent. Every A-student should then strive for 100% in all subjects which is considered complete mastery. After all, our children are gods! Not only should our children strive for excellence in academics, but also in their extracurricular activities: sports, drill, piano, stage performances, debate, martial arts, etc. Their commitment level to these disciplines should reflect a desire to achieve excellence. Even their assigned household chores should not be done haphazardly – they should be taught to pay attention to detail and not give their parents any reason to gripe. Parents must serve as examples for their children that the standard is no less than excellent with regards to our behavior, our manners, and our language.

If the standard of excellence is firmly established, we will see it reflected in whatever field of endeavor our children choose because they will be the Best at it! However, Black parents have to encourage their children to pursue challenging fields of study – Nation building disciplines. Remember, they are gods! The Honorable Minister Louis Farrakhan has visited countless college campuses and has always challenged students to declare majors in math, science, engineering, and agriculture. Liberal arts colleges and majors like psychology, sociology and African-American studies were intentionally designed to oppose Black intellectual focus towards mastering those disciplines which will allow us to build a Nation within a nation.

During the *State of the Black World Conference in New Orleans* (2008), The Honorable Minister Louis Farrakhan stated, *"To see us always in*
278

a begging stance, to see us always in a dependent stance feeds the notion of white supremacy. It's very difficult to feed that notion when Black excellence is on the scene. That's what you represent, Black excellence. But those of us who represent Black excellence are too few to stem the mounting tide of what is moving against the rise of our people."

Black excellence in every field of endeavor will be the death knell of white supremacy and racism – it simply cannot be sustained if Black excellence is everywhere because everyone would be constantly reminded at every turn that white people are not superior. The enemy will no longer be effective at stealing our songs, our inventions or appropriating our culture because he will be overwhelmed by the constant emergence of Black excellence coming out of every nook and cranny of society; not just in entertainment and sports – but from the sciences, medicine, education, law, agriculture, government, business, technology and media.

Every racist will be forced to bear witness that Black people are not now, nor were we ever three-fifths of a human being; but we are direct descendants of God Himself. They will be forced to bear witness that their former slaves actually descend from the most intelligent and advanced scientists and builders on the continent of Africa and not from savages. They will be forced to denounce every so-called study that promotes the lie that Black people are less intelligent than white people. Jews will be forced to admit that the Hamitic curse is an outright intentional lie and declare that Black people are in fact the chosen people of God. All will be forced to submit to a new educational paradigm, new leadership, and a new reality, all bathed in Black excellence.

THE SOUND OF MUSIC:

Nope, this section is NOT about the 1965 musical, starring Julie Andrews as the singing nun, who brings warmth and music into the home of the Von Trapp Family. But this section is about the incredible effects that music can have on the brain and the body.

You may have heard of the Mozart effect: *"A term that has been applied to the controversial conclusions from various research groups that listening to Mozart's music may make a person more intelligent. The effect, if real, has been attributed to short-term improvement in performing mental tasks that require spatial-temporal reasoning."* This concept, introduced in the early nineties, has led to several additional studies and books analyzing the correlation between classical music and brain development. The idea is that listening to certain types of music, particularly for infants and children, will lead to higher intelligence, primarily in the areas of math, memory, and language. The research is convincing, but while listening to classical music may be mentally advantageous, even more, impressive cognitive benefits are found when one actively learns how to play, read and create music.

The Most Honorable Elijah Muhammad said that music, medicine and the science of color are at the root or essence of God's true religion. The Honorable Minister Louis Farrakhan stated that he also said, *"Those who understood or knew music, medicine and the science of color would make his best ministers."* Music is not a man-made invention, only his discovery. Music – melodic sounds, rhythms, vibrations, and harmony have always existed, as they originated simultaneously with Allah's (God's) glorious creation.

No one was more attuned to the power of music than Mother Tynnetta Muhammad, who was not only one of our wisest scholars but also a self-taught musical genius. Her studies unveiled that the genetic coding of our DNA is linked to music. According to Mother Tynnetta Muhammad, *"We are all composed of the frequencies and vibrations of sound, light and the chemistry of our atomic and subatomic structure in space time. If we were able to properly apply this science, we would be able to heal ourselves completely of all illnesses and diseases."* So, the application of music not only stimulates brain activity but can also heal the body. This knowledge has led to the burgeoning field of musical therapy.

According to Harvard Medical School, there is now evidence that music is not just mentally therapeutic, but physically healing. Their research attests that music therapy improves invasive procedures, including lowering the use of opioid painkillers. Music therapy has helped to restore lost speech; it reduces the side effects of cancer treatment; it aids in pain relief, and it improves the quality of life for dementia patients. Additional studies have shown that music has beneficial effects on the heart rate, blood pressure, and the entire cardiovascular system. Extensive research by Fabien Maman reveals, *"Human blood cells respond to sound frequencies by changing color and shape. These findings demonstrate sick or rogue cells can be healed or harmonized with sound."* A similar study by Dr. Claudius Conrad found that patients' brains released 50 percent more pituitary growth hormones with music, which reduces inflammation and promotes healing.

For those particularly in the Black community who may have an aversion to classical music, it is important to disabuse ourselves of the notion that this is "white folks" music. Music, like mathematics, is a universal language. Furthermore, white people are guilty of stealing, repackaging and successfully selling classical music, opera, and ballet to the world as being exclusively European with white origins. The truth is that these artistic expressions are all a part of a massive stolen legacy from Black Africans which also included literature, architecture, science and a host of inventions.

The Honorable Minister Louis Farrakhan is a classically-trained violinist who was introduced to the violin at the age of five. He gave up playing the violin professionally and the entertainment industry as a whole just a few months after becoming a registered member of the Nation of Islam in the mid-1950s. However, he was blessed to return to his love of music in the early 1990s, a love that culminated in May 1993 with an acclaimed performance of Felix Mendelssohn's Violin Concerto in E minor, Opus 64 – he was accompanied by the New World Orchestra conducted by Michael Morgan. Nearly a decade later in 2002, he performed the Beethoven Violin Concerto in Los Angeles. A compilation album with many of today's well-known artists is now available, where the Minister's musical artistry is once again on display. The Honorable Minister Louis Farrakhan has stated that he wishes to inspire young Black children to consider learning how to play classical music and stringed instruments.

In the Bible, we read about David the Psalmist, who is said to have had a heart after God's heart. David played a stringed instrument, a harp or a lyre. According to 1 Samuel, King Saul sent for David who could heal him through music. King Saul was plagued with evil spirits and when those spirits came upon him, David would heal him by playing his instrument. Interestingly, David began as a popular musician who later became great by killing Goliath. Eventually, after King Saul's fall, David becomes King and takes the Kingdom to great heights. We also read in the Holy Qur'an where David and his heir, Solomon, are taught to understand the speech (singing) of birds (27: 15-16) – yet another sign of the ubiquitous essence of music.

There has not been an adequate number of studies with the music of other genres to draw sound conclusions about their cognitive benefits, but the brain does appear to respond to classical music primarily by boosting cognitive function. It is clear that babies and children benefit from listening to and engaging with classical music. We know that it is soothing – this is why so many baby toys, swings, and mobiles play classical sounds. But it also improves memory, verbal intelligence, math skills and promotes creativity. Music is intrinsically coded in the genetic make-up of the original people of the earth. That means it comes naturally to Black and native people. An immediate introduction to music as an infant proves this point. We are born with rhythm. It does not take a lot of effort on the part of parents to get children to gravitate toward melodic sounds. Just offer a simple initiation to classical music and watch nature take over.

Other studies have also shown that when non-musicians are given musical training, there is a marked change in their brain activity and function. This should encourage us not to stop at simply playing classical music for our babies, but to give them music lessons. The discipline, creativity, and cognitive skills that are required to read, interpret, play and then create music can be transferred to almost any field of endeavor.

The gift of music is given to all of us by Allah (God); so, it is difficult to find anyone who does not enjoy or at least appreciate good music. The difference is that the ability to express that gift lays dormant in most; while others have awakened to their genius and used it to heal and to advance mentally. And just as important, many have also found music to be a vehicle to communicate, to entertain and to unite. But what we all know for sure is that our quality of life is exponentially enhanced with the sound of music.

LOVE IS NOT AN EMOTION:

Over the years, The Honorable Minister Louis Farrakhan has been very candid in sharing the circumstances of his birth and the details surrounding his childhood. He speaks of his beloved mother with great reverence and honor. She was a strict disciplinarian who reared her sons to be respectful and truthful; to be God-fearing and to love Black people. He describes his mother as a woman who demonstrated her love for her children daily, through the manner in which she was determined to rear them. She was a single Black woman with the serious task of rearing two boys during the 30s and 40s, leaving little time for foolishness. She was not affectionate with her children, giving them hugs and kisses; or saying, *'I love you,'* with the regularity that children may desire. However, she was a dutiful devoted mother; and though they were poor, she made sure that her children did not want for anything.

Love is a word used far too casually – *I love ice cream; I love that song; I love my bestie!* However, we are taught that love is NOT an emotion. The dictionary's definition of *love* is simply inadequate; it does not capture the scope of the word. In its fullness, God is Love. Duty is Love. Love is a verb; it's action. Love is not something we merely feel; love is mostly seen. How do we know if we love our spouse? Our children? A critical examination of our actions will allow us to honestly ascertain whether or not our love is complete. The Honorable Minister Louis Farrakhan, a divinely guided man, dissected real love and offers a brilliant explanation.

In ***Self-Improvement: The Basis of Community Development (Study Guide 18: Rising Above Emotion into the Thinking of God)***, The Honorable Minister Louis Farrakhan wrote, *"Though 'Love' is equally defined as an emotion, I would say that Love is not an emotion; Love is the Mother of Emotion. Love is the Creative Force out of which all things come. Love can be broken down into 4 principles: Freedom, Justice, Equality, and Obedience to the Will of Allah (God). We call our intense feeling of like or dislike 'Love' and 'Hate.' But Love is not just an intense feeling. That is a limitation that*
284

this world has placed on it, making it our emotional reaction to something…We must not narrow Love to an emotional reaction. But when we say, 'God is Love,' the word 'is' is represented by the '=' symbol, then Love has to be complete because God is not an emotion. All of His Attributes are embodied in the Creative force we call Love; an intense like for something is only one of its manifestations."

Again, on the subject of 'Love,' The Minister writes in **Study Guide 16: The Law of God**, *"The Essence of Divine Law is Love…When one gains Love for Allah (God), and for His Creation, then in that Love is contained the Law. One willingly obeys Divine Law out of Love.* <u>*We need Love, but not without Law.*</u>*"*

Displaying love at this level is deliberate and purposeful, nothing is done haphazardly. Parents who unwisely seek the friendship of their children, and above all simply desire that their children are happy with them will acquiesce to their children's wishes even if it conflicts with what they know is right. This is the emotional aspect of love. Seeking favor from our children and not the favor of God is an unworthy goal because the reward is fleeting. How can we honestly profess our love for our children and allow them to engage in activities that are not good for them? It is a contradiction to say we love our children but will not discipline them or put restrictions in place to protect them. We are guilty of abdicating our God-given responsibilities as parents when we seek the path of least resistance.

The evidence that a mother or father love their children beyond the limitations of an intense emotional relationship is manifested in their actions. They will teach their children about God and righteous conduct. They will correct them when they deviate or rebel against the rules of the home because this reinforces discipline and builds respect and character. They will feed their children the best foods because this increases the likelihood of long life and good health. Parents who love completely will also take all necessary measures to keep negative influences away from their children; as well as teach and train them on how to navigate around those that seep through. This means that cell phones, social media, friends, and activities are all monitored.

It is in the nature of a child to be curious about the unknown; so, children will push boundaries until they are stopped. Children do what parents permit them to do. Therefore, we must BE THE PARENT and not the friend. Giving in to pressure is not love. Certainly, our children may feel that we are strict or even "mean" for keeping an ever-watchful eye over what they watch; listen to; the friends they keep; cell phone usage and all their comings and goings. But in the end – SO WHAT! Rest assured, they will not be children forever and will thank you later. If we love our children completely, we will do what is best for them; whether it leads to their displeasure or not. After all, the Holy Qur'an reads, *"It may be that you dislike a thing while it is good for you, and it may be that you love a thing while it is evil for you; and Allah knows while you know not."*

If love is freedom, justice, equality, and obedience to the Will of Allah (God); our children should be free to (respectfully) express themselves – we should welcome questions, comments, complaints, and conversation. Their concerns should not be dismissed. We must be just and fair in our dealings with them; and if they are right, we must bow down to the truth that they speak. If we parent with equity and justice, our children who are righteous by nature will grow to love God's law and His way. As they mature, they will be grateful for our obedience to the divine laws of Allah (God). We cannot parent our children, looking for instant gratification – our reward comes tomorrow.

All of this is not to say that we should not be affectionate with our children because we absolutely should. Children need to be hugged and

286

stroked and kissed. There is power in the touch; just a few seconds releases oxytocin, strengthening our natural bond and trust. Children also need to be reassured and validated by receiving positive affirmations and praise; and by hearing the words, *'I love you'* all of the time. But if we say it and don't show it, then our words are in vain. So, the greatest testament of our love is to be dutiful to Allah (God) and to rear our children in the best manner.

A LOVING PARENT, DISCIPLINES:

Several years ago, I was fortunate to attend a wonderful event hosted by the M.G.T. & G.C.C. (Women of the Nation of Islam) in Houston, Texas. During this event, I was blessed and privileged to be among a group of sisters who attended a workshop conducted by Mother Tynnetta Muhammad. Though it was not her specified topic, she shared profound advice and gave words of encouragement regarding the rearing of our children. I recall her tone being serious when she said, ***"Our children come through us, but they are NOT from us. They are from Allah (God)."*** Those words illuminated the proverbial light bulb over my head. As a new mother, I was simultaneously humbled and elevated at this affirmation of the divine value of motherhood.

Our children are from God, but He charges us with caring for what **He** created. How does one handle a gift from God? The Honorable Minister Louis Farrakhan has stated that mothers, in particular, are the supreme being in the lives of their children before the child is old enough to recognize the real Power - God. Any need the child signals, the mother provides – the child is not yet aware of the One that mother is depending upon. This gives parents tremendous authority, power, and responsibility. An unbalanced parent can easily abuse this authority; forgetting that the child is from Allah (God). Authority can make us arrogant and crazy if we do not respect the AUTHOR who gave us the authority in the first place. When we disrespect God by moving Him out of the equation of our parenting, abuse is inevitable – verbal, physical, and/or sexual.

Allah (God) is our Father; so, there is no better reference for parents to study than how God handles His people. God is balanced. Every decision He executes is justified. He punishes; He rewards; He chastises, and He elevates. He will straighten our means of subsistence; He will amplify our means; He gives us difficulty; then He gives us ease. We could go on and on. But according to the Holy Qur'an, His chief attribute is Mercy. Mercy takes precedence over punishment – this is God's way. Mercy is undeserved kindness, compassion, and forgiveness. If Allah's (God's) overarching attribute is Mercy, then shouldn't ours be as well? How do we know when mercy is required and when it should take a backseat to punishment? Study God.

The Honorable Minister Louis Farrakhan said, *"When children come out of a home where there is no discipline and go into a home where there is discipline, you will find that they like being where there is discipline. There is a human need to be disciplined, and, therefore, to discipline is a human right. As parents, we must have the right and authority to discipline our children."* Chaos and confusion are unnatural. The universe is governed by laws, order, and structure set in place by the Creator. The most energetic, active toddler craves structure and normalcy. He may not be able to communicate it, but his nature bears witness – there's a time for play, a time for rest; a time to learn, a time to eat; a time to bathe, a time to be comforted, etc.

In an article titled, *Family...From the Perspective of Children*, Minister Farrakhan wrote, *"Some of us think that disciplining our children is abuse, but everything in creation has its affair regulated by law. In the home, there is a need for rules, regulations or laws. Rules and regulations are a human need, and to deny our children the discipline of rules is to deny them that which ultimately will make them secure. There must be rules in the home. There must be rules that teach us how to relate to one another properly in the home. There must be rules of respect for parents, children, self and one another that are taught in the home because everywhere we go, we will find existing rules and regulations. Where there are no rules, there will be no order. Chaos will be the result. Where there is chaos, it will bring to an end the activity or the life of the home, school, community, nation, and the world."*

Why is it that being disciplined is positive if we are dealing with adults, but seen as negative if we are dealing with children? Discipline in any field involves instruction, training, structure, regulations, guidelines, correction – and yes, punishment. Those who undergo the process of discipline reap the benefits.

Neither the Holy Qur'an nor the Bible condones abusing children. Discipline is not synonymous with abuse. Punishment is not synonymous with abuse. Spanking or corporal punishment is not synonymous with abuse. The latter must be done in moderation and with the thought in mind of correction, not inflicting as must pain as possible. No sane parent takes pleasure from bringing pain to their child. However, the enemy is playing a dangerous game when he threatens to take the God-given rights of parents away for spanking and disciplining their children in an effort to correct or protect them. These are children given to them by God, not by governmental agencies. These same policymakers then have the audacity to look the other way when police officers brutally beat and murder our Brothers and Sisters without cause – the hypocrisy is sickening. Universal law demands that we are disciplined. At some point, we must all submit and humble ourselves to a higher authority. So, it is better that the parent is the one to regulate the child early in life, rather than the judicial system, fellow prisoners, a disease or terrible tragedy.

To be clear: If there is irrefutable evidence that parents or guardians are abusing their children, those children must be removed from that home. Those parents have misused their authority from God in the worst imaginable way. Not only should they lose their children, but in truth, those that commit the most egregious criminal acts against children are worthy of death.

The Minister makes it clear, *"Corporal punishment is not abuse if it is done with moderation, with the thought in mind of correction and not the thought of afflicting pain, but to bring about change in the behavior to make a better child and a better human being. Punishment must always be in accord with the violation, and devoid of anger. The love that we have for our children is the reason why we punish them because our desire is to make the child better."*

Corporal punishment has become a controversial topic, so it must be addressed. Physical discipline is not the only form of discipline, but it's very effective. However, let's be sure to follow God. Allah (God) is slow to anger; though He does get there. He is so patient with us and before His anger is unleashed, He could provide proof of ample reminders and warnings. So even though He is completely justified – when He finally punishes, His anger is still controlled. The Bible advises us to be quick to listen, slow to speak and slow to anger. We should never punish when we are out of control with anger; even if the reason is sound. Never should our frustrations be taken out on our children. Quick-tempered parents will soon abuse their children. Exercising patience helps us to be slow to anger. In other words, the disciplinarian must also be disciplined. Discipline should build character and establish regulation; not destroy self-worth. If we are impatient with our children, we will spank them for every single infraction, making our punishment ineffective.

The truth is that corporal punishment (spankings) should decrease as the child gets older; and at some point, it should end all together. Physical punishment is only productive at an early age. If we are still spanking our teenager, something was missed a long time ago. The Minister explains that in child psychology, there is a phase of human development called the animalistic stage; which is from birth to about five years old. During this phase of development, trying to reason with a child using logic, discussion and debate is a waste of time. However, they respond immediately to pleasure and pain. Animals and small children are creatures of instinct. It may sound crude, but just as animals are trained using pleasure and pain, it's just as effective for children. A spanking (on the behind) brings about immediate results. Can this be found in the scriptures? Absolutely.

If our children are from Allah (God), we should rear them in the manner He dictates. There are many scriptural references that admonish parents to discipline their children and our sincere love for them is questioned if we do not. Allah (God) says that those whom He loves, He chastens much. The most common reference is to Proverbs 13:24, *"Whoever spares the rod hates their children, but the one who loves their children is careful to discipline them"* (NIV). Modern translation: *Spare the rod, spoil the child.* The King James Version uses the term *"betimes"* – discipline the child *early, speedily.* Younger children must learn to submit to their parents; even if it is out of fear. We cannot protect what we cannot control. The Honorable Minister Louis Farrakhan said that fear is more constant than love. So, initially, fear is necessary, but it does not last because their submission will lead to understanding. Punishment, particularly for toddlers must be swift. If we wait to punish our child, chances are he will have forgotten why he is being spanked or reprimanded; which then makes his punishment ineffective and unjust.

The Honorable Minister Louis Farrakhan also stated, *"The more correction one is given, the greater the demonstration of love."* He went on to say that, *"There is no child who will not be comforted by the proper use of the rod and the staff,"* for as David said, *"Thy rod, and Thy staff, they comfort me."* As our children mature, understanding comes; so, the way we discipline has to also evolve. At this point, we should talk first and explain why such and such behavior is not allowed and what the consequences will be for persisting to disobey. This is when getting grounded, having stern conversations and employing reason becomes effective. It is imperative that we follow through with the punishment the next time it occurs. Every time we say we are going to do something and then do not follow through; our authority is weakened, and our children learn to manipulate us; getting away with more and more.

Parents must demonstrate a united front. Children should not see their parents disagree about the appropriate punishment. When Daddy is doing the punishing, Mommy has to stand down. She should not interfere physically or verbally. The same is true vice versa. Our children should be clear that if a particular behavior is not okay when Mommy is around; then it is equally not okay when Daddy is around.

There are real consequences for our children and for us when we choose not to discipline. So be careful about following the trends of the time. When in doubt, ask God. He is our example and He changes not. He makes it clear in the scripture that where there is no discipline, there is no love. So, let's all strive to *"Train up a child in the way he should go: and when he is old, he will not depart from it"* (Proverbs 22:6 KJV).

MOMMY'S FAVORITE:

The Honorable Minister Louis Farrakhan said that growing up, he believed that his older brother, Alvan, was their mother's favorite. Alvan was dark-skinned like their mother so he believed this similarity made their bond tighter. Likewise, he would later learn that his brother believed that the Minister was their mother's favorite because his skin complexion was much lighter, which was often preferred. It is probably safe to assume that she favored them both, equally.

Children cannot help but notice the obvious differences between themselves and others, particularly their siblings. They are constantly comparing and competing with one another. Therefore, if a parent overtly or even subtly differentiates treatment in any way and their children pick up on it, they will believe that favoritism exists. This will likely be based on noticeable superficial differences – gender, birth order, skin complexion, talent, height, etc. Most children do not look beyond the surface to analyze why there may have been a different reaction to what appeared to be the same behavior.

But, let's be honest, some parents do have favorites. Is this wrong? Or, is it natural to have a favorite? Is it possible to have a favorite without showing overt favoritism? Can we love equally and yet still have a favorite? As parents, we have tremendous power and influence over the lives of our children – these precious beings are from God, but He gives us authority and responsibility for them. In this preeminent role, Allah (God) authorizes us to serve as His '*khalifah*' or successor. So daily, parents are required to make decisions and judgments concerning their children. We can answer the aforementioned questions by studying the words and the example of Our Father.

Does Allah (God) have favorites? According to the scriptures, yes, He does; but not in the way we may commonly think about being one's favorite. Allah (God) never treats those who are not favored by Him unjustly. His judgment is always right and exact. And those who are favored by Him are chosen for a divine purpose, which often includes more responsibility and more trials. Allah (God) does not favor us based on our wealth, our status, degrees conferred, our beauty or even our religion. The Book of Isaiah reads, *"'Has not my hand made all these things, and so they came into being?' declares the Lord. 'These are the ones I look on with favor: those who are humble and contrite in spirit, and who tremble at my word'"* (66: 2, NIV).

Sometimes Allah (God) grants blessings and favors to some and not others to test both parties – and sometimes it is simply an expression of His Mercy. Throughout the Holy Qur'an and Bible, we read of those receiving favor from Allah (God) for various reasons. It is important to remember that His decisions are never arbitrary – every favor granted, blessing bestowed, a prayer answered, means amplified or rank elevated are all essential to His Master Plan. But this does not excuse us from striving mightily to position ourselves to be amongst His elect.

The Holy Qur'an opens with the oft-repeated prayer in which the supplicant closes with these words, *"Guide us on the right path, The path of those upon whom Thou hast bestowed favours, Not those upon whom wrath is brought down, nor those who go astray."* According to Islamic scholars, Allah (God) favors the prophets, the truthful, the faithful and the righteous. It is in this path that the Believer should strive to walk in order to be favored by God. This is the purpose of Allah (God) raising messengers and prophets. They come to teach us the *"Will of Allah (God) and to give us the privilege and the opportunity to submit our Will to do the Will of Allah (God) and come into favor with Allah (God)."*

294

In a similar vein, if parents express favor it should be based on righteous behavior – respect, obedience, discipline, hard work, and other favorable attributes. Unfortunately, there are in fact parents who have favorites based on the superficial – skin color, gender, athletic ability or the like. There is no justification for this; it is improper and unjust. Indiscriminate favoritism can produce jealousy and can even lead to envy and hatred. If our parenting practices are justified, then when our children reach the age where they are able to properly weigh cause and effect, we should take the time to explain our decision-making process. This way, our children are clear which actions reap punishment and which qualify for a reward. Allah (God) handles us in a like manner. How can we strive to seek His favor if we are ignorant of what pleases Him?

It takes a deliberate effort, but each child should know that he or she is loved immensely, even if a favorite resides in the heart of a parent. Parents, especially mothers have a unique capacity to effortlessly love multiple children. Allah (God) expands her breast to love equally regardless of how different each child may be. Just imagine being asked to choose between our lungs and our heart, we could not do it – both are vital. We require a beating heart as much as we need functioning lungs. Just the same, a loving mother cannot choose between her children, no matter their flaws – each is a part of her. Each child has strengths and challenges; skills and burdens – but each demonstrates functions and responsibilities that are integral to the balance of the family unit. Their differences should be respected and nurtured. Validate their uniqueness; it's what makes us each so special. Children, especially those who are not reared on swine, are very sensitive. They know when they are being treated differently and this will lead them to try to become more like the favored child, which is unnatural. Or, they may rebel completely – or perhaps even hate themselves for something that could not be controlled. Never make a child feel they are not as loved as the next.

Regularly express to each child how much they are loved. We should remind them of how thankful we are that Allah (God) blessed us with them. To hear Mommy and Daddy say, *"I love you,"* enriches the spirit of a young person and validates their existence. In the Black community, this seems to be more difficult from father to son. It is a cycle we must break. Begin to say, *"I love you,"* from the day the child is born so that these words will not become foreign in the home; but a natural, regular occurrence.

We may be familiar with the Biblical story of the brothers, Cain and Abel. The Bible reads, *"The Lord looked with favor on Abel and his offering, but on Cain and his offering he did not look with favor. So, Cain was very angry, and his face was downcast"* (Genesis 4:4, NIV). Although God does not explain His decision, He does give Cain a chance to be accepted if he *"does the right thing."* Of course, Cain is overcome by his anger and instead, kills his brother. Cain and Abel were the children of Adam and Eve; but at this point, they were not children – they were adults, well over 100 years old. Envy led to murder. Even as an adult Cain could not handle his brother's offering (actions) being favored over his; he saw it as a personal rejection.

If an adult could not handle what "appeared" to be a rejection without explanation, it is unlikely that a child would fare any better. Allah (God) was clearly testing Cain. However, unless we are intentionally testing our children, then we should help them in any way we can to understand our decisions. We have to listen to our children if they express feelings of rejection, abandonment, anxiety or pain. No child should feel unloved – real or perceived – by his or her parents. If there is a favorite and it is apparent to everyone; then as parents, we need to examine, analyze and correct how we parent. We may not be able to help having a favorite, but we should not show favoritism – those close to us should be none the wiser.

Prophet Muhammad (PBUH) had a favorite amongst his wives. A'ishah was reportedly his favorite. But Allah (God) warned him not to be *"disinclined (from one) of them with total disinclination, so that you leave her in suspense."* In other words – don't make it so obvious to the others that they are not the favorite.

Parents who practice extreme favoritism could be charged with abuse – nothing good comes from extreme favoritism. We must strive to be fair and just as parents, knowing that we will inevitably fall short. When we fail, and our failure is pointed out, let's humble ourselves – acknowledge our wrongs, then work to repair any damage that may have resulted. With the help of Allah (God), the pain inflicted will not leave any permanent scars.

FIGHTING PARENTS, A CHILD'S BURDEN:

On Sunday, August 27, 2017, at the Family Summit-Conference in Atlanta, Georgia, the Honorable Minister Louis Farrakhan made the following statement during his keynote address: *"There is going to be a perfect family as the perfect foundation to a perfect world. There has to be a perfect man to unite with a perfect woman to produce a perfect family that is so in harmony with The Nature of God and the nature of their own creation, that they will produce an exemplary family as the base of the unity of all families…"*

The Bible bears witness that this ultimate goal is in fact attainable. Jesus says in the Book of Matthew, *"Be ye therefore perfect, even as your Father which is in heaven is perfect"* (5:48). Isn't this the ideal life that we are all truly chasing if we say that we are "striving" to submit our entire Will to do the Will of Allah (God)? The same can be said for those who are following in the footsteps of Jesus. We are all seeking perfection! Though we are striving, even the best of us fall short. Perhaps we fall short because our entire being has not yet accepted that perfection is attainable, or maybe it's because we do not know what perfection looks like.

Children are the products of their parents and the environment in which they were reared. Ideally, children should one day be better than their parents; and the children they produce should be better than them, and this pattern should continue for generations until we attain perfection. In order to one-day produce, the exemplary family the Honorable Minister Louis Farrakhan referenced, we must eliminate everything that is not ideal. The list is very extensive; so, we should start with the most abhorrent behaviors, those actions farthest away from perfection are easiest to eliminate. One such behavior is arguing and fighting in the home around our children.

As a general principle, parents should never get in a heated argument or fight with one another in front of their children. It is very important that the moment couples agree to have children that they also agree not to argue in front of those children. Children literally worship their parents and love to imitate them whether their behavior is appropriate or not; this distinction is not drawn, particularly by younger children. No one makes a more indelible impression on children than parents. Parents model both good and bad behavior for their children every single day. There is a Nigerian proverb that states, ***"What the child says, he heard at home."*** Behavior is not genetic; behavior is learned. And the most influential teachers of behavior are parents.

Worse than imitation is the internal damage caused by witnessing parents fight. The impact that a heated argument or fight can have on a child does not discriminate by age or gender. Whether the child is male or female; age three or fifteen, the mental dialogue that plays out in the mind of a child has no redeeming qualities. The child's world is literally turned upside down.

At that very moment, their emotions can range from confused to sad; then from scared to devastated.

Every marriage will have disagreements, but the need to get one's point across regardless to whom or what, may give the individual an immediate temporary satisfaction, but the child experiences lingering insecurity stemmed from fear that their parents could separate. Children are instinctively drawn to listen, observe and analyze every word and every motion of an argument between their parents because it directly connects to the first law of nature – self-preservation. They see their security, wellness, happiness and survival as directly tied to the outcome of that specific argument, so every aspect is ingested. Though the argument may have nothing to do with them, they still feel threatened. This takes a huge emotional toll. The burden for the child is unnatural and undeserved. We all now know that continuous emotional and mental stress and turmoil will eventually show up physically.

Ideally, parents should be exemplary models and examples of a loving relationship and work effectively to demonstrate a stable and peaceful home environment. Children are not clueless, they know that adults argue and may fight verbally – but they should not be forced to witness their parents go at it. This causes anxiety for children and forces them to inwardly withdraw or to take sides; and in some of the more severe instances, interject themselves into the argument in an effort to try to settle the difference. Home should be a sanctuary, the safest environment for children; not a battle ground.

In the Holy Qur'an (16: 125) we are taught to argue in the best manner with those who disagree with our way of life and may have a harsh attitude towards what they do not fully understand. If we are taught to take this approach with strangers and with our rivals, then we certainly should treat our spouse with this same level of respect or greater. Truth should settle **all** arguing and disagreement, but sometimes as we journey toward the truth there is a debate. It is not that we should be silent when we feel strongly about an issue, but timing and environment are paramount. Couples will disagree, but it is completely dysfunctional to fight all the time. And to do so around our children is careless.

Another proverb states, ***"Work the clay while it is still wet."*** The clay in this proverb is our children. We strive to shape and mold them as best we can while we still have power and influence over them. Once the clay is dry, you cannot change its shape. Once our children are no longer in our homes and move on to start families of their own, our influence over them is almost nil. It is so interesting that the vast majority of our lives will be spent living as adults, away from our parents; yet most of us can attribute our personalities, our self-esteem, our successes and our failures to the fleeting moments of our childhood. This should make us alert and cognizant to the reality that what our children experience during their rearing is preparing them for the **majority** of their life. God-willing, they too will seek perfection and get closer than their parents to achieve the ideal.

PROFANITY WEAKENS THE IMMUNE SYSTEM:

Those of us of a certain age remember when the only way to bully someone was in person. We did not own cell phones and there was no internet. Most can recall being at the school playgrounds or in our neighborhood streets instigating, watching or participating in all-out fist fights; or at the very least "riding" (insulting) one another to the point of no return. We may also remember a certain chant circulating about – *'sticks and stones may break my bones, but words will never hurt me.'* This was a childlike way of saying that using words to demean, insult or humiliate someone will have no physical effect on the body. Well, today we know this may not necessarily be true. Harsh words certainly hurt us emotionally and psychologically, but they may also be hurting us physically.

In her book, *Weapons of Self-Destruction*, Dr. Ava Muhammad wrote, *"When the sound of filthy words travels through the physical realm, its effect is similar to the AIDS virus. It weakens the immune system. Every word we speak is reabsorbed into the subconscious mind where it originated. We cannot say a word unless we think it, which means it begins as a thought residing in the mind...This type of language is deadly, like bullets from a gun. It is disruptive to the universal order of things. It can injure the person it is aimed at or strike anyone within hearing range. When someone uses these names [b*tch, m*tha f-word, etc.] or is called such names repeatedly, the nervous system is worn down because they don't produce anything useful to humanity. We all know the Creator does not acknowledge profanity, so we don't connect with His power when we use it."*

The nervous system is very complex. It controls every part of the body. It is so complex that neurologists anatomize it as two major systems in one – central nervous system (brain and spinal cord) and peripheral nervous system (arms, hands, legs, and feet). The nervous system also includes two subsystems; autonomic nerves (lungs, heart, intestines, bladder, sex organs and stomach) and cranial nerves (eyes, mouth, ears, and other parts of the head). Our nervous system is our body's electrical grid, wired with over 45 miles of nerves, 60,000 miles of blood vessels and over 100 billion neurons (nerve cells). It has three primary functions: 1) to collect sensory input from the body and external environment; 2) to process and interpret the sensory input, and 3) to respond appropriately to sensory input. Sensory data in the form of words not only send messages, but they carry energy (electricity) and vibrations with them. Negative energy and vibrations cause discord instead of harmony, which stresses the nervous system – stresses the brain.

There is a direct link between our brain and our immune system. The primary function of the immune system is to defend the body against invaders (viruses, bacteria, fungi, etc.) which can cause illness and disease. A weakened immune system leaves every part of the body vulnerable to sickness. Our brains were created to think right by a Creator, Whom we just stated, does not acknowledge profanity. The Honorable Minister Louis Farrakhan said, *"Falsehood, which is untruth or deception produces a spiritual and chemical imbalance in the brain. And since the nine (9) systems of the human body all rely upon the brain, its imbalance results in a malfunctioning of the entire health system. Even though there may still be a regular heartbeat, normal blood pressure, etc., there is a very real dysfunction that ultimately shortens life – because Allah (God) intended for us not to be nearly balanced, but we are made to achieve exquisite balance"* (Study Guide 4: The Struggle for Balance).

There was a time when "shut-up" and "stupid" were the worst of words that parents reprimanded their children for using. But today, we have all seen it – that little two or three-year-old child who curses like a grown drunk sailor. Our first impulse is to reprimand the child until we remember that profanity is not hereditary like one's skin color or height. Profanity and the use of vulgar language are learned behavior – the culprit almost always being the parents. So, the next inclination is to stare down the parents with a piercing look of indignation and disgust. I guess we believe this will somehow shame them into correcting their child, and it may, but only for a moment. Many parents continue to curse freely and proudly because to them, words are just words and carry no measurable consequence. The hypocrisy in this scenario is that most are only disturbed when younger children let one go, but not at all offended when adults regularly spew foul obscenities during casual conversations – not to mention when they are angry or frustrated.

Our first exposure to language begins in the womb of our mothers. And it continues to be mother's voice and language that we hear the majority of our early formative years. We say the body is the real temple of God; but do we really believe that? When we behold any house of God – a mosque, temple, synagogue or church – defiled with graffiti, swastikas, offensive language, debris or any intentional damage, believers take this as a personal affront. We become livid with anger. But these beautiful structures were built by the hands of man – as opposed to the human body, which was created by the hands of Allah (God). Therefore, any defilement of the human body should garner the most outrage.

Allah (God) determined that the composition of our body would be 75% water. Studies like Dr. Emoto's Water Experiment illustrate the effects that negative and positive words have on water molecules. The study proves that words are alive! What we say and what we hear can either purify or corrode 75% of our being. If corroded, we are left susceptible to illness and disease.

The Honorable Minister Louis Farrakhan said, *"The misuse of language and/or the harshness of language in rebuke can hurt the emotional and psychological development of the child."* As a parent, one of the greatest misuses of language is profanity (curse words) directed towards our children in conjunction with personally degrading, belittling and humiliating them. We have to be so careful with our tongue because it is one of the most powerful muscles in our body and it can be used for good or for evil – to heal or to harm. Speech does not have to be directed at our children to be harmful; they just have to be within earshot.

The quality of speech and language that comes from our children is influenced by environmental factors and people, but none is more influential than parents. So, when we allow the uncivilized, lower reptilian mind to rule our thoughts and behaviors, profane language is the natural byproduct of this way of life. A regular dose of obscene, profanity-laced speech in the home from parents or music; video games or film will beget foul-mouthed children. Profanity weakens the immune system; but the highest form of communication – divine revelation, offers an opportunity to energize the brain, thereby energizing the entire being so that we may be more like The Father and become gods.

DINNERTIME TABLE TALKS:

The Most Honorable Elijah Muhammad and The Honorable Minister Louis Farrakhan are both lauded for their decades of steadfast, uncompromising commitment to teaching Black people the true knowledge of God, self and the enemy. Their sole mission is the spiritual and mental resurrection of our people, which will set us on the path to becoming gods. In order to be successful at this mission; which happens to be the hardest job ever given to any human being – both men understand that time cannot be wasted. Therefore, even dinnertime with these great men has never been just about the physical consumption of food. *Table talks*; or being spiritually fed with the Word of God at every meal, is a staple for every guest who is blessed to dine with The Most Honorable Elijah Muhammad or with The Honorable Minister Louis Farrakhan.

In his books *How to Eat to Live (Book One & Two)*, The Most Honorable Elijah Muhammad wrote, *"Eat the proper food as given in this book and eat at the proper time; one meal a day from 4 to 6 P.M."* He further expounds, *"If we eat one meal once every day at four o'clock or six o'clock (whatever is the best hour for your meal), then wait until that hour comes again before eating again."* Here, The Most Honorable Elijah Muhammad is emphasizing that we should eat only one meal a day. If we are able to eat that one meal from 4 to 6 pm, then we should do so; but what is most important is to eat one meal a day at the same time each day.

This is a practice that should be implemented in every home. We should also adopt the practice of eating together as a family at the dinner table as often as possible. We know that the reality of today's modern family often consists of two working parents and children who are involved in extracurricular activities which usually extend beyond the suggested dinnertime, but we should prioritize a minimum of one day per week where the entire family can dine together at a reasonable time.

One of the great-grandsons of The Most Honorable Elijah Muhammad, Imam Sultan Rahman Muhammad, along with others, worked to compile both audio and written transcripts of his great-grandfather's dinnertime *table talks*. The high level of knowledge and wisdom shared by The Most Honorable Elijah Muhammad in those dinner conversations remain unmatched. Seemingly basic questions and conversations reveal divine revelation and leave no doubt that the one at the head of the dinner table met with God. The lesson our families can learn by this example established by The Most Honorable Elijah Muhammad is that dinnertime affords an opportunity to not only dine well; but to enjoy the company of others, impart knowledge, practice table etiquette, good manners, and share a laugh.

Eating one-meal-a-day allows for the preparer of that meal not to become overwhelmed or exhausted by constantly preparing additional meals throughout the day. This also increases the likelihood that the one meal will be a full course – soup, salad, bread, main course, and dessert. Such a meal eaten over the span of two hours allows for great conversations. Every family member should have something to share – conversations are best when there is not a monopoly over the discussion. We will be amazed at what we can learn from and about our own children when they are given an extended opportunity to share freely without interruption.

Of course, the family should begin each meal with prayer – the Name of Allah (God) should always be invoked preceding a meal. The prayer is typically led by the head of the household. Televisions should be turned off and cell phones should not be at the dinner table. Cell phones were not an issue when The Most Honorable Elijah Muhammad was among us, but he did dismiss a believer from the dinner table who fell asleep. He said, *"If you are talking to someone, and they don't seem to be receptive to what you are trying to teach, it limits your will and desire to try to teach."* In that same vein, if our children are sharing a word at the dinner table, they should have our undivided attention and vice versa – no one wants to be ignored – no one wants to be second to a text message, social media post or television program. Dinnertime is family time!

In addition, do not be rushed at the dinner table. Taking our time does not only allow for great table talks, but it is also good for our health. As a society, we regularly see limits set on meal times – i.e. thirty-minute school lunches and short lunch breaks at work. The Most Honorable Elijah Muhammad wrote, *"If we expect to live from what we eat, we must be sure that what we eat is masticated so perfectly well, until the stomach juices (which have no teeth), with its hot acid can digest the food without too much work. THE AMERICAN EATERS, I believe, when it comes to a human being, are the fastest of all on the earth in eating their food...A man should chew his food (as many doctors teach us and agree with what is said here), until it slips away into the throat, before swallowing."*

There are many other advantages to dining together as a family. According to TheFamilyDinnerProject.org, there are physical, mental and emotional benefits to families regularly eating meals together; which include: *"Better academic performance, higher self-esteem, greater sense of resilience, lower risk of substance abuse, lower risk of teen pregnancy, lower risk of depression, lower likelihood of developing eating disorders, and lower rates of obesity."*

Keep in mind that our children are more likely to look forward to family dinnertime and be receptive to sharing if we keep the conversations light. Good, positive discussions lead to proper thoughts, which aid the digestive process. Both the Most Honorable Elijah Muhammad and The Honorable Minister Louis Farrakhan are masters at teaching deeply profound lessons by injecting a little levity. We close with this reflection from The Honorable Minister Louis Farrakhan when asked by Brother Jabril Muhammad to tell about the sense of humor of The Most Honorable Elijah Muhammad for those who didn't get a chance to see him or hear him or sit at his table. The Minister said:

"The Honorable Elijah Muhammad lived the majority of his life with a very heavy weight on his head. His heart was with the "weighty word" and the Mission that Allah (God) had given him. Those were great blessings, at his dinner table, where we were involved in discussions and in hearing him expound on the Wisdom of Allah (God), as found in the Bible and Holy Qur'an and methods of going after our people, to bring them into the light of a knowledge that had been kept from them. Our discussions with him at his table were of a serious nature. So, it was most refreshing to sit at his table sometimes and hear him tell a humorous anecdote and laugh. When he laughed his cheeks became so rosy. For me, it was a joy to see him laugh and sometimes he would laugh until tears welled up in his eyes. His sense of

humor was unique because one would not think a man of his station, of his tremendous wisdom, would even take the time to be humorous. But even in his humor, he was always teaching lessons."

A GIRL CHILD AIN'T SAFE IN A FAMILY OF MEN:

The 1985 epic movie, The Color Purple, based on Alice Walker's novel of the same title; had no shortage of memorable scenes and dialogue. Right up there at the top is the unforgettable confrontation between Sofia (portrayed by Oprah Winfrey) and Celie (portrayed by Whoopi Goldberg). As you may recall, Sofia was livid and hurt that Celie would tell her husband, Harpo, to beat her as a way of keeping her in check; more subdued. Sofia approaches Celie fuming with rage and exclaims, *"You told Harpo to beat me! All my life I had to fight. I had to fight my daddy; I had to fight my uncles; I had to fight my brothers. Girl child ain't safe in a family of mens [sic]. But I ain't never thought I'd have to fight in my own house. I loves Harpo – God knows I do...but I'll kill him, dead, before I let him beat me..."*

This movie is based on a fictional storyline, set in America's racist rural south, during the early 1900s; but the issue of incest that lingers throughout the tale is not fictional at all. There is no country, community, religion, income-level, status or race that has not been affected by the devastating impact of rape and incest. The Most Honorable Elijah Muhammad was concerned enough about the potential for incest that he told the Sisters in the Nation of Islam not to leave their daughters alone with their fathers. Most of us, when we hear this for the first time, probably react the same way the Honorable Minister Louis Farrakhan did when his wife first informed him of those instructions. He said that he became upset. As a father

308

of five daughters, he was very offended – he even thought someone was lying on Mr. Muhammad and that some "crazy" sister in the class made it all up.

It is completely understandable for a protective doting father, who would never think of abusing his daughter, to be initially offended by anyone saying that he should not be alone with his own flesh and blood. However, it did not take long for the Minister to understand the reality of sexual molestation in our community and why it was necessary for the Most Honorable Elijah Muhammad to give out such a directive. We cannot be more concerned about sparing someone's feelings than we are about protecting our precious daughters. It is not difficult to get over a bruised ego – but only God can completely restore a woman who suffers from the abuse she endured as a child. The primary goal is the protection of our daughters and the preservation of their innocence and chastity.

In his lecture, **The Sin of Child Molestation**, the Honorable Minister Louis Farrakhan said, *"I know what you think, brothers, especially if you're a good person…Sometimes, brothers, you are good, and the thought never enters your mind and God has to make a rule taking into consideration the total society. And we should obey it, not because we need it; but for the weak one in the society that needs it."*

As it was made evident in Sophia's case, we know that these instructions must extend beyond fathers. Every effort should be made not to leave our girls alone with any male – family or otherwise. Unfortunately, our natural God-centered mind is being overcome by a sick pleasure-seeking mind that is corrupting the innocence of our young girls, daily. The fastest way to destroy our future is to abuse children. It only takes a moment in time to ruin the hope, potential and countless successes destined in the span of someone's lifetime. As mothers, we are charged by God with being watchful, vigilant protectors of our children; and though the choices we make may appear to be extreme to others, enacting this discipline plants the seed that will help our girls to one day protect themselves.

They may not articulate it in this manner, but the thought is: *"If I can't be alone with my own father, nobody else stands a chance."* Not permitting our daughters to be alone with men in general, including their father, inoculates them against a feeling of ease and peace when found alone with a man. Since she is not accustomed to being in this type of situation, it should make her uncomfortable enough to rebel and seek to remove herself.

There are a few additional, yet simple and very effective instructions that we are taught to implement in our homes to provide added protection for our girls. As followers of the Most Honorable Elijah Muhammad, under the guidance and leadership of the Honorable Minister Louis Farrakhan; we do not permit our girls (or our boys) to sit in a man's lap. It matters not the relationship – our children sit with their mother or in a chair. We deal with science and nature; not with the fact that someone is "supposed" to know better. Clearly, too many men do not care to do what they know is right or else rape, incest and molestation would not be so prevalent. The male is easily stimulated by sight and touch. And a man whose mind in not wrapped in God may act on an impulse.

We also do not permit our husbands (or other males) to bathe our daughters or even change their diapers – that role is exclusively for mother. And this practice that we are now seeing, where parents are bathing / showering with their children is completely inappropriate! We are not to expose our own naked or half-naked bodies around our children of the opposite sex after they have reached the age of two. The Holy Qur'an states that we may only display our adornments to *"children who know not women's nakedness."* We should not even bathe our children together. In the name of saving time and/or water; we are exposing our children to habits that were once rightly considered taboo. The Honorable Minister Louis Farrakhan said that adults, as well as children, need space and privacy. He said that boys and girls should not share a bedroom and certainly, they should not share the same bed. Girls must have their own bedroom.

In addition, modest clothing should be worn at home as well as in the public. Every little girl in a family of men should own a robe and have decent night clothes that cover her developing body. These days, the onset of puberty is starting younger and younger due to our poor eating habits and the enemy's tampering with the food and water supply. As we mentioned, the Honorable Minister Louis Farrakhan has several daughters; and he said that after the age of two, he never saw so much as his daughters' legs. Their wonderful, diligent mother made sure that they were always covered in the presence of their father and brothers. What a great example for us all!

This is the ideal way of life that we must actively strive to attain. Yes, there will be exceptions, such as single fathers and emergencies or other situations that may prevent a perfect practice. But we must work to make this way of life the norm and not an anomaly. When our children are away from us, it is necessary that we assess them, physically and mentally for any signs of tampering. If we see ANY indication of such a violation, we must move heaven and earth until we expose the culprit, whoever he may be.

The Honorable Minister Louis Farrakhan said, *"This means that we (men) must help in the production of a righteous woman. As men, we must know that the little girls that come into this world come in pure and we as husbands, fathers, brothers, uncles, and cousins must commit ourselves to protect the purity of females that we come in contact with, particularly fathers, uncles, and brothers, for, oft-times it is family members that are destroying the virtue of our young girls."*

In 2016, the Honorable Minister Louis Farrakhan gave this divine warning on the popular New York based radio program, The Breakfast Club: *"In our world (of Islam) the penalty for abusing women and children is death. And unless we are willing at some point to kill those who rape our women; to kill those who destroy our children – that's going to come. Not now, because you have to be taught first and given a chance to reform your life. But you are not going to live among us and carry out that crap and not pay for it…I hope we never will have to do that."*

NO SLEEPOVERS:

The three predominant monotheistic religions – Judaism, Christianity, and Islam – all have several fundamental principles in common: Belief in One God, prayer, charity, fasting, struggling to overcome the weaknesses of self, doing unto others as you would have them do to you; and many more. In Islam, prayer is second only to our belief in One God. Prayer is so important that we are required to pray five times a day, at prescribed times. Depending on the time of year (and location), the distance between the first prayer at dawn and the second prayer could reach nearly 9 hours. However, after that second prayer, the time that lapses between each prayer gets shorter and shorter and shorter, as the night falls. Why is that?

Allah (God) requires us to pray to Him for many reasons; primarily as a demonstration of gratitude, but also to seek His guidance and protection. Our prayers increase as the light is replaced with darkness because nighttime can be very dangerous. Many use the darkness as a cover for participating in activities they perhaps would have reconsidered if their actions were visible to all. Darkness provides a cover that gives rise to an increase in crime, deviant behavior, sick impulses, and foolish shenanigans. When we allow our children to sleepover at a "friends" house, we make them vulnerable and expose them to a myriad of such risks that are just NOT WORTH IT!

We simply cannot be so trusting in a world like this – not when it comes to our children. We do not know people as well as we think. Often, when we hear of a child being molested or raped it was by someone they knew, not a complete stranger. This is true for boys and girls. The perpetrators are often the ones we least expect because they intentionally portray themselves as upstanding, respectable members of the community.

Already, there is so much in this world that our children are exposed to, that as parents, we have little control over. To compensate for this, we teach and train our children about potential vices and then "debrief" them after they have been away from us. BUT deciding who keeps our children overnight is an area in which we have complete control. There is no benefit to making sleepovers a part of our regular family practice. It is just not necessary.

In the nineties, the Honorable Minister Louis Farrakhan told the Sisters in the Nation of Islam not to engage in sleepovers…He was speaking to adult women! If there is a risk present for adults, certainly the danger is far greater for our children. We must realize that everyone does not parent the way we do; what is important to us may not be as important to others. At a sleepover, not only do we have to be wary of the supervising parents, but every other person that lives in the house as well. What about the other children coming to the sleepover? How well do we really know them and their families? What other relatives or friends of the family may be dropping by? And let's be honest, how much real supervision can adults provide in the wee hours of the night?

In his lecture, *How to Give Birth to a God* (Part 3), the Honorable Minister Louis Farrakhan warned, *"Passion is good, but young people –*

restrain it. And if you can't restrain it; mothers – fathers, keep watch. Your ever-present vigil will restrain the passion; because [it is] very difficult to get fired up with mom and dad looking. Mom and dad's presence kill passion. Just a quick turn on of the light will turnout dark thought."

When we accepted the responsibility to become parents, we accepted to take on a commitment that we do not get vacations from. Being physically present goes a long way towards the prevention of the unthinkable. On the surface, sleepovers appear harmless and fun; but just the fact that our children have to change clothes to get into their pajamas and then bathe away from home should be enough to make us cringe. These acts are far too intimate to permit them to take place just anywhere.

Unfortunately, it's parents, not children, who are the biggest promoters of sleepovers. They usually start hosting sleepovers when their children are very young – trying to help them make friends – and usually tying it to a birthday party. Sleepovers are foolishly seen as a rite of passage to some and give girls, in particular, an erroneous social status within a group. All of this could come at a steep price. The influence that our peers have on us at **any** age is formidable. For children, it is often difficult not to succumb. Sleepovers are breeding grounds for bad behavior. Curfews are extended or relinquished; mischievous pranks and games are played; television and social media rules are relaxed; sexual experimentation takes place; children have been hazed, sexually violated and worse. Yes, that's the reality for far too many. And if you or your children were fortunate enough to escape any of these horrors, we thank Allah (God). But still, was anything gained by sleeping over at someone's house just for "fun?"

While age-appropriate language should be used, we should definitely explain our concerns to our children. Knowing they are not permitted to attend sleepovers initially may not make them happy, but explaining the reason gives them an understanding that their safety and protection is the priority and we are not just being tyrants. Make this the family's way of life and stick to it! Soon, as a parent, we may not even hear about the sleepover invitations because our children will inform their friends that they *"don't do sleepovers!"* This way, no one's feelings are hurt because there is an understanding within their circle of friends that they cannot go to **anyone's** house for a sleepover – it's not personal. We cannot be afraid of being different in a world like this. Those of us who are striving to be righteous cannot simultaneously be seeking popularity and acceptance.

This world makes it difficult for parents to have a constant presence in the life of their children but fight and be willing to sacrifice to be with them. There will certainly be the occasional emergency or time with grandparents and other very close relatives, but even in these instances, we must use wisdom. There is a reason why Allah (God) chose **YOU** to be the parent for that child. Mother's intuition is REAL – do not ignore a warning from God. Usually, the first mind is your God-mind. The Holy Qur'an reads, *"And say: Praise be to Allah! He will show you His signs so that you shall recognize them. And thy Lord is not heedless of what you do"* (27:93).

Since we are all flawed individuals, we will inevitably make some parenting decisions which we will later bemoan. But saying, "NO," to sleepovers is one of those decisions we will NEVER regret.

REARING OUR GIRLS IS A CHORE:

In this age of gender-neutrality and an all-out rejection of gender-specific clothes, toys, sports, roles, and bathrooms; we offer a reality check. Boys and girls are not somewhat different; they are COMPLETELY different! And there is nothing wrong with that; it was designed this way by the Best Knower, God Himself. The Holy Qur'an reads, *"The male is not like the female."* Our deliberate rebellion against the nature in which God created the male and the female puts us in line for a divine whipping from Him. Today, there are no grey areas, God's Way is clearly distinct from error or Satan's way.

The title of this section, *"Rearing Our Girls is a Chore,"* should not be misinterpreted as harsh, chauvinistic or misogynistic. To state the obvious, the author of this book is a woman; she was born from a woman; LOVES Black women and is rearing a beautiful daughter. This title actually comes from the Honorable Minister Louis Farrakhan, who spoke these words to my husband during a dinner conversation – others were present who can bear witness. But before anyone gets upset with the Minister, let's delve into what he meant and why as parents we should approach rearing our girls with this divine insight.

Colloquially, the word "chore" has a negative connotation. But a chore is work that needs to be done **regularly**. Yes, this work is often difficult. It can be described as an assignment, a duty, job or a task. We can agree that the world in which we are rearing our girls is not one that respects, elevates and values the female as Allah (God) intended. This world constantly preys upon women and girls, physically and mentally. She is objectified, harassed, abused and discarded. If we approach the rearing of our girls as if this is not the reality, we will lose. As parents, we must be vigilant protectors of our girls – both mind and body, at all times. Rearing our girls is indeed a chore – it's constant and quite difficult. One blink could lead to being completely blindsided.

The Most Honorable Elijah Muhammad teaches us that, *"A Nation can rise no higher than its woman."* To the degree that the woman is reformed, refined, cultivated, civilized and educated in the Way of Allah (God) is to the same degree that the Nation will reflect this way of life. It will be directly proportional; no more, no less. So, the Most Honorable Elijah Muhammad said that 75 percent of his work of reform was with the Black woman, the Mother of Civilization. Seventy-five percent of the work must be with her because this is where 75 percent of the problem is found. Solve the problem of reforming the Black woman and you solve the problem of restoring a people to once again reflect the Glory of God, resulting in a superior Nation. This obligates anyone who has any role or duty whatsoever that involves rearing, educating or handling our girls in anyway to be painstakingly attentive, cautious and righteous in our methodology.

Master Fard Muhammad said, *"The hardest job ever given to any human being"* is the job of resurrecting the so-called American Negro. We can all debate as to what the second hardest job is; but somewhere high up on the list has to be, rearing our girls in a world where perverse behavior is in vogue. Regardless of how much the enemy tries to make evil fair-seeming, wise parents must resist and choose to rear their children in the nature in which they were created. This contrary way of life will not remain forever because the truth is always confirmed. The enemy clearly warns us in the Holy Qur'an, *"And the devil will say, when the matter is decided: Surely Allah promised you a promise of truth, and I promised you, then failed you. And I had no authority over you, except that I called you and you obeyed me; so, blame me not but blame yourselves. I cannot come to your help, nor can you come to my help. I deny your associating me with Allah before. Surely for the unjust is a painful chastisement"* (14:22).

We cannot take on the rearing of our boys and girls in the exact same manner because they are not the same. In her book, *Queen of the Planet Earth: The Rebirth and Rise of the Original Woman*, Minister Ava Muhammad writes, *"When a woman or man does not manifest feminine or masculine traits, it is the result of environment and experience, not nature.*

What we are looking at is the nature of things; that which Allah (God) intended."

A distinctive quality in the nature of the female is to be pleasing to Allah (God). This is why we also find in her nature a desire to equal herself up to man; up to God. Not because she wants to challenge God, but because she desires to be just like Him. Therefore, girls naturally seek to please the male figures in their lives who are exercising a degree of force and power (their godhood). Women and girls naturally gravitate to powerful men. This can be dangerous because most who manifest power in this world are unrighteous. Those unrighteous men take advantage of the nature of the female by showing their approval of her only in terms of her physical adornments. The vast number of so-called "compliments" given to girls are based solely on her appearance. This poses a serious challenge for parents because it is baked into the nature of the female to be beautiful. In her book, *Naturally Beautiful*, Minister Ava Muhammad writes, *"Understand that our primary goal as women is to be beautiful…The desire to be beautiful is innate; it was programmed into our DNA by the First God Who Created Himself in and from the triple darkness of space."*

Herein lies the great chore in rearing our girls. If found in her nature, given to her by Allah (God) Himself, is a primary goal to be beautiful; then how does she know that she has attained that goal if someone does not declare her to be *beautiful*. Subconsciously she is always seeking this confirmation. It is critical that this declaration initially comes from her father and the righteous men in her life or she will seek it elsewhere. It is also important that this affirmation not be one fleeting moment in time. She must be consistently reassured since she is simultaneously being bombarded with the warped standard of beauty set by the narrow lens of the enemy. Their definition of beauty is distorted and unnatural. Girls study their fathers and

318

the men around them, to see what pleases them. If parents, particularly fathers of daughters, buy into this world's ideal beauty – the scantily clad temptress; our daughters will seek to become that, thinking they are pleasing their father and indirectly pleasing God.

As our daughters get older and their bodies begin to mature and develop, it is increasingly important that they not wear short clothing, clothes that reveal their bosoms and backsides, or tight form-fitting attire. Now, why is all of this necessary? The Holy Qur'an reads, *"O Prophet, tell thy wives and thy daughters and the women of believers to let down upon them their over-garments. This is more proper, so that they may be **known**, and **not given trouble**. And Allah is ever Forgiving, Merciful"* (33:59).

Allah (God) desires for righteous women to be clearly distinguished so that she will not be harassed or assaulted by lustful undisciplined men. The way Allah (God) wants women to dress is protection for her, not a punishment. We have to make sure our daughters understand this. As children get older, they respond best when we approach them with reason and intelligence. Nagging and threatening will only drive them toward rebellion. The fact is, once our daughters reach a certain age, we can no longer guard their chastity for them; they must guard it themselves. The only way this will happen successfully is if they were taught and trained to value their sacredness from the cradle.

Naturally, girls have a stronger need to be accepted because they are innately more communal than boys, who are more individualistic. This means parents must be ever vigilant about how their girls go about trying to be acceptable in the eyes of their peers and society in general. Yes, there is a double standard in this world that puts the burden on women. We need to know it and understand it. The standard for women is higher, as it should be since we can birth a Nation of gods through our wombs.

Remember Maryam as our standard and let's teach our daughters about her. As we consistently impress upon them at an early age their immeasurable value, we are preparing them to one day give birth to a god. Preparation for motherhood and fatherhood begins as a child. God willing, our children will have the desire to one day produce someone better than themselves.

The Honorable Minister Louis Farrakhan described the value of our precious daughters as immeasurable and limitless. When we look at them, we too have to see that same quality; so, we will never be tempted to forsake the difficulty factor attached to rearing our girls and preserving their virtue.

A MOTHER'S ADVICE TO HER SON:

It goes without saying that every father has a duty to provide continual sound advice for his son, during the time of his youth and beyond. A good mother will naturally do the same for her daughter. However, the wisest of parents will partner as each other's reinforcement irrespective of the child's gender. The experience and knowledge of others, particularly one's parents, can be far more beneficial than going it alone if the successes and failures are studied and used as a tool to guide future decisions. There is a brief section in the Book of Proverbs where a mother offers such counsel to her son; but not just any son – her son is a king, King Lemuel.

A study of King Lemuel will offer very little in terms of concrete facts but will provide quite a bit of speculation and scholarly conjecture about his actual identity. Outside of nine brief verses, there is virtually no additional scriptural information about him. We know he was a ruler, somewhat of a poet and that he had a very wise mother. The latter is clear because within those nine brief verses we find three excellent pieces of advice from a Queen

Mother to her son. The prevailing view is that King Lemuel was actually King Solomon, who was known for his great wisdom. If true, this would then make the Queen Mother, who imparted such profound advice, Bathsheba. But, whomever the King was, we know he was a leader with great responsibilities and a great following, therefore the advice she gave to her son should be modeled by all mothers who want their sons to aspire to greatness. After all, the bloodline of the Black man and woman is regal, and our DNA is divine.

The Queen Mother first advises her son, *"Listen, my son! Listen, son of my womb! Listen, my son, the answer to my prayers! Do not spend your strength on women, your vigor on those who ruin kings"* (Proverbs 31: 2-3, NIV). According to linguists and scholars, the name Lemuel means, "for God" or "devoted to God." Here, we have a mother pleading with her son and reminding him of who he is, a man of God. Men of God are not promiscuous or casual about relations with women. Not only is this way of life immoral and sinful; but it will undoubtedly lead to the ruin of a great man and perhaps the destruction of his family and kingdom. Unfortunately, history (and present-day) provides us with a litany of examples of powerful men who have been taken down and trapped by their inordinate lust for women and lascivious behavior. One's strength and vigor are gradually weakened by succumbing to lower desires. Not only is his seed weakened with each unlawful act, but he also becomes mentally impotent and ineffective.

The Queen Mother's next piece of advice is a warning about the dangers of intoxicants: *"It is not for kings, Lemuel – it is not for kings to drink wine, not for rulers to crave beer, lest they drink and forget what has been decreed, and deprive all the oppressed of their rights"* (Proverbs 31: 4-5, NIV). It is not difficult to understand why the Queen Mother would warn her son against the dangers of alcohol. The ethanol in alcoholic beverages is mind altering and if overused leads to symptoms of intoxication – difficulty concentrating and processing information; memory loss; problems with planning and decision making; and having difficulty regulating emotions – not the characteristics one would expect from a great ruler. How can justice be fairly adjudicated by a lawless incoherent king?

Alcohol does not only have an adverse effect on the brain but also on the body. It overworks the liver. One of the primary functions of the liver is to remove toxins from the bloodstream. If the liver is constantly removing alcohol from the system, it cannot adequately remove the countless other poisons the body accumulates. In *How to Give Birth to a God: Part Two*, the Honorable Minister Louis Farrakhan also warns of the harmful effects that alcohol can have on the man's offspring, *"You must clean yourself up, Brother; because the sperm that you have, which represents the future of your life, that's a sacred thing. But you're poisoning it every time you drop alcohol, a cigarette, or dope into yourself – it's reflected in your sperm."*

The Holy Qur'an also bears witness that intoxicants are unclean, *"the devil's work."* Therefore, the Believers should shun strong drinks if they want to be successful. According to the Qur'an, intoxicants are one of the things the devil (wicked men and women) uses to create enmity and hatred among the righteous and to keep Believers from prayer and the remembrance of Allah (God). Therefore, the sin of intoxicants is greater than any advantage it may offer.

The Queen Mother's final words of wisdom for her son were regarding his responsibilities to the poor and the destitute. She instructs her son, *"Speak up for those who cannot speak for themselves, for the rights of all who are destitute. Speak up and judge fairly; defend the rights of the poor and the needy"* (Proverbs 31: 8-9, NIV). What a wonderful woman! What a wonderful mother! This advice reveals the true beauty of the heart and soul of this extraordinary woman of God. She is the Queen Mother; her son is a King and their family rules over others, but her concern remains focused on *the least of these*. Her first two pieces of advice were given so that ultimately, her son would be in a physical and mental position where he could execute her third instruction to the best of his ability.

The Honorable Minister Louis Farrakhan has reminded us that we cannot rise above the condition of our people. As long as there are others who lack the knowledge, wisdom, and understanding needed to improve their condition, our work is not done. Our concern should not be for our family alone, but for all of humanity. We should follow this Queen Mother's sound advice and the example of our Beloved Minister, who continues to speak for those who cannot speak for themselves; who advocates for the destitute; and who tirelessly defends the rights of the poor and the needy.

PRODUCING GOOD HUSBANDS AND FATHERS:

If you are the mother or father of a daughter, surely one of your many prayers for her is that she will one day have a meaningful courtship with an outstanding young man – which will ultimately lead to a healthy, strong marriage. The prayers, of course, are the same for our sons. The additional burden that parents carry when rearing a son is that they remain keenly aware that one day if it is the Will of Allah (God), their sons will have to be the head of their own households. This responsibility entails many things, but primarily the man is charged by Allah (God) as being the spiritual head of his family. He must also be a good provider, maintainer, and protector of his wife and children.

The head of anything leads the body. The body of an organization or family reflects the condition of the head. Black women and children are especially in need of good husbands and fathers to return to their God-given position as the natural head of the family. Every mother and father of a son is in a crucial position because preparation for manhood and fatherhood begins as a child. Learning how to be responsible for self and others should begin in our youth; not as adults. So, the role of parents is to prepare our children for adulthood, a time which will constitute approximately 85% of their lifespan!

The physical differences between boys and girls are obvious; but as early as the toddler years, the evidence is clear that there are distinctive differences in the character and behavior traits of boys and girls that bear witness to the nature in which God created them from the womb. The brain of a boy is structurally different from the brain of a girl. Allah (God) intentionally wired our brains differently to emphasize different character and behavior traits so that our natures would complement each other, not repel one another. Hundreds of studies have been done in various countries over the decades that highlight innate differences in boys and girls. These differences do not make one superior to the other but being aware of these natural differences allow parents to rear their children according to their nature and not societal trends.

According to some of these studies, girls are generally more in-tuned to people's emotions while boys are more interested in objects. However, girls that are exposed to higher than normal levels of testosterone in the womb also show an above average interest in trucks and cars – an interest that boys generally express naturally. Research shows that very early on, boys have an advantage when it comes to spatial skills, *"the ability to solve problems involving size, distance and the relationship between objects."* Boys are certainly faster and have more brute strength than their counterparts, but girls have more endurance and can withstand more heat. Beginning in the womb, boys are more physically active than girls and are also more aggressive. However, with environmental factors being equal, girls consistently begin talking sooner than boys and maintain larger vocabularies.

The Honorable Elijah Muhammad teaches that a woman should be a comforter and consoler to a man who is working to be a good provider, protector, and maintainer. The aforementioned differences make her the perfect candidate for this role. These physiological differences were clearly designed by Allah (God). Evidence of the nature in which He created us is also provided in the scriptures. The Holy Qur'an reads, *"He it is Who created you from a single soul, and of the same did He make his mate, that he might find comfort in her"* (7: 189). It also reads, *"And of His signs is this, that He created mates for you from yourselves that you might find quiet of mind in them, and He put between you love and compassion. Surely there are signs in this for a people who reflect"* (Holy Qur'an 30: 21). Referencing the man, the Holy Qur'an states, *"Men are the maintainers of women, with what Allah has made some of them to excel others and with what they spend out of their wealth"* (4: 34).

Every child, boy or girl, needs their mother to be the primary nurturer and most influential person in their life from birth through adolescence. She is the first nurse, teacher, and trainer for a reason. But as mothers, we must be careful to remain mindful of the nature in which our sons were created. The Honorable Minister Louis Farrakhan said that a concern in the Black community is that we are rearing our daughters to be strong and our sons to be weak. As a consequence, there are too few men in the community to show Black men how to be real men. So, what can we do to reverse this trend?

Boys are naturally aggressive; that aggression should not be destroyed, just redirected. In his book, **A Torchlight for America**, The Honorable Minister Louis Farrakhan wrote, *"We need to do more to curb and* *guide the natural aggressive tendencies among young men. In the wealthy communities the rich are able to channel the aggression of their young men into meaningful activities.* He mentions that boys, in particular, need athletic involvement – competition in league and team sports or camps; even regular access to an athletic facility used to channel their aggression will help.

There is also a need in our sons to prove to themselves and their parents that they can handle increased independence and responsibilities. Mothers of sons tend to be overly protective and doting – this can feed weakness and dependence instead of fostering strength and autonomy. Therefore, mothers must be careful not to spoil their sons while they bring the wrath down on their daughters. As mothers, we must make sure we parent with fairness and balance.

Our sons are not exempt from household chores. They should learn how to cook, wash dishes, clean, do laundry, etc. But more importantly, they must gain a level of comfort and mastery in those skills that involve serious labor – car maintenance, lawn care, appliance repairs, home restoration, and basic construction. This does not mean that our girls cannot also acquire these skills, but our boys MUST have them! It is also important for a young man to be physically fit and know how to defend himself and those he loves. He must always remain prepared by regularly practicing and training in the art of self-defense. Every woman wants the peace of mind of knowing that her husband is not just willing, but physically able to defend her.

While it may be ideal for our daughters not to leave the home of her parents until she is ready to move directly into the home of her husband; this is not necessarily ideal for our sons. Getting a handle on real-life responsibilities like sustaining an income, paying bills, saving and budgeting all while maintaining a household, outside of the protective bubble of his parents may be necessary before the addition of a family.

When our boys reach adolescence, which starts around age 10; he needs a man, ideally his father, to now become the primary and most influential person in his life. Mothers must let them go and not become possessive and overly protective. He will never become a responsible man if we continue to hold his hand. Turn him over to his father – a man can best teach another male how to be a real man. We know that there are exceptions – many single women have and are rearing boys to become outstanding men. The Honorable Minister Louis Farrakhan is a notable example that it can absolutely be done. But it is very difficult because it requires a special woman, who must be willing to go outside of her nature to teach and train a boy to become a man.

In the Nation of Islam, we are taught, *"Make all men and boys join the F.O.I. Train them fast and make them brave fighters willing at any time to give their lives for Allah's sake and righteousness."* The men's class in the Nation of Islam is called the Fruit of Islam (F.O.I.). It is the name given to the military Training of the men that belong to Islam in North America. This class is private, meaning women and girls are not allowed. The Sisters also have a private class that complements the Brothers' class, called the M.G.T. & G.C.C. (Muslim Girls' Training & General Civilization Class). Men must be properly taught and trained on how to become protectors, providers, and maintainers; all while being the spiritual head of their families. These skills will not be infused into them through osmosis, they must be taught and trained.

Consensual sex before marriage is also a concern. We have to pay attention to our children as their bodies mature and a natural interest in the opposite sex arises. We are obligated to emphasize abstinence until marriage with our sons as well as our daughters. This is God's way. Sex without purpose is a violation of the law of God and therefore has serious consequences. When the male is promiscuous, he is regularly emitting fluid with no purpose outside of sexual gratification. This is a violation. The consequence is that his life germ loses its potency and it actual become physically and spiritually weakened. As a result, his offspring will also be physically and spiritually weaker than what God intended. Due to the lack of knowledge, we foolishly allow our boys to indulge in sex, while we reprimand our daughters.

The enemy has us so messed up to the point that we will almost push our children to become sexually active out of fear that if they do not, it is a sign of homosexuality. STOP IT! We should encourage our children to restrain their sexual passions until they are married and help them to do so by not allowing intimate interactions with the opposite sex. Since our children are not to have boyfriends and girlfriends, period – we should not foster an environment that could lead to such relationships. Adolescent boys, in particular, need to practice *How to Eat to Live* – being able to discipline our diet helps to discipline the sexual appetite.

It is very difficult for most parents, especially mothers, to allow their children to venture out into adulthood. Rarely does a parent believe the child is ready because it is impossible to prepare them for every scenario they could possibly encounter – but that is not the objective. We cannot protect our children from all trials, difficulties or pain because struggle is ordained by Allah (God) for each and every one of us. They have to go through what Allah (God) has deemed necessary for their development. However, we can help them to not experience the **EXACT** same trials, difficulties, and pain that we endured by sharing our experiences and doing our best to give them an advantage through teaching and training.

Water seeks its own level. So, if we give our sons a strong foundation and help them to prepare as best we can, to become good husbands and fathers, then God-willing, they will attract a young woman whose parents have done the same – they will complement one another and be on their way to building a healthy and powerful union.

LYING FOR THE SAKE OF TRADITION?

People who lie repeatedly are called liars; classified as untrustworthy and considered despicable. On the other hand, people who lie repeatedly to children for the sake of some tradition are generally excused and even enabled to help to keep the lie going. Why is it justified to continuously lie to our children while it is frowned upon in most other circumstances? Who said this was okay? Admittedly, we are all guilty of lying; but when it comes to lying for the sake of traditions (which Black people have adopted from our former slave masters) the hoax becomes elaborate; and often lasts for many, many years. The three most consistent oft-repeated lies that American parents tell their children are concerning the existence of Santa Claus, the Easter Bunny and the Tooth Fairy – all made-up mythical, magical, imaginary characters.

It is never a good idea to lie to children; not in the name of playful fun or for the sake of preserving a fabricated tradition. Lying is anti-God; which also makes it anti-self. The Honorable Minister Louis Farrakhan stated, *"The Honorable Elijah Muhammad said that Allah (God) created within us **14 billion brain cells**. That's an awful lot of brain cells! 'And every brain cell,' the Honorable Elijah Muhammad said, 'is created by God to **think right.'** Allah (God) never created the brain to think wrong...when Falsehood is introduced, and men begin to entertain false ideas, false concepts; and take Falsehood for Truth; where men begin to think and meditate on that which is False, giving their lives and the power of their brain to that which is false, then you start destroying the power of the brain cell to bring up vision."*

The Bible teaches – *"Where there is no vision, the people perish..."* (Proverbs 29:18). How could we have visions while nursing from falsehood which goes against the grain of our brain, destroying its power, one lie at a time? The terrible irony is that the optimal time for children to learn, birth to six years old, is also the same span of time in which they are bombarded with the lies about Santa Claus, the Easter Bunny, and the Tooth Fairy. Babies and toddlers learn so much faster than adults because not only are their brains growing physically, but this is the time in which their cognitive development is accelerated. This means their brain is still being fashioned; but instead of taking advantage of this peaking mental acuity, we are introducing lies. Whatever goes on while something is being fashioned becomes a part of the very nature of the thing that is being fashioned. This goes for both truth and falsehood. Once brain cells have been destroyed, they cannot be restored; only Allah (God) has the power to replace our brain cells after their destruction. And nothing destroys the brain cells created with God's Truth, faster than Falsehood.

The Most Honorable Elijah Muhammad gave his followers *16 Restrictive Laws and 10 Guiding Rules of Conduct* which we strive to uphold everyday of our lives. One of his *Guiding Rules of Conduct* states, **"No lying (speak the truth regardless of circumstances)."** Regardless of the circumstance, the situation, the condition, the factor or the tradition; we should speak the truth! This is not easy to do, but it is required if we want to follow the example of the Father. We are taught that the one thing that God cannot do is lie. His very existence and the Truth that governs the creation of His Universe dictates that everything He says and every action He takes is THE TRUTH.

Good parenting does not involve lying. The external consequences of a so-called, "white lie," may not be immediately evident – but what is happening to the brain cells of the parent who tells the lie and the brain cells of the child that is forced to receive the lie and make sense out of the nonsensical? Reindeer cannot fly! Jolly Old Saint Nick does not deliver gifts to every child on earth in one night! There is no Tooth Fairy! And bunnies do not lay eggs! This is not innocent fun. An "innocent lie" is an oxymoron. Lies cannot be innocent; every lie is imbedded with a negative consequence.

We can easily prove that both Christmas and Easter were never intended to truly celebrate the birth and resurrection of Jesus Christ. But if one believes that they were – then at least celebrate the Lord on those days. This is why we say, **'Up with Jesus, Down with Santa!'** What is wrong with parents telling their children that they are responsible for those wonderful gifts? Tell them that it was mommy and daddy who put the money under their pillow. Then, tell them that Resurrection Sunday has nothing to do with bunnies, eggs, candy or new dresses; it is about our Savior, Jesus Christ!! Be honest with children. They will eventually learn the truth anyway. And when they do, how do we now explain this deception to our children – likely, with more lies? We should not give our children a reason to ever distrust us as parents. We are hypocrites if we expect our children to be truthful with us, but we are not willing to model honesty for them. Even when our children ask us general questions, if we do not know the answer, tell them, *'I don't know, but I will try to find out for you.'* Do not make up an answer to pacify them; this too is lying.

If the devil is a liar, then the righteous must be the truth-tellers. No excuses – we must stop this insanity. If we are being honest, keeping up these lies do more to serve parents in the eyes of their peers than it does for their children. The Honorable Minister Louis Farrakhan's mother would come down very hard on him and his brother for lying. She would say, *"I'm gonna beat you more for lying, because a liar will steal, and a thief will murder, so*

I'm gonna stop you at the lie." Child psychologists are now bearing witness. Studies show that the lies of a parent can have detrimental effects on their children's behavior. The children are more likely to lie themselves, become cheaters and increase in deviant behavior.

According to the scriptures, the truth is freeing for everyone who embraces it. It is the truth that makes us free. Lies keep us in mental and spiritual bondage. Let's stop feeding brilliant children foolishness and get away from deceiving our children for the sake of traditions. As we mature, we are supposed to grow closer and closer to Oneness with Allah (God). Immersing our children in falsehood for the first several years of their life is reversing their natural course towards God. *"The Lord detests lying lips, but He delights in people who are trustworthy"* (Proverbs 12:22, NIV). What a wonderful existence to be able to walk the earth secure because we know that we are among those whom Allah (God) delights!

STOP CALLING CHILDREN, 'KIDS':

Language has always shaped our thinking and vice versa – the way we think is expressed through our language. Every action is first preceded by a thought. The act of speech; our deliberate choice of word usage, in every instance is first preceded by a thought. The thought could be a lengthy internal deliberation or completed in an instant, but the eventual spoken word is rooted in our thinking. While the written word can be reviewed, edited, revised and perfected; casual, everyday vernacular will emerge solely from our personal vocabulary catalog, not from someone else's. The question is: Who is the originator of the words we select to file in our personal catalog?

It is fair to presume that those reading this book can also speak and write the English language. However, most of us are not self-taught English speakers. We learned to understand and speak the language primarily through immersion – everyone in our environment spoke English, so we picked it up. Later, we were instructively taught how to read and write the language. Somewhere during our rearing, we understood that certain words were considered vulgar or profane, so we either refrained from using them altogether or we were careful where and with whom we chose to use them. A powerful lesson that members of the Nation of Islam learn early in our studies is that many common words and phrases can be just as profane and vulgar as others if used improperly.

During, *The Time and What Must Be Done* Lecture Series (Part 16), The Honorable Minister Louis Farrakhan said, *"...A 'kid' is a young goat...Beloved brothers and sisters, stop calling your children 'kids!' When we understand the nature of the goat, why would you name your little children after something that is 'wild,' that is 'mischievous'—that is a 'trouble maker?' Goats are akin to the sheep, but the nature of the sheep is different from the nature of the goat. And so, Jesus used these two animals in his parable of 'The Separation between The Sheep and The Goat' found in the Book of Matthew, Chapter 25, verses 31-46."*

The word 'kid,' appears several times in the Bible, but it is only used to reference a young or baby goat; **never** a child. Though the origin of referring to our children as 'kids' seemingly goes back centuries, it was not used as a term of endearment. It was not until the 1960s and 1970s that referring to any and all children as 'kids' became commonplace and completely interchangeable with 'children.' A kid is the offspring of a goat. Our children are not baby goats or young goats, they are children of the Most High God. It is insulting and disrespectful to The Father to refer to His children as goats. Remember, our children come through us, but they are not from us – they are from Allah (God). Only a goat can give birth to a kid; humans produce children.

The Scripture reads, *"When the Son of Man comes in his glory, and all the angels with him, he will sit on his glorious throne. All the nations will be gathered before him, and he will separate the people one from another as a shepherd separates the sheep from the goats. He will put the sheep on his right and the goats on his left. Then the King will say to those on his right, 'Come, you who are blessed by my Father; take your inheritance, the kingdom prepared for you since the creation of the world...'"* (Matthew 25: 31-34). So, if there is a distinction between the sheep and the goat. The same distinction can be made between their offspring, the lamb and the kid. After such a pronouncement, why would anyone want any association with the goat, in name or in deed?

We certainly cannot make any valid comparison of our children to goats based on physical appearance; so, the only practical reason to begin referring to children as baby goats (kids) is that at some point, a correlation was made between the behavior and characteristics of goats to that of children. As the Minister stated, goats are wild mischievous troublemakers – they are unruly scavengers that are very difficult to tame. Goats are nearly impossible to discipline because they are born of a stubborn rebellious nature. Now, some may be reading this saying, *"Yep, I know some children that fit that description."* That may be true; but if a child had learning challenges, would we call him or her, 'stupid?' No! Not only would we skillfully teach the child, but we would consistently shower them with positive encouraging adjectives that speak into them their potential, so it may manifest one day. Words create reality; call them kids and they will behave like baby goats.

According to the dictionary, a person likened to a goat (particularly a man) is depicted as a libertine, a womanizer, a seducer, a pervert, a

334

philanderer, a dirty old man, a debauchee, an adulterer, etc. People who are characterized as *goatish* are lecherous, hypersexual, licentious, lustful, salacious, lewd and immoral. Even the term *scapegoat* comes from the Book of Leviticus (16: 9-10), where a goat symbolically took on all the sins of the people and was casted out into the wilderness.

Let's please do away with calling our precious children 'kids' and all of its variants…kiddos, kiddies, kidders, etc. We must challenge ourselves and others to make this correction – gentle reminders are all that is required. The term 'kid' is unworthy of our children; it is snide and dismissive. Our children are divine and far too sacred to be cheapened and lowered to the level of the beasts.

In the Holy Qur'an, Allah (God) says that He has made subservient to man whatever is in the heavens and whatever is in the earth and granted us His favors complete outwardly and inwardly (31:20). This means that nothing in creation is above or even equal to a man and woman. We should strive to reflect God in our appearance, our behavior, our character, our traditions, and our language. Children are not pets and should never be equated as such. We must elevate our language to draw the distinction. A kid will eventually become a mature goat. But the nature of a child is to one day manifest the Glory of God.

BIRTHDAYS 2.0:

The Honorable Minister Louis Farrakhan once said that the only thing that makes the date of our birth significant is if during our life, we accomplish something significant. Going further, he said, *"People expect that when they have a birthday, somebody's supposed to give them something—a life that has done nothing, expecting something. When your birthday rolls around, remember your mother. Because she's the one who bore you with fainting and pain. And every year that you are blessed to be alive, thank her."*

Interestingly, the early Christians did not celebrate birthdays; and presently, Orthodox Jews, Muslims, Jehovah's Witnesses, and many others do not participate in this practice. So, what is the origin of birthday celebrations? Why do we have parties, give gifts, eat cake, light a candle, make a wish and sing that song? But before we get into that – what do the scriptures say about birthdays?

There is no mention of birthday celebrations in the Holy Qur'an; but the Bible does, in fact, mention birthdays four times – what's recorded may surprise you! The first reference to a birthday celebration was that of Pharaoh's (Genesis 40:20-22). Pharaoh, as we know, was not a servant of God and actively worked to oppose Him. Consequently, being the ruthless man that he was, by the end of Pharaoh's birthday feast, he had hanged his chief baker, *hmm*. The second reference is found in the Book of Job (1:4-5). In the King James Version, the phrase *"every one his day"* is used, but the New International Version translates this to "birthdays." Here, there is a description of Job's sons who would also have feasts on their birthdays, inviting their sisters to join them. After the birthday feast, Job – a faithful servant of God – would arrange for his children to be purified because he feared that they had sinned, *wow*. Lastly, the final two references to birthdays are two accounts of the same celebration – Herod's birthday – another man who did not serve God. Similarly, at the end of Herod's birthday supper a man dies – John the Baptist – he was beheaded at the request of the daughter of Herodias (Matthew 14:6-10 and Mark 6:21-28).

So, according to the Bible, birthday celebrations involved feasts, large suppers or banquets – basically, modern-day parties. Emerging from this is a pagan-rooted practice that continues to this day. Pagans were spooky.

They believed that on the date of someone's birth they were more susceptible to being attacked by evil spirits, so the more people they had around them with presents, the more protection they had to ward off these spirits. Pagans also believed the candles were *"endowed with special magic for granting wishes."* Other scholars claim that we have the early Greeks to thank for the round cakes that represented the Goddess of the Moon, adding the candles was symbolic for moonlight. Modern rituals now include singing the "Happy Birthday" song and even giving birthday spankings or licks equivalent to the age of the recipient *(and one to grow on)*.

The Honorable Minister Louis Farrakhan teaches that all of this is rooted in a bigger practice of the enemy's attempt to mark time. His time is linear, it begins and ends; while ours is cyclical. Satan asks Allah (God) in the Holy Qur'an to respite him until the day they (the righteous) are raised (in consciousness). Birthdays, anniversaries, New Year's Day, and many holidays are an attempt for one who knows his end is near to keep track of how much more time he has left to cause havoc on the earth while keeping the people of God distracted and engaged in foolishness.

We are not saying that there is anything wrong with simply wishing someone well on the anniversary of their birth – that's fine. And if we so choose, we are certainly also free to give our children gifts. Just don't get carried away. Perhaps consider giving them a gift because they pleased us; or because they accomplished something great; or just because we felt like being generous – not because they *expect* a gift on their birthday. The only reason they have that expectation is that we taught them to have it.

Allah (God) is the Giver of Gifts and the ultimate gift He gave us was the gift of life. We should show Him gratitude and be reflective when He permits us to gain another year. We should commit to representing His Greatness even better as we add a year of maturity. The Minister's sentiments are also clear – a wonderful display of appreciation for our birth would be to show love, reverence, and gratitude for our mother, whose womb God used to bring us forth – she is worthy of receiving gifts DAILY!

How we choose to go forward from this day forward is our prerogative, but it is always more empowering when our actions are informed and made with a conscious mind. Keeping up traditions and rituals without understanding the root is unworthy of us in an era where information is easily accessible.

We close this section with a beautiful and profound perspective from Mother Tynnetta Muhammad: *"Normally, we are not enjoined to celebrate birthdays because they accent the aging process. According to the Divine Teachings of the Most Honorable Elijah Muhammad, Allah came to reverse the aging process and not to emphasize age in our evolution to be ever young. The idea of getting older makes you think older as opposed to getting younger because you are what you think. Every time we say, 'How old are you,' we are emphasizing the aging process and not the youthful, blissful days of our lives. We must celebrate our birth into the Work and Mission of our Nation's Resurrection into the New Life of the Hereafter in which we will be rejuvenated and made forever young."*

All praise is due to Allah (God)!

IT TAKES A VILLAGE:

Whether it's just a cliché or a genuine African proverb, it stands true – *"It takes a village to raise a child."* In its simplest terms, a village is "a place where people live that is usually smaller than a town." But a traditional authentic village is so much more. It is best described as an interdependent

338

society, comprised of an assemblage of several families, organized by agreed upon spiritual, economic, political and social laws, norms and values. If we visited any African village today, we would come with certain expectations. We would expect everyone to speak a common language; to practice the same religion, and to share a common lineage. We would also expect the members to have common political views; share a common code of conduct, and perhaps even physically resemble one another. Most importantly, we would expect to find every member of the village contributing in some way. Anything contrary to this would strike us as odd. In America, we call villages – communities.

Why does it take a village to raise a child? The Honorable Minister Louis Farrakhan said, *"Environment can influence heredity; therefore, we must be careful what environment we put ourselves in because no matter what is in you of good if you are in the wrong environment, that environment can affect the good that is in you and turn you into itself."* So, the environment can influence our biologic genetic make-up!

Conversely, the Minister also said, *"Whatever goes on while something is being made, goes into the make-up of the thing. You can't be making something in an environment and something from the environment drops into the thing and then you keep on going; it's made into the thing."* Based on these statements, we can see how a pregnant mother can affect the very genetic make-up of her child based on the environment she is in while pregnant AND once born, this same child's heredity can be influenced by the environment in which he/she is reared. That's powerful!

In the Nation of Islam, we have been blessed with several divinely inspired Study Guides by the Honorable Minister Louis Farrakhan that all fall under the title, *Self-Improvement: The Basis for Community Development*. These Study Guides are available to anyone who seeks them. One of the things we learn in this particular course of study is that *"There is no such thing as a member of a Nation who does not count."* The Minister said, *"Community development is not building buildings. Community development is building people and linking people with people."*

Consider this scenario: A beautiful, faithful couple has decided to expand their family. They have been planning physically, mentally and spiritually well in advance, as we are taught in ***How to Give Birth to a God***; and they are then blessed with a healthy, strong child – a potential god. Where will this god be reared; a daycare; or at home? Where will this god attend school? Where will the food come from to nourish the god? Who will be the god's doctor? Who will be the god's playmates and friends? Which extended family members will have access to the god? Who will coach or instruct the god in extracurricular activities? Where will the god go for spiritual guidance and rejuvenation? The answers to all of these questions and many more should be found in the village. And the strength of the village will be determined by the level of development of each member and how strongly linked they are to one another.

The Holy Qur'an reads, *"Surely this your community is a single community, and I am your Lord, so serve Me"* (21:92). Self-improvement is not for the sake of the individual alone, but for the good of the entire community. No matter how hard we may try, we do not and cannot live in a vacuum. We are taught that no man or woman can rise above the condition of his/her people. If we do not work to develop the community or the village, it will not matter how successful we appear, we will eventually be negatively impacted by that same village. Don't misunderstand – yes, it takes a village, but that does not absolve us of our personal responsibility to self and our immediate family. We are not to abuse this proverb by holding it up as evidence to exonerate us from bad behavior or poor parenting. The village becomes the beneficiary when we undertake **self**-examination, **self**-analysis, and **self**-correction. This process brings about personal balance, which has a positive impact on the community, making our personal contribution more effective.

We should ask ourselves: How am I personally contributing to the village? If we are all brothers and sisters, then we ALL have nieces and nephews that we can influence. Are we being good aunties and uncles? Do we want for our brothers and sisters what we want for ourselves? The Honorable Minister Louis Farrakhan once said that sometimes Aunty may have more success with a rebellious child where Mommy falls short.

A distinguishing characteristic of a village is that it is interdependent; we depend on each other. Our functions may differ, like the functions of the organs in our body, but they all depend on each other to operate at an optimum level. The heart and the liver have different functions, but the same goal – keep the body healthy and alive. Yet, we know that liver disease can weaken the heart and heart disease can impact the liver. Similarly, in the life of a child, the function of a parent is different than the function of the karate sensei; but the ultimate goal is the same – help the child to have a well-rounded and fulfilling quality of life. If either party neglects their role, there will be a ripple effect on the child's ability to operate effectively within the village.

We know that in order to have the ideal village comprised of ideal families we are going to have to separate from our enemy; it's the BEST and ONLY solution. In the meantime, however; we must increase our efforts to improve self, unite with those likeminded and make our communities a safe and decent place to live.

THE NOBILITY OF MA'AM & SIR:

Honorifics like *Ma'am* and *Sir* used to convey honor, respect, politeness and showed evidence of having good manners, but they are now being received with the offense of a four-letter word. The most offended on the spectrum appears to be "middle-aged" women, who misinterpret being called *Ma'am* as an indication that the speaker believes them to be of a more mature age than actual. And of course, there is no greater sin than aging a woman before her time - *smile*. In general, men who are not regularly called *Sir*, seem to be indifferent when extended the courtesy. Age is not and should not be the deciding factor when choosing to refer to someone as *Ma'am* or *Sir* - there is great wisdom behind restoring these expressions of status and nobility.

Not surprisingly, when we research the origin of *Ma'am* and *Sir*, we find that these abbreviations come from titles once reserved for British royalty. [Before going any further, please remember that the true kings and queens of the planet Earth are Black men and women; our blood is regal, and our essence is divine – but I digress.] *Sir* is short for 'sire' and *Ma'am* is short for ma dame (my lady) or madam. Today in the U.S., we commonly use madam and sir to indicate status in political, military and judicial institutions (i.e. Madam Secretary). So, while some of us 'regular folks' are peeved by symbols of gallantry, those who have worked for years to reach a high status in their profession believe they are not only deserving but have an expectation of the honor and respect that *Ma'am* and *Sir* yield.

Brothers and Sisters in the Nation of Islam can be found extending the respect and courtesy of *Ma'am* and *Sir* to a five-year-old just as quickly as they would to a ninety-year-old. Age is irrelevant. As direct descendants of Allah (God), we were born into the world with a divine status and therefore addressing one another in this dignified manner is our birthright to receive and our privilege to extend.

Good manners protect good morals. Manners and morality should not be regional, they are universal; so respectful speech is not exclusive to the South. All parents should teach their children to use *Ma'am* and *Sir* at the earliest age. No need for a formal lesson on the topic – if the use of *Ma'am* and *Sir* is a natural and regular occurrence in the home, our children will follow suit. This is especially the case if parents also respond to their children using *Ma'am* and *Sir*. After all, what's the alternative? Children replying to their parents with: what, huh, uh-huh, uh-uh, etc. As opposed to *ma'am, sir, no ma'am, no sir, yes ma'am, yes sir*.

Both the Bible and Holy Qur'an leave no ambiguity about how children should treat their parents. The Bible reads, *"Honour thy father and thy mother: that thy days may be long upon the land which the LORD thy God giveth thee"* (Exodus 20:12, KJV). This is actally quite a remarkable commandment – it draws a direct link between the length of our days and our relationship with our parents. The Holy Qur'an reads, *"And thy Lord has decreed that you serve none but Him, and do good to parents. If either or both of them reach old age with thee, say not 'Fie' to them, nor chide them, and speak to them a generous word. And lower to them the wing of humility out of mercy, and say: My Lord, have mercy on them as they brought me up (when I was) little"* (17:23-24). "Fie" is an expression of disgust and outrage, which should never be extended to those who sacrificed so much; to not only give us physical life but to care for us until we could care for ourselves.

Humility is a characteristic of the righteous. Children are required to be humble around their parents even when they surpass them in knowledge, wisdom, and understanding. We must demonstrate this example, so our children will come behind us and maintain the standard. The Honorable

Minister Louis Farrakhan said, *"Children today are growing up in homes where there is no discipline because there are no rules. Children today do what they please and their parents, mothers, in particular, allow this license not realizing that their unwillingness to train the children up in the way they should go will bring great pain to the parents in the future."*

On the surface, it appears to be such a small expression of deference – but in a world where respect is fleeting and disrespect, rudeness and incivility flourishes, small gestures make big impacts. So, let's get away from being so offended when we are called *Ma'am* or *Sir* and receive it with the noble intentions of the giver.

A MUSLIM CHILD:

Student Minister Nuri Muhammad (Indianapolis, IN) said, *"The child of a Muslim is not necessarily a Muslim child."* Hmm – let that sink in. The same can be said about the children of Christians and those of any other faith. Those of us who are striving to practice a way of life that is congruent with the principles of our faith, desire to reproduce children who will adopt those same righteous practices and principles. It is a challenge when the major institutions in this society – which we are forced to engage with – do not reflect our faith traditions and beliefs. This can make it difficult to reinforce the values taught at home or at the mosques and churches. There are no guarantees for any parent; but there is a direct correlation between effort and outcome – so our efforts must be intentional, strategic and consistent.

We cannot take for granted that our children will do as we say and as we do if we do not give them an understanding of WHY we do what we do. The Book of Proverbs 4:7 reads, *"Wisdom is the principal thing; therefore get wisdom: and with all thy getting get understanding"* (KJV). The New

International Version of the same scripture reads, *"The beginning of wisdom is this: Get wisdom. Though it cost all you have, get understanding"* (Proverbs 4:7). What we can extract from this verse is that wisdom is the prerequisite for understanding, which is the ultimate goal. Knowledge and wisdom start us on the right path – understanding keeps us there – and faith takes us to our god-potential. Knowledge, wisdom, and understanding can all be taught. However, faith is an experience. Faith can only be established through a personal journey and relationship with Allah (God). As parents, we are responsible for what can be taught.

Parents who faithfully immerse their children in the Teachings of the Most Honorable Elijah Muhammad by bringing them to mosque meetings and by living a disciplined lifestyle reflective of those Teachings may yet be surprised by the responses from their children to basic questions about what we believe and why we practice as we do. The breadth of the Teachings of the Most Honorable Elijah Muhammad goes far beyond universal principles such as, belief in One God, prayer, charity, fasting, personal struggle, and treating others the way we want to be treated. In addition, we are taught a specific body of knowledge and wisdom that is comprised of lessons which cover – the deportation of the moon; the 24-Scientists; the history of Yakub; the history of Shabazz; the Mother Plane; How to Eat to Live; and so much more. Our children must be taught this same body of knowledge.

In order for the children of Muslims to become Muslim children, they have to be directly taught the Teachings as we would teach them to the new converts. They cannot simply receive an influx of knowledge and wisdom; they need the same understanding we would give to a brand-new Believer. *"Do as I say, or else,"* only works for a finite period of time. And there is no such thing as magically consuming the Teachings of the Most Honorable Elijah Muhammad; it must be purposefully taught and studied.

CHILDREN OF THE MOST HIGH

Those cities who are blessed to have Muhammad Universities of Islam or affiliate schools fully operational, have to also be careful that the curriculum not only includes core academics (math, science, English/language arts, social studies); but also, the Lessons and the Teachings of the Most Honorable Elijah Muhammad. And those without fully operational schools are not off the hook. We have to cast down our buckets where we are and take baby steps. Churches have Sunday school – and every city with a Mosque or a Study Group should at least have the equivalent by having a Saturday School. Saturday Schools are a wonderful first step to expose our children to a structured, focused curriculum that covers the Teachings of the Most Honorable Elijah Muhammad.

Children love to be around other children and will be far more engaged and attentive than learning alone. Remember, the Most Honorable Elijah Muhammad said, *"You can have a university under a tree, as long as you are teaching subjects pertaining to the universe."* Our children are not only our future, but they are our present. We cannot wait for the complete establishment of desired institutions of learning before we pay attention to what our children need at present. They need The Teachings. The Originator created Himself and His home planet simultaneously. We must do the same. We will discover that what we desire for our children is the same desire that other Believers have for theirs – like-minds must come together. Simply start by teaching the children what you already know. Then, follow every lesson by checking for understanding and giving a practical application exercise.

The Honorable Minister Louis Farrakhan said, *"Even the little babies can be taught about the Original Man and the Colored Man and the difference between the two. Why should we wait until they are graduating from high school to learn the Teachings?"* He went on to say, *"You are being carved out to be a standard of something new to reflect back to the old to bring the*

346

old forward into the new. That takes great courage, great strength, great conviction, great faith in what you have been given."

Do not let this world's grand institutions get us starry-eyed so that we lose focus. What we have been given is a superior Teaching, intended to produce the Kingdom of Allah (God). Our children will not accept this way of life simply because they were born into it – they must know it as we know it – understand it as we understand it – and then establish their personal faith by trying Allah (God).

RAMADAN GOALS FOR CHILDREN:

The Holy Month of Ramadan commences annually during the ninth month of the lunar calendar year. Each year, approximately 1.8 billion Muslims all over the world observe this Holy Month by fasting (abstaining) from food and drink during the daylight hours. This sacrifice is obligatory for every Muslim who has reached puberty and is free from health conditions that would prevent them from fasting. In addition to fasting, Muslims are mindful to make their daily prayers; read the entire Holy Qur'an; increase charitable contributions; refrain from quarreling; commit no unscrupulous acts – and married couples do not engage in sexual intercourse during the daylight hours. Nearly one-quarter of the world's population will unite and observe this strict discipline for 30 days.

The Holy Qur'an reads, *"O you who believe, fasting is prescribed for you, as it was prescribed for those before you, so that you may guard against evil"* (2: 183). This verse addresses those who "believe." So, the principles of Ramadan are not exclusive to those who identify as Muslims. A Muslim is simply one who submits his or her will to do the Will of Allah (God). So, by nature, we could argue that every Black man and woman is a Muslim. But regardless of our labels, every believer in God should desire to guard against

347

evil; so, we invite and encourage all of our Brothers and Sisters to join us every year for a beautiful month of fasting and prayer.

Children who are too young to abstain from eating and drinking during the daylight hours, do NOT have to be excluded from receiving the tremendous reward gained from self-imposed discipline. Below we list seven ways in which younger children can participate and benefit during this month. These are only suggestions. It is advised to first have a conversation about them with your children, then implement some – or all. Each goal should be adjusted as needed so it's age-appropriate. We pray that all will be encouraged to make every Holy Month of Ramadan a family affair!

1. **One good deed a day / Charity**: Now this is a worthy goal that can be accomplished at almost any age. Every religion and even those who claim to be agnostic believe in the "Golden Rule" – or variations of *"do unto others as you would have them do unto you."* It is never too early to teach and train our children to be kind and considerate of others. There is no greater deed than one that has a direct positive impact on another person, but they are not limited to this. Good deeds or acts of kindness are boundless, but if children need a jumpstart, be sure to offer suggestions. Anything from picking up trash in the neighborhood to giving their sibling a compliment – or making a "thank you" card for their teacher, to completing an unassigned chore, are all considered good deeds. Monetary charity, clothes or toys can also be donated to a worthy cause. Charity can also be expressed through volunteering one's time to feed the hungry, keep company with the elderly, or visit with children who are ill. At the end of each day, make time for each child to share their good deed for the day and its impact.

2. **Prayer**: Prayer is a pillar of Islam second only to Belief in One God. Depending on their age and/or their level of discipline, prayer at

348

best is probably inconsistent for very young children. They usually either pray only with their family or in the congregation. Or, they may only pray before a meal or right before bed. Whatever the level of prayer, the goal is to increase. If a child does not pray at all, they should be encouraged to pray at least once a day. If they only pray once, increase it to twice a day; if twice, then increase to three times; and so on. At a minimum, regardless of what time our children rise in the morning, it is best to begin their day with prayer. It is never too early to build a personal relationship with Allah (God).

3.   **Read Holy Qur'an**: The Holy Qur'an is compartmentalized in many different ways. One way is division by 'Parts' – it has a total of 30 Parts. Adults and teens who fully observe Ramadan are required to read one Part each day; so, by the end of Ramadan, the entire revelation has been read from cover to cover. Simply include the younger children in the daily readings. It would be wonderful if schedules and time would permit the entire family to read the Holy Qur'an aloud together every day. The family can have a designated shared reading time and even the children who are not yet able to read should be invited to listen to the revealed Words of Allah (God) being read. One does not have to be able to read to benefit from being immersed in the Word – it is all being recorded in the brain and mentally absorbed.

4.   **No fighting or arguing**: Fighting is strictly forbidden during the Holy Month of Ramadan. The only exception is if we must defend the life of self or others. We are to avoid arguing and quarreling as well because it robs us of the peaceful spirit of God. Depending on the number of children in a household, their ages, gender, and other family dynamics; this could be quite the achievement for siblings. Imagine 30 days without any bickering

and all differences settled in the best manner – now that's a small glimpse of heaven!

5. **Personal sacrifice:** The most difficult aspect of the observance of Ramadan for most is the abstention from food and drink during the daylight hours. This is because we are abstaining from something that is natural – it is natural and necessary to eat and drink if we want to live, but we are asked to suppress this natural instinct for 30 days (during the daylight hours). A sacrifice such as this is too great for very young children. However, they can sacrifice and strengthen discipline in other ways. They can forgo indulgences that may be personally enjoyable, but not a necessity. So perhaps children can sacrifice eating sweets or junk food; sodas or land animals – allow them to choose but encourage them to choose something that will really challenge them. They can also sacrifice the amount of time spent watching television, playing video games, surfing the internet, going to the movies or aimless socializing. The goal of personal sacrifice and abstention is self-control, self-mastery. If we begin this practice in our youth, not only will we be able to master self, but eventually our immediate environment.

6. **Overcome one bad habit**: According to the scholars and experts, it takes about 21 days to break a bad habit and form a new one. This rule is not exclusive to adults; which means that during the month of Ramadan our children can rid themselves of at least one bad habit. It is important to first have a clear understanding of why the specific habit is not good for them, so they will stay the course. It is also imperative to get started on this goal right away as time is a factor that dictates their success.

7.   **<u>Set one worthy goal</u>**: The idea here is not to have the goal accomplished by the end of Ramadan, but rather for our children to be in a position physically, spiritually and mentally to be ready to take on a worthy goal. This goal may take a week or several months to accomplish; but they will be well prepared and have actual evidence it can be done, having disciplined themselves for the last 30 days. It is no small feat for a child to accomplish these seven goals and successfully observe Ramadan. The Honorable Minister Louis Farrakhan said that the Most Honorable Elijah Muhammad wanted to see his followers *"supremely disciplined."* It takes a disciplined individual to accomplish any goal worthwhile.

SWEET SIXTEEN:

The Honorable Minister Louis Farrakhan was asked via Twitter what was the best advice he gave to his children and grandchildren when they were young. He answered: *"The best advice is found in the words of Solomon where he advised young people to believe, follow and commit to their Creator in the days of their youth. Unfortunately, many of us live to get old before we finally submit. But if young people realize how important it is to submit to God in their youth, then their lives will be a great and productive life for the good of self, family and our people."*

It is the greatest honor and privilege to successfully complete the process of becoming a registered member of the Nation of Islam. This distinction is second to none regardless of how one found their way to Islam. There is one school of thought that believes it is a greater challenge to "convert" to Islam after having practiced another way of life for years or even decades; whereas others believe it is more of a challenge for those who have never experience a life outside of Islam to remain in the faith. The debate is pointless when we understand that none of us were self-guided and that our individually unique paths were all orchestrated by the hands of Allah (God). However, in a world like this; there is something to be said about a young person who may be in the world but makes a conscious decision not to be of it.

According to the Holy Qur'an (chapter 46, verse 15), the age of maturity is forty years. Prophet Muhammad (PBUH) received his first revelation at the age of 40. Based on that fact alone we know that more than one's biology must certainly be factored when measuring maturity. A mature man or woman is a fully developed and capable adult – mentally, spiritually and emotionally. A mature person is also one who has reached or attained their final stage of development required to fully embrace, pursue and achieve success in his or her life's purpose. Therefore, it is no coincidence that so many of our great revolutionary leaders were assassinated before reaching the age of forty: Malcolm X (39), Dr. Martin Luther King, Jr. (39), Medgar Evers (37), Thomas Sankara (37), Patrice Lumumba (35), Steve Biko (30), Fred Hampton (21), and others.

However, reaching the age of forty does not mean we are somehow magically disciplined and begin to exhibit the characteristics and principles of maturity and responsibility. The process begins in our youth. So, while 40 is the age of maturity; 16 is the age of decision in the Nation of Islam. Traditionally in the Nation of Islam, we permit our youth to formally accept the Teachings of the Most Honorable Elijah Muhammad and take the steps to officially become a registered member of the Nation of Islam at the age of 16 (age 15, with parental consent). This allowance is scientific and strategic.

In his book, ***Our Saviour Has Arrived***, The Most Honorable Elijah Muhammad wrote, *"In the Bible Isaiah mentions the long life of the righteous in these words: 'that a person one hundred (100) years old will be like a child' ...meaning that their age will never cause them to look old. They will have* *the freshness of youth says the prophet, Isaiah. And the Holy Qur'an, also verifies the same.* **Allah (God) in the Person of Master Fard Muhammad, to Whom Praises are Due forever – out of His Own Mouth – Said to me that He Causes us to Grow into a New Growth. And that we would have the look and the energy of one who is sixteen (16) years of age and our youth and energy of a sixteen-year-old would last forever"** (Chapter 23 – He (Allah) Makes All Things New). Why sixteen and not thirteen? Why sixteen and not twenty-one?

The age of sixteen is significant for more than just driving legally, getting that first job, and visiting colleges (though all important). At the age of sixteen, children are at their optimum in mental potential, physical vitality, and spiritual realization. The brain makes tremendous leaps in cognitive skills and competencies during adolescence. The energy of a sixteen-year-old is tangible in all domains. There are truly no limits to what can be conceived and therefore achieved at this special age.

Sixteen is also the age where most teenagers meet a crossroads. Although we have all had the capacity to make small personal decisions since the age of two – those decisions were not at the level where the impact was life altering. However, the decisions we make at the age of sixteen can potentially affect us far beyond the age of maturity. Choosing to go left instead of right; saying yes instead of no; selecting one acquaintance over the other – every moment of our lives we are making decisions.

At the age of sixteen, we unequivocally know the difference between right and wrong; yet are fearless enough to face the consequences of either. We confuse our limitless energy with a belief that we are somehow immortal, so we are willing to take risks that we would have never taken as a seven-year-old and would never take again as an adult. Researchers say that when given time and access to information, teenagers start to have the

353

computational and decision-making skills of an adult. This state of mind is beneficial and necessary to one's success, but it needs to be guided because teens are highly emotional people. One should NEVER make important decisions during an intensely emotional period; but teenagers left unguided, do it all of the time. These decisions that are made around the age of sixteen can affect the trajectory of one's entire life.

We have a lesson in the Nation of Islam that states, *"Make all men and boys join the F.O.I...."* Why should we make a boy or a girl join the Nation of Islam? Because it is our submission to the law of God that gives us the understanding of His law. For example, you can explain to someone for hours about the benefits of fasting, but until one experiences fasting for himself; he cannot bear witness to its benefits – but after submitting to a fast, the individual then understands why it is beneficial. So, it is with the Restrictive Laws of Islam which all registered members of the Nation of Islam are bound by; regardless of age. By making our youth submit to a way of life free from premarital sex, drugs, alcohol, cigarettes, gambling, slack talk, and gossip, etc. allows understanding to come sooner.

The Bible teaches that the fear of God is the beginning of wisdom. Fear precedes love and is more constant than love. Fear of consequences and discipline is protection for us in our youth. Soon we will understand the law, grow to love the law, and no longer fear it. Loving the law makes obedience to the law effortless.

As parents, we all collectively hold our breath when our children near the age of sixteen, wondering what decisions will be made today; tomorrow? Peers are very influential at this age, but an overwhelming percentage of teenagers admit that they enjoy spending time with their parents and prefer to have rules and structure. What we model as parents still remain dominant in the hearts and minds of our teens.

Submitting to righteous conduct and behavior during our youth does not insulate us from struggle, difficulty, and trials; but it allows us to join the company of those who are favored and protected by Allah (God). This we should seek because it enables us to be perfected by our trials, instead of destroyed by them. The earlier this process begins, the sooner the benefits of our productivity will be manifested within the self, our family and our people.

The ultimate decision to become a registered member of the Nation of Islam should not be made by parents; but parents should support, encourage, inspire, motivate and promote this way of life. This does not mean we should give our teens free range and treat them as adults, because they are not – but they do need the autonomy to make this particular decision on their own. But make no mistake about it, our children should have NO question about their parent's desire for them to become a follower of The Most Honorable Elijah Muhammad and a helper of The Honorable Minister Louis Farrakhan!

VALUING OUR CHILDREN'S FRIENDS:

The moment a couple realizes they have conceived, their innate instinct is to do anything within their power to protect the new life. The need to protect our children is an intensely powerful drive that really never goes away; particularly for mothers, although the balance is required as the children get older. When our children are little, all of those first milestones are celebrated and welcomed – their first time rolling over, their first tooth, their first words, their first steps; being potty-trained, their first day of school, taking the training wheels off the bicycle…you get the idea. Then, they get a little older and all those firsts now produce anxiety and trepidation for parents – their first cell phone, their first time driving, their first job, their first fight, their first unsupervised outing with friends…goodness!

355

I am sure that if parents were told they could keep their children in a protective bubble until adulthood and somehow, they would still come out sane and well-adapted, we would have quite a bit of takers. Unfortunately, no such cocoon exists. The scope of our duty as parents is to prepare our children for adulthood. And since our children do not live with us in isolation, we know they will certainly develop relationships outside of the home. However, these friendships do not have to be scary for parents. In fact, they should be encouraged because the right friendships can be helpful and exceedingly valuable.

As our children approach their adolescent and teen years, the influence of their peers will rival the influence of their parents. This can be particularly challenging for the children of Believers because the vast majority of the world practices a lifestyle contrary to the one in which they are being reared. And quite honestly, it is not easy to be different from others during your youth. This is a time in everyone's life when the opinion of others matters more than they should. And the peers who matter most to our children are those who are most like them; same race, same gender, same age. This reality makes it very helpful if the primary friendships established for children of Believers be with the children of other Believers. The Holy Qur'an reads, *"Only Allah is your Friend and His Messenger and those who believe, those who keep up prayer and pay the poor-rate, and they bow down"* (5: 55).

We all benefit from having genuine strong friendships throughout our lifetime. But at the juncture of our lives when the thought of being left out may cause one to make poor choices with lasting consequences; it is even more important that those friendships be with young people who have a similar way of life, faith, intention, and mission. Our children's friendships are simply more important than we may realize. Children are not excluded from universal laws and truths. When two persons that have diametrically opposed viewpoints, goals, values, and ideas of morality become "friends," their relationship can only be sustained within that framework for a short period of time before one of two things eventually has to happen. Either, one friend will have to adopt the other's way of life; or the friendship will end – it's that simple, *birds of a feather flock together.*

When our young Brothers and Sisters in the Nation of Islam go out into the community dressed in their sharp suits and beautiful garments, heads literally turn. Overwhelmingly, the response, particularly from our people, is one of respect, gratitude, and admiration. There is nothing like the sight of well-dressed young Brothers and Sisters serving the community and being an example! When these young Brothers and Sisters are out in public together, we witness that they walk with more confidence, ease, security, and enjoyment because, even though their attire and purpose is not the norm, there is strength in numbers. This is especially the case for our young Sisters, who choose to dress modestly and wear the headpiece; which unmistakably identifies the wearer as a follower of the Most Honorable Elijah Muhammad, under the leadership of the Honorable Minister Louis Farrakhan. It takes a lot of courage for our young girls to proudly step out in the garment solo; but put seven or eight of them together and watch them exude added confidence and pride, feeding on the power of the sisterhood.

Unfortunately, parents cannot make friends for their children. When our children are little, we can set up playdates and outings; but as they get older, the most we can do is encourage good choices and help with arrangements and resources. This effort can also be fostered if the entire family attends the mosque or church together; along with other affiliated activities. Striving families have to make a better effort of being around each other more often. As the Most Honorable Elijah Muhammad wrote, *"Seek first the friendship of your own people."*

This is just one reason why it is so important to have a god-centered school in your city where natural friendships can develop. But whether that exists or not, as parents we have the right and a duty to inquire about the dynamics of all friendships. And when necessary, as long as our children live under our roof, we still have a measure of control and should exercise it by forbidding those "friendships" that are clearly unhealthy.

We have to check-in regularly with our children and see if their friendships are honest enough to correct one another when needed and strong enough to encourage righteous conduct. If so, they are fortunate because having a friendship with others who are also striving reduces stress and protects their mental health. Teenagers are not going to come to their parents for everything, but it should give parents comfort to know they have positive friends to confide in – a peer who can relate to their difficulties and challenges. It is not necessary for our children to have a lot of friends, but the righteousness of those friendships is the key.

Have you ever noticed how happy teens and children are when they are with their friends? Quality friendships play a pivotal role in boosting happiness, developing self-confidence and solidifying a sense of belonging. We cannot stop our children from maturing to social beings, so let's promote friendships that encourage healthy lifestyle habits, academic success, the pursuit of their purposes and love of God. Children are never too young to know the reality of God and His Messenger.

The Honorable Minister Louis Farrakhan was asked about friendship during an interview. In part, he said, *"Take Allah. Allah is—only Allah and His Messenger. Well, we know those Two. They have given us a supreme act of friendship. We know the Qur'an is right. 'Only Allah and His Messenger are your friends and those who believe.' But the question is who are they? So, in such a time of trial as this is and the sorting out that is going on, soon we will be able to unite believer with believer and we would know that the believer is the friend of the believer."*

RIGHTEOUS NEPOTISM:

It was necessary to add specificity to this section's topic by adding the adjective, "righteous," to its title since generally speaking, nepotism is frowned upon and even illegal in certain sectors of employment. While several may argue that nepotism has no redeeming qualities; one could argue that the Black community, in particular, needs to reassess the practice of nepotism because it may have utility. Our resistance to nepotism is understandable – it is seen as an exclusionary practice; which unfairly benefits those who may be *connected*, but not necessarily qualified. Largely, this has not included the Black man and woman. A basic definition of nepotism is, *"the practice among those with power or influence of favoring relatives or friends, especially by giving them jobs."*

It is ironic that a practice considered to be so disagreeable received its name from the western world's oldest religious institution, Catholicism. According to the history, Catholic bishops would *"bequeath wealth, property, and priesthood to their 'nephews'"* – hence the word, 'nepotism.' The only problem was that these so-called nephews were not their nephews at all, but they were, in fact, their biological sons; born out of wedlock and kept secret. This was all an effort by the church clergy to own land and property, but mostly to keep all the power within their lineage. Though the modern name for this practice has sinister roots, the practice of favoring relatives and friends over others goes back tens of thousands of years.

There is no aspect of life or history not covered by The Teachings of the Most Honorable Elijah Muhammad. This includes an in-depth body of knowledge, which covers the most ancient of days – a time long before the white man ever walked the earth; and a time when Black men and women were truly gods, capable of predicting and writing what would happen 25,000 years in the future. Prior to the coming of Master Fard Muhammad, the identity and knowledge of God was a closely guarded secret by twelve very wise Scientists.

In *Our Saviour Has Arrived*, The Most Honorable Elijah Muhammad wrote, *"The knowledge of God has been kept a secret by twelve men on our planet for many thousands of years. The twelve pass their knowledge on from son to son, but the number possessing this knowledge is never more than twelve; and they are not to ever reveal it"* (p.61). There is so much to be extracted from this one statement of his; but for the purpose of our topic, we will focus on the fact that the answer to the most important question of all questions that one could ask, "Who is God?" – was kept secret from son to son. There is no doubt this decision had nothing to do with our colloquial understanding of nepotism today. These men were certain that their sons were qualified to hold this secret, so there was no need to look elsewhere.

Righteous men and women are our example; not President Trump, who skirts anti-nepotism clauses by allowing his daughter and son-in-law to serve in governmental positions, which they are in no way qualified to hold. Optics are probably the most negative aspect of nepotism – there will always be an unfavorable perception by some who believe that no one else ever stood a chance at a particular position because they were not highly connected.

Nepotism done properly, by righteous families, can be extremely advantageous in the Black community. Honestly, how are we ever going to make sustainable progress at Nation building if each generation has to start from scratch, decade after decade after decade? We leave our children no real wealth; no land; no businesses; no established institutions – only debt. We cannot blame our youth for going in another direction if we have not established a solid foundation from which they can continue to build. If we study wise white folks (and other ethnicities), one of the many things we will discover is that they plan for generations into the future. In the United States alone, we will find several powerful family dynasties in a range of industries – politics, business, banking, media, law, and entertainment. These families are few compared to the overall U.S. population, but the wealth and influence they garner affect the masses.

We should take a page from their 'family first' playbook – minus the greed, corruption, fraud, dishonesty and general immorality – and look at the benefits of nepotism. We should not only pass on knowledge, wisdom, and understanding to our offspring; but we must begin to pass on tangible assets as well. Children must be the beneficiaries of their parents! Keep in mind that we are not just referring to an inheritance. Unless otherwise stated, children will automatically inherit what their parents leave behind – the good and the bad. If we wait until a parent or grandparent passes, there are no guarantees that their offspring will carry the vision forward. However, if we are blessed to have offspring and family who are willing, then preparation, training, and grooming must begin as soon as possible.

Our first option should always be family – our children, then relatives and friends who share our vision. Those closest to us, know us best; so, they do not have to figure us out nor we them. We know their strengths and weakness; personalities and characteristics exceptionally well. We are comforted because they thoroughly understand the vision and the mission; so, time is not lost with additional education and training. Almost always, we can count on them to be truthful – and loyalty is unwavering.

There is an assumption that if we work with those whom we are closest, the standard or expectation is somehow lowered. No! Not with ethical, highly-principled Black men and women. God is always the standard for the righteous; therefore, our criterion will always remain high. And those who refuse to abide by such standard – family or not – will have to be dismissed. If the desire from our offspring is fervent and we are determined to prepare our children and family to help secure unlimited progress through our businesses, our institutions, and our mission; then there is no doubt they *will* be the *most* qualified and the most deserving of these positions of power and influence.

So, let's get started! The Most Honorable Elijah Muhammad gave us a sound economic program to help fight against poverty and want, which the Honorable Minister Louis Farrakhan and the Nation of Islam continue to promote today; but we need everyone's help! The Most Honorable Elijah Muhammad wrote, *"The white man spends his money with his own, which is natural. You, too, must do this. Help to make jobs for your own kind. Take a lesson from the Chinese and Japanese and go give employment and assistance to your own kind when they are in need. This is the first law of nature. Defend and support your own kind."*

The Honorable Minister Louis Farrakhan said, *"God wants to bless us. We ought to put ourselves in a position to be blessed."*

SARAH MAE MANNING:

Anyone who has ever had an opportunity to hear a lecture by the Honorable Minister Louis Farrakhan, in its entirety, can bear witness that he is a man that does not waste words nor time. His words and actions are driven by divine intention and purpose. It is evident that his motives are purely anchored in his commitment to raising the consciousness of our people. The Minister consistently delivers a clear message and offers us guidance that we may live a life more pleasing to Allah (God). He is indeed a divine Reminder and Warner in our midst. A man like this is not made haphazardly. Allah (God) saw him long before he was born and meticulously designed the circumstances surrounding his birth and his rearing so at the specified time, he would be receptive to his ultimate purpose in life. However, before Allah (God) could make a man like Farrakhan, He had to first make a great woman, whose womb He would use as the laboratory to produce a man of this caliber.

The Honorable Minister Louis Farrakhan speaks of his beloved mother, Mother Sumayyah Farrakhan, quite often and it is clear that his love and reverence for her is profound. He has a genuine appreciation and understanding of his mother, whose care laid the perfect foundation for his higher purpose. So, when we hear him speak of her publicly it is not based in mere nostalgia or to simply reminisce. He is always teaching us and is willing to be very open and honest about aspects of his childrearing that we may benefit. There are lessons to be both modeled and learned from Mother Sumayyah Farrakhan's parenting, that should be studied and applied. After all, look at what she produced!

During the time she was rearing the Honorable Minister Louis Farrakhan and his older brother, Alvan; her name was Sarah Mae Manning, and the Minister was Louis Eugene Walcott. The Minister describes her pregnancy with him like this: *"My mother bore me with pain and sorrow because she tried to abort me three times. Because she was living with my brother's father – but my father, whom she married and never divorced came back into her life momentarily, and she became pregnant with me. So, all the time she was carrying me, she was in sorrow, because she tried to kill me, and then she decided to have me. You don't do that unless you are in pain. And the pain and fear of what the child would look like, that he who she was living with, my brother's father, would become aware that her husband had*

363

slipped back in and had an affair with his wife, who had left him, but was living with my brother's father. So, she bore him in sorrow. She bore him in pain and she bore him in fear and she bore him in great insecurity. And she, therefore, became very committed in prayer that God would save her – her life; her relationship with the man. So, she was prayerful out of great insecurity."

There are countless women who have experienced similar emotions when discovering that they are pregnant and do not want to be. It can be so terrifying that the woman believes that ending the pregnancy is easier than bearing the consequences. But Allah (God) is REAL and there is **nothing** that we cannot overcome with His help – Sarah Mae Manning came to see that as well. The Minister said, *"My mother knew she was in trouble. She went to God 'Lord, Help me.' The more she prayed, all of her supplications and prayers were going on down into the womb. She was making me a man of God without even knowing what she was making...I am here to tell you, if you do not have a man, remember God. My mother did not know that the circumstances around which I was conceived in her womb would make me the man that I am today."*

Sarah Mae Manning was a very beautiful dark-skinned woman and the man in her life, Alvan's father, was also dark skinned. However, the Minister's father was light-skinned. So, though she decided to carry the pregnancy to term, she prayed that the baby she was carrying would be a girl and also that her baby would be dark-skinned – this way, perhaps she could still hide her baby's true parentage. As we know, she did not have a girl and her baby was not dark-skinned. The Minister stated, *"Now, she wanted a girl. What does that mean? It means that she would make a child with characteristics that represent the feminine side of the Nature of God: Mercy,*

Compassion, Forgiveness, Long-suffering. It takes that kind of person to redeem a people in the condition that we are in."

To her anguish, the truth had come to light causing the end of her relationship. But what is so remarkable about Sarah Mae Manning is how she soldiered on – she had to rear two sons as a single Black woman in the 1930s and 1940s, and she did not relegate this responsibility one iota. When necessary, she would go without, so her boys could have. We learn from the Minister that she was also a strict disciplinarian. She kept a clean house – everything had its place and there were consequences for not keeping it just so. She worked hard as a domestic, cleaning other people's homes and also as a seamstress. The Minister said she never went to bed before her children and was up in the morning before they were.

However, Sarah Mae Manning wanted so much more for her sons. She knew that they needed skill and discipline early on, so she gave them both music – The Minister was only five years old at the time. He stated, *"The first thing that I remember that my mother gave me to play with was a violin. She was not about mindless pursuits. When she brought me toys, it was like Chinese checkers, something that engaged me. Or, a puzzle, something that engaged my mind and then something to read. I thank God Allah for my mother who never, ever, engaged me with mindless stupidity and called it fun."* She clearly understood the scripture, *"A wise son maketh a glad father: but a foolish son is the heaviness of his mother"* (Proverbs 10:1).

The Honorable Minister Louis Farrakhan was reared to love God and to love his people. His foundation was in the Episcopal Church, but even then, he was always looking for a savior for Black people because his heart ached to see us free. This too was fostered in him by his mother: *"I remember once a Filipino man came to our door; he was selling Bibles. And as he was opening the Bibles, showing my mother all these 'White' prophets and angels, when he got to 'The Last Supper' my mother asked him: 'You mean to tell me there's no Black people at all in this book?' – and she ran him out of the house. So, after I talked to my uncle who told me my dad was a follower of Marcus Garvey, and my mother was on the fringe of The Garvey Movement, that was, for me, a sign that my mother was very 'Black conscious.' And, I thank God for that because she instilled in me love for our people."* We thank God for that as well!

The Honorable Minister Louis Farrakhan was born in New York, but he was reared in Massachusetts and was not exposed first-hand to the horrors of the racist South. Sarah Mae Manning helped to connect her children to the struggles of Black people by making sure they read from Black publications. The Minister said he read the writings of W.E.B. Du Bois in the *Crisis Magazine*; as well as regularly reading *The Afro-American* and *The Pittsburgh Courier*. He said, *"In those papers there were stories of lynching and mistreatment of our people. Of course, that deepened my desire to see someone who would come along who would free our people. That's what led to my questioning my Sunday school teacher, that if God had raised Moses for his people and He always sent some prophet or somebody to deliver people who were oppressed, why hasn't God sent somebody to deliver us?"* The Minister was about seven or eight at the time.

Knowing the man of God that the Honorable Minister Louis Farrakhan is today and witnessing his unwavering commitment to serving his people for over six decades, makes it reasonable to presume that this journey began as a child. What is difficult to imagine is that he was just like most children in that he misbehaved on occasion and was involved in wrongdoing, but he was. However, it did not last long because Sarah Mae Manning was not having it! She would say, *"Alvan and Gene, come! I'm gonna whip your behind... 'No. 1,' for disobeying my instruction; and 'No. 2,' I'm gonna beat you more for lying, because a liar will steal, and a thief will murder, so I'm gonna stop you at the lie!"* The Minister said, *"She was making me a man who would not be afraid of the consequences of telling the truth. God cannot use you if you fear men as you ought to fear Allah. If we were unafraid, we could raise a Nation better than what we are doing."*

Truly, there is so much more that could be said about this magnificent woman and Mother. Sarah Mae Manning was not perfect, but she was perfect enough. She was both mother and father to her boys and reared them to become fine men. Her style was not one of showing affection with words or hugs, but her LOVE for her children was on display with every action she took. This was a woman who got up early each morning to make sure her sons had a hearty breakfast before school each day and would warm her children's underclothes to prevent them from having to endure the cold against their bodies – now that's love!

Preparation for manhood and womanhood begins as a child. It takes a strong uncompromising woman to make a man-child for God. The Most Honorable Elijah Muhammad said of the Biblical Sarah, *"Our women who are sitting under guidance into righteousness use Sarah as a very good woman they could pattern after."* We believe the same can be said for Sarah Mae Manning. Throughout the earth, today, Mary, the Mother of Jesus, is known and honored because of what she produced. We also honor the life and example of Sarah Mae Manning [later known as Mother Sumayyah Farrakhan] because of what she produced. May Allah (God) forever be pleased with her!

THE BLESSING OF REBELLION:

The Honorable Minister Louis Farrakhan's five-part lecture series, *How to Give Birth to a God*, illuminate the majesty of the relationship between the woman and God. Throughout the lecture series, The Minister emphasizes that a woman who has been awakened to her divine spiritual, mental and physical potential can co-operate and co-create with the Supreme Being and produce little gods from her womb, never missing. This special relationship between the woman and God involves a supreme level of mathematics and science, which she can access without limits when she chooses to submit her entire will to do the Will of Allah (God).

The opposite of submission is *defiance, resistance, disobedience, opposition*, and *rebellion*. The price of rebellion against God is death. This book intentionally highlights the ideal in terms of parenting, childrearing and giving birth to gods. This is done to offer a yardstick to use when determining how close or far we are to the goal. Some of us may read this book with a little angst, knowing full well that our parents did not do most of what is described or suggested. Herein lies the blessing of rebellion. Rebelling against God, righteousness, and truth does NOT produce blessings – it unleashes God's Curse; His Wrath and His Chastisement. But when we rebel against Satan, against evil and wickedness; and against the devil within, we are rewarded by Allah (God) and receive His favor and limitless blessings. So, if the punishment for rebelling against God is DEATH, then the reward for rebelling against Satan is LIFE!

The Honorable Minister Louis Farrakhan wrote a powerful article for The Final Call newspaper titled, *Accepting Responsibility for Our Failure*. In this article he wrote, *"No matter what failure, we as parents have made in the rearing of our children, if, or when our children learn to seek refuge in the 'God of men,' they will be freed…When we seek refuge in Allah (God), the God of men, we will cease to blame others for any failures in our life, but, we will take the responsibility that Allah (God) gave us when He gave us life, and, that is, to take charge of our lives and to live our lives in accord with the Will and the Way of Allah (God)."*

According to the Holy Qur'an, everything in creation is made to submit to Allah (God) except the rebellious devil. The human being is different from everything else in creation, in that we have free will – we can choose to submit, or we can choose to rebel. Everything else in creation must submit to the nature in which it was created. The sun, the trees, the birds, the elephants, all must submit. Animals have innate instincts, and when activated they cause them to resist or submit, but they do not have the capacity to reason. Humans do. This is actually a blessing because many of us need to consciously rebel against the negative inclinations that were impressed upon us in the womb.

We should each personally reflect on our life and how we were reared. If we are blessed to have our mothers with us, or other close relatives, we should ask about our mother's pregnancy and what conditions were prevalent surrounding our conception, birth and early rearing. This must be handled delicately and should never be approached in an accusatory or judgmental way; the intention is to understand ourselves. Many of us may discover that the conditions that brought us into existence have scarred us with innate negative inclinations and predispositions. But regardless of what we learn, we do not have to continue on a collision course of destruction. This knowledge is empowering because once we know, with the help of Allah (God), it can all be reversed.

The Honorable Minister Louis Farrakhan said *"will"* and *"thought"* can reverse this process; it can even change our genetic structure. So, the only person who is doomed is the one who does not have the desire to make positive, righteous changes. Rebellion against the negative influences that have affected our choices and behavior can turn a potential devil into a god.

The Minister has gone in front of us as an example of one who has reversed the trauma done while he was in the womb while preserving the positive. We know that the Honorable Minister Louis Farrakhan's mother fashioned him to love God from the womb, through her sincere supplications and prayers. But we also know that before she submitted to Allah's (God's) Will, she attempted to abort her son three times. She was so fearful of the consequences of his birth that she was willing to commit murder. This significantly marked the Minister.

During his lecture, *How to Give Birth to a God: Part Five*, the Honorable Minister Louis Farrakhan shared his personal struggle. He stated, "*I wondered to myself – why it was so easy for me to reject myself. Listen carefully. You can come in my house and go in any of my rooms, you don't find a picture of me nowhere in my house. Things have been written about me that you could stack up from the time I was a little boy, I don't have none of them. If my mother didn't keep the record, I wouldn't know where it is. I've made recordings and don't know where the masters are. Something about self-rejection. Something about self-negation. Listen to me good, now.*

"*When I met Malcolm X, I met the first man in my life and because Malcolm touched me – the Honorable Elijah Muhammad converted me – but Malcolm was my teacher. I fell in-love with Malcolm because Malcolm was the strong man that I always wished I could be. And so, to deny me, I became him. It's a part of murder and this is why there's so much imitation and nobody wants to be whom and what God made you to be. So, when I met the Honorable Elijah Muhammad and got closer to him and Malcolm was in disfavor, I wanted to be Elijah Muhammad because there wasn't nothing to me. So, all the time I was murdering myself, but it's not my fault as such; I was programmed from the womb to do this…*

"I want you to hear something, so you can understand yourself, man, and start looking into yourself and discover who you are, and how to correct the condition that was in the womb... I've taken abuse, man – that only a fool or a man of God would take and never fought you back, though I know what you were thinking about me! It's the womb, man! Prepared from the womb to die for a people! Prepared from the womb to die!"

He goes on to say of himself, *"He never was trained from the womb to think a damn thing of himself and anything you thought of arrogance and self-conceited was only a self-conceited show to hide a deep-seated inferiority feeling that came from self-negation, starting from the womb. But God in His infinite Mercy knows how to use a defective thing and make it something of value. To show you, Brothers and Sisters, that we can overturn the womb with the right kind of heart; the right kind of will to struggle."*

All praise is due to Allah (God) for free will and the capacity to correct the mistakes made while in the womb. We do not have to allow the errors of our parents to keep us in chains for one more second. And just the same, we are obligated to empower our own children by sharing the circumstances surrounding their development so that God-willing they will choose to submit to the good and rebel against the bad; allowing the god within to rule.

GOD – FAMILY – NATION:

God – Family – Nation. In that order. A recent statement by the Honorable Minister Louis Farrakhan via Twitter stated, *"Family is the essence of the Nation. When you neglect your family, you have neglected the Nation. When you uphold your family and look out for your family, you're looking out for the Nation."* This statement makes it very clear that family and Nation are inextricably linked. Strong, healthy, successful families are

371

the foundation of a great Nation. However, to ensure that our families experience the fullness of success, we must put God first. For some, misunderstanding and confusion exists about what it means to put God first; and what it means to put God before family and family before Nation.

Allah (God) must be the exclusive object of our worship. No one is worthy of worship except Allah (God). As much as we revere, honor, respect and love our parents or our spouses, they are not worthy of worship. We can discern when we are placing others before God by recognizing a willingness within self to compromise righteous principles in order to gain favor with others – all at the risk of displeasing Allah (God). Will we lie to protect our reputation, or in an effort to avert punishment? Will we steal in order to impress someone we admire? Will we sacrifice our character or integrity in order to earn acceptance or popularity? If we answered 'yes,' to any of the aforementioned or can relate to similar circumstances, then we have work to do before we can claim that God is first and foremost in our lives. As we move throughout the days, the weeks, and the years; our self-accusing spirit must be quickened by constantly measuring our thoughts and our actions against the standard of what is pleasing to God.

God, then family. Does this mean that if we are praying and the baby starts to cry, we should finish praying first before attending to the baby? NO! We are duty bound by Allah (God) to answer the cry of our baby, a gift from Him. However, it does mean that we should never think of proclaiming to a spouse or a loved one, *"I can't live without you."* We shouldn't even think it. First, it's not true…you can. But most importantly, it's idolatry, a sign of worshipping someone other than God. The scripture reads, *"The Lord, whose name is Jealous, is a jealous God."* Polytheism is the gravest of sins. You do not have to be a worshipper of animals, celestial bodies or statues to be guilty of polytheism. Loss through abandonment is indeed a great trial and loss of life is even greater. There is perhaps no greater loss than the loss of a child. Initially, the pain can be so debilitating that we truly believe we will not overcome it. But, Allah (God) is so Merciful that He does not give us more than we can handle. There is no trial we cannot overcome if we put Him first. The only Being we cannot live without is Allah (God).

So, as much as we love and adore our family, we cannot worship them. But they should hold a high position on the hierarchy of life. After duty to Allah (God) and duty to self, our family is next. Family, then Nation. If we do not pay attention to the spiritual, mental and physical health of our family, disease will emanate on all planes. The Honorable Minister Louis Farrakhan said, *"Divorce is a threat to National Security."* In order to protect our Nation from external foes and forces it must be strengthened internally. Anything that threatens the health of our marriages must be examined, analyzed and corrected. Lack of communication, quality time, and quantity time must be addressed. Inadequate support, affection, or encouragement must be remedied. If not, this can lead to increased arguing, abuse and straying from the marriage. All of this threatens the very existence of our Nation.

Brothers are often charged with putting the Nation before family and quite often the charge is justified. Student Minister Dr. Ava Muhammad wrote, *"He [Allah] put it in the nature of the woman to 'demand good treatment' from the man because consideration of her wants and needs do not come to the man naturally. So, though it is not in his nature, it is like many of the Divine Attributes: it is an acquired trait."* This means that Brothers certainly have the capacity to be considerate of specific wants and needs, but in order to develop these qualities, they must be taught and trained. This training is delivered through the Teachings of the Most Honorable Elijah Muhammad.

During the *Theology of Time* lecture series (1972), The Most Honorable Elijah Muhammad said, *"Any man loves his family. If he doesn't, he shouldn't have a family. All men that have families, they should love them. Do good to the wife who brings an increase of yourself into the world. We can't do [anything] but plant seeds, but we should watch the seed and help it to grow. One thing we must remember again is that we are up from slavery with slave ideas towards self and towards our wives. Our wives are far more better than we think they are, if we show better to them. So, let us do that. Let us show them good and that we are good men. They won't want to go away from you. I don't see [anything] out of your house that you should go after. If you have a Black woman there, you have the best."*

BE WHAT YOU WANT THEM TO BE:

There was a brief, yet exceptional article published in *The Final Call* newspaper several years ago, featured in Brother Abdul Allah Muhammad's column, *Eleven Fifty-Five*; the article was titled, *I Believe the Children Are Our Future.* In this article, Brother Abdul Allah wrote about a time when he asked the Most Honorable Elijah Muhammad to teach him how to be a leader and produce good followers for him. The Most Honorable Elijah Muhammad said, *"Be what you want them to be."* As the article continued, Brother Abdul Allah quoted a passage from a book titled, *All the Children of the Bible*, by Herbert Lockyer, which read: *"An old saying has it, 'Be what you would make others.' It is in the daily life of the parents that the children gain their most indelible impressions."*

One way to measure the quality of our parenting is to continually take a critical and thorough self-assessment. We cannot separate how we parent from who we are. Self-examination, self-analysis, and self-correction should be ongoing processes. Parenting is improved only by continuing to improve ourselves. Our children are watching us more than they are listening to us. Therefore, our example is more effective than our expectations. What do our children see? Does what they see line-up with what we preach? Could we be asking our children to do what we are not willing to do ourselves?

The Most Honorable Elijah Muhammad said, *"Be what you want them to be."* We acknowledge that this is easier said than done, but it is a principle that should be applied to any person who serves in a position of authority. Parents must strive to be examples for their children. We must practice and exemplify the discipline we desire for our children to exhibit. How can we expect our children to pray when they never see us praying? How can we expect children to study when they never see their parents studying to increase their level of knowledge and understanding? How can we expect children not to use profanity and to respect others when they witness their parents tear into each other on a regular basis? How can we expect our girls to dress modestly when mommy leaves nothing to the imagination? And how can we expect our children to pursue their purpose in life when we won't go after ours? In other words, we can't be hypocrites! We should be able to tell our children to do as we say AND as we do.

I am reminded of one of my favorite poems, which I first came across during my freshman year in college. I loved it so much, that I had it framed and put it up in my room. Though I never made the connection at the time, it applies perfectly to the parent-child relationship. Written by Edgar A. Guest, the poem is titled, "I'd Rather See a Sermon Than Hear One Any Day." The first two stanzas read:

I'd rather see a sermon than hear one any day;
I'd rather one should walk with me than merely tell the way.
The eye is a better pupil, more willing than the ear;

375

Fine counsel is confusing, but example is always clear,

And the best of all the preachers are the men who live their creeds,

For to see a good put in action is what everybody needs.

I can soon learn how to do it if you will let me see it done;

I can watch your hand in action, but your tongue too fast may run.

And the lectures you deliver may be very wise and true,

But I'd rather get my lesson by observing what you do.

For I may misunderstand you and the high advice you give,

But there is no misunderstanding how you act and how you live.

Self-imposed discipline is not easy, but it is a requirement for every parent. Our duty to ourselves is second only to our duty to Allah (God). The Honorable Minister Louis Farrakhan said, *"You have a duty and an obligation to God. He's number one. You have a duty and an obligation to yourself...And if you will not be dutiful to yourself, then there is nobody that you will be dutiful towards."* The health and vitality of the parent are critical to sustaining the life of the child. This is why in cases of an emergency; the flight attendant always instructs parents to first put their oxygen mask on before placing a mask on their child.

If we do not challenge ourselves to be closer reflections of God; then not only will we not benefit, but we deny our spouse, our children, our community and our Nation the advantages that come with being who Allah (God) created us to be.

Many of us are inclined to rear our children in the same manner in which we were reared – we assume that our parents knew what was best. The most difficult and important thing we will ever do is to produce and rear

376

children. Every parent regardless of their shortcomings deserves and has earned the respect and gratitude of their children. We should never fault our parents because more often than not, they truly did the best they could with what they knew. When we know better, only then are we required to do better.

As our children get older, they will become less and less dependent on mommy and daddy for their needs, so we must begin to teach them about the reality of Allah (God), Whom they will always be dependent upon. Never think they are too young to learn about submission to the Will of Allah (God). The Most Honorable Elijah Muhammad teaches that we should order our children say their prayers at the age of seven and at the age of ten, they should be spanked if they refuse. The earlier we begin introducing prayer by inviting our children to join us, the more natural it becomes for our children; so that perhaps spanking will not be necessary. As our children are encouraged to pray and begin to build a relationship with Allah (God), they are on their way to experiencing first-hand the benefits of peace and contentment of mind.

Student Minister Ava Muhammad has taught in depth about the power of prayer and study to restore us to our original greatness by actually changing our genetic structure. For thousands of years, she said, our memory banks have been closed to the knowledge of how to master the forces of the universe. Most of us have no idea where to begin if we wanted to build the great civilizations of yesterday. But worse than that, many of us have no idea that these highly advanced civilizations ever existed. However, she said that in this millennium, our memory banks will be opened, and we will once again remember how to achieve what we once had. She said that our ability to acquire knowledge will be multiplied by ten and our DNA will advance from being comprised of only two helixes to twelve.

There is new information to be attained daily – the universe is ever expanding. Only through sincere, regular prayer and intense study, will Allah

377

(God) reveal this new information through our children and through us. We will soon bear witness to the Scriptures, which speak of a world being established that *"Eye hath not seen, nor ear heard, neither have entered into the heart of man, the things which God hath prepared for them that love Him"* (1 Corinthians 2:9). We must pray for the righteous to prosper and for the Kingdom of God to be established through men and women. We should continue to impress this reality into the hearts and minds of our children!

The Holy Qur'an states that we (parents) pray to Allah (God) for a good one (child), but when He gives us a good one, we then set up with Allah (God) associates. Since it was Allah (God) who blessed us with this precious gift, then we must maintain the life of that child in the manner He prescribes. Any gift from Allah (God) must be accepted and given special care. The Honorable Minister Louis Farrakhan said, *"The best thing you can do with a gift is unwrap it and give it right back to the one who gave it to you."* We do this by vowing that the life in our womb will be devoted to the service of God.

Again, there is a difficulty factor attached to everything of value. Childrearing is not easy on any level; but if we are disciplined and determined to follow Allah's (God's) way we can persevere. We will minimize self-imposed misfortunes and allow the trials to come from Allah (God).

As Jesus is referred to as the Son of Mary, The Honorable Minister Louis Farrakhan said, *"Every time they talk about your child, they will speak of you. You will be remembered by what you produce."*

SECTION 6: CHILD SPACING

"And those who believe and whose offspring follow them in faith –
We unite with them their offspring and We shall deprive them of naught of
their work. Every man is pledged for what he does."
Holy Qur'an 52:21

CHILD SPACING:

The Honorable Minister Louis Farrakhan said that if you have not yet had children, you should consider yourself fortunate because you still have an opportunity to prepare and plan for a family; whereas others may not have had that chance. Though we are all here intentionally by the Will of Allah (God); from the perspective of our parents, most of us were unintended accidents conceived from lust and passion; not through any deliberate or calculated planning.

Child spacing commonly refers to the length of time we allow between the birth of one child to the conception of the next child. The Most Honorable Elijah Muhammad teaches that it takes two whole years for a woman's body to completely heal and be restored after giving birth. But before we deal with adequate time between the birth of multiple children, consider that child spacing also refers to the time allowed after marriage before having the first child.

It is recommended that couples take at least two to three years after marriage before trying to conceive. The number three represents trial. In marriage, the first three years are often fraught with difficulty, struggle, and trials – but trials purify, and hard trials are necessary to establish truth. So, if we can overcome those first three years; we know that our marriage can survive if we so desire.

The Honorable Minister Louis Farrakhan said, *"Some of you got married six months ago and it's over now. You got married five years ago and it's over, been over; was over the first year, but you hung out [and] let the marriage get cold and stale and dead and you were grumbling and cussing each other. And then you finally said, 'Well to heck with it, I'm just leaving.' Leaving the children torn and divided; not wishing to choose between the mother and the father, loving both. But unfortunately, having to choose because we did not struggle at the most difficult time in that marriage."*

The more we are able to overcome obstacles as a couple, the stronger our marriage. Strong marriages are the cornerstone of strong families. It takes time to adjust to marriage. Couples should enjoy quality and quantity time together before the tremendous demands of parenthood become the new reality. It is important to get to know one another and begin to build a solid foundation organically. We must understand the nature of a man and the nature of a woman; how to please one another and also working to avoid those things that annoy. Our children will enjoy a more loving and peaceful household if major issues are worked out before they arrive.

We have to better prepare and plan all future pregnancies. The closer our pregnancies, the more likely we are to have complications and the more serious ones can lead to a miscarriage or impact the health of the mother. Nutrients, hormones, muscle strength, body composition, and organs all have to be replenished and restored after pregnancy – this takes time. As we have been sharing throughout this book, a woman's mental, spiritual, moral, emotional and physical condition are crucial to giving birth to a god.

After enduring nine months of pregnancy, intense labor and delivery, followed by the demands of caring for a new life; only to discover that you must go through it all over again before you have had a chance to catch your breath, is a lot for any woman to endure. If pregnancy is not planned, it is difficult to be joyous instantaneously. Unplanned pregnancies often bring about immediate stress and unhappy thoughts towards the pregnancy, which are transferred to the baby. We have now already had our first set back towards giving birth to a god.

Having children back to back not only causes stress on the mother, but it can also put a strain on the marriage. Women could actually fear having intercourse and therefore avoid intimacy with their spouse because they do not want to get pregnant to soon. Or, she may take drastic measures of unnatural and unhealthy birth control; which can have long-term side effects, impacting her health and the health of any future children.

Child spacing is also beneficial for our children. Remember, babies are born selfish and this does not change for years. They are not concerned with anyone else's needs or wants, including that of their siblings. Children need and want their mother's time and full attention for the first few years of life. It takes most children close to three years before feeling secure and reassured enough by their parents, where short periods of separation will not cause them distress or anxiety. Some toddlers actually want to hurt the new baby, who is seen as an intruder. Conversely, if the next pregnancy is spaced, when the new baby comes, the older child is not jealous or angry about the new addition to the family; but happy, peaceful and excited. Ideally, we want older siblings to be eager and actually want to help their parents care for the new baby.

The Holy Qur'an reads, *"Man prays for evil as he ought to pray for good."* So to avoid that prayer – 'Oh Allah (God), please don't let me get pregnant' – before intimacy with our spouse, we need to make the proper preparations and plan our pregnancies. If it takes two years for our bodies to heal after giving birth and close to three years for our children to feel secure, then we should plan for the birth of our children to be spaced at a minimum of two years, nine months. By studying our body and understanding ovulation and fertility, we can plan each child's conception to the day.

The Holy Qur'an confirms that there should be adequate space between our children – Allah (God) exhorts mothers to nurse their babies for two whole years. Breastfeeding suppresses ovulation in many women for the duration of the time she nurses. As long as a woman is breastfeeding frequently, she will not ovulate and sometimes she also will not menstruate. If one is not ovulating, conception is not possible. Once breastfeeding decreases or stops, ovulation resumes. Breastfeeding can be a natural child spacing option for many women. If conception takes place too soon, breastfeeding should be aborted. The continuous action of drawing milk from the breasts causes the womb to contract. If she is pregnant and nursing a baby at the same time, there is a small risk of miscarriage. This is why some health care practioners recommend that a pregnant woman not continue to nurse a baby.

Did you know that there is such a thing as having too many children? Only in the sense that the woman's body will begin to break down a lot faster than otherwise. An experienced Sister in holistic health and wellness told me and a group of sisters that for a woman to bear more than four children could be considered physical abuse of the body. The Honorable Minister Louis Farrakhan bore witness that had they not had so many children (nine), his wife would be physically stronger today.

Brother Minister Jabril Muhammad shared that in the Hereafter, women will ultimately be able to bear a multitude of children during their lifetime without issue and without violating nature. This will be possible not only because we will be so much healthier and therefore able to heal much sooner; but also because our lifespan will equal or surpass those whom we read about in the scriptures; they lived for centuries!

BIRTH CONTROL:

The topic of birth control continues to be highly controversial and is often a politicized issue. As with most societal concerns in this country, we rarely factor into the discussion the Will of God in our decision-making. The generally accepted definition of birth control is: *"The act of preventing pregnancy. Methods include medications, procedures, devices, and behaviors."* **Prevention** of pregnancy is the ultimate goal for those staunch promoters and champions of any and all forms of contraception. These advocates are usually the same people who encourage abortions, should the contraception fail. Birth control in that sense is not even considered in Islam. However, birth control in Islam means what is says, controlling when you give birth. Planning as many aspects of parenthood as possible before conceiving; including spiritually, mentally, physically and financially – this is all birth control. Birth control should not center on preventing pregnancy by any means necessary. We should plan, to the best of our ability, when we choose to conceive – always remembering that Allah (God) is the Best of Planners, therefore we are willing to surrender to His plan should it not turn out to be the same as ours.

So, it is a misconception that Muslims in the Nation of Islam do not "believe" in birth control. We absolutely do. We practice writing our history then walk into it – meaning, we plan our future and then seek to fulfill it. But we are not willing to abuse our bodies by disturbing our natural biological chemistry or interrupting the woman's menstrual cycle for the sake of preventing pregnancy. Any artificial form of contraception that alters the blood, affects hormone levels, or interferes with menstruation and ovulation are discouraged. This includes birth control pills, birth control patches, IUDs, Depo-Provera shots, the vaginal ring, the Morning After pill (Plan B), and others. The immediate side effects and long-term consequences of these artificial methods can be dangerous.

In *Message to the Blackman in America*, the Most Honorable Elijah Muhammad wrote, *"Using birth control for a social purpose is a sin. Using the birth control law against production of human beings is a sin that Allah*

(God) is against and for which He will punish the guilty on the Day of Judgment. Both the Bible and Holy Qur'an's teachings are against birth control. So, you and I, too, should be against it...The motive behind these schemes is not designed to promote the welfare of black families, but to eliminate these families in the future" (p. 64-65).

In *How to Eat to Live: Book One*, he wrote, *"This pill is a bold offer of death, openly made...It is accepting extermination through a harmless looking pill, designed to take away the future birth of our Nation...Once you have swallowed the birth control pill, it is death"* (p.86-87).

The Most Honorable Elijah Muhammad once told Minister Farrakhan, *"Brother, you can't fathom the depth of Satan."* We cannot fathom his level of evil because our nature is righteousness, but he is not! The enemy of God has a focused agenda *"to cull between 2-3 billion people from the face of the Earth!"* The Honorable Minister Louis Farrakhan reminded us that Zbigniew Brzezinski, former national security advisor, said, *"Today, it is infinitely easier to kill a million people than to control a million people."* So, the wicked are on a mission to kill millions by using our natural urges for both food and sex. They genetically modify and poison our food supply; and then promote "temporary" birth control, which is actually gradual sterilization, in hopes of eventual extinction. Their father, Yakub, is the originator of this birth control methodology which has now evolved into deceptive agencies like Planned Parenthood; the name itself is clearly false advertisement. Planned Parenthood is primarily found in poor communities populated by Black and Brown people. They do not help women **plan** to become parents – they help women prevent and end their pregnancies.

The Holy Qur'an reads, *"And Allah has made the earth a wide expanse for you, that you may go along therein in spacious paths"* (71:19-20). There is ample space and ample resources for every living person and creature on the earth. Any control to the population that must take place will take place by the hands of God; He does not need our help. He does not permit life to come forth without creating a way to maintain the life. While we should definitely plan, we must always see the hand of God in everything. If it is His Will that we conceive; then we should embrace the pregnancy and allow it to come to term – no abortions. But family planning is the key. We control who we marry and with whom we decide to engage in sexual intercourse. After that decision is made, we are mandated by God to bear the consequences of our actions.

If we study how exquisitely Allah (God) designed the female – there are clear signs that He had every intention of the woman knowing exactly when she is ovulating so that she could plan when to conceive. We cannot begin to master anything outside of ourselves if we do not first study self, beginning with our physical make-up. A clean diet, regular exercise and adequate rest help to regulate a woman's cycle, which then makes her study of self a lot easier to analyze. Sometimes she does need outside help; but if that is the case, consider consulting a naturopathic or holistic health practitioner to meet those specific needs – whether trying to conceive or trying to space pregnancies. This knowledge can be vital because women need adequate time between births to completely heal before conceiving again. The best naturopathic practitioners will be able to help women meet their specific needs, by balancing their personal body chemistry with those elements that the earth naturally supplies.

The Honorable Minister Louis Farrakhan echoes both the Bible and the Holy Qur'an when he said that premarital sex is forbidden: *"Among the righteous, those of high moral values, premarital sex is forbidden. In this world premarital sex is the order of the day and anyone who forbids premarital sex is looked at as archaic, old fashioned, and not thinking in the best interest of the individuals."* He teaches us that in the mosques [or any houses of worship] and in our schools, the only message that we should teach and promote is abstinence until marriage - period. Unfortunately, in a world like this, our children are exposed to and bombarded with sexually explicit images and subliminal messages constantly. So, it sometimes takes a miracle (divine favor or God's active intervention) to keep our youth away from premarital sex.

Therefore, The Minister has also stated that we should study our children as parents. No one knows our children better than we so if we see that they are engaging or likely to engage in premarital sex, we have a duty as parents to teach them how to protect themselves. This role is reserved for parents and guardians. It is not for the mosques, churches or schools. Prevention of pregnancy is not the primary goal here; but rather protecting our children from sexually transmitted infections and diseases, which can sometimes be a life sentence.

Doing our very best every day to live a life pleasing to Allah (God) and trusting His guidance assures our success. So, let's get better at controlling (planning) our births naturally and be sure to teach the young sisters and brothers coming behind us to do the same. The enemy's way is dying out and the righteous must replace it with something new, something better – a Nation that will last forever!

ACCEPTABLE BIRTH CONTROL OPTIONS:

Before we share two completely natural methods of child spacing or birth control, we will briefly emphasize what is NOT recommended and also those methods that are not considered "natural," but are safe and acceptable.

The methods of birth control that are strongly advised against include anything that is hormonal, affects the blood or natural body chemistry long term; also, generally, anything that requires permanently altering the body. Those methods include, but are not limited to – birth control pills, implants, shots (Depo-Provera), patches or the vaginal ring. They also include IUDs and Norplant. Other methods of birth control which are surgical and also NOT recommended are forms of permanent sterilization: Tubal ligation, which is the tying of the fallopian tubes; full or partial hysterectomies (the removal of parts of the female reproductive system or the entire womb); and vasectomies for men.

Everything in our body serves a purpose, including the womb (uterus) – post childbearing years. When a part of our body is removed or altered, it has a ripple-effect on the rest of the body since each part of the body connects to another. Not one cell or organ in the body is suspended in mid-air. Some doctors will actually tell us that we do not need our tonsils or our appendix; and that we only need one kidney to survive. It is true that the removal of any of the aforementioned organs will not lead to our instant death but be assured that Allah (God) would not have given them to us if we did not need them. Since our knowledge is limited, we may not know the full purpose of every organ or body part beyond the obvious, but to say it is not necessary simply because we have not figured out God's vast purpose is extremely arrogant and foolish.

Safer options of birth control that are acceptable include those methods that are external, used only at the time of intercourse, or have no lasting effect on our biological composition. Some of these methods include a condom, female condom, diaphragm, sponge, or cervical cap. It is important that spermicidal gel that is **hormone-free** be used in combination with these methods.

However, the HEALTHIEST options for child spacing or birth control are those two methods that are completely natural: (1) Breastfeeding and (2) Family Awareness Method (AKA – rhythm method).

Breastfeeding cost nothing and is 98% effective at suppressing ovulation in most women for the duration of her time nursing. As long as a woman is breastfeeding frequently (every 4-5 hours), she will not ovulate and sometimes she also will not menstruate. If one is not ovulating, conception is not possible. Once breastfeeding decreases or stops, ovulation resumes. So, the more often the mother nurses, the more likely ovulation is suppressed; and the less she nurses, the more likely ovulation will resume. This works out quite nicely if the mother nurses for the recommended, two whole years. We must stress this warning…EVERY WOMAN IS DIFFERENT. It is critical that we study and get in-tuned with our own biological rhythm. If a woman chooses to use breastfeeding as her primary method of child spacing, we strongly recommend investing in books and material that will offer a better understanding of all the dynamics involved. One such book is **Breastfeeding and Natural Child Spacing**, by Sheila Kippley.

Now suppose breastfeeding is not an option for the mother because she is one of the unlucky few who continues to ovulate while breastfeeding; or because she wants to plan the birth of her first child and therefore has no baby to breastfeed. Or, perhaps husband and wife simply do not wish to have any more children. In such instances, if we do not want to use any commercial forms of birth control, the woman must learn how to detect ovulation and avoid intercourse during her fertile period. This is called the Family Awareness Method (FAM).

As mentioned previously, when we violate nature, we cause unnecessary complications for ourselves. In the book, *Planning for Pregnancy, Birth, and Beyond*, the American College of Obstetricians and

Gynecologists is quoted to describe the process of ovulation: *"Each month, hormones cause the lining of the uterus [womb] to build up and an egg to mature in a follicle – tiny clusters of cells in the ovaries. When an egg is mature it is released from the ovary."* While ovulation is 24 hours, there are several days out of every month (5-7 days for most women) during and around ovulation when a woman is fertile and can, therefore, become pregnant.

The FAM option is most effective if **all three** of the following techniques are incorporated and used together:

1. ***CALENDAR METHOD***: A simple way to understand the concept of a woman's monthly (or menstrual) cycle is that it covers a span of time that begins on the first day of menstrual discharge to the first day of the next menstrual discharge, and in between ovulation takes place. The average monthly cycle lasts 28 days, however, to have a cycle that lasts from 21 to 35 days is also within the "normal" range. Menstruation lasts for two to seven days. About mid-cycle ovulation takes place and lasts about 24 hours. However, a woman can be fertile for up to six or seven days.

Before we continue, understand that this method only works for women who have regular monthly cycles – menstruation and ovulation cannot be irregular. If our cycle was 26 days 2 months ago and then 35 days the next month, and then 19 days the next – this method will not be effective. A calendar record of the woman's monthly cycle must be kept for several months and if it is determined that menstruation and ovulation are regular; then the woman can predict cycle by cycle when the first day of menstruation should begin. Ovulation occurs approximately 12-14 days before the first day of menstruation. Use a calendar to count back 12-14 days from the first day of the anticipated start of the next menstruation. This is most likely ovulation day and certainly within the fertile period.

Again, ovulation lasts for 24 hours, but a woman's fertile period can actually last for about six or seven days. To increase the likelihood of **not** conceiving, couples should abstain from intercourse at least five days prior to ovulation and of course on the day of ovulation, and to be extra cautious, the day after (seven days total). This is recommended because studies confirm that sperm can live up to five days in the uterus. In other words, a woman can conceive even if she did not have intercourse on the day of ovulation. *However, for those trying to get pregnant, then this is the best time for conception.* The safest time for intercourse when trying **not** to conceive are during the days immediately following menstruation, and even safer are the days immediately preceding the next menstruation.

2.   ***CERVICAL MUCUS METHOD***: Every healthy woman has a regular odorless discharge, which is completely natural and necessary. Women have to record or chart their cervical mucus discharge for any changes each day for at least 1-2 cycles. During and around ovulation, the cervical mucus changes dramatically (color, amount, texture). For most women, it looks like the white of a raw egg and is very plentiful and slippery. Ovulation starts with the first sign of this change and continues for approximately 24 hours. If a couple is trying to conceive this is the best time to be intimate. If a couple is **not** trying to conceive, intercourse should be avoided at this time.

3.   ***BODY TEMPERATURE METHOD***: There is a slight rise in body temperature just **after** ovulation. In order to use this method to detect ovulation, the woman must take her temperature at the same time every morning for at least three full cycles (it helps to use a graph of some sort to record the results). This will show a pattern which can be used to detect ovulation during future cycles.

Another indication of ovulation that many women experience is the physical discomfort that shows up during ovulation. Many women experience cramping and/or tender breasts. During ovulation, the womb contracts slightly as the egg is being released. This process causes some women to cramp in the lower pelvic region near the ovaries. This cramping is similar, but not as severe as the cramping that some women may experience during menstruation. Many women may also notice that their breasts are also very tender and sensitive to the touch during ovulation.

All of these methods of detecting ovulation are very effective especially when used together. There are also ovulation kits and monitors available. Ovulation kits work by detecting the increase of LH (luteinizing hormone) that happens just before ovulation. The instructions to these kits must be followed precisely. Remember, it takes two to conceive a baby, so it is important that both husband and wife are aware when the woman is ovulating and when she is not.

Keep in mind that every woman's body is different; so, it is critical that every woman get to know herself by studying her physiological patterns. A regular, healthy diet and steady exercise routine, without dramatic fluctuations, will help us to better understand our biologic rhythms. Any extreme variations from the norm will affect both ovulation and menstruation.

It goes without saying that we should always pray for what we need. But there is nothing wrong with praying for what you want. Planning is essential but bear in mind that Allah (God) is the Best of Planners. So, should Allah (God) decide that another plan is better for us, then we should let go and let God intervene in our affairs. He knows us better than we know ourselves. He knows tomorrow better than we understand yesterday. Allah (God) created each of us and gave each of us a place in His universal plan.

Do not attempt to alter Allah's (God's) plan. Always pray that He sees us through and perhaps one day He will give us some understanding of His decisions.

ATTAINMENT OF PERFECTION

We conclude this book with a beautiful picture from the Holy Qur'an of the Kingdom of God. It is found in Chapter 76, Al-Insān (The Man) and it comes from the section titled, *Attainment of Perfection*:

"So Allah will ward off from them the evil of that day, and cause them to meet with splendour and happiness; And reward them, for their steadfastness, with a Garden and with silk, Reclining therein on raised couches; they will see therein neither (excessive heat of) sun nor intense cold. And close down upon them are its shadow, and its fruits are made near (to them), easy to reach. And round about them are made to go vessels of silver and goblets of glass, Crystal-clear, made of silver – they have measured them according to a measure. And they are made to drink therein a cup tempered with ginger – (Of) a fountain therein called Salsabīl. And round about them will go youths, never altering in age; when thou seest them thou wilt think them to be scattered pearls. And when thou lookest thither, thou seest blessings and a great kingdom. On them are garments of fine green silk and thick brocade, and they are adorned with bracelets of silver, and their Lord makes them to drink a pure drink. Surely this is a reward for you, and your striving is recompensed."
Holy Qur'an 76:11-22

MAY ALLAH BLESS US ALL TO GIVE BIRTH TO GODS!

NAVY BEAN SOUP RECIPE

INGREDIENTS (Organic, Non-GMO):

2 lbs. dry navy beans	1 tsp. curry (optional)
½ onion diced	½ tsp. basil
½ bell pepper diced	½ tsp. oregano
5-6 garlic cloves diced	cayenne pepper (4 dashes or to taste)
1 celery stalk diced	1 tsp. parsley
3 tsp. Celtic sea salt	¼ cup olive oil
1 tsp. turmeric	1 bay leaf

PREPARATION:

Sort beans and remove any discolored or bruised beans. Wash beans thoroughly several times. Soak beans in a large bowl overnight (or for at least 8 hours) in the refrigerator.

Rinse and drain beans. Place in a large pot; beans should be completely covered with 3-4 inches of water above the beans. Add the bay leaf. Cook on medium to high heat. Keep lid ajar. As beans begin to cook and boil, remove the accumulating foam from the pot. When beans begin to get tender, add all vegetables. Reduce heat to medium. When beans and vegetables are completely tender, add seasonings one at a time, stirring in between each seasoning. Turn heat to low. Add olive oil. Let soup simmer on low heat for about 30 minutes. Serve hot.

For very young children, the soup should not be overly seasoned; and it should be pureed (or blended). Eat daily!

REFERENCES

Articles / Letters

Farrakhan, The Honorable Minister Louis (2000, August 1). Accepting Responsibility for Our Failure. The Final Call. Retrieved from https://www.finalcall.com

Farrakhan, The Honorable Minister Louis (2000, June 6). Allah's (God's) Choice of Jesus. The Final Call. Retrieved from https://www.finalcall.com

Farrakhan, The Honorable Minister Louis (2014, May 27). 'Family'…From the Perspective of Children. The Final Call. Retrieved from https://www.finalcall.com

Farrakhan, The Honorable Minister Louis (2002, May 14). Heaven Lies at the Foot of Mother. The Final Call. Retrieved from https://www.finalcall.com

Farrakhan, The Honorable Minister Louis (2000, September 14). Men of This World Do Not Desire a Righteous Woman. The Final Call. Retrieved from https://www.finalcall.com

Farrakhan, The Honorable Minister Louis. "The Most Honored Woman in History: Mary, The Mother of Jesus." The Final Call, volume 19, number 43, 2000.

Farrakhan, The Honorable Minister Louis (2009, October 10). No Discipline, No Love. The Final Call. Retrieved from https://www.finalcall.com

Farrakhan, The Honorable Minister Louis (2000, July 10). The Pain of Infidelity. The Final Call. Retrieved from https://www.finalcall.com

Farrakhan, The Honorable Minister Louis (2000, August 22). A Proper View of the Woman in Building the Family. The Final Call. Retrieved from https://www.finalcall.com

Farrakhan, The Honorable Minister Louis (2000, May 2). Rebuilding the Family: What Are Allah's (God's) Thoughts and His Ways? The Final Call. Retrieved from https://www.finalcall.com

Farrakhan, The Honorable Minister Louis (2010, April 18). The Sacredness of the Female. The Final Call. Retrieved from https://www.finalcall.com

Farrakhan, The Honorable Minister Louis. Statement in Support of NFL Player Colin Kaepernick, 30 Aug. 2016.

Farrakhan, The Honorable Minister Louis (2000, June 20). What is the Purpose for Sex in Marriage? The Final Call. Retrieved from https://www.finalcall.com

Muhammad, Abdul Allah. "I Believe the Children are Our Future…" The Final Call, volume 17, number 41, 1998.

Muhammad, Jabril (2017, August 25). A Birth Rooted in Prophecy. The Final Call. Retrieved from https://www.finalcall.com

Books

The American College of Obstetricians and Gynecologists. Planning for Pregnancy, Birth, and Beyond. The American College of Obstetricians and Gynecologists, 1995.

Clarke, Alison J. Maternity and Materiality: Becoming a Mother in Consumer Culture. Rutgers University Press, 2004.

Clymer, R. Swinburne. How to Create the Perfect Baby. Philosophical Publishing Company, 1902.

Eisenberg, Arlene; Hathaway, Sandee Eisenberg; Murkoff, Heidi Eisenberg. What to Expect When You're Expecting. Workman Publishing, 1984.

Emoto, Masaru. The Hidden Messages in Water. Atria Books, 2005.

Farrakhan, The Honorable Minister Louis. Education is The Key. FCN Publishing, 2006.

---. The Restrictive Law of Islam is Our Success. Minister Louis Farrakhan, 2012.

---. Self-Improvement: The Basis for Community Development [Study Guides]. The Honorable Minister Louis Farrakhan, 1986.

---. A Torchlight for America. FCN Publishing Co., 1993.

Holy Qur'an, Maulana Muhammad Ali Translation. Lahore, Inc., 1991.

King James Version Bible. Thomas Nelson Publishers, 1984.

Kippley, Sheila. Breastfeeding and Natural Child Spacing: The Ecology of Natural Mothering. Sheila Kippley, 2008.

Merriam-Webster Dictionary. Merriam-Webster.com. Web.

Muhammad, Betty. Dear Holy Apostle. Photo Grafix, Design Express, 2002.

Muhammad, Jabril. Closing the Gap: Inner Views of the Heart, Mind & Soul of the Honorable Minister Louis Farrakhan. FCN Publishing, Co., 2006.

---. This is the One. Jabril Muhammad, 1993.

Muhammad, Master Fard. The Supreme Wisdom Lessons. The Final Call, 1994.

Muhammad, Minister Ava. The Force and Power of Being: Lift Yourself to a Higher State of Energy and Expression. LoveKare Productions, 1997.

---. Naturally Beautiful. Ava Muhammad, 2014.

---. Queen of the Planet Earth: The Rebirth and Rise of the Original Woman. LoveKare Inc., 1997.

---. Weapons of Self-Destruction. Profits Publishing, 2005.

Muhammad, The Most Honorable Elijah. How to Eat to Live: Book One. Muhammad's Temple of Islam No. 2, 1967.

---. How to Eat to Live: Book Two. Muhammad's Temple of Islam No. 2, 1972.

---. Message to the Blackman in America. Muhammad's Temple No. 2, 1965.

---. Our Saviour has Arrived. Muhammad's Temple of Islam No. 2, 1974.

Muhammad, S., Muhammad A., Muhammad, B., Muhammad, K., X M., Muhammad N.,

Muhammad R., Muhammad S. M.G.T. & G.C.C. A Look at the Feminine Side of the Culture of Islam. Nation of Islam, 2013.

Muhammad, Tynnetta. The Women in Islam Educational Series, Part III: The Divine Light:

The Origin and Reproduction of Life in Ourselves and in Our Universe / Articles Based on Muhammad's History and The Holy Qur'an. Under the Auspices of The H.E.M.E.F., 1994.

Muhammad, Wesley. Understanding the Assault on The Black Man, Black Manhood and Black Masculinity. A-Team Publishing, 2017.

New International Version Bible. Zondervan, 2001.

New King James Version Bible. Biblegateway.com. Web.

Reader's Digest. ABCs of the Human Body: A Family Answer Book. Readers Digest Association Inc., 1987.

Women Partners in Health. Midwives Expand Your Options. Women Partners in Health., 1998.

Interviews / Lectures / Presentations / Press Conferences

Farrakhan, The Honorable Minister Louis. "The Call to Faith and Struggle: State of the Black

World Conference II." Ernest N. Morial Convention Center, New Orleans. 23 Nov. 2008. Lecture.

---. "How to Give Birth to a God: Part One." Lecture Series. The Final Call Administration Building, Chicago. 26 Jul. 1987. Lecture.

---. "How to Give Birth to a God: Part Two." Lecture Series. The Final Call Administration Building, Chicago. 29 Jul. 1987. Lecture.

---. "How to Give Birth to a God: Part Three." Lecture Series. The Final Call Administration Building, Chicago. 2 Aug. 1987. Lecture.

---. "How to Give Birth to a God: Part Four." Lecture Series. The Final Call Administration Building, Chicago. 5 Aug. 1987. Lecture.

---. "How to Give Birth to a God: Part Five." Lecture Series. Muhammad Temple Number 7, New York. 9 Aug. 1987. Lecture.

---. "Press Conference." Watergate Hotel, Washington, D.C. 16 Nov. 2017. Press Conference.

---. "The Problem of Suicide and the Causes of Homosexuality." Muhammad University of Islam, Chicago. 7 Apr. 1993. Lecture.

---. "The Sin of Child Molestation." The Final Call Administration Building, Chicago. 20 May 1984. Lecture.

---. "Strong Families: The Foundation of a Great Nation – Message at the Family Summit Conference." Sheraton Atlanta Hotel, Atlanta. 27 Aug. 2017. Lecture.

---. "The Time and What Must Be Done: 2013 Lecture Series, Part 16." Online video. NOI.org/TheTime. 27 Apr. 2013 (released). Web.

---. "Un-Masking of Satan." Mosque Maryam, Chicago. 27 May 2018. Lecture.

---. "Who is God?: Saviours' Day 1991." Christ Universal Temple, Chicago. 24 Feb. 1991. Lecture.

"Interview with The Honorable Minister Louis Farrakhan." Interview by Charlamagne Tha God, DJ Envy and Angela Yee. The Breakfast Club - Power1051.iheart.com. 24 May 2016. Web.

"Interview with The Honorable Minister Louis Farrakhan." Interview by David Broder and Tim Russert. Meet the Press - NBC Television. 13 Apr. 1997. Television.

"Interview with Minister Tony Muhammad: The Hidden Enemy and the Plot to Kill all Black Boys." Interview by Ebony Safiyyah Muhammad. Hurt 2 Healing Magazine hurt2healingmag.com. 28 Jun. 2016. Web.

Muhammad, The Most Honorable Elijah. "The Theology of Time." The National Center, Chicago. 24 Sept. 1972. Lecture.

Roussell, Jasmine. "Presentation on Doulas." Texas Empowerment Academy, Austin. 2 June 2018. Presentation.

Organization Websites / Research Studies / Social Media

American Academy of Pediatrics. (n.d.). Website - https://www.aap.org/

The American College of Obstetricians and Gynecologists. (n.d.). Website – https://www.acog.org/

Andrea, Coleman. (n.d.). Music benefits the brain, research reveals. Nature Reviews Neuroscience. Retrieved from https://en.calameo.com/read/0008203917a0f3afdddb3

Black Mamas Matter Alliance (n.d.). Website - https://blackmamasmatter.org/

Black Women Birthing Justice (n.d.). Website - http://www.blackwomenbirthingjustice.org/

Centers for Disease Control and Prevention. (n.d.). Website - https://www.cdc.gov/

Davis, D.R., Epp, M.D., Riordan, H.D. (2004, December). Changes in USDA food composition data for 43 garden crops, 1950-1999. The Journal of the American College of Nutrition.

DONA International. (n.d.). Website - https://www.dona.org/

The Family Dinner Project. (n.d.). Website - https://thefamilydinnerproject.org/

Focus on the Family. (n.d.). Website - https://www.focusonthefamily.com/

Greenwood, Brad N., Carnahan, S., Huang, L. (2018, August 21). Patient-physician gender concordance and increased mortality among female heart attack patients. Proceedings of the National Academy of Science.

Gruber, Kenneth J., Cupito, Susan H. Dobson, Christina F. (Winter 2013). Impact of doulas on healthy birth outcomes. The Journal of Perinatal Education: Advancing Normal Birth. Retrieved from https://www.ncbi.nlm.nih.gov/pmc/articles/PMC3647727/

Johnson, Nathanael (2010, September 13). For-profit hospitals performing more c-sections. California Watch. Retrieved from https://khn.org/news/californiawatch-profit-hospitals-performing-more-c-sections/

La Leche League USA. (n.d.). Website - https://www.lllusa.org/

LouisFarrakhan. (2012, December 28). @Alisbride Women who are pregnant, as they grow in their pregnancy it becomes uncomfortable for them to sit…[Tweet]. https://twitter.com/Alisbride/status/274902605069692928

LouisFarrakhan. (2012, December 28). @Alisbride and the Honorable Elijah Muhammad did not want the sisters to be spectacles of the brothers…[Tweet]. https://twitter.com/Alisbride/status/274902605069692928

LouisFarrakhan. (2012, December 28). @Alisbride It is wise that she's in an environment where her husband sees her evolving, where her husband loves & nurtures & cares for her [Tweet]. https://twitter.com/Alisbride/status/274902605069692928

LouisFarrakhan. (2012, December 28). @Alisbride …where her friends in the M.G.T. Class come and visit her! And where she's constantly feeding on The Word without… [Tweet]. https://twitter.com/Alisbride/status/274902605069692928

LouisFarrakhan. (2012, December 28). @Alisbride …others "feeding their eyes" on her. After birth: That's a critical time for the mother and the child to begin bonding. [Tweet]. https://twitter.com/Alisbride/status/274902605069692928

LouisFarrakhan. (2019, January 17). Family is the essence of the Nation. When you neglect your family, you have neglected the Nation. When you uphold your family and look out for your family, you're looking out for the Nation. [Tweet]. https://twitter.com/LouisFarrakhan/status/1085880767954055169

Mamas on Bedrest & Beyond. (n.d.). Website - https://mamasonbedrest.com/

National Black Doulas Association. (n.d.). Website - https://blackdoulas.org/

National Healthy Marriage Resource Center. (n.d.). Website -

http://www.healthymarriageinfo.org/

Nestlé. (n.d.). Website - https://www.nestle.com/

Radical Doula. (n.d.). Website - https://radicaldoula.com/

RouCares. (n.d.). Website - https://www.roucares.love/

Selim, Leah (2018, July 31). Breastfeed from the first hour of birth: What Works and What Hurts. UNICEF. Retrieved from https://www.unicef.org/stories/breastfeeding-first-hour-birth-what-works-and-what-hurts

Similac. (n.d.). Website - https://similac.com/

Surgeon General. (n.d.). Website - https://www.surgeongeneral.gov/

Tama-Do: The Academy of Sound, Color and Movement. (n.d.). Website - https://tama-do.com/index.html

Texas Public Law. (n.d.). Texas Education Code Sec. 25.082 Pledges of Allegiance; Minute of Silence. Retrieved from https://texas.public.law/statutes/tex._educ._code_section_25.082

U.S. Department of Health & Human Services. (n.d.). Website - https://www.hhs.gov/

U.S. Food & Drug Administration. (n.d.). Website - https://www.fda.gov/

Villarosa, Linda (2018, April 11). Why America's black mothers and babies are in a life-or-death crisis. New York Times. Retrieved from https://www.nytimes.com

Warner Bros. Home Entertainment. (2011, January 10). The Color Purple: Fight My Whole Life. Retrieved from https://www.youtube.com/watch?v=rnSbUuCEvrQ

World Health Organization (2018, July 31). Breastfeeding within an hour after birth is critical for saving newborn lives. WHO. https://www.who.int/news-room/detail/31-07-2018-3-in-5-babies-not-breastfed-in-the-first-hour-of-life

INDEX

216, 217, 218, 219, 220, 221, 223, 224, 243, 253, 288, 304, 305, 306, 307, 311, 328, 336, 345, 348, 350, 388, 397
Ectopic 54
Eczema 180, 185
Educate 56, 83, 178, 264
Education 22, 23, 36, 37, 91, 117, 142, 144, 145, 147, 193, 239, 240, 241, 245, 255, 256, 258, 259, 260, 261, 263, 264, 265, 267, 268, 272, 279, 361
Educational 109, 146, 254, 263, 264, 267, 279
Effeminate 101
Egg 30, 46, 48, 49, 55, 56, 61, 64, 65, 124, 183, 226, 236, 331, 393, 394, 395
Ego 309
Elevate 9, 22, 31, 56, 62, 91, 98, 287, 288, 294, 316, 335
Elijah 2, 5, 7, 9, 14, 15, 22, 24, 26, 28, 31, 34, 37, 47, 50, 51, 59, 63, 72, 73, 82, 87, 89, 96, 103, 108, 109, 116, 121, 123, 124, 126, 129, 136, 139, 140, 154, 168, 176, 178, 181, 182, 186, 193, 206, 208, 211, 214, 215, 216, 217, 218, 219, 221, 223, 224, 226, 233, 235, 237, 241, 245, 248, 251, 252, 256, 261, 263, 264, 265, 266, 267, 270, 272, 273, 276, 277, 280, 304, 305, 306, 307, 308, 309, 310, 316, 317, 325, 329, 330, 338, 345, 346, 351, 352, 355, 357, 359, 360, 362, 367, 370, 373, 374, 375, 377, 383, 387, 388
Eliminate 2, 34, 49, 54, 92, 124, 151, 178, 182, 187, 222, 229, 234, 236, 260, 277, 298, 388
Embryo 54, 55, 66

Emergency 137, 138, 145, 148, 151, 152, 220, 260, 311, 315, 376
Emit 39, 64, 226, 328
Emotion 23, 36, 40, 76, 80, 81, 97, 98, 110, 119, 120, 125, 140, 141, 143, 146, 155, 211, 212, 227, 234, 274, 283, 284, 285, 299, 301, 303, 307, 322, 324, 352, 354, 364, 384
Enamel 223
Encourage 6, 23, 24, 34, 80, 83, 91, 102, 104, 106, 122, 138, 141, 155, 157, 159, 178, 181, 187, 188, 196, 204, 213, 238, 253, 257, 276, 278, 283, 328, 334, 348, 349, 350, 355, 356, 357, 358, 377, 387
Encouragement 196, 263, 287, 373
Endocrine 214
Enemy 15, 16, 25, 28, 78, 95, 99, 105, 129, 130, 157, 161, 177, 185, 209, 223, 224, 225, 245, 250, 251, 259, 264, 267, 273, 277, 279, 289, 304, 311, 317, 318, 328, 337, 341, 388, 390
Enfamil 177
Engagement 35, 44
Engorged 189
Enjoy 61, 100, 234, 252, 253, 283, 305, 354, 384
Enlarge 137
Entertain 92, 93, 94, 95, 193, 246, 256, 279, 282, 283, 329, 361
Environment 17, 22, 26, 30, 54, 55, 72, 93, 94, 96, 97, 98, 103, 106, 149, 150, 208, 209, 211, 225, 226, 227, 236, 245, 254, 258, 261, 262, 274, 275, 298, 299, 300, 301, 317, 328, 333, 339, 350

False 250, 266, 329, 388

Falsehood(s) 4, 86, 87, 96, 217, 245, 250, 251, 275, 302, 329, 330, 332

Family 17, 24, 26, 34, 36, 37, 43, 44, 46, 63, 66, 106, 112, 144, 147, 150, 165, 168, 185, 197, 205, 207, 209, 217, 219, 226, 234, 240, 252, 253, 280, 288, 295, 297, 298, 305, 306, 307, 308, 309, 311, 313, 315, 321, 323, 324, 326, 340, 348, 349, 351, 355, 357, 361, 362, 371, 372, 373, 374, 383, 385, 389, 392

Fard 52, 63, 64, 92, 95, 219, 235, 237, 238, 250, 263, 265, 273, 317, 353, 360

Farrakhan 1, 2, 3, 4, 5, 6, 8, 14, 15, 18, 19, 21, 22, 23, 24, 25, 27, 28, 32, 33, 36, 37, 39, 40, 41, 43, 44, 46, 48, 49, 52, 55, 56, 57, 60, 62, 67, 72, 76, 80, 82, 83, 86, 88, 89, 91, 92, 94, 96, 100, 103, 105, 106, 107, 108, 112, 113, 115, 116, 118, 120, 121, 122, 127, 136, 148, 154, 155, 159, 161, 164, 168, 169, 174, 177, 180, 183, 197, 202, 205, 206, 208, 211, 212, 213, 218, 225, 228, 234, 235, 236, 239, 240, 243, 244, 246, 251, 252, 254, 255, 256, 257, 258, 259, 260, 261, 265, 267, 269, 270, 272, 274, 276, 277, 278, 280, 282, 283, 284, 287, 288, 291, 292, 293, 297, 298, 302, 303, 304, 307, 308, 309, 310, 311, 312, 313, 316, 320, 322, 323, 325, 327, 329, 331, 333, 335, 337, 339, 341, 344, 346, 351, 355, 357, 358, 362,

363, 365, 366, 367, 368, 369, 370, 371, 373, 376, 378, 383, 386, 388, 389

Fashion 100, 102, 110, 127, 258

Fasting 51, 124, 215, 312, 345, 347, 348, 354

Father 9, 15, 23, 43, 56, 58, 63, 64, 66, 67, 79, 86, 119, 120, 121, 122, 129, 130, 151, 153, 154, 155, 156, 159, 162, 179, 196, 197, 202, 210, 211, 273, 285, 288, 293, 296, 297, 304, 308, 309, 310, 311, 314, 318, 319, 320, 323, 324, 327, 329, 330, 333, 334, 343, 363, 364, 365, 367, 384, 388

Fats 126, 180

Favorites 293, 294, 295

Favoritism 293, 295, 297

FDA (Food and Drug Administration) 157

Fear 29, 44, 58, 75, 76, 78, 79, 80, 82, 120, 121, 156, 175, 291, 299, 328, 354, 363, 364, 367, 384

Fearless 353

Feed 3, 48, 95, 98, 127, 177, 178, 188, 190, 191, 192, 197, 215, 216, 217, 237, 244, 279, 285, 326, 348

Feel 31, 39, 48, 72, 78, 91, 110, 119, 121, 191, 197, 219, 233, 252, 284, 286, 296, 299, 300, 385

Feelings 44, 75, 76, 110, 115, 190, 232, 296, 309, 315

Feet 31, 101, 120, 121, 237, 301

Female 14, 15, 17, 18, 19, 27, 38, 41, 49, 54, 57, 64, 65, 66, 67, 72, 73, 76, 78, 88, 89, 99, 100, 101, 102, 104, 113, 120, 130, 131, 139, 145, 154, 156, 160,

415

163, 165, 179, 183, 192, 209, 257, 260, 262, 263, 298, 311, 316, 318, 389, 391
Feminine 91, 100, 101, 102, 104, 129, 130, 168, 317, 364
Feminist 21
Fertile 61, 64, 392, 393, 394
Fertility 385
Fertilization 66
Fertilize 64, 65, 226, 236
Fetal 137
Fetus 66, 96, 103, 110
Fever 99, 158, 220
FGC (Female Genital Cutting) 165
Filth 93, 94, 95, 109, 301
Finances 44, 45
Fish 103, 124, 217
Fit 2, 23, 47, 100, 139, 224, 258, 326, 334
Food 2, 49, 50, 51, 52, 61, 72, 91, 92, 99, 112, 120, 123, 124, 125, 126, 127, 157, 161, 175, 177, 178, 180, 181, 185, 187, 189, 195, 215, 216, 217, 218, 219, 222, 223, 252, 285, 304, 306, 311, 340, 347, 350, 388
Fool 4, 15, 33, 50, 56, 79, 81, 93, 97, 121, 211, 244, 246, 254, 276, 277, 312, 314, 328, 365, 371, 391
Forbid 22, 28, 29, 30, 32, 42, 49, 79, 121, 349, 358, 389
Force 4, 8, 9, 35, 57, 74, 85, 87, 111, 112, 122, 124, 160, 161, 182, 184, 189, 191, 194, 196, 210, 212, 218, 240, 248, 255, 267, 268, 271, 279, 284, 285, 299, 318, 331, 344, 373, 377
Forceps 137, 150, 151
Foremost 19, 113, 146, 233, 372

Foreskin 161, 162, 163, 164
Forgiveness 101, 288, 365
Formula 59, 152, 174, 175, 176, 177, 180, 181, 184, 185, 186, 187, 190, 191, 193, 215, 216
Formula-fed 185, 187
Fornication 28, 29, 30, 31, 32
Friendship 285, 356, 357, 358
Fruit 76, 77, 78, 79, 80, 98, 125, 126, 127, 217, 218, 222, 223, 224, 327, 396
Funeral 26, 95, 96, 97
Fungi 302

Garlic 55, 397
Garment 357, 396
Gay 102, 104
GCC (General Civilization Class) 168
Gender 19, 63, 65, 78, 99, 100, 102, 104, 130, 168, 257, 260, 261, 293, 295, 298, 320, 349, 356
Gene 366
Genetic 46, 49, 52, 66, 77, 78, 81, 86, 224, 225, 240, 281, 283, 298, 339, 369, 377, 388
Genital 165
Gerber 174, 177
Germ 179, 210, 328
Gestational 83
Girl 22, 23, 24, 27, 33, 34, 63, 65, 66, 67, 82, 99, 100, 101, 102, 119, 168, 203, 219, 250, 257, 258, 261, 262, 263, 308, 309, 310, 311, 313, 314, 315, 316, 317, 318, 319, 320, 324, 325, 326, 327, 354, 357, 364, 375
Girlfriend 20, 42, 328
Gland 79, 124, 160, 178, 179, 182
Glans 161, 163, 164

Infection 54, 158, 163, 164, 179, 188, 214, 390
Infertility 54, 192, 193
Inflammation 163, 164, 281
Insemination 66
Intercourse 28, 30, 54, 59, 60, 64, 65, 347, 385, 389, 391, 392, 394
Intervention 103, 118, 136, 150, 151, 183, 390
Intestine 185, 301
Intimacy 61, 385
Intoxicants 321, 322
Intravenous 137
Invasive 281
Irradiation 160

Jealous 48, 210, 295, 372, 385
Jesus 3, 17, 18, 19, 20, 24, 25, 26, 28, 31, 86, 106, 113, 139, 161, 163, 169, 239, 271, 297, 298, 331, 333, 367, 378
Juice 187, 216, 222, 223, 306
Justice 43, 91, 117, 120, 148, 268, 269, 270, 284, 286, 322

Kid 333, 334, 335
Kindergarten 239, 242, 243, 278
Kindness 288, 348
Kissed 287
Kisses 284

Labor 47, 52, 90, 120, 127, 132, 137, 139, 141, 142, 143, 144, 148, 149, 150, 153, 154, 156, 268, 326, 384
Laboratory 53, 73, 74, 85, 111, 277, 363
Lactation 189, 192, 194
Lactoglobulin, Beta 188
Latex 213

Law 22, 27, 28, 29, 30, 31, 32, 41, 66, 78, 87, 91, 98, 104, 108, 110, 112, 118, 121, 123, 140, 142, 162, 163, 164, 178, 197, 223, 248, 252, 261, 270, 271, 274, 275, 277, 279, 285, 286, 288, 289, 299, 327, 330, 339, 354, 356, 361, 362, 387
Leader 40, 251, 321, 352, 374
Leaky 180
Leche 174
Lewd 335
Liar 81, 83, 86, 88, 91, 111, 329, 331, 367
Lie 9, 40, 41, 62, 74, 79, 81, 82, 84, 85, 86, 87, 90, 93, 154, 159, 165, 190, 232, 244, 251, 259, 268, 277, 279, 318, 329, 330, 331, 332, 367, 368, 372
Ligation, Tubal 391
Lineage 17, 339, 359
Literacy 115, 241, 242, 259
Liver 97, 185, 322, 341
Loss 23, 203, 322, 372, 373
Love(s) 14, 15, 21, 33, 34, 35, 36, 37, 38, 39, 40, 44, 49, 53, 60, 62, 66, 72, 73, 76, 88, 90, 95, 97, 102, 105, 110, 113, 117, 120, 121, 122, 156, 166, 169, 176, 177, 186, 187, 197, 208, 211, 214, 215, 233, 243, 247, 249, 256, 269, 271, 282, 283, 284, 285, 286, 287, 290, 291, 292, 293, 295, 296, 298, 308, 316, 325, 326, 338, 346, 354, 358, 363, 365, 366, 367, 370, 372, 373, 374, 378
Loyalty 361
Lump 111, 114
Lungs 97, 221, 295, 301
Lust 31, 58, 60, 62, 86, 109, 319, 321, 335, 383

Meatitis 164
Meconium 180
Medicaid 144
Medication 2, 46, 49, 92, 99, 136, 137, 139, 150, 191, 387
Medicine 8, 102, 138, 161, 192, 195, 220, 260, 279, 280
Meditate 57, 58, 249, 268, 329
Membrane 74, 85
Memory 140, 274, 280, 283, 322, 377
Men 1, 7, 12, 14, 17, 20, 23, 27, 28, 29, 30, 32, 33, 34, 38, 39, 40, 42, 44, 46, 47, 52, 53, 56, 65, 67, 89, 90, 91, 95, 102, 119, 150, 156, 158, 162, 197, 203, 204, 237, 255, 260, 262, 304, 308, 310, 311, 318, 319, 321, 322, 325, 326, 327, 329, 342, 354, 360, 362, 367, 368, 374, 376, 378, 391
Menopause 183
Menstrual 53, 219, 387, 393
Menstruate 47, 53, 54, 90, 182, 219, 386, 387, 392, 393, 394, 395
Messenger 7, 97, 123, 154, 294, 356, 358
Messiah 20
Metabolism 180
Midwife 46, 124, 125, 141, 142, 143, 144, 147, 148, 149, 150, 151, 153, 155, 156, 189
Midwifery 141, 142
Miscarriage 55, 96, 384, 386
Mischievous 314, 333, 334
Misogyny 91, 316
Mistreatment 14, 97, 121, 366
Mistress 194
Molecule(s) 73, 219, 303
Molested (Molestation) 309, 310, 313

Mom 136, 168, 188, 212, 238, 247, 292, 293, 296, 314, 331, 341, 375, 377
Money 38, 59, 109, 142, 143, 160, 162, 193, 204, 241, 252, 253, 331, 362
Monoxide, Carbon 96
Moral(s) 21, 30, 31, 57, 63, 169, 192, 211, 343, 384, 389
Mother 3, 4, 15, 17, 20, 23, 24, 25, 34, 35, 40, 41, 43, 56, 60, 72, 75, 76, 77, 79, 80, 81, 82, 84, 90, 91, 92, 94, 96, 97, 98, 99, 100, 101, 102, 103, 104, 105, 107, 109, 113, 115, 116, 117, 118, 119, 120, 121, 124, 125, 126, 127, 129, 130, 137, 139, 140, 141, 142, 143, 144, 145, 146, 147, 148, 149, 150, 151, 152, 153, 154, 155, 156, 159, 160, 161, 165, 166, 167, 168, 169, 172, 174, 175, 176, 177, 178, 179, 180, 181, 182, 183, 184, 185, 186, 187, 188, 189, 190, 191, 192, 193, 194, 195, 196, 200, 202, 207, 208, 209, 210, 211, 212, 213, 214, 215, 216, 217, 225, 226, 227, 229, 230, 235, 237, 239, 243, 244, 246, 250, 251, 274, 280, 281, 284, 285, 287, 293, 295, 303, 309, 310, 311, 314, 315, 317, 320, 321, 322, 323, 324, 325, 326, 327, 328, 331, 336, 338, 339, 343, 344, 345, 355, 363, 364, 365, 366, 367, 369, 370, 384, 385, 392
Motherhood 166, 176, 207, 212, 226, 287, 320
Motive(s) 63, 169, 362, 388
Mucus 47, 394

Ointments 153
Opioid 281
Oppressed 269, 321, 366
Oral Hygiene 46
Organ(s) 100, 111, 114, 116, 124, 158, 221, 301, 341, 384, 391
Organic 126, 223, 232, 397
Osteoporosis 183
Ovarian 183
Ovary (Ovaries) 183, 393, 395
Overdose 159
Ovulate 47, 386, 392
Ovulating 386, 389, 392, 395
Ovulation 47, 48, 61, 64, 65, 182, 385, 386, 387, 392, 393, 394, 395
Oxytocin 155, 287

Pacifier 152, 186, 194, 211, 212, 213, 214, 215, 246
Pacify 97, 213, 331
Pads, Nursing 166
Parent 21, 31, 35, 36, 37, 42, 45, 58, 59, 60, 82, 84, 88, 91, 120, 129, 130, 152, 157, 158, 160, 164, 172, 174, 191, 202, 203, 204, 205, 206, 207, 215, 217, 219, 225, 226, 227, 228, 229, 230, 232, 233, 234, 235, 238, 242, 244, 245, 246, 249, 252, 253, 258, 259, 263, 269, 275, 278, 283, 285, 286, 287, 288, 289, 290, 291, 292, 293, 295, 296, 297, 298, 299, 300, 302, 303, 304, 305, 310, 313, 314, 315, 316, 317, 318, 319, 320, 323, 324, 326, 328, 329, 330, 331, 332, 340, 341, 343, 344, 345, 354, 355, 356, 357, 358, 361, 363, 368, 371, 372, 374, 375, 376, 377, 378, 383, 385, 388, 390

Partner 6, 163, 192, 320
Party 150, 165, 166, 192, 314, 341
Passion 6, 30, 32, 62, 313, 314, 383
Pathogens 195
Peace 15, 45, 57, 58, 98, 108, 112, 114, 119, 139, 141, 153, 154, 175, 181, 183, 197, 212, 220, 256, 258, 310, 326, 377
Peaceful 61, 119, 150, 180, 299, 349, 384, 385
Pediatrician(s) 160, 210, 220, 228, 230
Pediatrics 174
Peer(s) 262, 314, 319, 331, 354, 356, 358
Pelvic 54, 395
Penetrates 74, 85
Penile 163
Penis 161, 165
Pentothal, Sodium 85
Perfection 204, 298, 300, 396
Perineal 151
Perverse 317
Pervert 334
Pharmaceutical 136, 159, 220
Phimosis 163
Phonics 115, 242, 243
Phthalates 214
Physician 46, 138, 141, 142, 151, 164, 260
Physics 241, 277
Physiological 57, 97, 155, 183, 325, 395
Pituitary 281
Placenta 85, 96, 111, 151, 152, 251
Plant 41, 89, 196, 374
Plasma 221
Play 97, 103, 138, 149, 188, 233, 245, 246, 251, 252, 253, 254,

Psychokinesis 8
Psychological 81, 156, 224, 263, 301, 303
Psychology 1, 241, 245, 278, 291
Puberty 311, 347
Public-school 254, 255, 256, 261
Punish 22, 28, 29, 30, 33, 40, 139, 288, 289, 290, 291, 292, 295, 319, 368, 372, 388
Pure 19, 21, 24, 25, 26, 66, 124, 126, 159, 182, 217, 224, 311, 396
Pureed 216, 397
Purity 21, 311
PVC (Polyvinyl Chloride) 214

Quarreling 347, 349
Queen 14, 110, 317, 320, 321, 322, 323, 342
Qur'an 12, 15, 17, 20, 24, 25, 27, 29, 30, 31, 40, 42, 53, 57, 59, 63, 66, 70, 72, 73, 76, 78, 79, 87, 89, 95, 107, 111, 113, 114, 116, 123, 126, 130, 134, 139, 143, 145, 152, 162, 163, 172, 175, 181, 191, 192, 193, 200, 204, 209, 213, 224, 231, 235, 238, 244, 247, 263, 267, 271, 272, 282, 286, 288, 289, 294, 299, 307, 310, 315, 317, 319, 322, 325, 335, 336, 337, 340, 343, 347, 349, 352, 353, 356, 358, 369, 378, 381, 385, 388, 389, 396

Racism 88, 89, 228, 261, 272, 276, 277, 279
Racist 145, 269, 279, 308, 366
Radiation 126
Rape 33, 34, 60, 77, 105, 308, 310, 312, 313
Rapist 81, 91

Raw 124, 126, 223, 394
Rebel 83, 103, 105, 285, 295, 310, 368, 369, 371
Rebellion 22, 79, 83, 316, 319, 367, 368, 369
Rebellious 23, 79, 91, 224, 225, 334, 341, 369
Rebirth 110, 317
Recover 182
Recovery 138, 144, 153, 164, 220
Recreation 60, 251, 254
Reform 15, 157, 259, 277, 312, 316, 317
Regret 21, 77, 141, 252, 315
Relationship 12, 23, 38, 44, 57, 58, 60, 61, 62, 119, 121, 146, 182, 232, 234, 236, 245, 285, 299, 310, 324, 328, 343, 345, 349, 356, 357, 364, 365, 367, 368, 375, 377
Relatives 35, 37, 167, 263, 313, 315, 359, 361, 369
Relax 58, 197, 254, 314
Religion 88, 91, 95, 162, 165, 178, 249, 270, 280, 294, 308, 312, 339, 348
Religious 28, 33, 89, 95, 157, 160, 271, 359
Remarry 42
Reproduce 15, 40, 45, 50, 60, 82, 104, 203, 204, 344
Reproductive 53, 391
Reputation 35, 44, 129, 372
Respect 17, 59, 86, 106, 148, 176, 186, 209, 254, 256, 257, 263, 270, 285, 287, 289, 295, 299, 342, 344, 357, 372, 375, 377
Respiratory 158
Responsibilities 84, 285, 295, 321, 322, 326
Responsibility 47, 60, 77, 78, 79, 82, 90, 130, 144, 146, 176, 189,

Secure 55, 119, 143, 161, 233, 289, 332, 362, 385
Security 119, 153, 175, 227, 258, 299, 357, 373, 388
Seed 31, 82, 156, 161, 162, 217, 310, 321, 374
Self 4, 9, 15, 157, 240, 255, 256, 263, 280, 289, 304, 312, 324, 340, 341, 349, 350, 351, 355, 372, 373, 374, 389
Sensitive 100, 190, 202, 210, 216, 295, 395
Separate 42, 73, 161, 250, 257, 261, 262, 299, 334, 341, 374
Separation 255, 333, 385
Serotonin 97
Serum 85
Sex 22, 23, 29, 30, 31, 32, 33, 41, 42, 43, 60, 62, 63, 64, 65, 66, 77, 80, 93, 94, 234, 262, 263, 301, 310, 327, 328, 354, 388, 389, 390
Sexes 29, 260, 262, 263
Sexism 88, 89, 261
Sexual 28, 32, 41, 53, 54, 60, 288, 309, 314, 328, 347, 389
Sexually 31, 53, 54, 102, 163, 314, 328, 390
Shower 14, 95, 117, 122, 150, 165, 166, 167, 168, 169, 310, 334
Sibling 122, 185, 253, 263, 293, 348, 349, 385
Sick 51, 109, 116, 177, 193, 210, 230, 281, 309, 312
Similac 174, 177, 181, 184, 191
Sin 23, 105, 120, 191, 263, 309, 322, 335, 342, 372, 387
Single-sex 260, 262, 263
Sister 1, 6, 14, 21, 22, 31, 37, 39, 44, 53, 83, 91, 92, 94, 103, 128, 142, 146, 147, 150, 166, 167,

168, 169, 191, 192, 194, 205, 207, 208, 226, 250, 252, 274, 287, 289, 308, 309, 313, 327, 333, 336, 341, 342, 348, 357, 371, 386, 390
Sisterhood 357
Skin 52, 104, 130, 138, 151, 165, 185, 221, 293, 295, 302
Skin-to-skin 179
Slave 15, 36, 41, 59, 130, 160, 194, 268, 269, 276, 279, 329, 374
Sleep 62, 89, 156, 182, 212, 249, 250
Sleepover 312, 313, 314, 315
Smile 65, 107, 111, 122, 194, 227, 239, 342
Smoking 2, 96
Social 37, 80, 166, 167, 234, 261, 286, 306, 314, 339, 346, 358, 387
Soda 55, 222, 223, 350
Son 24, 26, 35, 48, 63, 64, 66, 91, 102, 107, 128, 159, 191, 238, 284, 296, 320, 321, 322, 323, 324, 325, 326, 327, 328, 334, 336, 359, 360, 365, 367, 370, 378
Sore 189
Soul 15, 25, 49, 60, 98, 152, 162, 209, 240, 254, 323, 325
Soymilk 177, 188
Spank 289, 291, 292, 337, 377
Spatial-temporal 280
Sperm 30, 46, 49, 52, 55, 61, 64, 65, 73, 226, 236, 322, 394
Spermicidal 391
Spinal 137, 301
Spoil 92, 213, 291, 326
Sponge 391

Urinary 163
Urinate 120, 190, 229
Urine 47
Uterine 54, 55
Utero 87, 96, 110, 156, 225, 237
Uterus 2, 53, 391, 393, 394

Vacation 205, 253, 314
Vaccinate 153, 157, 158, 159, 160, 161
Vaccine 153, 157, 158, 159, 179
Vaginal 53, 54, 55, 136, 137, 138, 150, 151, 236, 387, 391
Vaginosis 54
Vasectomies 391
Vegetables 125, 126, 127, 217, 218, 223, 224, 397
Vegetarian 50, 217
Violence 93, 94, 98, 104, 122, 259
Violent 97, 138
Virgin 21, 22, 23, 24
Virtue 21, 22, 23, 25, 27, 31, 32, 33, 311, 320
Virtuous 20, 21, 23, 40, 41
Virus 54, 159, 301, 302
Vomiting 120
Vulgar 106, 302, 333
Vulvovaginal 54

Washing, Vaginal 54
Water 16, 51, 56, 73, 103, 110, 143, 150, 152, 187, 189, 221, 222, 223, 224, 226, 237, 303, 310, 311, 328, 397
Wealth 34, 38, 45, 204, 259, 294, 325, 326, 359, 360, 361
Wean 2, 172, 217, 231

Wife 20, 21, 23, 37, 39, 40, 46, 61, 62, 90, 93, 119, 120, 121, 122, 140, 154, 156, 197, 226, 308, 323, 364, 374, 386, 392, 395
Wise 1, 4, 8, 15, 32, 37, 53, 56, 59, 63, 130, 131, 157, 203, 208, 220, 265, 267, 317, 320, 360, 361, 365, 376
Wives 40, 53, 121, 197, 297, 319, 374
Womanizer 334
Womb 1, 2, 3, 4, 5, 17, 18, 19, 25, 40, 41, 48, 53, 54, 56, 72, 73, 76, 77, 78, 79, 80, 81, 83, 84, 85, 88, 89, 90, 91, 92, 95, 97, 98, 101, 104, 107, 109, 111, 113, 114, 115, 117, 118, 121, 122, 126, 130, 138, 139, 143, 145, 148, 153, 176, 181, 182, 184, 185, 192, 200, 210, 211, 217, 225, 227, 235, 237, 239, 241, 242, 275, 277, 303, 319, 321, 324, 338, 363, 364, 368, 369, 370, 371, 378, 386, 391, 393, 395
Worship 33, 37, 298, 372, 373, 390

X-sperm 64

Y-sperm 64
Yoked 45
Youth 30, 207, 253, 257, 268, 320, 324, 350, 351, 352, 353, 354, 355, 356, 361, 390

About the Author

Sister Fudia Muhammad is a student of The Teachings of the Most Honorable Elijah Muhammad under the leadership and guidance of the Honorable Minister Louis Farrakhan. She has been a registered member of The Nation of Islam at Muhammad Mosque No. 64 in Austin, Texas since February 1995. She previously served as the city's local Student M.G.T. & G.C.C. Captain. Sister Fudia has been happily married to Student Minister Robert L. Muhammad since 1996 and they have been blessed with four wonderful children.

Professionally, Sister Fudia has taught at the elementary and middle school levels. She holds a master's degree in Education and was a former elementary school principal. She has also served as the M.U.I. Austin Saturday School instructress for many years and at present continues in that capacity. An advocate for God-centered childrearing, her work has been published in The Final Call newspaper, NOKOA The Observer newspaper, and Virtue Today Magazine. Her weekly column, "Children of the Most High," can be found at BrotherJesseBlog.com.

Made in the USA
Columbia, SC
22 August 2019